Danish Lights

For Trine and Sebastian
and in loving memory of my
mother, Kirsten Lytken

Published with generous support from

AUGUSTINUS FONDEN

Beckett-Fonden
Bergiafonden
Bestles Fond
Ernst and Vibeke Husman's Foundation
Lemvigh-Müller Fonden
The Nikolai and Felix Foundation

POLITIKEN-FONDEN

Danish Lights
—1920 to Now

Malene Lytken

Strandberg Publishing

Contents

Preface—8

Lamps, lighting and *hygge* in the right light—10

One hundred stories about Danish lamp design

Poul Henningsen:
Slotsholmen lamp—34

Poul Henningsen:
System PH—36

Poul Henningsen:
PH lamp—38

Frits Schlegel and Vilhelm Lauritzen:
Fritzsche's Universal lamp—40

Arne Jacobsen:
AJ reading lamp—42

Poul Henningsen:
Chandelier with PH lamps—44

Niels Rasmussen Thykier:
T3—46

Piet Hein:
Ra lamp—48

Vilhelm Lauritzen:
Radiohus pendant—50

Vilhelm Lauritzen:
B&G pendant—52

Tage Klint:
Model 1—54

Kaare Klint:
Fruit Lantern, Model 101—56

Bent Karlby:
Peanut lamp, Model P162—58

Jørn Utzon:
Sundowner and
Tivoli pendants—60

Poul Henningsen:
Tivoli lamp—62

Arne Jacobsen:
AJ lamp—64

Poul Henningsen:
PH 5—66

Poul Henningsen:
Artichoke lamp—68

Jørgen Bo and Vilhelm Wohlert:
Louisiana pendant—70

Verner Panton:
Topan—72

Lars Eiler Schiøler:
Pearlshade—74

Hans J. Wegner:
Wegner pendant,
Model JH604—76

Poul Henningsen:
Contrast lamp—78

Simon P. Henningsen:
Divan 2—80

Henning Koppel:
Petronella—82

Jo Hammerborg:
Orient—84

Jens Møller-Jensen:
Albertslund Post—86

Friis & Moltke:
Pendant—88

Finn Juhl:
Table lamp—90

Louis Weisdorf:
Conch—92

Jacob E. Bang:
Bang pendant—94

Andreas Hansen:
Pine Cone lamp, Model 153—96

Verner Panton:
Shell lamp—98

Bent Gantzel-Boysen:
LamPetit—100

Jo Hammerborg:
Trombone—102

Benny Frandsen:
Ball Model 1300—104

Verner Panton:
Flowerpot—106

Sven Middelboe:
Verona—108

Torsten Thorup and
Claus Bonderup:
Semi—110

Verner Panton:
Spiegel Fittings—112

Verner Panton:
Ilumesa—114

Verner Panton:
VP Globe—116

Bent Karlby:
Pantre—118

Michael Bang:
Parasol—120

Poul Christiansen:
SinusLine Model 172A—122

Verner Panton:
Panthella—124

Bent Gantzel-Boysen:
Unispot—126

Jørgen Gammelgaard:
Tip Top pendant—128

Henning Koppel:
Bubi—130

Hans Due:
Optima—132

Hans Jørgen Berthel and
Hans Erik Vestergård Schmidt:
Abo Mag, Model H 63—134

Louis Weisdorf:
Multi-Lite—136

Hans J. Wegner:
Opala—138

Torsten Thorup and
Claus Bonderup:
Pendel no. 1, Calot and
Confetti—140

Alfred Homann:
Nyhavn Wall—142

Torsten Thorup and
Claus Bonderup:
Floor Lamp and Table Lamp—144

Ebbe Christensen and
Sophus Frandsen after PH:
Charlottenborg 6½-6—146

Erik Magnussen:
Porcelight—148

Erik Magnussen:
Ship's lamp and EM oil lamp—150

Jørgen Gammelgaard:
VIP—152

Stig Gerlach:
String Light—154

Sidse Werner:
Phoenix—156

Alfred Homann:
Rappe Louis—158

Piet Hein:
Sinus lamp—160

Peter Bysted:
Rubbie—162

Sofie Refer:
Bulb—164

Simon Karkov:
Norm 69—166

Olafur Eliasson:
Opera House Chandeliers—168

Louise Campbell:
Campbell—170

Philip Bro Ludvigsen:
UnderCover—172

Cecilie Manz:
Caravaggio—174

Jørn Utzon:
Opera—176

Stig Gerlach:
LED candle—178

Louise Campbell:
Collage—180

Tom Rossau:
TR7—182

Poul Christiansen:
Elysion—184

Louise Campbell:
Snow—186

Salto & Sigsgaard:
Nosy—188

Salto & Sigsgaard:
Wet Bell—190

Ole Jensen:
OJ lamp—192

Norm Architects:
Milk—194

Maria Berntsen:
Design with Light lantern—196

Louise Campbell:
LC Shutters—198

Olafur Eliasson and
Frederik Ottesen:
Little Sun—200

Anne Qvist:
Outfit L905—202

Øivind Slaatto:
Swirl—204

Øivind Slaatto:
Patera—206

Jonas Edvard:
Gesso—208

Norm Architects:
Carrie—210

GamFratesi:
Suspence—212

Anne Qvist:
AQ01—214

GamFratesi:
Yuh—216

Philip Bro Ludvigsen:
Hiti—218

Sofie Refer:
Blossi 8—220

Design by BIG:
Gople Lamp RWB—222

Cecilie Bendixen:
Volume Yellow—224

Maria Berntsen:
Stay—226

Olafur Eliasson:
OE Quasi Light—228

Design by BIG:
La Linea—230

Øivind Slaatto:
Shade Pendant ØS1—232

Thanks—234

Notes—236

Interviews and literature—263

Index—269

Preface

'In the lamp, mankind has forever sought to manifest their most sublime technical ability, coupled with the aesthetic ideals of the time.'[1] This statement, from a book on the history of oil lamps written in 1964, captures precisely what has characterized lamp design from the earliest beginnings to the present day. Now as then, designers find lamp design fascinating and challenging, and many design enthusiasts similarly have lamp design as their particular field of interest.

While architects and lamp designers can now delight in all the new possibilities afforded by the increasingly sophisticated LED light sources, the recent years' retro wave has also led to renewed interest in early electric lamp designs. Original lamps fetch high prices, and models from previous decades are continually being relaunched. Just during the writing of this book, several older lamp designs were put back into production, a trend that seems set to continue.

In Denmark, the lamps created by Poul Henningsen — or PH, as he was widely known — are found throughout public and private settings, and although there are many other Danish lamp designs, PH and his 'System PH' naturally occupy a key place in the introduction essay and in the book's early stories because PH defined the DNA of Danish lamp design. Like the impact Kaare Klint's furniture school had on the development of the now iconic mid-century modern Danish furniture designs, PH's system laid the foundation of the development of modern Danish lamp design, and its influence continues to be felt today.

The book opens with a historical introduction to the inventions that paved the way for the first new and groundbreaking light sources, from the development of oil and gas lamps to the culmination in the late 19th century: electric lighting. It took time before all Danish homes were electrified. The first electric lamps were lit in the late 19th century, but it was not until around the time of the breakthrough of functionalism in Scandinavia that most Danish had electric lighting installed. Thus, one of the ambitions of the introductory essay is to place modern lighting into the context of this transitional period.

In PH's opinion, the incandescent light bulb was not suited to constituting a 'lamp' in its own right, as an independent and complete luminaire, or 'luminous body', as he also called it: 'It is too small to produce glare-free light. (...) Thus, the light has to be modified by a particular luminaire that encloses the incandescent lamp.'[2]

PH thus took the innovative step of shielding the new light source, and his earliest lamps are the topic of the first three stories. They are followed by another 97 stories about Danish lamp design, each focusing on a specific lamp. As the texts follow a chronological sequence, PH reappears in later stories too. Several other designers also feature in more than one story — for example, Verner Panton appears in seven. The book thus offers a chronological overview of the development of Danish lamps from the 1920s up to the latest new luminaires from the present day.

In 1921, the Danish weekly magazine *Vore Damer* (Our Ladies) presented a 'beautiful lamp', although the writer lamented that, regrettably, the photo could not depict its 'ability to provide illumination — although that would be the principal purpose of a lamp. It is a photographic impossibility to provide an honest depiction of a luminous lamp'.[3] That has remained a challenge for printed magazines and books to this day. The present book is no exception; the many photos show the form of the lamps, while the text attempts to describe the light itself.

Just as there is no way to reproduce 'an honest depiction of a luminous lamp', there is also no way to show all the many Danish lamp designs. It was decided to include 100 lamp stories in the book, which sharply limits the field. The initial list of 100 stories was revised throughout the process, sometimes because it proved impossible to find sufficient documentation to base even a brief story on, particularly for some of the older lamps, such was the premise of the book. In other cases, extensive detective work actually made it possible to piece the story together.

The 100 stories that you find here portray some of the Danish luminaires that – as groundbreaking iconic designs, as popular designs and/or as pioneering and ambitious designs – define Danish lamp design.

Once I realized how difficult it was in some cases to find the stories and the correct data for the selected designs, I began to contact the designers themselves and, in the cases where the designer had passed away, the family members who now manage their design legacy.

The emphasis in the book is on interesting and fascinating designs with good stories, and it was important for me to include both some of the historical milestones and the designers' own stories. As a result, there are sometimes several lamps from the same year, while at other times, a few years are missing from the chronology – sometimes even a longer span of years. During the 1980s and 1990s, much of the new design that was popular in Denmark came from abroad, not least from Italy, including lamps. After 2000, however, the New Nordic wave and new lighting challenges have revitalized Danish lighting design. That trend is reflected in the high number of stories from the current millennium.

These latter stories also, finally, shine a light on more female designers. There is no escaping the fact that female designers are only the focus of 15 of the stories, and that the first story to feature a woman is no. 62. That is not to say that there were no earlier lamps designed by women, but it paints a clear picture that women were also underrepresented in the field of lighting design, as in so many other fields. Fortunately, the stories included here also illustrate that the situation is changing radically.

In text and images, the stories behind the individual lamps are unfolded in a panoramic view of the development of Danish lamp design over time – from the time when the bright incandescent light bulb first made it into Danish homes and immediately had to be shielded until the present day, when the incandescent light bulb has been switched off for good and designers are now creating lamps for LEDs, light-emitting diodes.

The light sources are not a main focus, but still they are the component that the luminaires both shield and light up with, and so they have been given a place in the introduction and in the individual stories.

Indoor lighting, specifically lamps for private homes, is the main focus of the book, but outdoor lighting is included too. Streetlights are part of our common frame of reference, and often streetlamps lit the way before the new light sources were invited in.

When PH created his first design solutions for electric light bulbs during the 1920s, he approached light from the point of view of human needs, not as a technical task. In recent years, lighting technology has developed in leaps and bounds, providing new possibilities but also giving rise to concerns about how to provide suitable lighting. The principal purpose of a lamp is to provide light; ideally, good light – but what is good light? In some situations, a bright light is preferable, in others, a cosy, atmospheric one. PH's goal was to create a lamp for the incandescent light bulb that would regulate the intensity and the tone of the light. In addition to its tendency to produce glare, the then novel incandescent light bulb was too white and too cold to meet consumer demands, and PH consistently underscored the importance of warm lighting in the home.

Today, *hygge*, the Danish word for a cosy atmosphere, is a trending term, also outside Denmark – Danish lamp design has never been exclusively about form. The young functionalist architects may have claimed that purpose – function alone – should determine form; however, as in furniture design, a wide range of other factors had to be considered, and thus the Danish approach to lighting arose, with *hygge* as a crucial design parameter. Thus, the purpose of modern Danish lamps is not only to provide light but still, to this day, the dual purpose of being decorative and providing cosy lighting in the home. Hence, the concept of *hygge* is a recurring feature in many of the 100 stories.

The writing process was made particularly rewarding and enjoyable by the dialogue that played such a key role throughout. So many people contributed to this process, and I am indebted to you all. I extend my most sincere thanks to each and every one of you; please see the long list of acknowledgements at the back of the book.

The notes accompanying the introductory essay and the 100 stories are also placed at the back of the book. In addition to references, they contain many additional stories about the designers, the lamps or other topics that lay outside the scope of the core story. The reader is thus invited to consult this additional source of information!

It is now time to dive into the main text. The book's core focus – which, by the way, is the Latin word for domestic hearth – is on the 100 stories that, with 1920 as the start date, put the lamps into the context of their time, with the varying design ideals and the ever-changing conditions for design solutions based on technological developments over the past century. The story opens with a brief look at the past and at the particular Danish lighting conditions, going all the way back to a time when the glow of the fire was the common focal point.

Malene Lytken

In loving memory of Alfred Homann, Benny Frandsen, Claus Bonderup, Claus Julin, Hans Jørgen Berthel, Jens Møller-Jensen and Louis Weisdorf, who all contributed with their personal stories about lamp designs in 2019 – thank you all for the light you gave us.

Lamps, lighting and *hygge* in the right light

'In Denmark, the light source is so important because we spend so much time indoors – light defines our life. As a result, we might be slightly more pernickety about our light. We are not content with simply having a bright light source placed close to the ceiling in the centre of the room; that doesn't work for us.'
—Jonas Edvard, 2019[4]

Hygge by candlelight. Candle holder designed by the architect Arne Jacobsen for the SAS Royal Hotel. Originally produced by A. Michelsen in silverplated brass hollowware. Relaunched by Georg Jensen in 2002 in cast aluminium with clear lacquer.

Today we agree what a lamp is, since that is the everyday word most of us use to refer to the design around the light source. Originally, a lamp was a vessel with oil and a wick, and that was the case for thousands of years. The fuel and wick improved, and the design of the vessel varied, but the principle remained the same. When the flame turned into an electric glow in a glass orb, the new light source was called a lamp, and today the word 'glow lamp' is still sometimes in use. In Danish usage, the term 'bulb' gradually replaced 'lamp' in reference to the light source because the orb containing the filament was typically bulb-shaped. With this shift, 'lamp' came to mean the device as a whole: the fitting or luminaire around the bulb.

Whatever the term, the topic is artificial light as opposed to natural light. In 1915, the Danish engineer R. Theilgaard defined light as follows in the Danish encyclopaedia *Salmonsens Konversationsleksikon*: 'A distinction is drawn between natural and artificial light. Natural light is sunlight, daylight; (...) Artificial light comes from a variety of light sources, such as a) wax candles, tallow candles, paraffin wax candles and similar, b) oil (vegetable or mineral), c) various gas mixtures (...), d) electric light.'[5]

When electric light is brought indoors, the Danish phenomenon of *hygge*, a cosy atmosphere, is crucial. The prominence of the concept in Denmark is associated both with our culture and with our northern latitude, with long winters and short days for much of the year. In Denmark, as in the rest of Scandinavia, people put an effort into making their homes warm, secure and cosy.

A study found that the average Dane spends between 80 and 90% of their time indoors,[6] in many cases because we prefer it since the outdoors is often cold and dark. Interior lighting typically aims to imitate the light we experience outdoors. During the day, sunlight provides a pleasant working light. When it fails us, we use lamps to replicate the effect of daylight, an energizing light that makes us active and efficient. However, when it is time for rest, recreation and relaxing with friends and family, we prefer a warmer light with a more reddish tone. Again, we seek to replicate the natural light.

The artist Olafur Eliasson (b. 1967) specifically drew on this knowledge when he created the lighting for his 2018 project Fjordenhus (Fjord House) in the Danish city of Vejle, in south-eastern Jutland:

The lighting in the middle of the office space is warmer than standard office lighting because we aimed for a sort of 'campfire mood' in the areas where people work together. By contrast, the light in the circular offices on the periphery of the open-plan space have more blue notes; this is where people go when they want to work on their own.[7]

In Denmark, we see the sun move from east to west in the southern sky every day. At noon, it reaches its zenith before it begins to slide down the arc. The sun's meridian altitude is highest at the summer solstice. However, it never climbs as high as it does in more southerly reaches. This is particularly noticeable in winter, when the sun stays low in the sky all day.[8] Even at the summer solstice, the noontime sun does not go beyond 57 degrees above the horizon. The many hours of morning and evening twilight are a phenomenon that only occurs in the high north (or similarly far south in the southern hemisphere). Around midsummer on the equator, dusk lasts about an hour, while in Denmark it lasts all night.[9]

The astrophysicist Cecilie Sand Nørholm at the Tycho Brahe Planetarium in Copenhagen explains that the light from the sun is refracted slightly differently in

Denmark compared to at the equator. When the sun is lower in the sky, the sunlight passes through a slightly thicker layer of atmosphere before it reaches us, compared to locations on the equator, where the sun reaches its maximum altitude. At noon, the effect is not normally visible because the sunlight is refracted equally (that is why the sky is blue). However, at sunset and sunrise, we see what the added refraction does to the light. Then the sun is close to the horizon, and the refraction turns the light red: 'In that sense, the lower in the sky the sun is, the more the light is refracted – and that makes the reddish colours dominant. So it makes good sense that we prefer a warm light, particularly at night.'[10]

In Denmark, the duration of daylight varies between about 17.5 hours at summer solstice and 7 hours at winter solstice. Before the invention of brighter light sources, the pace and rhythm of our daily life followed the arc of the sun. During the summer, people rose with the sun and worked into the evening to make the most of the daylight.[11] In the wintertime, the working day was correspondingly shorter. Technological advances that enabled bright lighting made a dramatic difference. Our everyday life changed radically, and so did our use of artificial light. New options were available, including the possibility of dimming the light, something we still do when we want cosier 'mood lighting' – a term that was defined in the 1948 *Dansk Husmoderleksikon* (Danish Homemaker's Encyclopaedia) as lighting that is *not* intended to 'serve as working light but aims to contribute to a pleasant or festive mood in the room in connection with rest, conversation, parties or similar'.[12]

Thus, although Danish lamp design is influenced by advances in lighting technology and international trends and developments, Danish designers have also been guided by a persistent desire to provide warm and cosy light – at least when designing for private homes. *Hygge* has long been an ideal in interior design. The concept arose within the Danish upper middle class during the romantic era in the early 19th century as a celebration of warm, close relations in the home.[13] The same associations persist today, and when *hygge* is visualized in home design magazines, the images typically show soft, dimmed lighting, often featuring candles and lamps creating little islands of warm light around groups of furniture.

Tallow or wax candles were once the primary source of lighting, but today candles are used exclusively for ambience, and Danes have the world's highest average consumption of candles.[14] Even though we know that candles emit harmful particles, we enjoy candlelight and are increasingly replacing or supplementing the polluting candles with battery-driven imitations where LEDs recreate the flickering flame. These imitation 'candles' (or lamps), whose technological content is embedded in paraffin, avoid the fire hazard and the emission of substances that are harmful for our health and indoor climate. The question is whether they convey the same sense of *hygge* (see page 178).

Since electric light bulbs became commonplace in Denmark, popular demand has called for warm light, similar to the kind of light people were used to from the open flame. As PH put it in 1928, people didn't want to 'sit in that that damned cold light'.[15] Light is not just technology packaged in design. Light is an integral part of our cultural concepts of homeliness and *hygge* and has a crucial impact on our well-being. The director of the Danish Center for Light, Anne Bay, points out that

Danes are currently being overexposed to everything to do with *hygge*, and Poul Henningsen's role as an exponent of Danish lighting design is so established that it has almost become a cliché. However, the best Danish lamps are classics because they manage to shape the light to meet human needs. In a strictly functionalist approach, the direction, amount and colour of light are shaped around human needs – and that includes a natural, self-explanatory quality with regard to the operation and aesthetic of the lamp. Light affects us, and that is not just about how we look in different kinds of light. Light also affects our mood, our diurnal rhythm, sleep, stress levels and activities and, ultimately, our health.[16]

The study of light touches on essential areas of life. It rests on the ancient knowledge that the body needs light to function. The ancient Greeks were aware of the healing effects of sunlight, and as early as 400 BCE, the Greek doctor Hippocrates recommended 'heliotherapy', the therapeutic use of sunlight. Daylight is important to our well-being, but, as mentioned above, many Danes spend most of their time indoors, which makes quality lighting even more important. Today, the options for achieving that are legion, but that was not always the case.

The history of lighting

'The basic history of light during the millennia before the invention of electricity can be written in just a few words. I will skip the brief intermezzo of gaslight. During these many years, light was the flame. Since then, the flame has been replaced by a glowing fibre – first by a carbon filament, then a metal filament'[17] – thus the succinct summary of the history of lighting, as told by Poul Henningsen (1894–1967) in 1945. Today, PH is himself an important part of Danish design history, but the history of lighting begins long before, and this background helps explain our current relationship with lighting and lamp design.

Seen in the context of a span of several millennia, PH was right to call the era of gaslight a brief intermezzo. Recently, we concluded the era of the incandescent light bulb. In order to reduce CO_2 emissions and fight climate change, we have, for some years now, been replacing incandescent light bulbs in both indoor and outdoor lamps with more energy-efficient alternatives: from large energy-efficient bulbs to tiny diodes. Critics found the early alternatives much too bright and cold for Danish homes, while the light from the incandescent light bulb was nostalgically characterized as the warm, pleasant light we should be striving for. A century ago, when the incandescent light bulb was introduced into Danish homes, it was the light from the open flame that was described as warm and pleasant, and the incandescent light bulb was regarded as being much too cold and bright. Going back another century, the first oil lamp was accused of being too bright compared to the pleasant light of the wax candle. Hence, the need for a lampshade.

Almost every important step in the development of artificial lighting has been made outside Denmark. The Industrial Revolution, and thus the new technical possibilities of machine production, began abroad. Hence, the story of lamps and lighting naturally has to transcend Denmark's borders – as lamp design did and still does – but

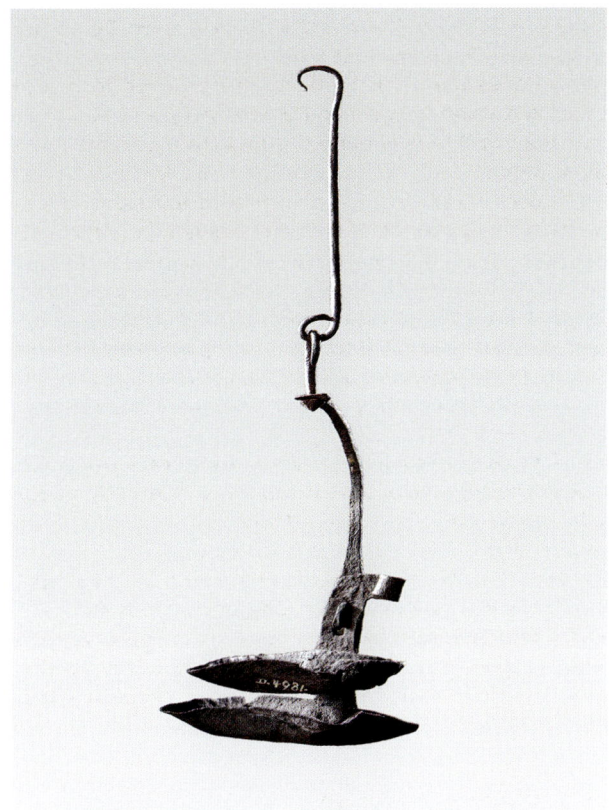

Train-oil lamp from the Renaissance, ca. 16th–17th century. The lamp is 47.6 cm tall and consists of a flat four-sided dish with a vertical rod that is riveted on. On the rod is a peg that supports a loose upper dish. National Museum of Denmark.

Gothic chandelier from the 15th century. National Museum of Denmark.

be told primarily from a Danish angle and with reference to Danish sources and conditions.

Fire – from glowing campfire to resinous pinewood sticks

It is difficult to pinpoint the earliest human use of fire, and in recent years the date has been moved back repeatedly. Most recently, the timeline was adjusted based on finds in the Wonderwerk Cave in South Africa, which pushed the presumed origin of the controlled use of fire back to around one million years ago. Presumably, fire began to be regularly used in Europe 300,000–400,000 years ago, and that gave rise to the possibility of lighting up the dark hours on our northerly latitude.

In his novel *Bræen. Myter om Istiden og det Første Menneske* (The Glacier. A New Myth of the First Man) from 1908, Johannes V. Jensen imagines the discovery of fire, which in a split second transformed daily life: 'In the evening, the cave was lit! A campfire on the floor showed them, for the first time, the interior of a home where they had been used to feeling their way with their hands. A new time began.'[18] Cultural expression began for real when humanity tamed fire to make a campfire and, around it, a home. Fire served three principal functions: heat, cooking, light.

Thus, the first luminous flames in lighting history came from the campfire, and mastery of fire was a transformative breakthrough. The designer Øivind Slaatto (b. 1978) comments in 2019:

Controlled fire is a natural focal point that offers protection from the cold, the dark and dangerous animals, as long as it is controlled – but wields devastating power if it is released. Today, LEDs and radiators have taken over the function of fire as lighting and heating, but the open fireplace preserves the fascinating and unifying power of fire. Lamps can play a similar role, not only as a source of light but also as a source of fascination, safety, hygge – something that we gather around.[19]

The glowing fire prolonged the day and broke the power of the dark. But what did people do if they needed to see something beyond the circle of light provided by the flames? The historian Johan Hedemann Baagøe imagined the following scenario:

One probably does not stray beyond the realms of probability if one imagines that the cave dweller would have taken a stick and lit it in the flames or embers, using it to light his way, and if he needed light for a longer time, he might well have pushed it into a crack in the wall or in a bifurcated branch that he pushed into the ground.[20]

Baagøe's story forms a transition to the rest of the story about lamps in private homes: from the stationary to the portable and the installable light source.

First, however, the log paved the way for the down-scaled, versatile and portable primitive torch. The Danish historian Troels Frederik Troels-Lund (1840–1921) wrote in 1884 of the sparse lighting in the Nordic countries during the 16th century: 'After dark, the country's poor as well as poor people in the cities seem to have made do with the light from the fireplace.'[21] He explains that when people could afford a little more 'luxury', they would light a lamp or a resinous pinewood stick, adding that in Denmark, the latter was the most common option, at least when someone just needed a quick light.[22]

Troels-Lund noted that in late-16th-century Denmark, resinous sticks were sold in bundles alongside candles, which were 'a luxury that only the more affluent indulged in'.[23] Unlike the resinous sticks, candles were thus a real extravagance. What stands out is that lamps, candles and sticks were available as parallel options. Old Danish iron candlesticks often have a place for both a resinous stick and a candle, so that people could use the sticks for everyday use and tallow candles for special occasions.[24]

The first improvement on the resinous stick was the torch, a precursor of the wick. Artificial lighting in the earliest stages of history was almost entirely dependent on the natural availability of wood, while this next phase represents a modest yet tangible technical advance in the form of a branch or a stick with one end coated or soaked in a flammable material: resin, pitch or wax. Later, the end of the branch was wrapped in strips of leather or fabric impregnated with a flammable material. Thus, the wood was no longer fuel but a handle. In candles and oil lamps, this functional division is even more pronounced, with the wick as the important innovation.

The resinous stick and the torch allowed us to move away from the light of the stationary campfire, and the wick enabled a range of other portable solutions.

Early oil lamps

Just as Johannes V. Jensen imagined the early human use of fire, in 1917 the writer Nils Filskov imagined the first lamp: 'One day it happened that a man thought to put a wick into a dish filled with thick, smelly oil. And so, the first lamp was invented. Accompanied by the inevitable acrid smoke, it illuminated peasant huts and imperial palaces.'[25] Scholars of human culture date the earliest lamps to the Ice Age, when Neolithic humans filled a vessel with rich vegetable oil or animal fat and added a wick made of lichen or dried moss. Lamps gradually became more sophisticated, and regional differences emerged, but a technical challenge with all oil lamps is to enable the wick to absorb the thick fat or oil effectively and convey it from the vessel to the flame. As the distance could be no more than a few centimetres, the early oil lamps were shallow. The lamps were portable and could be raised to the desired level by being suspended or placed on a shelf. They were rarely placed directly on a table, because the light was better when they were raised up, and so they were often mounted on a rod with a stabilizing base. In the Nordic region, train-oil lamps were hung from the ceiling, provided there was a beam at the right place and height.

A typical early Danish train-oil lamp model in iron that was in use for centuries consisted of two bowls. Train-oil was poured into the upper bowl, and a wick was added and lit. As the train-oil heated up, it expanded, spilled over and was caught in the lower bowl. In addition to preventing sticky spills, the lower bowl also served as a reservoir so the oil did not go to waste. There were more elaborate models, but all these early lamps produced acrid smoke and dim light, and the only way to have more light was to add more lamps.[26]

Tallow and wax candles

Candles appear to have existed since 700–500 BCE.[27] They are derived from the torch, with the important difference that the torch acts as a thick wick dipped in beeswax or tallow for a better burn, while the candle has a thin wick to prevent the molten wax or tallow from catching fire.

During the Middle Ages, the expensive wax candles were increasingly used in churches, placed in candlesticks or chandeliers. The National Museum of Denmark has in its collection a Gothic cast-iron chandelier from Gimlinge Church near Slagelse, in south-western Zealand. The chandelier, which hung from three chains, is divided into three sections and designed to hold four large altar candles. The short arms on the lower ring of the chandelier hold flat bowls with prickets (sharp points on which the candle is fixed). The smaller rings protruding from the chains of the lower section are a clever design detail that supported the long and fairly soft wax candles until they had burnt to a lower height. These chandeliers were widespread in medieval Danish churches. Unlike the plain iron train-oil lamps in people's homes, the chandeliers were ornamented and would have been a prestigious task for medieval smiths.[28]

From liturgical use, wax candles began to spread to the royal courts and the homes of wealthy nobles from the early 16th century, and from the 17th century candles became a more widespread, if still exclusive form of lighting.

The dipped tallow candles, which emerged in the 12th century, were cheaper than wax candles and thus accessible for a wider audience. Unlike a cast candle, a dipped candle is made by repeatedly dipping a wick into melted tallow from oxen, goats or, not least, sheep.[29] Although cast wax candles were the most exclusive, dipped or cast tallow candles were also considered a valuable and precious commodity. In 1870, Hans Christian Andersen (1805–1875) wrote the fairy tale 'The Candles', which aptly captures the different perceptions of wax and tallow candles at the time:

'I,' he said, 'am made of the purest wax, cast in the best mold. I burn more brilliantly than any other candle, and I outlast them all. I belong in the high chandelier or the silver candlestick.' 'What a delightful life you must lead,' the tallow candle admitted. 'I am only tallow. Just a tallow dip. But it's a comfort to think how much better off I am than the taper. He's only dipped twice, while I am dipped eight times to make a thick and respectable candle of me.'[30]

In everyday life, both country and city households would gather after dark around a single candle placed on a table in the middle of the room. For dinner parties in urban

The Heiberg lamp shown in Vilhelm Hammershøi's painting *Interior With Woman at Piano*, 1901. Private collection.

This marked an important stage in lighting history, as the light intensity improved considerably.

The breakthrough was achieved by the Swiss physicist François-Pierre Ami Argand (1750–1803), who conducted experiments to improve the luminosity of oil lamps. Argand was motivated by a personal need to continue working after dark, and with a technically innovative construction he managed to develop a lamp that was far more efficient and, not least, emitted a clear, white light in a far superior quality to all existing sources of light. In 1784, Argand presented his new lamp, whose superior combustion was further supported by another important innovation, namely that the flame was enclosed in a glass cylinder, which made the flame stronger and prevented flickering.[33]

The later American president Thomas Jefferson (1743–1826) was in Paris in 1784. He saw Argand's lamp, and in a letter home he wrote that it emitted a light equal to six or eight candles, a huge improvement on the feeble light from the early oil lamps: 'Numerous reports convey the sensation caused by the lamp's – for its time – almost magically brilliant light.'[34] In connection with the presentation of the lamp, a Paris newspaper wrote that its white, almost dazzling light was so beautiful that it surpassed all previous lamps and even the human imagination. However, another contemporary newspaper report sounded the alarm:

With lamps becoming so fashionable, it is now the youth who wear spectacles, and the best eyesight is found among the elderly, who have preserved the habit of reading and writing in the light from a single candle, surrounded by a shade. One has to admit that lamps impose an anaemic risk on the eyes and that their smell is a hazard, particularly to the nerves, but never mind such trivial matters, since a lamp is found to be more elegant than a beautiful candle![35]

Considering that lighting had for centuries consisted in dim lamps and candles, the assumption that lighting ought to be dim should come as no surprise. The quote implies that lamps continued to be used without a shade, while candles, on the other hand, were shaded when they were used as a reading light – because a shade directs the light onto the paper. Shades were not a new invention but had been in use since the 17th century when wax or tallow candles were used for studying. The shades on the study lamps, however, had never been intended to diffuse, dim or soften the light but merely to shield the flame so it flickered less and, not least, to focus it on a text or working task.[36] That was also the purpose of the lampshades that were soon added to the Argand lamps.

At the threshold to the 19th century, the Paris-based British physicist Count Rumford (1753–1814) wrote 'Of the Management of Light in Illumination'.[37] Rumford explains that Parisian shops offered beautiful versions of the Argand lamp, with a base that was either gilt or painted to imitate marble or granite. To dim the powerful upwards light, they were equipped with conical tin shades with the exterior decorated to match the base. The inside of the shade was painted to better reflect the light. These painted tin reflectors directed the light downwards but also led to a significant loss of light. Rumford acknowledged that the unshielded light was too bright to be pleasant and thus needed to be moderated.[38] In his opinion, however, a more 'elegant' solution would be desirable, using a shade of a translucent material, for example white silk or

upper-middle-class homes, however, the rooms were lit with many candles, in part to create a festive atmosphere and in part to show off the family's wealth.[31] It takes 50 candles to produce the same amount of light as the now obsolete 60-watt incandescent light bulb, and one candle emits almost the same amount of heat as such a bulb. That gives us an impression of the vast number of candles needed to light up the large ballrooms. It was expensive to light the big chandeliers in palaces and mansions, and during the 18th century and the early 19th century, candles were the biggest expense at these events. In addition, it was a labour-intensive task to light all the candles, trim them and replace them when they had burnt down – not to mention the cost and labour involved in cleaning the elegant robes afterwards, since few women could avoid wax stains on their dresses.[32]

The perfected oil lamp

It would take a long time before a superior lamp model was invented, but in the late 18th century efforts to improve the oil lamp intensified. The first improvement was the invention of a superior wick; next, the lamp itself was improved.

Electric versions of Heiberg lamps made of opaline glass and porcelain, respectively, both with brass trim. H. incl. socket: 41 and 27 cm. 20th century.

A Danish version of the moderator lamp found its way into many Danish homes. Eventually, the tall oil lamp with the angular base was nicknamed the Heiberg lamp after a famous painting by Wilhelm Marstrand (1810–1873) showing the Heiberg family gathered around a moderator lamp. The twelve-sided porcelain base hides the cylindrical oil reservoir, while the oil tube and a rack are placed inside the narrow octagonal porcelain column. Mounted on the column is a brass fitting with an adjustable wick; the brass fitting also serves as the mount for a tall glass chimney. A frosted glass orb encloses the burner and chimney. In Marstrand's painting, the orb has a decorative floral design. Vilhelm Hammershøi (1864–1916) also included the lamp in his paintings, but his lamps are clean and unadorned, like everything else in his home interiors.

In the 1860s, the popular oil lamp model was modified to burn kerosene, and later yet it was converted to electricity. The Heiberg lamp is thus an early Danish standardized lamp design that survived for many years. The angular (never patented) base was originally made in both opal glass (by the Holmegaard glassworks, among others) and porcelain, and now a ceramic version was added (made by Søholm Keramik, among others). One of the companies that sold many of the Heiberg lamps modified for electricity was the lighting company P.J. Høyrup (see page 74).[41]

The improved wick and Argand's lamp construction, including the later variants, such as the moderator lamp, had improved the light from the oil lamp. The original Argand lamp from the 1780s was an expensive luxury design, but Argand's burner – the technical component – was so functional that it could also be used in later, much more affordable kerosene lamps. Thus, Argand's invention improved and refined the oil lamp, leading to a complete system of components that come together in a good and useable design solution. In that sense, it represents an innovation on level with Thomas Edison's invention of electric light a century later.

The Argand lamp remained an oil lamp (albeit highly improved), in which a flame burns around a wick. However, it marks the time when the flame began to lose some of its gentle character, turning into a bright light that, in Rumford's opinion, was too powerful to be pleasant. That is the first time in lighting history that this issue arises.

Until then, everyone had struggled with dim lighting, and the main challenge had been to make the light as bright as possible. Even the light from an improved oil (and later kerosene) lamp was not always bright enough for tasks that required good eyesight and strong light. To address this problem, a glass sphere could be used to draw daylight indoors and optimize indoor lighting. When the glass orbs were filled with water, they acted as a lens, concentrating and enhancing the light. In a shoemaker's workshop, the globe would be placed near a candle or lamp to focus the light and direct it to the work (shoe) at hand, hence the name cobbler's or shoemaker's globe. The globes were used by many artisans, either placed on the table or hanging from the ceiling in front of the individual masters and apprentices.[42]

white paper – a solution known from Japanese lanterns – as the 'too powerful brightness' of the lamp could then be diffused and softened to produce a gentler, calmer and more pleasant light with no significant loss of luminosity. Furthermore, he argued that the shade would help conceal the lamp's overly technical – machine-like – appearance, since 'all that is ugly and disgusting in a lamp may be concealed'.[39] Rumford stated that the necessary technical developments were now in place to allow for the design of 'an entirely new system of domestic illumination'.[40] The right design for the light of a new era – a topic we shall revisit later.

Argand's original lamp was expensive, both in acquisition and use, as it required a constant flow of quality oil, so a market for mass-produced Argand-inspired oil lamps soon emerged, including more or less successful copies. Gradually, better-designed variants also appeared, such as the astral lamp (1804) and the moderator lamp (1837). These latter lamps addressed some of the shortcomings of the Argand lamp, which worked well with a shade as a reading lamp but was less ideal as a table lamp providing general lighting.

Candles are improved and industrialized

Candles were also improved. In 1823, the French chemist Michel Eugene Chevreul (1786–1889) discovered a pro-

The so-called shoemaker's globe, a sphere filled with water that was used to intensify the light from a tallow candle or an oil lamp.

cess for extracting stearic acid from animal fat. That led to the development of stearin, a tough, stable material that burnt with a clean flame.[43]

In Denmark, stearin candles were introduced in the mid 19th century, an early example of a light source that was not made in the home but purchased. The introduction of mechanized candle making made these cheaper and higher-quality candles more affordable, although they were still a fairly expensive item for the average Dane.

In 1904, the physicists Helge Holst (1871–1944) and Poul la Cour (1846–1908) wrote in the popular-science magazine *Menneskeaandens Sejre* (Triumphs of the Human Spirit): 'However, it was neither stearin nor wax candles that would replace the tallow candles as the daily source of lighting in the home; instead, they were made obsolete by the lamp, which had been its competitor from ancient times.'[44] The stearin candles never played the key role in lighting that the expensive wax and cheaper tallow candles had. They had a different role to play, and the reason why the stearin candles soon lost ground was the next important improvement of everyday lighting: the kerosene lamp.

From oil to kerosene lamps

Despite improvements to the oil lamps, their efficiency was restricted by the oil itself, which was both expensive and low grade. As the demand for superior lamps increased, innovators therefore sought to develop a cleaner fuel with a clearer flame.[45] Kerosene was the new high-quality fuel that, for a time, improved artificial light in many homes.

In 1859, oil prospectors in the United States struck a rich vein of 'rock oil'. The oil could not be used in its raw state but was heated in primitive retorts, and in just a few years the distillation process was effective enough that 75% of the crude oil could be refined to make kerosene.[46] Soon, Scandinavia began to import kerosene for lamps, and as early as 1861 kerosene arrived in Copenhagen. It became popular almost overnight because it was much cheaper, cleaner and almost without smell, compared to the animal and vegetable oils that it replaced. Although the kerosene lamp was simply a more advanced type of oil lamp, it offered, for the first time in history, an artificial light source that was easy to handle, affordable and provided fairly bright and clear illumination.

Whether the lamp was suspended or stood on a base, the kerosene reservoir was at the bottom. Above the reservoir sat the burner, which held the wick, which was moved forward through the burner's wick tube as it was consumed by fire or to adjust the size of the flame and, thus, the intensity of the light. The necessary intake of light was also controlled via the burner. On top of the burner sat the glass chimney, adapted in form and size to the burner type to ensure the right flame and the cleanest combustion. The flash point was normally placed inside a frosted glass globe to diffuse the light into the room – exactly as in previous oil lamps.[47]

The kerosene lamps were created during the historicist design period with its lavish ornamentation, and the lamps followed this fashion. They became a widespread device in Danish homes and found many different uses, not only as table or pendant lamps but also, for example, as piano lamps and even bicycle lights.[48] They were popular because they produced less smoke and odour than previous oil lamps and required less attention than candles in candlesticks or chandeliers. However, it was well known that kerosene was 'on the other hand, quite a fire hazard'.[49] In Jeppe Aakjær's 1900 short story 'Da Lampen tændtes – et minde fra firserne' (When the Lamp Was Lit – A Recollection from the Eighties), the risk associated with the new lamp is a key theme: 'He for one dared not set foot in a room where such a device was hung, as one could never feel safe for life and limb or know whenever one's house might just go up in flames.'[50] Because the light was a result of combustion, the kerosene lamp produced a significant amount of heat and, still, a fair amount of soot, and its efficiency in terms of the fuel-to-light ratio was quite poor compared both to electric light, which came later, and to gaslights, which were introduced in Danish cities in parallel with kerosene lights.[51]

Around 1912, the turning point occurred in Denmark, as the cost curves for gaslight, kerosene light and electric light intersected. From that time, the cost of electricity continued to drop, and that determined the path forward.[52] Kerosene lamps had been very popular, and as late as 1948 the architect and lighting expert Mogens Voltelen (1908–1995) wrote in his article in the *Dansk Husmoderleksikon* that the kerosene lamp 'was the most widely used source of lighting where there is no electric light', and that it 'provides a suitably warm, coloured light, usually bright enough for use in the home'.[53] This awareness of the need for suitably warm, coloured light had emerged after the bright electric light had been installed in many homes.

The Danish lighting expert Michael Schrøder concluded in his 1964 book *Olielampen i den Vestlige Verdens Kulturområde* (The Oil Lamp in the Cultural Realm of the Western World),

All that remains now is memories of a cosy time in the glow of the kerosene lamp. But while relics from the light sources of previous eras are mainly defective or chipped remains that only hold an interest to a museum, many thousands of beautiful kerosene lamps still remain in our homes. And (...) new kerosene lamps are being made and sold in growing numbers. Everyone agrees that their live flame lends a pleasant ambient mood to the room.[54]

As late as the 1960s, kerosene lamps were widely used in summer cottages that did not have electricity. That was also why a modern version of the kerosene lamp was launched in 1962, two years before the release of Schrøder's book: Henning Koppel's Petronella, produced by Louis Poulsen (see page 82).

The kerosene lamp was a big improvement of the lighting in many Danish homes and the first important source of lighting that everyone needed to buy. As such, it was one of the first pieces of merchandise that many households became dependent on. However, its introduction coincided with the introduction of gas that could be used in streetlights and chandeliers, and the brighter gaslight was an important alternative to the kerosene lamp. A single gaslight could illuminate an entire room, which was a dramatic development – and an advantage because unlike the kerosene lamps, gaslights were stationary.

Gaslights: an important intermezzo

'Coinciding with the growing perfection of the oil lamp, another source of lighting gradually began to play a role: gas.'[55] With these words in the weekly magazine *Hjemmet* (The Home) in 1917, Filskov introduces the next stage in the development towards electric lighting. The historian Hanne Thomsen, who is the director of GASmuseet, points out that what made gaslighting such a revolution was that 'the new white, intense gaslight gave rise to a new physical world, where streets and squares, buildings and rooms could now be used in a new and unprecedented way at night'.[56]

The first gaslights illuminated the streets of London in 1814, and the technology soon spread to other European capitals, but gas was not used for domestic lighting until the 1840s.[57] In the Nordic region, it took even longer, simply because gas was introduced here much later. Thus, gaslighting was not introduced in Copenhagen until 1857.[58] Between 1857 and 1868, 38 gasworks were built throughout Denmark, until most major cities in Denmark had their own plant.[59] Gas had to be piped into homes, so unless there was a gasworks nearby, there was no gaslight.[60] Thus, gaslights were an urban phenomenon.

In a Danish context, gas lamps were installed in private homes fairly soon after the introduction of gas. In other countries, home use was delayed because gas was considered dangerous. Gaslight was still a flame, and the explosive gas posed an even greater risk than the other light sources.[61]

Around 1850, gaslight was becoming fairly common in English homes, and *The Great Exhibition* in London in 1851 featured many of the new impressive gas lamps. The lamps highlighted a key concern with regard to their use in the home. The distinction between the lamp's technical and decorative aspects that had been highlighted by the Argand lamp was further stressed by the many kerosene lamps that people now used in their homes. The base and reservoir might be created by an artist, while the mechanical components (burner and cylinder) were pure, cool technology. A frosted glass globe or a lampshade might camouflage the latter, but the gas pipes presented a new aesthetic challenge. By imitating older styles in the decoration around the pipes, manufacturers tried to make the industrial product appeal to the public.[62]

The Great Exhibition at Crystal Palace in London in 1851 revolved around the explosive development within science and industry.[63] The exhibition's impressive and richly illustrated catalogue, with more than 300 pages of etchings, showed the finest exhibits and contained a vast number of lavishly ornamented candelabra, chandeliers, oil and gas lamps and, not least, impressive gas chandeliers with shades in crystal glass. The exhibition catalogue confirmed the status of gaslight and also showed that highly ornamented surfaces imitating historical styles were a general trend in industrial products at this time.[64]

The German architect Gottfried Semper (1803–1879) criticized these attempts at dressing new technology in historical garb. After the exhibition, Semper wrote the following, with direct reference to the gas lamps: 'What a glorious discovery is the gaslight! How its brilliance enhances our festivities, not to mention its enormous importance to everyday life! Yet in imitating candles or oil lamps in our salons, we hide the apertures of the gas pipes.'[65]

The gas lamps and chandeliers in Danish homes were less impressive than the ones in *The Great Exhibition*, but the trend was the same: new technology was manifested in traditional designs. In Danish homes, gas and kerosene lamps were in sharp competition, and new and improved lamps, both for kerosene and for gas, regularly reached the market. Around 1890, gas lamps received a boost thanks to a new technological breakthrough: the Welsbach gas mantle, which solved the problem of soot in the lamps and provided brighter, clearer and more pleasant light. However, by then, gas was already being replaced by electricity for lighting purposes.[66]

Gas lamps began to enter Danish homes during the 1860s, and together with kerosene lamps they dominated lighting for a time. Both types had their pros and cons. Kerosene was odourless, kerosene lamps were mobile, and kerosene was cheaper. Gas was more expensive, because one not only needed to pay for the gas and buy new lamps but also had to invest in fixed installations. Thus, gas was mostly installed in more affluent households during the 1860s and 1870s.[67] Gaslight also had significant qualitative advantages: in addition to a brighter light, which many favoured, it was now, for the first time in history, easy to switch the light on and off as needed. There was no reservoir to be refilled, no wick to be adjusted, and, moreover, gaslight was widely associated with higher social status. Gaslight thus managed to preserve its place in the more exclusive segment of the lighting market, while the kerosene lamp was the main replacement for tallow candles in more common homes.[68]

Up to and including gaslight, all artificial light, including all lamp light, came from a live flame that had to be treated with care. Gaslight was the first very bright light – even brighter than Argand's lamp, which sprang from his own need for proper working light after sunset. Gaslighting was so bright that it was possible to introduce night shifts in industry, which meant that many now had to work after dark. Gaslight thus impacted people's home life in both indirect and direct ways. Indirect, as altered working conditions changed the structure of the day for many people. Direct, as the individual members of the family no longer had to gather around the lamp but were free to retreat into the corners of the room, without needing to bring a light. That was a new development. However, the stark light also led to modifications, either with the addition of a lampshade or, more simply, by opting not to use the bright light. In 1904, the physicists Holst and la Cour wrote,

While even the dim light from a tallow, wax or stearin taper might suffice for use in the home – since, if necessary, each person could have his own light and place it close to him – bright light is an irrefutable condition for

The catalogue for *The Great Exhibition* in London in 1851 stated about this American gas chandelier, 'The design is very rich in ornament, and possesses some novelty in the succession of curves ingeniously and tastefully united: the gas-key represent bunches of fruit, thus combining beauty with utility' (*The Great Exhibition*, 1851).

good street lighting. (...) As the kerosene lamps now, further, offered sufficient light to meet domestic needs, it is little wonder that domestic gaslighting has only gained modest popularity.[69]

From flaming lamps to electric glow

Electricity was both a product of industrialization and a key factor in its continued development. In a 1917 issue of *Hjemmet*, Filskov called the invention of electric 'the greatest triumph of the past century' and explained that the British chemists Humpry Davy's (1778–1829) and Michael Faraday's (1791–1867) experiments had laid the groundwork, which was subsequently perfected by other inventors.[70] In closing, he recognized the accomplishment of the 'brilliant inventor' Thomas Edison for perfecting 'the electric glow lamp' and declared that 'with this lamp, the ideal source of lighting has been found'.[71]

Just as the older lamps had enclosed a flaming wick, a glass globe now enclosed a glowing filament. Hence, the term 'glow lamp' was used about the light source itself, but gradually the term 'bulb' prevailed, and 'lamp' was once again used to refer to the entire luminaire, including the

Illustration for Hans Christian Andersen's fairy tale 'Godfather's Picture Book' (1868). Artist: Lorenz Frølich.

shade and base, as had been the case for the train-old, oil, kerosene and gas lamps.

Edison's filament or glow lamps were bulb-shaped, but the early globes also existed in other forms, including tapers, spheres, mushrooms and tubes. Regardless of form, from the outset and until today the globes have been made in ordinary glass, finished in various ways, depending on their purpose.

Edison is often recognized as the inventor of the electric light bulb because he developed a workable concept for not only an incandescent light bulb but also for a socket that remains in use today and allows for easy replacement. Edison and his team also devised the cords, dynamos, fuses and switches needed to produce and distribute electricity for lighting in public and private settings.[72]

In 1878, Edison had announced that he was experimenting with a safe and affordable incandescent light bulb that could connect to an electric grid and bring the new light into any room in a building, where it could be switched on and off as needed, without any of the drawbacks of gas: 'The electric light is the light of the future – and it will be my light – unless some other fellow gets up a better one.'[73]

In Denmark, Bernhard Olsen, the director of the Tivoli Gardens, had read about Edison's experiments, and in 1878 he wrote in the Danish weekly *Illustreret Tidende* (Illustrated Magazine), 'Whether he has truly managed to split the electric current to a degree that makes it possible to bring tempered and dimmed electric light into our living rooms (...) we shall see in the near future'.[74]

Edison developed a light source capable of competing with gaslight. In 1879, he therefore applied for a patent on an incandescent light that would burn for many hours and produce a good light. In contrast to other lighting options, it was not a fire hazard, and it was odourless and smoke-free.

After *The Great Exhibition* at Crystal Palace in London in 1851, international exhibitions became a recurring forum for showcasing and thus disseminating advances in industrial art, design and technology. In 1881, the new amazing artificial light was presented in a large-scale international electricity exhibition in Paris.[75] Among the exhibits were many other types of electric light bulbs. In fact, 19 companies presented 159 different types of incandescent light bulbs. So Edison was neither the first nor the only one, but his company, The Edison Electric Light Company, received a Diploma of Honour for being the only company to present a complete lighting system with every detail worked out: the bulb could be screwed into the socket, and when the switch was pushed, the lamp lit up.

At the Paris exhibition, Edison presented his light bulbs in an impressive two-ton crystal chandelier from the renowned French crystal company Baccarat. The crystal chandelier was originally made for gaslights. Again, the distinction between the lamp's technical and decorative aspects deserve mention. In the early 19th century, Rumford had underscored that 'all that is ugly and disgusting in a lamp may be concealed' (see page 16). However, while Edison concealed the cords in the gas pipes, the incandescent light bulbs were unshielded to produce the most impressive and bright light possible, further intensified by the many crystal prisms.

That Edison chose, in 1881, to install his new light bulbs in a gas chandelier illustrates the absence of an 'entirely new system of domestic illumination' – see Rumford's words from 1806 about the shade on the Argand lamp (page 16). Thus, the new manifestation of modernity could not be presented in a new garb, as luminaires for the bulbs had yet to be developed, and the chandelier itself, above all, reflected simply what was fashionable at the time. Siemens also presented incandescent light bulbs in a chandelier in Paris,[76] and a Danish book on interior decoration from 1891 underscores that one would be unlikely to find a (wealthy) home where 'the chandelier is missing in the living room'.[77]

In the late summer of 1881, the large electricity show in Paris was the talk of Europe, and *Illustreret Tidende* published a feature article about 'the electric exhibition' in Paris written by the magazine's special correspondent, Franz Woaz. He concluded that 'the main outcome of this unique special exhibition' was bound to be that the electric light would make its way out of the exhibition halls and 'push its way into the houses, into the families'.[78]

Over the next ten years, Edison's direct-current (DC) system formed the basis of the electro-technical industry in the United States and around the world. However, in Denmark there was reluctance, probably for fear of destroying the gas utility, which was a good business. The resistance was in part due to the efforts of the gas lobby.[79] In 1891, however, the first incandescent light bulbs were lit in Denmark, in the city of Odense, and in 1892 the first homes in Copenhagen installed electric lamps. By 1905, 28 power plants had been constructed, and their supply of power to private consumers gave electrification a real boost.[80]

It took time to bring electric light into private homes, and it was not until 1938 that most households in Denmark had been electrified. Even after the Second World War, some households, particularly farms, still did not have electricity, and the many summer cottage environs followed much later.[81] Gaslight may have been merely an intermezzo, but the kerosene lamps remained in use in private homes for years. The live flame that had throughout most of history served as the source of domestic lighting retained its place, but circumstances had changed, and over time the live flame went from necessity to a deliberate choice with the purpose of creating a cosy ambience.

Streetlights illuminate the city

The first streetlights were installed in Copenhagen around 1680. They were constructed as oil lamps and fuelled by train-oil, which was the most effective choice for the Danish climate.[82] In 1681, King Christian V signed a decree requiring the city's street lamps to be made of copper and equipped with horn windows. In 1771, J.F. Struensee (1737–1772) had the latter replaced with glass.[83] The train-oil lamps would continue to illuminate the city and make it safe to be outside after dark, until they were replaced by gaslights.

In 1913, the writer Emma Gad (1852–1921) wrote about the advances that had happened during her lifetime. She pointed to street lighting as an example of a significant improvement of everyday life – from the relatively dim train-oil lamps to electric street lamps: 'Where in my childhood the train-oil lamp dimly lit the mostly deserted streets, the electric lights now illuminate lively city traffic and busy commerce.'[84] However, in between the two types of lamps, gaslight had been an important intermezzo. It first illuminated the streets of London in the early 19th century, but in the Danish capital, gaslighting was not installed until 1857. Emma Gad skipped the big leap from train-oil lamps to gaslight; she may have been unable to recollect, but the switch was experienced as a significant event for the much older Andersen, who made it the core theme of his fairy tale 'Godfather's Picture Book': 'It was the very last evening on which the oil lamps were to be lighted; the town had gas, and it was so bright that the old street lamps seemed quite lost in it.'[85] Andersen had one of the old train-oil lampposts describe the new gas lamps:

Indeed, they shine a little stronger than we old fellows, but that's nothing; when you're molded like a gas chandelier, and have the connections they have, the one pours into the other. They have pipes going in all directions and can get strength from both inside the town and outside it. But each one of us oil lamps shines because of what he has in himself, and not because of any family connections.[86]

These lines highlight a crucial difference between train-oil and gas lamps: that the gas lamps were interconnected via tubes, thus drawing 'strength from both inside the town and outside it' – that is, from the gasworks. The first lamps, which came from England, were made of sheet iron and mounted on cast-iron arms on the facades of buildings and on cast-iron posts along the pavements.[87] The more brightly illuminated streets made people feel safer when they ventured out at night, for example to go to the theatre, to visit friends or to go to (night) work.[88]

In Andersen's fairy tale, the old train-oil lamp makes a startlingly precise prediction of a not so distant future: 'People are certain to find a better light than gas.'[89] As early as 1892, 35 years after the gaslights were lit in the streets of Copenhagen, the first electric streetlights were installed on the central square of Kongens Nytorv.[90] The lampposts were Danish: the four initial lamps were suspended from candelabra designed by the architect J.V. Dahlerup (1836–1907) and cast at the F. Mogensens Jernstøberi (F. Mogensen's Iron Foundry).[91] As one of the most prolific architects in 19th-century Copenhagen, Dahlerup has left a strong imprint on the cityscape; he was no stylistic innovator but a follower of European historicism. In keeping with the ideals of the time, his lampposts were ornamented, but, most importantly, at the top of the just over 11-metre-tall post, the electric carbon-filament bulbs were installed facing downwards, illuminating the pavement.[92] While a flame invariably strives upwards, electric light now made a downwards light source possible. That will have been a startling sight at the time, and the luminosity, not least, will have seemed overwhelming.[93]

Just how overwhelming the electric light appeared outdoors in the dark of night was described in a review in *Illustreret Tidende* when the reporter first experienced electric streetlights in Paris: 'How radiant everything was in the building's immediate surroundings! (…) Some pulled their newspaper out of their pockets to read. "As if by daylight!" they were heard saying, and then they returned their attention to the light that was so clear and bright.'[94] A day after the lights were lit on Kongens Nytorv, a Danish newspaper wrote, 'For many in the street, the experience was such a complete shock that they were reduced to tears.'[95]

The new bright, clear light defined yet another new era in the history of lighting, indoors as well as on the street. Initially, only a small number of streetlights were installed, which shone with a bright carbon-arc light. This type of lighting was well suited for large open squares, but from 1898 they were replaced by incandescent/metal-filament lamps that produced a more moderate light and could be used even in narrower streets, where the gaslights had so far been the only possible source of lighting.[96]

At the same time, more power plants were being built; in 1920, the new H.C. Ørstedsværket (the H.C. Ørsted Plant) initiated high-capacity production that made electricity affordable. At this time, a young PH designed a lamppost that, unlike Dahlerup's, was without ornamentation and, not least, much shorter. It held an ultramodern lamp head, shaped for and around the incandescent light bulb and based on the lighting engineering experiments that would guide PH's future efforts to design the glare-free light that he would become renowned for (see page 34).

When the electric light came into the Victorian home

The electric streetlights in Kongens Nytorv were first lit on the day of King Christian IX and Queen Louise's golden wedding anniversary, on 26 May 1892; on this day, the first

The first electrical street lighting in Copenhagen, designed by the architect J.V. Dahlerup and installed on Kongens Nytorv in 1892.

interior design objects of poor industrial manufacture.[97] This shift in style, which ultimately led to radical changes in ideals and taste, occurred at different times and places in different countries – but nowhere did it happen overnight.

Housing conditions in Denmark during the latter decades of the 19th century varied dramatically between different segments of society. One key distinction was that between city and country, another was people's economic standing in society. In the city, workers occupied the small flats in backyard buildings, while upper-middle-class families lived in the larger flats in the first row of buildings towards the street. It was in the biggest flats, with their wealthy occupants, that the eclectic Victorian style developed during the final decades of the 19th century.[98]

The emergence of factories and offices led to a desire for a physical as well as mental distinction between the workplace and home. While the city was becoming increasingly bustling and hectic, the home was seen as a refuge of calm, and that was reflected in furnishing styles. In 1947, the film director Peter Urban Gad (1879–1947), who grew up in one of the Copenhagen's leading families, reminisced about the padded, cluttered style and explained that living rooms were supposed to be 'warm and cosy, the home in general was supposed to be a nest, where one could feel safe and secure, after the heavy curtains had been drawn close against the cold and dark outside – and, in a sense, against the growing social tension knocking on the windows'. Gad summed up the mood of the period as 'a persistent attempt to create *hygge*'.[99]

In the Victorian living rooms, little daylight was allowed to pass through the curtains and portières and into the living rooms, and in the evening, candles and shaded oil and gas lamps provided soft, muted lighting.

The fashion generally called for plenty of textiles. As it said in the Danish book on interior decoration *Kunsten at Møblere sin Lejlighed* (The Art of Furnishing One's Flat) from 1892, textiles created 'the quintessence of *hygge*', so a lamp had to have 'one of the pleasant, voluminous, coloured shades'.[100] *Hygge* is a recurring concept in texts about home design written during the Victorian era. With regard to lighting, the book suggests that, for the sake of *hygge*, the new bright incandescent light should be dimmed with shades, and generally one should stick to the use of candles.

The merchant Rudolf Christensen and his family were among the first in Copenhagen to have electric lighting installed. In 1890, the family moved into a stately ten-bedroom flat by Frederiksholms Kanal in Copenhagen after comprehensive renovation and decoration by some of the finest artisans in the city (stucco workers, paperhangers, upholsterers and cabinetmakers).[101] The flat was decorated in the most exquisite style of the time with furniture in many different historical styles – depending on the function of the individual room – and multiple layers of textiles, not least in the form of heavily draped curtains and portières with trimmings, fringes and tassels.

At the same time as the Danish royal family in 1892 had electric light installed at the palace, the merchant family's stately home was the first and only in the building to be electrified, via a cable attached to the main cable at the nearby square Vandkunsten.[102] In their salon, the Christensen family could thus enjoy the light from the lavish crystal chandelier (H: 135 cm, D: 100 cm), which had been converted from gas to electricity (just like Edison's exhi-

Copenhagen power plant in Gothersgade was put into operation, making it possible for the Danish royal family to have electric light installed at the palace. And they were not the only ones to bring the innovation into their homes. For it was now, at the height of the Victorian era, that the first Danish homes had electric lighting installed.

The Argand lamp was the first lamp design that was (too) technical in appearance, a practical object divided into a decorative part and a 'machine' part. This remained a persistent dilemma throughout the Victorian era, with designs divided between two worlds: a cluttered, highly ornamented domestic world versus a world outside the home dominated by dramatic developments with industrial, technological and scientific advances that were also manifested in lamp design. From its place in the middle of the living room, the lamp should, ideally, tie the two worlds together.

While electric light gained ground, leading to drastic changes in home lighting from a technological point of view, interior decoration ideals changed too. Fashions changed from the lavish and overwhelming eclecticism of historicism to functionalism, which was, at its core, a rejection of cluttered rooms and an excessive number of

French electric table lamp in bronzed zinc, purchased by the Christensen family in 1892. The Victorian Home, National Museum of Denmark.

The crystal chandelier in the Christensen family's salon was converted from gaslight to electricity in 1892. The Victorian Home, National Museum of Denmark.

bition chandelier in 1881). The crystals were mounted on a frame made of brass tubes, perfect for concealing the cords, and the chandelier had five arms fitted with lights. The downward-facing frosted glass shades were shaped like flowers, each enclosing the brilliant flower bud, which in 1892 was a carbon-filament light bulb.[103]

The family also purchased new lamps for the home. In 1892, a bronze chandelier was bought for the study, listed in the accounts as '1 electric chandelier. 4 flames' – the terminology still referring to the gas flame.[104] That same year, the family also bought a sculptural table lamp in bronzed zinc depicting a young woman holding an oversized plant in her hand. The cord is concealed inside the long flower stem, this design too ending in a flower consisting of the socket, the incandescent light bulb and a ruffled white frosted glass shade. None of the lamps were Danish. The crystal chandelier, the bronze chandelier and the table lamp all had downward-facing bulbs, a design feature that could never have been achieved with a flame.[105] The lamps would have been a spectacular feature in the home, thus serving the dual purpose of lighting the rooms and demonstrating the merchant's economic prowess and the family's position in the upper echelons of society. Like the rest of the home design, the lamps will have contributed to framing and displaying the family's image.

Danish home decor long followed the heavily furnished, richly ornamented and fairly dark (and, actually, rather cosy) style. Many who had installed electric lighting found the new light much too stark and revealing, as described in an article in *Vore Damer* in 1913:

Until just a few years ago, when even the biggest dinner parties were lit entirely by kerosene and candlelight, it was a fairly simple matter for a lady to match the colours of her evening wear by daylight. One could always be certain that the warm lamp light would only enhance the look. However, since the advent of electricity and gas, the choice of colour for evening wear has become a problem. Every colour has its own properties, and even the most careful choice may lead to unanticipated surprises. Modern lighting is so rich in nuances that a lady who dresses for a party in an unknown setting can never anticipate the effect with any certainty.[106]

Thus, the lampshade became more important – as did the importance of its styling, which followed current fashions, as outlined in a description of the lamp and its shade in another article in *Vore Damer* in 1913. Here, the latest new lampshades from the department store Magasin du Nord are described:

> Whether the lamp is a central focal point of the living room, drawing it together – as it rarely is in our electric age, now that the hanging lamp is usually a bright and highly hung chandelier – or it stands on a desk or in a corner, serving the individual, it is always a bit of a favourite child, and since we are always happy to show extra care to our favourite children, it is only fair that we now, at the start of the winter season, immediately begin to think of dressing up the lamp. It deserves a new dress, but not one of the tucked-up and elaborately decorated dancer's robes that were the fashion for some time, but rather a stylish, calm yet elegant form that seems less eccentric but therefore doubly distinguished.[107]

The quote from *Vore Damer* illustrates that by 1913, tastes were changing in favour of a simpler expression, as reflected in the writer's disparaging description of a recent period's ostentatious fashion. Simplicity may not be the most apt term, however, as the text clearly refers to shades that any functionalist would call lavishly decorated: 'a dream in champagne silk garnished with violet-flower border; trimmed with a serrated beaded fringe in purple notes' and 'a crimped rose-coloured silk shade trimmed with white lace inserts and motifs; fringed with white and rose-coloured beads'.[108]

The terms used in the review show that lighting fashion at the time favoured golden and reddish notes that led to a warm light but also reflected the effort to domesticate and personify the lamp and tone down the aspect of pure, cool technology; wrapped in silk, the incandescent light bulb blended into the homely scene, like a beloved member of the family. A later article from *Vore Damer* in 1921 similarly personifies the lamp:

> Now comes the cosy time when the lamp is once again in focus, the lamp, our dear friend, whether at a dinner party for our closest friends or pleasant and quiet everyday evenings. There is nothing better suited to bringing a cosy ambience to a living room, a salon, a lobby than a lamp selected with the right, insightful taste and understanding of the harmony between the components of the interior – as today's public has such a wide range of options, catering to anyone's particular taste. Here, we present a few examples of original electric lamps.[109]

'Original' does not refer to lamps that were designed for electric light. The illustrations in the magazine in no way suggest that the new technology, the incandescent light bulb, had been embraced as inspiration for the new designs. Rather, 'original' refers to an artistic or eccentric expression: highly curious lamps with bases shaped like bird's legs and dark textile shades inspired by the Orient.

A few years later, the presentation of the PH lamp (personified by carrying the maker's initials!) marked a real revolution – this was an 'original lamp' indeed, a carefully considered design solution customized to the electric light bulb to ensure quality lighting, which was the focus of the task and, thus, of the form. PH's lamps transformed modern lamp design, but initially they were mainly adopted by avant-garde architects. The architect and glass designer Jacob E. Bang spoke of the excitement about the PH lamps: 'It somehow released something in us, and there was an almost cultish element to the enthusiasm and adoration it was met with. Hanging it from the ceiling affirmed one's standing as an intellectual and an avant-gardist.'[110]

One of the 'Original electrical lamps' shown in Vore Damer, no. 21, 1921.

Kaare Klint was another admirer: 'With the glow lamps currently available, the result Poul Henningsen has achieved with matt shades in glass and metal is the best I know of.'[111]

From the mid 1920s, Danish architects stepped up their challenge to 'beaded fringes' and 'lace inserts' and similar superfluous trimmings, and the modernist PH lamps became a symbol of modern design. PH was a pioneer, embarking on electric lighting design at a time when the electrification of Denmark was rapidly progressing, but many homes had still to embrace electric light.

Functionalism – and PH's lamps for a new approach to lighting

'The purpose of a lamp is to give light,' stated the functionalist architect Edvard Heiberg in the magazine *Kritisk Revy* (Critical Review) in 1927.[112] He wrote this in an article arguing, in the functionalist spirit, that it was up to the architects to educate people, to make them embrace a modern home design – rational and natural interiors that were not about taste or lack of taste but about taking a fresh look and considering the original purpose of furnishings: 'A chair is for sitting, and the purpose of a lamp is to give light – if the objects we live with in our home are clear and logical, they will help form a truly modern culture.'[113]

Heiberg was one of the early Scandinavian functionalists. In 1924, with direct inspiration from a Bauhaus experimental house, he built his own home, which was Denmark's first functionalist house.[114] Later, he installed PH lamps, but before we turn to those, it is time to take a brief look at the spirit of the time.

After the First World War, Central Europe was in ruins, both physically and culturally – and out of the ashes, new trends within design and architecture emerged. These trends continued developments that had emerged around the turn of the century, when visionary architects had begun, in theory as well as in practice, to focus on creating an authentic expression using new technologies and materials. The Paris-based architect Le Corbusier (1887–1965) was a key figure, and in Weimar, Germany, Walter Gropius (1883–1969) founded Bauhaus with a goal of fusing art, architecture and crafts into a unified discipline.[115]

The functionalist ideals spread from France and Germany to Scandinavia, where the *Stockholm Exhibition* in 1930 marked the functionalist breakthrough in the Nordic region. The exhibition presented complete home interiors: light, airy, with bright colours and simple and practical furniture. A new approach to home design and decor intended for the general public adjusted to meet their specific needs. The Swedish architect Gunner Asplund (1885–1940), who was the lead architect for the exhibition, embraced the rational expression of Le Corbusier and Bauhaus but rejected the functionalist call for standardization and the tendency to treat all human beings as identical.[116]

The *Stockholm Exhibition* was a 'must-see' for Scandinavian architects in the summer of 1930, and PH wrote with great enthusiasm about Asplund's exhibition buildings in *Nyt Tidsskrift for Kunstindustri* (New Magazine for Industrial Art): 'I know of no greater artistic experience than when task and solution match, and this is the first time in the history of functionalism that I have encountered that.'[117]

PH did not write about the light in the exhibition, although Swedish lamp design for modern electric light was on display in Hall 17. In keeping with the functionalist ethos – see Le Corbusier's mantra that 'the house is a machine for living in'[118] – these were presented as 'lighting devices'.[119] Characteristically for the time and the exhibition approach, they were thus presented with reference to their function rather than as 'lamps'.[120] 'Lamps' ran counter to the spirit of the event, as it might point back to the old lamp forms, and besides, it was ambiguous, as it might refer either to the light source itself or to the design around it.

The other Danish architects who reviewed the exhibition shared PH's enthusiasm but were not impressed by the 'lighting devices'. The architect Willy Hansen's (1899–1979) review in *Arkitekten* (The Architect) praised the exhibition set-up, where people could switch the lights on and off, but he found the lamps themselves 'rather unsuccessful'.[121] Ole Wanscher (1903–1985) elaborated in his review, applauding the effort to give the individual pieces of furniture new form but lamenting that the issue of lighting was not taken seriously at all: 'There are nice, cheap luminaires, but generally the lamps appear to be applied-art objects, no more technically determined than tin candlesticks and ashtrays in the modern style.'[122]

Copy of PH's Model I from the Paris exhibition in 1925. Made in 1974 in connection with a retrospective exhibition on PH's work at Sophienholm.

Three decades later, in 1960, PH wrote in the design magazine *Mobilia*: 'A revolutionary approach to applied art must contain the attempt at improving our utilitarian objects.'[123] In PH's own case, this effort had been directed at lighting design, an effort that had begun several years before the Stockholm event. His streetlight from 1920–1921 was mentioned earlier, but in 1925 PH had presented new multi-shade lamps at the International Exhibition of Modern Decorative and Industrial Arts in Paris.

The Paris exhibition was an international display of modern decorative luxury goods, but functionalism was represented too, in Le Corbusier's *Le Pavillon de l'Esprit Nouveau* (The New Spirit Pavilion), a demonstration of his architectural theories, as outlined in the book *Towards a New Architecture* (published in French in 1923) and the magazine *L'Esprit Nouveau* (1920–1925).[124] There were pavilions from 21 countries, including a Danish pavilion, designed by Kay Fisker (1893–1965) and Tyge Hvass (1885–1963), which displayed PH's lamps, designed for the lighting company Louis Poulsen & Co.

PH wanted to improve electric light, and the shades that he created for the electric light source were the physical manifestation of the theoretical challenges that he had

Walter Gropius's office at the Bauhaus in Weimar, originally designed in 1923. Note the ceiling lamp, which PH did not care for. The table lamp on the desk is Carl Jakob Jucker (1902–1997) and Wilhelm Wagenfeld's (1900–1990) iconic Bauhaus lamp from 1923–1924.

Table lamp by Carl Jakob Jucker and Wilhelm Wagenfeld from 1923–1924.

defined himself, since lighting engineering remained, at that point, fairly uncharted territory.

The lamps in the Victorian home from 1892, shown above, used carbon-filament bulbs (like the ones used in Edison's chandelier in Paris 11 years earlier), and they were not unpleasant to look at directly. However, the increasing use of the brighter metal filaments made it necessary to shield the light. PH sought to find a way to prevent glare without dimming the light too much. That was not quite accomplished in the solutions he presented in Paris in 1925, but less than a year later he had arrived at a simple triple-shade design that concealed the filament.

It was these triple-shade lamps that Heiberg installed in his functionalist house. He was excited about PH's lamps when he saw them in Paris. Unlike most other designs he saw at the exhibition, these luminaires were guided by the technical possibilities of the time; they aimed to solve a specific task and were not just decorative.[125] When Heiberg was interviewed about the design of his own home a few years later, he explained that he had chosen PH lamps because 'of all the lamps I have seen, in Denmark and abroad, none seem better suited to their purpose than this one; it is practical and beautiful!'[126]

In Denmark, the functionalist era had begun in the 1920s, spearheaded by architects such as Heiberg, Klint and Henningsen. In 1924, Klint was appointed the head of the newly established School of Furniture Design at the Royal Danish Academy of Fine Arts, School of Architecture. Klint felt that by categorically rejecting prior design approaches, Bauhaus designers cut themselves off from a useful source of accumulated experience. He thus required his students to study older designs and systematically analyse their functionality before creating their own solutions. Klint also folded paper lamps, as described on page 56.[127]

While Klint thus saw the benefits of embracing tradition, PH took a more critical stance. He had himself ventured into a new, almost uncharted field, and he carefully documented all his studies and thoughts. He also wrote about the new spirit of the time that shaped the light, initially in *Kritisk Revy*, which was published from 1926 to 1929.

This cultural magazine, which is identified closely with PH and his thinking, became a manifesto for what PH called realism – rational approaches for a modern era.[128] The editorial team behind *Kritisk Revy*, which also included Heiberg, among others, was fully updated on the latest international trends. However, although PH and the rest of the editorial team supported the rejection of a 'phoney culture' and decorative form, they also took a critical view of new ideas.¹²⁹ And while PH agreed with Le Corbusier's statement in *Towards a New Architecture* – 'In his struggle against a phoney culture, Le Corbusier does not write a single word that is not also ours'¹³⁰ – he criticized Bauhaus and, in particular, had a harsh assessment of Walter Gropius's ceiling lamp in the director's office: 'That has nothing to do with lighting, with technique, with skill and careful reflection on the issue.'¹³¹

On the desk in the director's office stood Carl Jakob Juncker (1902–1997) and Wilhelm Wagenfeld's (1900–1990) Bauhaus lamp from 1923–1924. The table lamp adheres closely to the original Bauhaus design concept, and although it looks simple, it is complicated and costly to produce.¹³² The lamp reflects a greater emphasis on the industrial aspect than on lighting quality, and in PH's opinion, that ran contrary to good lamp design. PH believed that the task had to revolve exclusively around achieving good lighting.

Kritisk Revy was primarily an architecture magazine, but it was also a forum for PH's thoughts on contemporary design and a medium for promoting the PH lamp. PH's two longest articles in the magazine deal with electric lighting. In the premiere issue of *Kritisk Revy*, in 1926, there is a 22-page article titled 'Moderne belysning af rum' (Modern Lighting of Rooms).¹³³ The PH lamp is not mentioned in the title, but almost every single page features an advertisement for the PH lamp. The article revolved around PH's efforts to develop his own lamp system, and the article is illustrated with photos of the lamps from the Danish section of the Paris exhibition. When PH followed up on the article a year later with an even longer article of 36 pages, the title was more explicit: 'Rummets belysning – med særligt Henblik paa Anvendelsen af P.H.-Lampen' (Interior Lighting – With a Particular View on the Use of the P.H. Lamp).¹³⁴ In fact, both articles were thorough descriptions of the PH lamps as tangible examples of the criteria of good lighting.

In the 1926 article, PH explains that the development from wax or stearin to kerosene and gas and further to carbon-filament and later metal-filament light bulbs had raised the temperature of the light. The light from the carbon-filament bulb was still warm and red, but that from the metal-filament bulb was not, because a higher temperature meant the emission of fewer red rays, which are also costly because of the heat emission. Thus, the more affordable light was of a poorer quality in the sense that it was less warm and less red, hence the need to shield the new light bulbs with textile in warm colours. PH wrote that although people initially exaggerated the size of the red and yellow silk shades, he was sympathetic. It was a fact that people wanted warm home lighting. In 1926, there were only two ways to achieve better lighting: reducing the temperature or shading the cold light bulbs – and since the light bulbs currently were what they were, the only solution was to construct suitable luminaires. It was important to educate people to enable them to install the right kind of lighting, one that spared their eyesight and enhanced their rooms, as well as to see the value of a simple, unadorned lamp.¹³⁵

In the 1927 article, PH thus defines a series of criteria for suitable lighting:

PH lamps in Carl Jensen's cartoon, captioned 'An architect passed through the living room'. *Blæksprutten*, 1943.

*We demand mainly downwards light, which makes the use of downwards-curving shades a natural choice. We demand glare-free light, which requires a luminaire of a certain size, which in turn depends on the nature of the task. We demand that the luminaire be luminous without being dazzling, which makes it a natural choice to divide it into multiple shades, so that a dim reflected light illuminates the outsides of the shade, even when it is made of an opaque material. For we want to be able to see where the light comes from. We further demand light with a pleasant composition and a warm main colour.*¹³⁶

As for the demand for mainly warm light, PH underscored that he did not call for light to resemble daylight: the lamp illuminated the room at night, and evening light had its own value and beauty and promoted a sense of calm.¹³⁷

In the article, PH discussed and analysed these demands and ended by comparing them to the construction of the PH lamp and concluded that the lamp, whose form resembled no other style, fully lived up to the criteria. Aesthetically, the beauty of the lamp lay in the fact that it was an object that accomplished its task and did not pretend to be something other than what it was.¹³⁸

Apart from Heiberg, architects such as Mies van der Rohe (1886–1969), Gropius, Alvar Aalto (1898–1976), Le Corbusier and Hannes Meyer (1889–1954) immediately began to use the PH lamp in their radical modernist interiors (see page 38). The general Danish public, however, did not embrace the lamp until 1930 when it was marketed more directly to private buyers and became more affordable thanks to an industrial manufacturing process. At the same time, the frame was lighter, the shades were made in a warm, golden colour, and several chandeliers with multiple light sources were launched, since that – a slightly less pared-down form – was what people wanted.

Functionalism aimed to make homes more hygienic, aesthetic, economical and rational in order to give many more people access to healthy living conditions. However, the new 'clinical' style was far from universally embraced, and many felt that all sense of homeliness and *hygge* was eliminated in the cold sterile interior. This point of view is reflected in a drawing from the satirical yearbook *Blæksprutten* (The Octopus) from as late as 1943. It clearly illustrates the paradox of patronizing architects and design reformers seeking to guide a sceptical public to embrace proper functional interior design. Most people preferred cosy homes with warm lighting. 'An architect passed through the room,' says the caption, which continued, 'Young architects are determined to improve Danish homes.'[139] In the drawing, the elderly couple is enjoying their cosy, cluttered Victorian living room in the light of the kerosene lamp; after the architect's visit, they sit, clearly uncomfortable in every way, in their cold, airy living room with its PH lamps. In all fairness, it should be noted that the story features an elderly couple, since no young couple furnishing their home in the 1940s would ever have opted for the stuffy Victorian style.

Although the PH lamp has become synonymous with modern interior design, it was in fact based on established conventions for the sensory qualities of lighting: lighting in the home should not just be glare-free but should also feel cosy, at the same time as the design should reflect contemporary demands for functional and practical 'applied art'. While the modernists had a negative view of *hygge*, associating it with the dark, cluttered, highly ornamented style that they wanted to leave behind, PH was sympathetic to people's desire to use lighting to create a cosy ambience. The key was to understand the concept in the right way: '*Hygge* is character, restfulness, comfort, not superficial style,' he stated in an article in 1928; in another he wrote that 'very often, *hygge* is confused with daintiness'.[140] Thus, the point was not to take *hygge* out of lighting but to take daintiness out of *hygge*. *Hygge* was another word for the desirable warm light. PH repeated the demand for warm light over and over again, from his earliest articles in *Kritisk Revy* until an interview he gave a few months prior to his death, where he stated that there is nothing as ghastly as overly bright rooms:

It is a misunderstanding that artificial light should be an imitation of sunlight, of daylight. Day and night were never supposed to be alike. It doesn't suit us. Of course, we need light in the evening – human beings are scared by total darkness – but when our cave-dwelling ancestors huddled around the fire at night, it was the heat – including the visually perceived heat from the flames – that made them feel safe. (...) Warm light also transforms

PH 6/5 from a trial hanging at the Danish Museum of Art & Design in Copenhagen in 1926. The lamp in the photo has been stripped of the white lacquer that was used in 1926.

its surroundings. (...) The human eye is more familiar with warm colours, and they suit us better.[141]

With this comparison PH returns to the Neolithic campfire as the origin of artificial light. Thus, even though his lamp design was conceived as a new form for a new era, the light from the lamps was rooted in history. To PH, it was never about form for form's sake; it was always about creating forms for the light to achieve better-quality lighting – light based on human needs rather than a technical issue. This is well aligned with the general Danish approach to functionalism, an approach that can be summarized as 'functional tradition' and can also be applied to a wider Nordic adaptation of international modernism.[142]

As evident from the stories in the book, PH continued to design lamps and to write and give lectures on lighting throughout his life. He wrote about lighting in Louis Poulsen's magazine *LP & Co. NYT*, which he also edited from the premiere issue in 1941 until his death in 1967. He also wrote about lighting in *Mobilia* and elsewhere and gave interviews to newspapers and magazines, contributing to an important ongoing debate about lighting design. The architect Finn Juhl (1912–1989) acknowledged in 1954 that there were many bad lamps which were more form

PH's Artichoke lamp from 1958, which concealed the incandescent light bulb.

than good function, but he also hints that perhaps he felt that he had heard plenty from PH:

It should probably be acknowledged that there are few very good luminaires available in the world today. (...) Most of them serve such a simple function in terms of lighting engineering that the task is largely restricted to the external form. Few designers in this field have any knowledge of lighting engineering, but some of them are quite fanatical in their effort to establish their own unique standing.[143]

PH's ideas have dominated the field, but they have also been instrumental in inspiring quality lamp design. In 2019, the designer Maria Berntsen (b. 1961) said of her view of PH and his role for the Danish design tradition,

There's no escaping PH's influence! I have mostly been fascinated with the beauty in PH's approach to proportions, and most importantly there were no modern Danish lamps when he made his first shades. He was a pioneer, creating a new form for a new light source and bringing good lamps into so many rooms.[144]

The continued development of light sources

In 1926, PH explained in the article 'Moderne belysning af rum' that the development from wax or stearin to kerosene to gas to incandescent light bulbs – carbon filament followed by metal filament – had raised the temperature of the light. From today's perspective, Edison's carbon-filament bulb was not very efficient, but it did emit a warm, red light. Since then, increasingly efficient metal-filament bulbs have led to more but colder light, and in PH's opinion, that was not a good development. The light had fewer red rays, and it was dazzling. From the early technical experiments PH conducted when he designed a streetlight (see page 34), he strived to achieve the glare-free light that would earn him world fame.

PH arrived at the right light by using multiple shades, either translucent (for example opal glass) or opaque (for example copper). The key was to position the shades to conceal the dazzling filament in the bulb. The sizes of the shades were determined by sight lines that went from the outer edge of a shade to the filament. These lines had to be run from the upper edge of the shade to the lower edge of the next shade to prevent dazzling light from hitting the eye.[145]

Another way to prevent both direct glare and contrast glare is to shield the light source using paper or matt, opal or flash glass, as shown in many of the examples throughout the book; this diffuses the light through the shade, so that it lights both the luminaire itself and the room around it.

Warmer light can also be achieved by using lower-wattage light bulbs. In his 1942 interior design book *Bo for To* (A Home for Two), the architect Bent Karlby (1912–1998) highlighted the benefit of 'chandeliers or, rather, luminaires with multiple lights', which is that they can be fitted with multiple low-wattage bulbs instead of just a single high-wattage one (for example, multiple 25-watt bulbs versus one 100-watt bulb): 'To produce a warm light – which seems to suit most people best – it is better to use multi-light luminaires.'[146] An example of Karlby's own luminaires with multiple light sources is seen on page 117.

In 1958, PH wrote in *Mobilia* in connection with the launch of the PH 5 and Artichoke lamps that 'whether we put a lady's hat of tin over it or place it inside a rational luminaire, we thus acknowledge that it is not in itself suited for home lighting'.[147]

The purpose of the lamp is to guide the light where it is needed and to prevent glare. Thus, PH underscored in 1958 that 'the luminaire constructor' should base the design on the currently available light source.[148] The earliest electric bulbs were made of clear glass, emitting a direct, dazzling light from the glowing filament. Later, matt light sources – both incandescent bulbs and strip lights – came to dominate the market. PH thus had to edit his 30-year-old triple-shade solution in order to hide the entire light bulb, not just the filament (see pages 66–69 and 78–79).

The stories in the book first present a large number of lamp designs – more or less closed or open – all created for the incandescent light bulb. When Verner Panton (1926–1998) in the late 1960s flouted the functionalists' rules and idea about making rooms as simple and bright as possible and instead created unconventional and warm

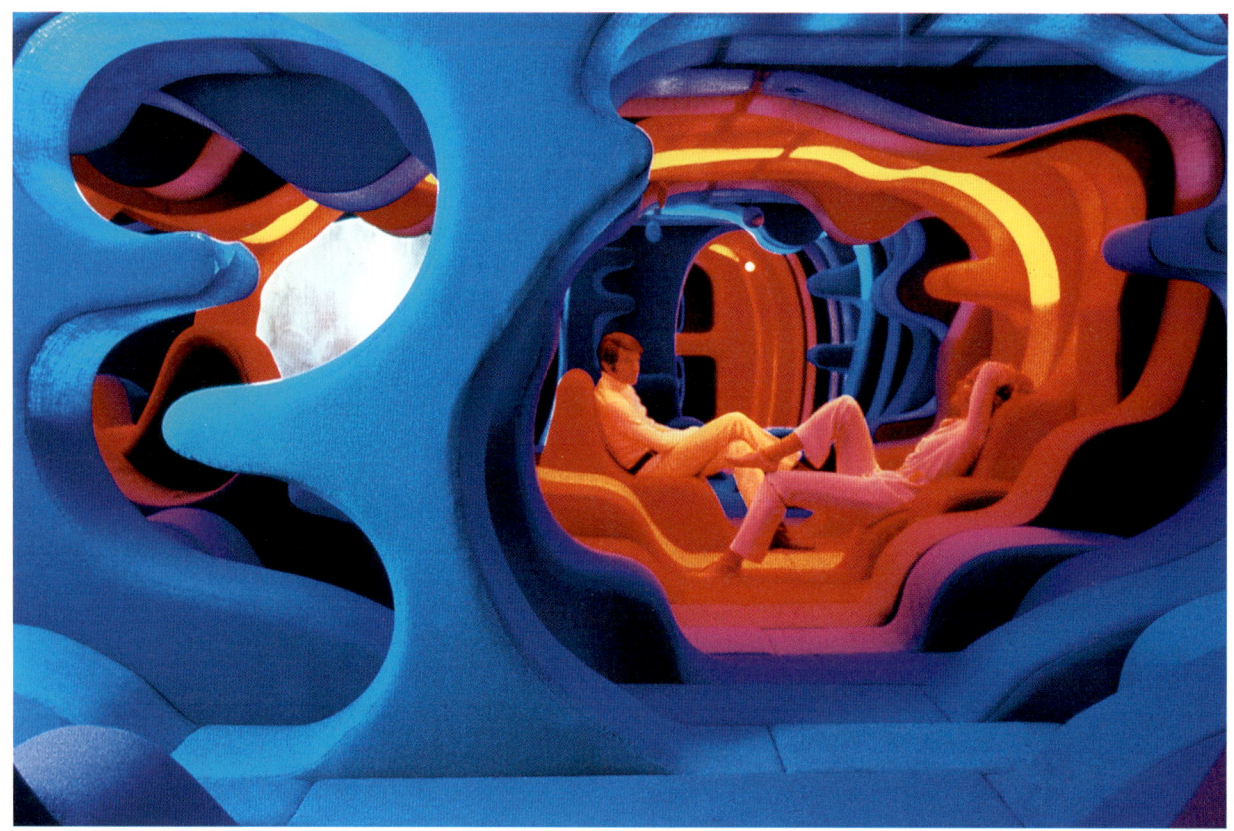

Verner Panton's luminous, polychrome total interior design Visiona II from 1970.

lighting experiences, his designs too were based on the incandescent light bulb.

During the 1970s, a new type of incandescent light bulb appeared, the halogen bulb, but it did not gain a real position on the Danish market until the 1980s.[149] The halogen bulbs used slightly less energy and were smaller than the ordinary light bulbs, which transformed lamp design. Now, the lamp head could be smaller and still conceal the bulb, and that provided wider design options. A new challenge, however, was to find room for the transformer (see pages 144 and 188). The fairly white light of the halogen bulb was used side by side with the warmer light of the traditional light bulb, which remained the preferred light source in Denmark until it was no longer an option.

In order to reduce CO_2 emissions and combat climate change, in 2008 the European Union decided to phase out incandescent light bulbs gradually, from September 2009 to September 2012, in favour of energy-efficient light sources. Since 1 September 2012, the sale of virtually all incandescent light bulbs has therefore been banned in the EU, with the exception of a few select halogen bulb types.

Both lamp designers and consumers now had to get used to the new options. The first was the energy-efficient light bulb – in principle, a bent strip light. The spiral-shaped light source had been available since the 1990s and was thus the first of many possibilities that were explored in a rapid development where the LED technology ultimately prevailed.[150] Neither designers nor consumers were happy with the new light sources, however, as none of them provided the desired light. The book has several examples of attempts to accommodate the new light sources.

In 1941, PH had optimistically written, 'One day we may well see the next development: electric light of such high quality that we can treat every single beam of light carefully instead of wrapping everything up in yellow cloths'.[151] Today, we are almost at that stage, for since the first LED lights were put into the lamps, the quality has improved dramatically. Today, LEDs[152] can be made for virtually any specific purpose and, importantly, in a fully polychrome palette. The diodes are often placed inside classic bulb-shaped globes and can therefore be used in all the old lamps with their E27 and E14 sockets, but they do not have to. The diodes are so small that they allow for truly

Innovative design for LED lighting: BIG's La Linea from 2019.

innovative lamp design – as described in some of the last stories in the book.

Another aspect of the new light sources that may transform lamp design completely is their much longer lifetime. While incandescent light bulbs had to be replaced frequently, the diodes are so durable that they may, in principle, outlast the lamp. This also makes it possible to seal them inside a closed luminaire, so that the consumer has no access to the light source.

However, it is not only lamp design that may be rethought. We also had to get used to new concepts. When the electric light was new, and lamps went from an open flame to an incandescent filament, we began to measure light output in watts. However, that is really like using fuel consumption to measure the speed of an aeroplane. With the many new energy-efficient light sources, we have now begun to measure light output in lumens, which is much more correct. An old-fashioned 25-watt light bulb produces about 250 lumens, 40 watt about 470 lumens and 60 watt about 800 lumens. By comparison, a candle produces 10–15 lumens.

In addition to the output, it is also important to consider colour rendering and colour temperature. Colour rendering is indicated by the so-called Ra index, where perfect colour rendering is equal to 100.[153] Daylight is Ra 100. The higher the Ra value, the better colour rendering, with 80 being considered the lower quality threshold. Light sources in general retail have to be at least Ra 80. Many of the earliest energy-efficient light bulbs had notoriously inferior colour rendering.

Colour temperature, measured in Kelvin (K), reflects whether the light, on average, is perceived as cold or warm, with lower colour temperatures meaning warmer light, and vice versa. A colour temperature of 2,700–3,000 K is recommended for cosy ambient lighting, while 3,000 K and above provide good working light. In LED lighting, 2,700 K corresponds to the familiar warm light of the traditional incandescent light bulb. LED bulbs on the retail market typically have a colour temperature of 2,700–3,000 K.[154]

The designer Sofie Refer (b. 1974) made this comment on our current lighting situation in 2019:

We are still in a phase where it's easiest to compare everything to a 60-watt bulb, but gradually people are getting used to using lumens and prefer that as a reference. We are still in a transition period, and many things have been frustrating. The positive point is that the rules are there to protect the environment. There are also huge savings involved. That's important to remember when we cuss about it and then try to buy quality light bulbs.[155]

In the many stories from after 2008, the designers deal with the new lighting situation and the options afforded by the new light sources in very different ways. With high-quality LED lights and the ability to control the light, the designers have really embraced sustainable lighting, and more and more designers go one step further and design sustainable luminaires for LEDs.

Today, LED lighting is used in almost all the old lamps, indoors and out. Even Dahlerup's lampposts, whose bright carbon-arc lamps impressed Copenhageners in 1892 and which were reinstalled on Kongens Nytorv in 2019 after the completion of the new metro station, now use modern LEDs.

In 1917, *Hjemmet* marvelled at the fact that all people now had to do was push a button or throw a switch for the new electric lamp to turn 'night to day!' as if by magic.[156] Since then, lighting technology has gone from low-tech solutions with a light switch on the wall and a small selection of light sources to a high-tech stage with programmable light and a wide range of light sources. This transformation has given lamp designers new possibilities.

Although all new houses and flats now have multiple outlets, and most people have lamps throughout their home, there has been and continues to be a demand for a light we can bring with us – also outdoors, to the balcony, the patio or the garden. A portable lamp is thus a theme that designers continue to address, and some of the 100 stories cover lanterns, modern versions of versatile oil lamps (pages 150, 196 and 210), a lamp with a very long cord (page 212) and a portable light with a diode flame and battery (pages 178–179). You can also read about a solar-powered lamp created specially for people living in conditions where they cannot, to this day, simply flick a switch to have electric light (pages 200–201).

Now, in the first story of the book, we go back 100 years to a time when electric light was still a novel innovation in Denmark and good design solutions were needed to create the right light.

One hundred
stories
about Danish
lamp design

Poul Henningsen: Slotsholmen lamp

Københavns Belysningsvæsen—1920-1921

When the first electric street lamps were lit in the central Copenhagen square Kongens Nytorv in 1892, it was a manifestation that electric lighting had arrived in Denmark. The lamps were designed, in the highly ornamented style of the time, by the established architect Jens Vilhelm Dahlerup (see page 22), who had a penchant for historicist design. Their installation coincided with the opening of the first Copenhagen power plant in Gothersgade, also in 1892, which also made it possible for the Danish royal family to have electric lighting at the palace. It would take some time, however, before electric lighting reached the many living rooms and streets throughout the country and before Danish luminaires were developed for the new light source.

By 1920, the proliferation of power plants had made electric lighting more widely affordable, and electric lamps began to show up in greater numbers, both in private homes and in the streets. In extension of this development, in 1920 Københavns Belysningsvæsen (Copenhagen Municipal Lighting Co.) launched a competition for new electric street lamps. The young architect Poul Henningsen (1894–1967) seized this opportunity to create a new form for a new era. Like many other contemporary designers, Poul Henningsen, commonly known as PH, did not have an academic degree from the Royal Danish Academy of Fine Arts, School of Architecture, but had attended the Technical Society's School in 1911–1917, supplemented with three semesters at the College of Advanced Technology.

PH began to experiment with shielding incandescent light in 1919, the same year that he founded his design firm. He designed a modern, 4.3-metre-tall street lamp, comprised of a post and a luminaire for the light bulb. Existing fittings designed for gaslight or carbon-arc light had become obsolete, and the lighting company expected a simple glass globe with a top cover to protect the electric components from the elements. PH, however, wanted to refine the technical properties and spread the light as far as possible. His solution was a glass cylinder covered by a large enamelled shade in a parable form that reflected the incandescent light evenly. The upper shade and five smaller, interior shades directed the beams so they hit the street at an oblique angle, the beam extending halfway to the next lamppost, which was 30 metres away.[1]

In 1921, seven of PH's street lamps were installed on Slotsholmen (Castle Islet) in central Copenhagen. The 1920s were a period of transition for street lighting. In the city streets, gas and electricity were in competition, but most street lamps still used gas. PH wrote in the Danish newspaper *Politiken* in 1921:

The trial lamps are now in situ along the canal from Højbro to Holmen. I have shaped them (...) as a solid of rotation (...) second, as concisely as possible without letting myself be overtly influenced by associations from old lamps, since the problems associated with the electric lamp and the gas lamp are completely different. (...) With its height, its narrow head and large shade it in no way corresponds to the fixed image we carry in our minds of the concept lamp.[2]

After the initial seven test lights had been installed, the Slotsholmen lamp was subsequently installed in several locations around Copenhagen.[3] However, when Københavns Belysningsvæsen decided to remove the interior reflectors and shades, the bulb was exposed, which resulted in too much glare through the clear glass: 'Then, as now, no one took any interest in glare-free lighting, and the public thought it was dreadful,' as PH later concluded.[4] Although the lamp was thus largely absent from the streets, it remained in use on Slotsholmen until 1972. Most importantly, PH's work with the modern luminaire served as a springboard for his continuing work with lighting and for later designers' successful streetlights (see page 86). Not least, the issue of glare had captured PH's interest, and he continued to explore the distribution of light and had his first, almost glare-free lamp ready and fit for a gold medal at the International Exhibition of Modern Decorative and Industrial Arts in Paris in 1925. Thus, the technical experiments PH carried out in connection with the design of the now all but forgotten Slotsholmen light laid the groundwork for his future efforts to achieve glare-free lighting that would later earn him world renown.

The Slotsholmen lamp debuted in Louis Poulsen's magazine *LP & Co. NYT* in 1947. The photo shows that Københavns Belysningsvæsen had removed its interior reflectors and shades.
→ Reconstruction of the Slotsholmen lamp from 2019. Seven of the original lamp heads are being restored and reinstalled with a view to possibly relaunching production.

'When the lamp is lit, the post and lamp form an energetic whole; this is a new form of beauty.'
—Professor Wilhelm Wanscher, 1921[5]

Poul Henningsen: System PH

Louis Poulsen—1925

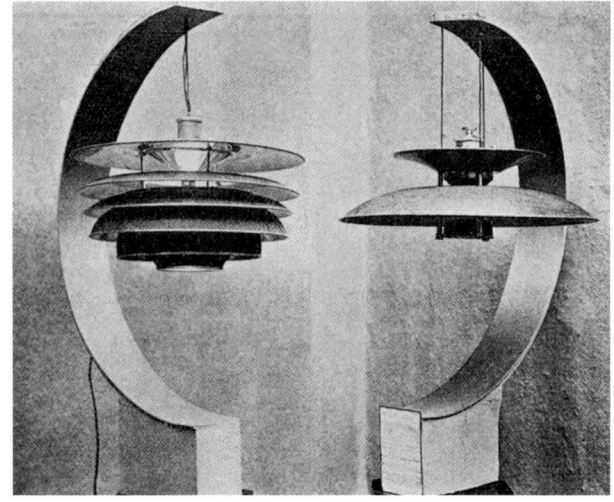

System PH lamps at their debut in Paris, 1925.
→ The lamps from the Paris exhibition were used in 1925 in the newly opened restaurant Schucani & à Porta in Copenhagen in a version with matt gilding to reduce glare. The shades were decorated by the Danish ceramicist Axel Salto.

From 1905 to 1920, so many new power plants were built that electric lighting became widely affordable. By 1920, half of Danish households had had electric light installed, but in PH's childhood home it had been introduced as early as 1907. It was a mixed blessing, however. PH later explained, 'Mother was so intensely unhappy with electric lighting. (...) The transition from the kerosene lamp was rough for her.'[1] PH later wrote that it was at this young age that his interest in lighting was sparked.

New lighting called for new luminaires: 'The electric chandelier is a new thing that calls for a new form.'[2] PH made this observation in 1926, but his first chandelier designs, ten years earlier, reflected a less revolutionizing approach. At the time, electric lighting had not yet come into its own with regard to uses and properties. The luminaires therefore largely copied previous forms designed for gas, kerosene or wax candles, the electric light bulbs being simply retrofitted.

Following this pattern, PH's earliest lamps did not break new ground in terms of form or technical properties. They were crystal chandeliers with frosted glass shades decorated with painted gold ornamentation in a geometric pattern, all in keeping with the prevailing design paradigm.[3] In winter 1918–1919, he designed a crystal chandelier with an outer ring of candles around an electric light bulb in the middle covered by a conical matt glass shade that made the bulb almost glare-free.[4] Marking a transition from live flame to electric lighting, the chandelier actually offered a welcome degree of versatility.

It soon became clear to PH that the new electric light source, the modern incandescent light bulb, necessitated new types of lamps that shielded the stark light, lent it a pleasant, golden hue and directed it to where it was needed. From 1920, PH's early lamp designs moved towards actual studies in lighting technology; at the time, there was neither theory nor practice to rely on, and he therefore engaged in extensive experimentation to develop methods and gain experience firsthand. In 1921, PH introduced the first lamps with glossy metal shades that reflected the light from the bulb for added brightness. The first globe he designed was made of shiny brass; the next featured reflective silver slats and was thus the first lamp to implement multiple shades as a design principle.

In his search for a solution, PH arrived at a design system based on multiple shades with curves designed to direct the light. His experiments resulted in a series of pendant and table lamps, all carefully designed around a constructive principle that achieved the desired light distribution. Despite the designer's best attempts, the lamps were not glare-free, however. This was in part because PH used shiny, reflective shades as the mirror effect helped him guide the direction of the light with great precision. It was these lamp models, designed to meet 'modern aesthetic demands', that PH, in partnership with the electric wholesale company Louis Poulsen, presented at the *International Exhibition of Modern Decorative and Industrial Arts* in Paris in spring 1925.

In the Danish pavilion, PH presented street lamps and interior lamps under the common brand 'System PH'.[5] PH had also designed the ceiling lights in the Danish pavilion: seven-shade chandeliers in three sizes made in shiny, reflective silver, which therefore produced glare. The lamps attracted considerable attention in Paris, and PH was awarded a gold medal and received widespread recognition for the multi-shade lamps. He had, however, failed in his endeavour to create glare-free luminaires, and after the exhibition he continued to pursue his theory of hiding the light source from view. As early as the coming winter, of 1925–1926, he arrived at the final form of his new, glare-free lamp type: the triple-shade PH lamp that provided the basis for subsequent lamp models and ultimately came to be seen as the quintessence of Danish functionalism.

'The thing should be beautiful in its connection between the form and the task at hand.' —Poul Henningsen, 1927⁶

Poul Henningsen: PH lamp

Louis Poulsen—1926

During the winter of 1925–1926, after the 1925 World's Fair in Paris, PH completed the construction that would become one of the most durable luminaires of all time. A functional, simple and, not least, glare-free lamp, now with a matt shade, it achieved the dual purpose of diffusing the light and concealing the light bulb filament: 'a precise and unfailing form'.[1]

In 1926, PH reduced the number of shades to three. The curves in the three simple shades were based on the logarithmic spiral, with the light bulb filament positioned in the origin of the spiral, so that every beam of light strikes the shade at the same angle. Later, he modified the shades, making the central shade narrower than the upper shade, and the lower shade narrower than the middle shade: 'The upper shade has a flat plate shape, the middle shade an oblique bowl shape and the lower shade a deep cup shape.'[2] The size and positioning of the shades were guided by considerations of glare, the distribution of light across the shade and demands for light diffusion based on a simple but effective formula: the upper shade reflecting 50% of the light from the light bulb, the middle shade 25% and the lower shade 25%.[3]

In 1926, the first triple-shade lamps lit up the new exhibition hall Forum in the Copenhagen enclave of Frederiksberg: 'The success was indisputable; modesty forbids me from quoting the newspaper reviews,'[4] PH commented 40 years later. The Forum pendants were soon developed into a complete lamp system, including multiple models and shade sizes, all marketed as PH lamps. The first lamp that was available in general retail, from June 1926, was the white opal-glass 5/5 lamp, but both metal and glass shades were developed in varying transparency and a range of matt to shiny surfaces.[5] The variable lamp system, which solved the lighting challenges that had initially inspired PH, is described in detail by PH in two long articles in the architecture magazine *Kritisk Revy* (Critical Review), which PH founded in 1926, edited and, over the years, used as a platform for sharing his ideas on contemporary design – not least as manifested in lamp designs.[6]

PH's key requirement of lighting was that it should be glare-free and directed downwards while still revealing where the light emanated from; further, the shades should regulate the intensity and colour of the light. He often underscored the importance of warm lighting in domestic settings, since cold daylight was not conducive to rest and relaxation:

One commonly hears fabulations that the task must be to replicate daylight as closely as possible. What on earth for? The difference is, after all, that in the evening, the light source is right there in the room with us, while during the day it is outside and at a considerable distance. The evening light has its own quality and beauty – and a much more calming effect on the nerves. It would be a cultural loss if we were to replace it with imitation daylight.[7]

PH wrote in 1927 that the most surprising aspect of the success of the PH lamp was that so many had recognized 'the beauty of an object that wholly fulfils its task and does not pretend to be anything other than what it is'.[8] Apart from selling well in Denmark, PH lamps were now available from no fewer than 60 German retailers and featured in German interior design magazines as examples of lighting in trendy art deco or functionalist homes. The lamp was also presented at the World's Fair in Barcelona in spring 1929, where it received the highest award.[9] The PH lamps revolutionized modern lamp design. The rational multi-shade lamp not only eliminated glare but also did away with superfluous details and historical design references. That is why it was used in many of the prestigious architect-designed homes built during the late 1920s – from Edvard Heiberg's house near Lyngby (1924) to Le Corbusier's Villa Savoye (1929) and Mies van der Rohe's Haus Tugendhat (1928–1930). Henry van de Velde, Hannes Meyer and Alvar Aalto also used the lamps in the buildings they designed around 1930. PH's primary focus was on finding the best and, from the users' point of view, most pleasant use of the new electric light source. The lamp design revolved around the human users and their experience of rooms and objects. Function determined form.

PH lamp in a Belgian catalogue from 1929.

PH table lamp (1927) with green lacquered metal shades and stem and a shiny brass base. H: 54 cm, Ø: 40 cm. The lamp in the photo dates from ca. 1930.

'We demand that the luminaire produce light without producing glare, and so it is natural to divide it into multiple shades, so that a faint reflected light illuminates the exteriors of the shades, even when they are made of an opaque material. We want to be able see where the light emanates from.'

—Poul Henningsen, 1927[10]

Frits Schlegel and Vilhelm Lauritzen: Fritzsche's Universal lamp

C.E. Fritzsche—1928

The conical shade of the reading lamp is cut oa at an angle to optimize the cone of light.

The architects Vilhelm Lauritzen (1894–1984) and Frits Schlegel (1896–1965) both attended the Royal Danish Academy of Fine Arts, School of Architecture, in 1916–1921 and 1916–1922, respectively.[1] They became friends, and shortly after graduation they did their first joint project in 1922, when they entered a competition to renovate the Copenhagen department store Daells Varehus. Lauritzen and Schlegel won first prize, and when the renovation began the following year, they established a joint studio. The big, new department store, designed in the prevailing neoclassical style, opened in 1924.[2]

The two designers' first three luminaires were also created as joint projects: Fritzsche's Universal lamp, a pendant lamp and a reading lamp were designed from 1926 and put into production in 1928 by the glass manufacturer and retailer C.E. Fritzsche, purveyor to the Royal Danish Court. The following year, the former two lamps won exhibition prizes at the *Bygge og Bolig Udstillingen i 50 Aaret for Stiftelsen af Akademisk Arkitektforening* (Building and Housing Exhibition for the 50th Anniversary of the Founding of the Danish Architects' Association) at Forum, in Copenhagen. The two young, progressive architects embraced functionalism, and the lamps in their clear, stereometric forms were presented at Fritzsche's stand and in a domestic setting in a modern one-story model home designed by Vilhelm Lauritzen. Next, the lamps were awarded a gold medal at the 1929 World's Fair in Barcelona. In 1930, all three lamps received awards at the *Belysningsudstillingen* (Lighting Exhibition) in Tivoli, in Copenhagen.[3]

The Universal lamp was a two-shade luminaire, and according to PH it was inspired by a Swedish acorn-shaped lamp that was the earliest example of a diffused-lighting design based on a system of shades.[4] In Schlegel & Lauritzen's Universal lamp, the concept underwent a modernistic redesign that abandoned the organic acorn shape in favour of a geometric combination of cone and sphere: an open, conical shiny opal-glass shade on top of a closed glass globe that conceals the light bulb. The globe is bisected horizontally straight through the filament of the bulb. Like the shade, the lower half of the globe is made of shiny opal glass and emits a diffused light. The light emitted from the top half is reflected downwards by the conical shade. Like PH, and the many who embraced his system approach, Schlegel and Lauritzen aimed to utilize the light as efficiently as possible while eliminating glare. In Lauritzen's assessment, the lamp gave out more light than the PH lamp. However, according to the architect Mogens Voltelen, Lauritzen and Schlegel had not managed to eliminate glare completely.[5] The glass shade was topped by a small metal plate that concealed the socket, which was cast in one piece with a small tube for the cord. Voltelen applauded this construction feature, which made it easy to dust the lamp and to replace the light bulb.[6]

The Fritzsche pendant lamp also had an opal-glass shade, only with a steeper cone shape. In this simple lamp, the upper section of the shade is designed as a tight-fitting top that facilitates cleaning by covering the socket and thus preventing dust from collecting there. The reading lamp has an obliquely cut-off conical shade in either metal or glass. The stem is mounted on a circular plate. It was made in 'quality materials', one critic commented in 1930.[7] The lamp came in an adjustable and a fixed version: 'To avoid unnecessary cost for buyers who only read and write, the lamp also comes in a cheaper, nonadjustable form.'[8]

The two architects, each of whom would go on to design important modernist buildings, both remained interested in lighting (see pages 50–52 and 76). Of the two, however, it was mainly Lauritzen who would subsequently design iconic lamps for the buildings he created.

'Lamp model, designed by the architects Frits Schlegel and Vilh. Lauritzen, appears to be made of higher-quality materials.'
—Review of Fritzche's reading lamp, 1930[9]

Arne Jacobsen: AJ reading lamp

1929

Arne Jacobsen's Texaco petrol station near the Bellevue Theatre, also designed by Jacobsen, on Strandvejen, north of Copenhagen.
→ The AJ reading lamp was recently relaunched by &Tradition under the name Bellevue.

A complete works list for the architect and designer Arne Jacobsen (1902–1971) would be long indeed. Most of Jacobsen's design contributions were created as part of his architectural projects. Meticulous care for the larger whole as well as the details is a characteristic of many architects, but Jacobsen took it to a new level. His holistic focus was so all-encompassing that he would have preferred to design every single item that went into his buildings.

Two years after Jacobsen's graduation, in 1927, from the Royal Danish Academy of Fine Arts, School of Architecture, in Copenhagen, he founded his own studio. That same year, he designed a floor lamp that was one of the first of his designs to go into production. The lamp had an expression characteristic for its time, showing a kinship with both Schlegel and Lauritzen's reading lamp (see page 40) and the German silversmith and designer Christian Dell's contemporary Goethe lamp.[1] Jacobsen's floor lamp was height-adjustable with a head mounted on a flexible gooseneck, which made it easy to direct the light where it was needed. The upper section of the lamp head encloses the socket and expands into a new form: a large, softly rounded cone that envelops the bulb and shields the light. The shade was cut off at a 45-degree angle to optimize the cone of light. The lamp, which came in a standard version with a white-painted shade and base and a matt brass pole and gooseneck, was featured in Louis Poulsen's catalogues during the 1950s. In 1929, it was named the AJ reading lamp.[2] The current name, Bellevue, sparks associations to Jacobsen's design of the Bellevue theatre (1935–1937) and the area around it.[3] Jacobsen often repeated forms, and a similar shade – without the top part – was used as outdoor lighting at Jacobsen's functionalist Texaco petrol station from 1936 on the coastal road Strandvejen, close to Bellevue, up the coast from Copenhagen. At the petrol station, a series of white shades was mounted upside down to highlight the white circular roof above the petrol stands.

In his 1934–1937 design of Stelling House, a retail space for the paint company A. Stelling, at Gammeltorv, in central Copenhagen, Jacobsen once again turned to the materials and expressions of functionalism. He designed all the furnishings in the retail space, including the lighting, reusing the same shade now on table lamps affixed to the counters.[4] Two large shades were mounted on the exterior of the building, one on either side of the shop door, to shine a spotlight on the elegantly curved, light and transparent entrance, which had the same modern and functionalist expression as Stelling House overall. On the two lower floors and in the shop windows, Jacobsen used opal-glass pendants. Produced by Louis Poulsen, the design was marketed as the Stelling pendant.[5]

From the late 1920s, Jacobsen turned to functionalism, which was already a prominent trend in international architecture. In 1929, the Danish Architects' Association held a building and housing exhibition at Forum, in Copenhagen, where Arne Jacobsen and the architect Mogens Lassen (1901–1987) won a competition for House of the Future with a futuristic, round house where the food was not cooked in-house but delivered from a central kitchen – possibly by helicopter via the roof-top landing pad. In a review, the architect and hardcore functionalist Edvard Heiberg (1897–1958) called Jacobsen and Lassen's house a 'bluff!' but assured his readers that, that notwithstanding, progress would occur and make 'things simpler and more natural'.[6] Jacobsen's reading lamp was designed for the 1:1 model of the house, which was demolished after the exhibition. The reading lamp, which had not yet shed all elements of 'cosiness', was put into production but did not receive the same degree of attention as Jacobsen's later, more clear-cut geometric lamps (see pages 64–65).

'We live in a time of profound conflict between the demands for cosy and rational design. It is, not least, staggeringly difficult to make people understand that a house has to be practical, as they often have demands for a cosy atmosphere that can make it difficult for architects to do their job.'—Arne Jacobsen 1929[7]

Poul Henningsen: Chandelier with PH lamps

Louis Poulsen—1929

The triple-shade PH lamp, which had found its basic form in 1926, was promoted on the Danish market in the popular building and housing exhibitions of the 1930s and, for example, in the design shop and showroom Den Permanente, which opened in Copenhagen in 1931.[1] PH's primary focus had not been on the lamp's appearance but on achieving the best and most pleasant lighting for a room and the items in it. Although the avant-garde immediately embraced the new form, many people, in PH's own words, found his lamps 'a little too technical'.[2] It would be some years before he achieved his main goal of improving home lighting. With their 'modern appearance',[3] his lamps were initially used mainly in offices and public settings and in the homes of the progressive upper middle class and well-to-do intellectuals, who were bold and affluent enough to embrace the new simple functionalist style. Many felt that the PH lamp was too plain compared to traditional lamps and chandeliers. For this large consumer segment, PH's designs were too novel and too expensive.[4] Thus, if PH wanted to market his lamps as standard items for a modern home, he would have to accommodate the demands of the average consumer.

In pursuit of the overall goal of educating people to embrace a simple design expression while meeting prevailing tastes half-way, around 1930 PH and Louis Poulsen introduced new lamp types aimed at a broader audience. The new range, which had required PH to compromise, included several lamps designed to stand on tables and bureaus to light up the corners of the living room and, not least, chandeliers in various sizes and models with *funkis* (Nordic functionalist) and art deco frames. Some bespoke models even included prisms.[5] Thus, despite PH's claim that large chandeliers were becoming obsolete, they remained in demand. One advantage of chandeliers was that they could be fitted with several, dimmer, light bulbs rather than a single bright one, which gave a warmer and more pleasant light.[6] The most popular were the Bombardment chandeliers, which came in several sizes with a range of different shades.[7]

Lighter, coloured shades were also introduced. In 1927, PH commented that in an attempt to achieve a warm, muted light from the electric light bulbs, people went 'so far as to completely exaggerate the size of the red, fraise and saffron silk lampshades they used in their homes'.[8] Of course, PH's lampshades also came in golden and reddish tones, as this led to a warmer light.[9] PH explained that warm light could be achieved in two ways: either by 'using special incandescent light bulbs that emit a warm light or by using lampshades that make the light warmer'.[10] PH opted for the latter solution. A 1931 Louis Poulsen catalogue described the new amber lampshades as giving out a 'warm, golden light. Not an ideal working light underneath the lamp but good general lighting', while the red lampshades produced an 'entirely reddish light (...) good, intimate lighting'.[11] The new lamps were more saleable thanks to the golden and reddish lampshades and, not least, lower prices due to cheaper materials and more efficient industrial manufacturing.[12] As a result, more people invited the lamps into their living room. The initiative had worked, and, as PH repeatedly underscored, 'The P.H. lamp is, above all, constructed for use in the home.'[13]

In interior design books from the 1930s, Louis Poulsen's PH lamps were shown side by side with luminaires from their competitor, Kjøbenhavns Lampe- og Lysekronefabrik.[14] The latter was making a name for itself with lamps that were so close to PH's that it was sued for plagiarism. The verdict in 1930 rejected the claim for all but one of the lamps: PH's large table lamp, which was re-

PH-inspired chandelier with two-shade lamps from Kjøbenhavns Lampe- og Lysekronefabrik, 1934.
→ Reluctantly, PH accepted the launch of a range of chandeliers with PH lamps. Shown in the photo is the Bombardment chandelier with ten times three golden glass shades.

garded as more artistic than technical and hence covered by copyright law.[15] However, the similarities between PH's lamps and some of the competitors' designs also reflected that they were taking his words to heart. In two long articles in *Kritisk Revy* in 1926 and 1927, PH had described the ideal lighting design solution, a topic he continued to write about throughout his life. His normative criteria for good lighting and shade designs were embraced by many designers, who created their own designs to achieve 'modern room lighting' – the title of PH's first article from 1926.[16]

'Development is moving away from the traditional chandelier, hung high in the centre of the room, but where it is still in use it should emit a faint, general light as a mere supplement to the otherwise localized and defining lighting.'
—Poul Henningsen, ca. 1928[17]

Niels Rasmussen Thykier: T3

Thykiers Lampefabrik—1929–1930

The sculptor Niels Rasmussen Thykier (1883–1978) is believed to have designed his first lamp in 1928, thus beginning a production of lamps in his own small company.[1] His highly popular T3 lamp was put into production in 1930. The following year, it was featured in the ad man Ove Boesdal's book *Hvordan skal vi bo? Vejledning i sund og naturlig boligindretning* (How Should We Live? A Guide on Healthy and Natural Home Design).

'Interest in the simplicity, beauty, practicality and authenticity of modern home design continues to grow.'[2] Thus the opening lines, and these concepts and the book's title underscore its functionalist spirit. Five pages are dedicated to 'the modern lamp'. Here, the author concludes that few things could rival the transformative impact of electric lighting on the character of the home, although it had taken a long time for designers to learn to use the new light source properly:

The first technically correct lamp to reach widespread use in Denmark was the P.H. lamp. Although it clashed with the fraise-coloured style, it prevailed and paved the way for many other sensible lamps that distributed the light properly without wasting expensive electricity. The transition from unhygienic silk to the purely technical lamp was facilitated by the invention of the cheap pleated paper shades. They are excellent and cosy, both on ceiling lamps and on stem-mounted lamps.[3]

Boesdal dismissed the multilayered silk shades, with their frivolous ornamental features, for obscuring the light and thus wasting electricity. By contrast, he saw the technically correct PH lamp as a trailblazer for the rational lamps of a new era. Interestingly, he highlighted paper shades as a good compromise, ensuring excellent light and a cosy atmosphere. Boesdal acknowledged the Danish demand for *hygge*. His text was illustrated with photos of a PH floor lamp with white glass shades and Thykier's lamp with a paper shade. Boesdal praised the latter for its 'good light and beautiful, calm lines'.[4] The lamp in the photo has a decorated shade; the text explains that buyers could choose between a plain white shade and shades decorated by the artists Jais Nielsen (1885–1961) and Einar Utzon-Frank (1888–1955).[5]

The lamp has a simple and geometric design: a circular base supports the smooth stem, which is thicker at both ends to accommodate the continuous switch and, at the top, the socket and the shade frame. The lamp was made of bronzed, matt-brushed or chromed brass; this included the upper and lower rim of the open, conical shade. Originally, Thykier used white Schoellershammer drawing paper for the shade, which was impregnated after the rims were fitted. Into the 1940s, it was available with either crowd-pleasing flowers or Utzon-Frank's bold cubist patterns.[6] Most of the light fell on the tabletop, while the translucent shade diffused the rest into the room. Clearly a less technical luminaire than the PH lamp, the T3 has a simple, modern expression.

Thykier produced the lamps himself with the lighting company Fog & Mørup as his wholesaler. In 1936, the lamp was mentioned in *Bygge og Bo, Tidsskrift for Moderne Hjem* (Building and Living, Magazine for Modern Homes), which advocated a simple functionalist style. The article 'Moderne Belysning' (Modern Lighting) characterizes Thykier's design as Denmark's most beautiful and natural table lamp.[7]

The following year, when King Christian X celebrated his 25th year on the throne. Reportedly, Fog & Mørup presented the monarch with a lamp, which was launched in 1940 as Kongelys (literally 'royal light' and also the name of the plant great mullein). Despite the close similarity, Kongelys has nothing to with med Thykier; it is one of copies that major manufacturers produce, based on his popular design.[8] In 1991, the lighting company Horn Belysning acquired the production rights for the Kongelys lamp, relaunching it in 1999. In April 2000, Horn Belysning gifted a 'royal light' to Queen Margrethe II on her 60th birthday. In 2004, the Kongelys came out in a limited edition of 200 lamps in brushed steel and opal glass to mark the occasion of Crown Prince Frederik's wedding to Mary Donaldson. The base features the couple's monogram (designed for the occasion by Queen Margrethe) and a unique number. The bride and groom received Kongelys No. 1 — by then, both T3 and Thykier had been forgotten.[9]

Shade for T3 Minor with decorative pattern designed by E. Utzon Frank. Fog & Mørup, 1939–1941.

'The T3 lamp: without a doubt the most beautiful and natural table lamp ever made in Denmark.'—'Moderne Belysning', 1936[10]

Piet Hein: Ra lamp

Kjøbenhavns Lampe- og Lysekronefabrik— 1934

The Ra lamps were relaunched in 2007 by the Piet Hein company. Both lamps shown here are from this new collection.

In 1936, the mathematician and designer Piet Hein (1905–1996) described his solution for the optimal use of electric lighting in the year's first issue of *Arkitekten. Ugehæfte* (The Architect. Weekly).[1] His solution was the Ra lamp, which he had begun to sketch in 1931. He presented it at the exhibition *Danske Opfindelser og Konstruktioner* (Danish Inventions and Constructions) at Industribygningen in 1933, where it attracted considerable attention.[2] Hein was thus working on his own ideas about quality lighting around the same time as the PH lamps were becoming popular, although his approach to glare-free lighting was quite different from PH's.

In contrast to PH, Hein saw the popular globe lamp, which emitted light in a uniform pattern through opaque glass, as an ideal solution for minimizing glare. Hein sought to combine this glare-free quality with the predominantly downwards light emitted from a lamp with an opaque shade. In the early 1930s, based on the complex mathematical calculations that became a hallmark of his design approach, Hein arrived at a model that combined the benefits of the closed globe and the open shade. In Hein's model, the big metal shade, its shape defined by a flat, mathematically determined curve, shielded the bulb, which is mounted inside a smaller hemisphere, thus preventing direct downwards light and glare. The lamp emits an evenly distributed, indirect and mainly downwards light with minimal loss of brightness. Satisfied with the result, Hein named the lamp after the Egyptian sun god, who, according to tradition, traversed the sky in a boat by day and was swallowed up by the sky goddess Nut at night.[3]

In addition to the Ra lamp's obvious qualities – good and glare-free lighting – Hein emphasized 'two other important advantages: it does not gather dust in hard-to-get-to places, and the bulb is easily replaced with one hand'.[4]

The Ra lamp was selected for the sales hall in the White Meat District, a new section that was added to Copenhagen's existing meat market in 1931–1934 and named after the colour of the buildings. The weekly newspaper *Ingeniøren* (The Engineer) wrote in 1934 that the task of lighting the hall was 'exceptionally beautifully handled'. The paper noted that in addition to the 600 Ra lamps in the Meat District, the lamp was already in use in other settings too: 'This lamp will likely soon be widely used in all settings which call for a lamp that is both glare-free and focused and also produces very soft shadows.'[5] Hein and Kjøbenhavns Lampe- og Lysekronefabrik (Copenhagen Lamp and Chandelier Factory), which put the Ra lamp into production, presented the lamp at the 1935 World's Fair in Brussels, where it was awarded a gold medal. This international launch is highlighted in sales catalogues from subsequent years, which also include Hein's comments from 1932:

The Ra lamp does not purport to be the only viable option. (...) However, when a luminaire, by means of a particular shade form, manages to combine the globe lamp's absolute minimum of glare with the shade lamp's economy of light and ability to distribute the light appropriately, it would seem fair to assume the superiority of this luminaire in a wide variety of cases. There is, further, aesthetic value in the fact that the lamp form is not based on a passing fad but is strictly determined by the mathematical surface that comes closest to the ideal.[6]

The lamp was available in shops from 1934. In 1936, Kjøbenhavns Lampe- og Lysekronefabrik produced the Ra lamp in ten different models with a white or yellow shade ranging from 16 to 80 cm in diameter.[7] Later, the lamp head was also used in wall- or ceiling-mounted lamps or, mounted on different stems, in floor and table lamps. After being out of production for some time, the lamp was relaunched by Lyfa in 1969, now with shades in bright, trendy colours. In the new millennium, production returned to the company that bears the inventor's own name, Piet Hein.[8] The shape has indeed outlasted passing fads, and the formula has demonstrated its staying power.

'After the invention of the incandescent light bulb, the lighting problem is no longer one of ensuring sufficient light at an affordable cost but of making the best possible use of the light.'
—Piet Hein, 1936[9]

Vilhelm Lauritzen: Radiohus pendant

Louis Poulsen—1941

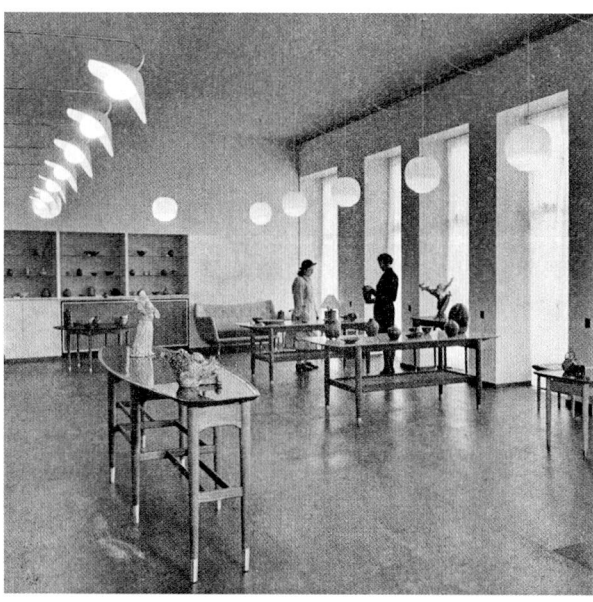

When the architect Finn Juhl decorated Bing & Grøndahl's showrooms on Amagertorv in Copenhagen in 1947, he used the Radiohus pendant with an acid-frosted shade that would not compete with the shiny porcelain or bounce stark reflections on the walls.

In the early decades of the 20th century, two innovative commodities, electric lighting and the novel electronic medium of the radio, were becoming commonplace in Danish homes.

With radio becoming a mass medium, the state broadcasting service needed more spacious premises. In 1934, the Danish architect Vilhelm Lauritzen was invited to join the team charged with designing the new radio building on a site across from the Forum event venue in Copenhagen. In 1936, work began on what is now considered a principal example of modernist architecture. The building was completed in 1942, but due to the war the official opening was postponed until 1945. Radiohuset (the Radio Building) was designed as a *Gesamtkunstwerk*, a total work of art, with specially designed furnishings and fittings throughout. This included the many lamps, except for the Universal lamp, which Lauritzen had co-designed with Frits Schlegel in 1928, although the version that was used was a custom-designed variant of the original. Lauritzen always designed lamps to complement his architectural designs, and the lamps for Radiohuset are accomplished examples of this practice.

Lauritzen designed the wide range of lamps in close dialogue with architect Mogens Voltelen, who worked in Lauritzen's firm from 1937 to 1947. Lauritzen focused on the form of the lamps, while the technical details were handled by Voltelen, who later taught lighting engineering at the Royal Danish Academy of Fine Arts, School of Architecture. All the lamps were produced by Louis Poulsen, and several were included in the retail catalogue, thus appearing alongside the PH lamps that had previously defined the company. Now, Lauritzen and PH shared the position as originators of the vast majority of the lighting company's models during the 1940s and 1950s.[1]

The Radiohus pendant was a less technical lamp, and soon after the launch, in 1941, it had become a bestseller. The exterior form of the elliptic opal-glass shade shows a close kinship with Radiohus Studio lamp, which combined diffuse general lighting with a more intense, downwards beam to provided good working light. Moreover, it was designed to provide pleasant glare-free lighting for the long hours spent in the studio. The Studio lamp had an ingenious design with a two-part glass construction, while the Radiohus pendant was a simpler, and more affordable, version with a single lampshade: 'We began with a globe pendant and had Louis Poulsen cut off the lower section so you could get at the bulb, and then we added a reflector to guide the light downwards.'[2] The solution worked, and the lamp is glare-free unless one stands directly underneath it looking up at the bulb through the opening at the bottom.

In 1954, Lauritzen described his lamp design criteria in Louis Poulsen's magazine *LP & Co. NYT*: 'It should be easy to clean, not gather dust in the base, not shatter with the first knock, offer simple bulb replacement, minimize glare (without adjustments) and be available for downward as well as evenly distributed light, as needed. And it should look nice.'[3] The magazine editor, PH, who always enjoyed a debate with Lauritzen, mentioned that he found the elliptic glass shade too much a fashion dictate, too 'nice' and shaped by a soft pencil rather than by the eternal laws of physics — unlike PH's own lamps, which were based on the natural principle of the logarithmic spiral.[4] That Lauritzen's design drew on a contemporary form is borne out by the similar but chubbier Søllerød pendant, designed by Arne Jacobsen and Flemming Lassen only two years earlier, and by the variants of the open glass globe that were subsequently launched (see page 58). These designs all draw inspiration from traditional Japanese and Chinese paper lanterns.[5] Today, the Radiohus pendant in shiny opal glass with the small brass fitting has come back in style, and since 2016, it has been available from Louis Poulsen under the name VL45 Radiohus pendant in three different sizes.

50

'We found the form to be beautiful and natural.'—Vilhelm Lauritzen, 1954[6]

Vilhelm Lauritzen: B&G pendant

Louis Poulsen—1941

'It is not quite as simple as PH would have it to determine when the design of a lamp represents an artistic effort.'—Vilhelm Lauritzen, 1954[1]

Vilhelm Lauritzen's architecture firm designed many lamps for the Radiohuset building on Rosenørns Allé as well as a series of lampshades in shiny opal glass, including two small ones measuring approximately 20 x 20 cm, that could be used on wall-mounted bracket lamps, on floor lamps or in chandeliers of various sizes. In technical terms, the two small lampshades are quite similar, both filtering the light through opal glass to emit a soft, glare-free light, while the opening directs bright, unfiltered light to the surface below. The shade used on floor lamps in the lobby and on the large Radiohus ring chandelier in the Radio Council Chamber had the larger opening of the two, thus providing good lighting for people coming and going and for the meetings in the Chamber. Unlike the others, the ten shades on the ring chandelier were acid-frosted. The shape of the lampshade resembles the head of an anglepoise lamp – for example, the Norwegian designer Jacob Jacobsen's classic Luxo from 1937. A key difference is that Lauritzen's shade – whether shiny or matt – is translucent.

The other of the two small lampshades has a more rounded shape and thus a smaller opening. It was used in the restaurant and concert hall, among other places, but was named the B&G shade because the architect Finn Juhl had used it and several other lamps from 'Radiohuset's wealth of luminaires' in his design of the porcelain factory Bing & Grøndahl's showroom and shop on Amagertorv in central Copenhagen in 1947.[2] Juhl used acid-frosted pendants throughout in the B&G interior in order 'not to compete with the shiny porcelain and cast stark reflections on the walls'.[3] The frosted shade was also the one that was used in the Christiansborg ring chandelier that Lauritzen designed in 1951 for the Danish Parliament building. The chandelier was produced in several sizes, from three all the way up to twenty-four lamps. The latter is an impressive luminaire, with its large brass ring, but in form it is much simpler than the chandeliers that Lauritzen installed in 1960 in the Danish embassy building in Washington, DC, with hundreds of small, delicate glass bells that cast their enchanting light on reception guests and cocktail glasses.[4]

The chubby B&G shade is quite similar to the one that was used in Radiohuset for a small working lamp (see page 90) and a record-player bracket lamp in metal, only cut off at an oblique angle to direct the light onto the work area. The record-player lamp was made in brass, while the table working lamp used a combination of brass and white-painted metal, the arm made in brass and the interior of the shade painted in a warm white to produce a soft, pleasant light.[5]

Lauritzen continued to design new lamps and to develop and improve on earlier models and thus always had a ready supply of lamps that were perfectly suited for the modernist buildings he designed. The architect Morten Lund has described how Lauritzen was able to transfer his ideas about the use of daylight in rooms into the design of good lighting: *in his architecture, he always made optimal use of daylight, merging warm, bright sunlight with the cooler, gentler skylight. This highlights the space itself rather than its delimiting wall, floor and ceiling surfaces, and the sculptural light illuminates people and furnishings with subtlety and nuance. Lauritzen's lighting designs draw on the same concept. They merge a bright, directed light that creates distinct shadows with a diffuse light that softens and adds new qualities to the rooms.*[6]

Lauritzen's lamps for Radiohuset were put into production in 1941, and, parallel with Lauritzen's large architectural projects, the selection presented in Louis Poulsen's catalogues expanded throughout the 1950s. For some years, Lauritzen's lamps went out of production, but in 2016 Louis Poulsen relaunched the Radiohus pendant and the VL38 table, floor and wall-mounted lamps. A black version of the latter was launched in 2017.

The original Radiohus chandelier in the Radio Council Chamber, its curvature matching the form of the table. The acid-frosted shades are mounted on matt brass tubes.
→ In 1951, the B&G shades from 1941 were used on the Christiansborg ring chandelier, relaunched in 2019 by Louis Poulsen as the VL Ring Crown series, which also includes a solitary pendant lamp.

Tage Klint: Model 1

Le Klint—1942

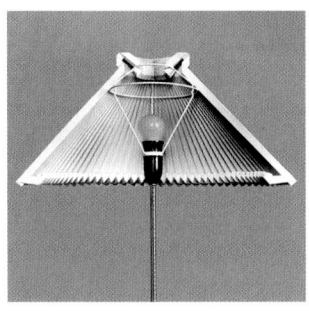

P.V. Jensen-Klint's kerosene lamp, ca. 1901.
↙ Tage Klint's collar design, patented in 1938. The natural elasticity of the folded paper holds the shade in place on the frame.

The art of paper folding and of making paper lamps has Asian roots. Originating as a Chinese tradition, paper folding was perfected in the Japanese art of origami. Both countries also have a proud, centuries-long tradition for crafting paper lamps and lanterns. In the West, the use of paper shades to filter and soften the light of the new, brighter kerosene lamps began in the 19th century. With inspiration from Japanese paper lanterns, the British physicist Benjamin Thompson in 1806 recommended the use of paper lampshades to avoid 'dazzling the eyes (...) without darkening the room or sensibly diminishing the beauty of the illumination'.[1]

In Denmark, light smooth or pleated parchment or paper shades became particularly popular after 1930. Like opal-glass globes and lampshades, they emitted a soft, warm light and matched the contemporary lighter interior design style. Moreover, paper was a low-cost and widely accessible material, even during the Second World War, when textile, glass and metal were in short supply.

Most paper lampshades were handcrafted in the home. Like many other families, the Klint family folded their own paper shades. They had begun this practice in the early 20th century when the architect and engineer P.V. Jensen-Klint (1853–1930) had designed a kerosene lamp in *skønvirke* (Danish art nouveau) style and wanted a pleated shade for it. To make the lampshade easier to fit on the shade ring and ensure the necessary distance to the flame inside the hot chimney glass, he designed the pleat to include a collar at a right angle to the shade itself – an innovative and effective solution.

The first of the Klint lampshades, it stood out from most other paper shades due to the level of refinement of the pleat. Kaare Klint (1888–1954) said in 1943 that he was about 12 years old when his father created the collar design and that although the whole family eventually caught the lamp-folding bug, his older brother, Tage Klint (1884–1953), was the keenest:

My brother was the most energetic, initially just for the family's use, but later as a hobby, an evening pastime, resulting in presents for friends. The shades would unfold like sea anemones in his hands, the technique developed and he figured out how to shape the collar in such a way that the shade could be secured to a standard lamp ring based on its own elasticity alone, with no need for a support.[2]

P.V. Jensen-Klint's eldest son thus refined the collar to be able to grip the ring without needing a drawstring to pull it tight. Tage Klint patented the principle behind the collar construction in 1938. In 1942, the finished lampshade had its premiere in an exhibition at Svenskt Tenn in Stockholm, and the following year, in the middle of the war, he founded the company Le Klint – named after his daughter Le – near the docks in the Danish city of Odense as well as a 'small shop in Copenhagen'.[3] Tage Klint's Model 1 laid the foundation for the commercial production of the Le Klint lampshades. It was followed up by the many other models that become highly successful both on the Danish market and abroad. In most historical accounts of Danish lighting design, Le Klint's lampshades and the PH lamps are the most prominent highlights.

Tage Klint's hand-pleated design was ready for production in 1942, and in 1943 the task of crafting the lampshades was handed over to workers in Odense. In a systematic, factory-like set-up, the shades were hand-folded by professional 'pleating girls', just as in most homes the task of pleating or embroidering lampshades had mainly been a female activity. To this day, the Le Klint shades are pleated by hand in an efficient large-scale production process – and still by an all-female staff.[4]

'This development, from an inherited utilitarian form through handicraft to commercial production, is not without tradition in Danish business history.'
—Kaare Klint, 1943[5]

Kaare Klint: Fruit Lantern, Model 101

Le Klint—1944

The architect Kaare Klint continued his father's work on a large scale when he took over the task of completing the Grundtvig's Church in Copenhagen's north-west district after P.V. Jensen-Klint's death in 1930. While his older brother, Tage Klint, was the entrepreneur who laid the foundation for the family-owned company Le Klint, Kaare Klint focused on his architectural firm and his work as head of the School of Furniture Design at the Royal Danish Academy of Fine Arts. Founded in 1924, the school inspired a new Danish furniture tradition.[1] However, he was also very involved in the Le Klint company – designing the retail space in Store Kirkestræde, in Copenhagen, writing the copy for the first catalogue and designing both the company logo and a number of lamps.

In 1930, Kaare Klint lamented that modern design had been too quick to jettison tradition in order to start over from scratch: 'This aversion to everything old obscures one's sense of the big picture and causes one to eschew the best help one can find, which is to build on the experiences that have been accumulated over the centuries. Problems are not so new; in many cases they have been dealt with before.'[2] In both form and material, Kaare Klint's lamps reference Chinese and Japanese paper lanterns, but he refined the craft to create beautiful, unique and complicated structures.[3]

In 1944, he folded four paper lamps. One of them was the Fruit Lantern: a rounded geometric – specifically, 16-sided – lamp with a collar. The lamp has a more refined pleat than the round Model 107, which his son, Esben Klint (1915–1969) created for Le Klint i 1942, and which Kaare Klint used in the company logo. The folding was based on cross pleats, and that led to a dispute between PH and the Klint family. While exiled in Sweden during the war, PH too had begun to make pleated paper lampshades, and in 1943 he took out a Swedish patent for a paper lamp design. In autumn 1946, Louis Poulsen launched PH's pleated globe in four sizes and four colours in addition to white: light yellow, light blue, pink and red. In connection with the launch, PH confrontationally described pleated lampshades as something that 'many have of course taken up'.[4] The dispute wound up in court but was concluded amicably.[5] Kaare Klint also experimented with lampshades in both reds and greens. As it turned out, they faded quickly, not least due to the heat from the light bulb, so the Fruit Lantern and the other Le Klint lampshades remained white.

↖ PH's pleated spheres, Louis Poulsen, 1946.
↑ The shade was designed by Tage Klint, the tubular frame by Kaare Klint. This Kiplampe Model 306 from 1945 doubles as a table lamp and a wall lamp.

The architect Finn Juhl had intervened in the dispute between PH and Klint, and he clearly favoured Kaare Klint's design over PH's. Generally, Juhl felt the paper lamps had too many drawbacks: they got dirty, they faded, and they provided only 'general lighting, with equally dim light in all directions'.[6] However, the Fruit Lantern does more than that. The paper filters the light to produce gentle and harmonious illumination, and Klint's application of the cross-pleating technique adds strength to the fragile paper and gives rise to an exquisite form, while the combination of translucence and structure creates soft, beautiful shadow effects. To top it all off, the Fruit Lantern is finished with a beautiful collar, as noted by Juhl in 1947.

Just as Kaare Klint strove for perfection in his wooden designs, he also explored the potential of pleated paper. He was a democratically minded designer, but although his mahogany furniture designs were based on an ideal of simplification, it was not cheap, and the buyers came from the upper middle class. Paper, on the other hand, is a humble material, and that gave the Fruit Lantern a more democratic reach. It remains one of Le Klint's best-selling lampshades. In 1945, Kaare Klint also designed a small brass-rod bracket for his brother's lampshade. The frame for the Kiplampe (Tilt lamp) has a clever tilt mechanism that locks into two different positions for easy conversion between wall and table lamp – a versatile and, for its time, innovative solution.

'I find the shape of Klint's lamp much more refined, probably due to the proportioning of the pleat that finishes the upper part of the form.'—Finn Juhl, 1946[7]

Bent Karlby: Peanut lamp, Model P162

Lyfa—1946

In 1934, two years after graduating as a building technician from the Bygmesterskolen (Building School) at Aarhus Technical School, the architect Bent Karlby (1912–1998) joined Vilhelm Lauritzen's architecture firm,[1] where he worked until 1939, a period that overlapped with the design of the Radiohuset building and its furnishings. After a few other, briefer, periods of employment, Karlby founded his own firm, focusing initially on an extensive line of wallpapers and lamps. Shortly after the start, in the early 1940s, he established a collaboration with the lighting company Lyfa. From the late 1940s, the collaboration expanded, and it came to last almost 40 years. In 1943–1944, Karlby designed the China lamp, launched by Lyfa in 1950.

Bent Karlby's China lamp was a popular item and sold in large numbers.

In its basic form, the oval, almost elliptic, opal-glass globe is not very different from the Radiohus pendant, which may have been on the drawing table during Karlby's time at Lauritzen's office. Karlby's model is slightly slimmer and has a narrow, openwork brass rim around the lower lip of the globe. The rim did not affect the quality of the light but was strictly decorative. In 1949, Karlby commented:

It is most definitely not enough to ensure the technical quality of the light; in a furnishing element such as interior lighting for the home, the decorative aspect should be given the same weight as the rational: decorative in the best sense of the word, not as pasted-on tinsel and glitter, but in the form of moderately applied and always motivated effects. After all, we are all romantics to some degree.[2]

Karlby's lamps from the late 1940s were criticized for having a romantic and nostalgic expression and, in some cases, a form that had more in common with Victorian-era kerosene lamps than with modern electric lamps. Karlby replied that he was not alone in embracing 'pastiche in modern lamps. (...) People want a cosy home (...) and there is nothing cosy about the most functionalist lighting of our time – the fluorescent tube'.[3] Unlike PH, Karlby rarely offered technical arguments for his designs, although his book Bo for To (A Home for Two) shows insight into the use of lighting in home design (see more on page 116). Karlby's views on what an architect-designed luminaire should look like were almost diametrically opposite to PH's. Here, however, the two men found common ground. PH too was a fierce critic of strip lights, and in 1928 he lamented lighting engineers' focus on providing ever brighter lighting, which ignored that people did not want to spend time in 'that damned cold light'.[4] Still, PH treated Karlby's designs with ironic detachment: 'How lovely they are, Bent Karlby's frilly lace trims! Is there anyone alive who can put a corset on a jar with similar sensitivity.'[5]

Karlby often used the openwork brass rim from the China lamp in a modified crenulated or lace-like version. He used the original openwork ribbon in his 1946 opal-glass lamp P162, which was renamed the Peanut lamp in 1952, in an obvious reference to its form. Two years earlier, Kaare Klint had presented his own Peanut lamp, folded in paper. Its launch coincided with the launch of the Fruit Lantern, and in fact the Peanut lamp was really two Fruit Lanterns combined. The Peanut model was only in production during the Le Klint company's early years. Karlby's glass Peanut was launched in three chubby variants, all with a 'corset', although the resulting waist was a far cry from the New Look silhouette.[6]

Technically, the P162 and the China lamp had similar properties, but the latter was the commercial success. It came in several sizes and could be combined into clusters of lamps. In 1953, Nordisk Solar Compagni launched an opal-glass pendant with a brass rim designed by Sigvard Bernadotte that was the spitting image of Karlby's China lamp, only slightly more barrel-shaped. Lyfa and Karlby sued for plagiarism, but Bernadotte insisted he had no prior knowledge of Karlby's model.[7]

'True, the lamp is visible during the day and should make a nice addition to the living room, but surely lighting must be the top priority.' —Bent Karlby, 1942[8]

Jørn Utzon: Sundowner and Tivoli pendants

Sven Middelboe / Nordisk Solar Compagni—ca. 1949

The architect Jørn Utzon (1918–2008) graduated from the Royal Danish Academy of Fine Arts, School of Architecture, in 1942. He later underscored the positive impact of the programme's emphasis on practice and craftsmanship, as this supported students' grasp of construction and spatial concepts.[1] In the late 1940s, concurrent with architectural design, Utzon also took on design in the smaller scale of lamp construction to secure some much-needed income for his family, and because lighting was a passion of his.

His son, the architect Jan Utzon (b. 1944), explains: 'This was right after the war, most construction materials were rationed, and you couldn't buy things because production had been halted; so, true to his creative nature, my father began to design lamps.' Jan Utzon says that lamp design was his father's own initiative but that Jørn Utzon contacted the lamp maker Sven Middelboe, who helped him with production.[2] Initially, conditions were fairly primitive, with the two men lacquering and assembling the shades in the sports facility KB-hallen in Frederiksberg (see page 146). They managed a couple of hundred luminaires a day.[3]

Jørn Utzon was pleased with the result. He gave a Sundowner pendant to his idol, the American architect Frank Lloyd Wright (1857–1969), on a visit to his home in Wisconsin in 1949. Lloyd Wright is said to have been very enthusiastic about the lamp and even asked if he could have one more.[4] Utzon naturally also installed his own lamps in the family's newbuilt house in the coastal town of Hellebæk, north of Copenhagen, in 1951. To this day, the Sundowner and Tivoli pendants are in use in the house. They are widely held to be among Utzon's earliest lamps.[5] They were probably first sold through Middelboe's company; later, both were available from Nordisk Solar Compagni, and the Tivoli pendant was also featured in Kemp & Lauritzen's catalogue.[6]

The Sundowner and Tivoli lamps were popular, and Utzon's architectural approach is evident in their geometric lines and flexible shade system, which allowed for varied colourways and expressions.[7] While the Tivoli design is based on a cylinder and a truncated cone, the Sundowner is more rounded with a fashionable New Look waist.[8] Both provide good downwards lighting but also emit light from the top and in between the shades, highlighting the shape of the lamp. The light slips out in between the middle screens, illuminating the shades above and below the gap. Thus, all four shades serve a purpose. The pendants are not glare-free, but the bulb is placed high inside the shade, so it is not directly visible when hung above a table, and the balanced contrast makes for a pleasant light. The Tivoli lamp also came as a ceiling lamp without the top shade. This latter version was named Halsskov because it was used in large numbers in the interiors of the ferries then crossing the Great Belt strait between the ports of Halsskov and Nyborg.[9] Whereas the Tivoli and Halsskov pendants came assembled, the Sundowner came as four separate shades. People then had to assemble the shades and place them over the socket, an easy task that required no screws.[10]

The names Sundowner, Tivoli and Satchmo, the latter the name of a 1957 pendant, suggest a note of laid-back leisure, but for Utzon the lamps provided an important source of income during this early part of his career.[11] After winning the architectural competition for the Sydney Opera House in 1957 and later moving to Australia with his family, Utzon largely gave up lamp design. There is, however, one more chapter to this story, as described on page 176.

After being discontinued for a number of years, the Sundowner was relaunched by the Finnish company Artek, founded by Alvar and Aino Aalto, while the Tivoli pendant is now in production at the Danish lighting manufacturer &Tradition, now under the name JU1.

Sundowner and Tivoli pendant (right) in Utzon's home in Hellebæk.

'It almost makes you feel sorry for the architects, that they just do computer drawings now. You miss the craftsmanship, I think. That was excellent.' —Jørn Utzon, 2004[12]

Poul Henningsen: Tivoli lamp

Louis Poulsen—1949

PH inspects the revolving luminaire by the Tivoli lake in May 1949.
→ Tivoli lamp in front of the Japanese Pagoda in the Tivoli Gardens, in the heart of Copenhagen.

In the heart of Copenhagen lie the Tivoli Gardens, the unique amusement park that so many Danes have fond memories of. On a grey, gloomy day, the gardens are a wonderful and exhilarating burst of colour, and when darkness falls, the atmospheric lighting creates a magical atmosphere.

PH lit many a light in Tivoli, also during the darkest times. On 9 April 1940, Denmark was occupied by Nazi Germany, an occupation that would last until Germany's surrender on 5 May 1945. It was at the beginning of this dark period that PH became Tivoli's architect, and during the war he created several lamps for the gardens. Throughout the occupation, a country-wide blackout order required everybody to cover their windows with blackout curtains, and cities to modify the street lamps so only a small fraction of light would escape. Naturally, the order also applied to the Tivoli Gardens; the first war-time season began just three weeks into the occupation, and throughout the first summer Tivoli closed at sunset, when the blackout came into effect. That changed in 1941, when PH designed a lamp that met the blackout requirements.

The existing blackout lamps encased the (already dim) light bulb in a white-painted capsule topped by a shade that directed the scant light downwards at a 45-degree angle. However, wet pavement or puddles would reflect the light upwards, which meant air crews might spot them – the very thing the blackout was intended to avoid. PH designed a special blackout shade lamp where all the light was emitted horizontally. Thus, it lit up the gardens and the guests but was not reflected upwards,[1] and from the opening of the second season in 1941, Tivoli was again able to stay open until midnight. PH had designed the lamp for 40-watt bulbs, but initially only 5-watt bulbs were allowed. In 1944, Tivoli was finally allowed to use 40-watt bulbs.[2] By then, PH had had to leave Denmark for Sweden due to his explicit anti-Nazi stance.

When PH returned from his exile after the war, he noted, with regret, 'During my almost two-year-long stay in Sweden, I saw no new advances in lighting engineering. To my knowledge, nothing happened in Denmark either. Light is treated as a taken-for-granted Christmas tree to be laden with ornaments.'[3] In 1949, PH constructed a lamp that was both quintessentially PH and highly decorative and unusual – and which could be rotated! PH based the design on the Spiral lamp that he had created in 1942 for Aarhus University. In the Spiral lamp, PH aimed to design a luminaire that appeared as a single long, spiralling line. His new design put this idea into motion.

The lamps were to be placed around the Tivoli lake, and PH found that 'a rotating spiral lamp' would be suitable; it would add a nice effect because there is 'something about the spiral that heightens or anticipates the form of the mirror image'.[4] The interior construction of the Tivoli lamp is based on a clear acrylic tube with a painted red spiral. A motor installed at the top of the lamp keeps the acrylic spiral tube spinning one way, while an exterior white-and-green spiral shade spins in the opposite direction. When the Tivoli lamps first lit up the Tivoli lake, in spring 1950, impressed visitors stopped to watch the spinning shades. Only, the shades did not always spin, because, although the small electromotor was powerful enough to maintain the rotary motion, it was not powerful enough to get it going again if something got stuck and interfered with the motion. It simply seized up. It took several years before the problem was finally solved, and for some time the lamps stood still. However, in 1982 12 lamps once again spun slowly on and around the Tivoli lake, and at the opening of the 2008 season, there were no fewer than 101 updated spiralling Tivoli lamps, now powered by sustainable motors.[5]

'When I was asked to design new lighting for the Tivoli lake, it struck me that a slowly rotating spiral lamp would make for a nice, subtle effect. A subtle touch is important, since too much rotation would make people feel drunk.'
—Poul Henningsen, 1949[6]

Arne Jacobsen: AJ lamp

Louis Poulsen—1957

The retail edition of the AJ pendant was made in lacquered aluminium. Today, all AJ lamps are made in lacquered steel.
↑ At the SAS Hotel, the wall model was used in two sizes, like the AJ table lamp.

In 1956, Arne Jacobsen was commissioned to design a hotel and an airport terminal for the SAS airline. When the SAS Royal Hotel opened in 1960, it was Denmark's first skyscraper and the world's first designer hotel. Jacobsen was given a free hand to design every last detail. Nothing was left to chance – or to others. Jacobsen designed everything, from chairs, rugs and curtains to door handles, drinking glasses, cutlery, even the ball at the end of the roller-blind drawstring – and, naturally, the lighting. This made the hotel one of the most accomplished total works of art in modern architectural history.[1]

A Danish exponent of the international style, the SAS building is a block rising from a base. Inside, this image was repeated on a smaller scale in the AJ floor lamp rising from its tiny base. A whole range of lamps was designed for the many different purposes at the hotel. Here, the focus is on the geometrically playful AJ lamps and the hemispherical AJ pendant. First, the AJ lamps:

While most of Jacobsen's earlier luminaires had soft, sensuous curves (see pages 42–43), the AJ floor, table and wall lamps had clear-cut geometric shapes. The lamp head consists of two geometric forms: a cylinder enclosing the socket and a cone enclosing the light bulb. Unlike the 1929 AJ reading lamp, where the two components of the shade had a common axis, the axis of this conical lampshade tilts, so that the upper side continues the line of the cylinder. Thus, the upper side of the lamp head forms a straight line, while the lower side has a sharp kink. The cone is cut off at an oblique angle, so that the lower edge of the shade is parallel with the horizontal surface the light falls on. In the table and floor lamps, the cylinder around the socket is mounted on a thin, slightly angled metal rod on a drop-shaped base with a circular cut-out that lightens the base and echoes the round lampshade opening. The cylinder enclosing the socket in the wall lamp is mounted on a short, thin metal arm attached to a round mounting plate. The latter lamp is less striking in appearance than the almost floating table and floor lamps, the floor lamp seemingly on the verge of tipping. From the outset, all the models had a functional built-in tilt joint inside the cylinder to make it easy to direct the light to where it was needed.[2] The inside of all the shades was painted white to optimize the light in the hotel rooms.[3]

For the common areas of the hotel, Jacobsen designed the similarly geometric AJ pendant, its shade a spherical segment with slits near the top. The slits make the lamp itself slightly luminous and emit diffused illumination upwards for general lighting. Most of the light is emitted downwards through the large opening in the hemispherical shade. The pendant was subsequently produced in two sizes, with three or four light bulbs.[4] The larger pendant, with a diameter of 50 cm, was designed to hang low, while the smaller one, with a diameter of 37 cm, was designed to hang high. The first, larger pendant had five slats while the later, smaller 37-cm version had four. The large pendants in solid brass were used in the hotel lounge areas and in the top-floor panorama salon.[5]

PH criticized Jacobsen for being too preoccupied with aesthetic perfection.[6] And indeed, Jacobsen sought to imbue his designs with visual and metaphoric attributes that lent them a sculptural quality. This is evident in his famous Egg and Swan chairs, which were designed for the hotel, as well as in his lamps. However, while the organic chairs and the hemispherical AJ pendant with its carefully calculated light distribution contrast the building's stringent, rectangular lines, the AJ floor, table and wall lamps with their oblique angles engage in a dialogue with both the chairs and the architectural space.

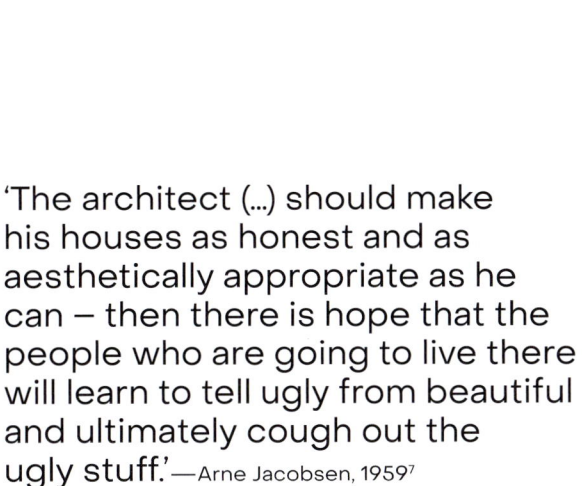

'The architect (...) should make his houses as honest and as aesthetically appropriate as he can – then there is hope that the people who are going to live there will learn to tell ugly from beautiful and ultimately cough out the ugly stuff.' —Arne Jacobsen, 1959[7]

Poul Henningsen: PH 5

Louis Poulsen—1958

To PH, a design had found its final form when any further change would be a detraction. Although the PH lamp had found its final form in 1926, PH continued to modify the number, form and size of shades and to experiment with other materials. In the late 1950s, he designed new models with a contemporary expression. What follows is the short version of the story about the best-selling PH lamp ever.

In 1958, Louis Poulsen launched the PH 5 lamp, which PH had designed two years earlier. The design of this new PH lamp, intended for private homes, was guided by the acknowledgement that the, in his words, 'unpleasant incandescent light bulb' was not going to get any better. The earliest electric light bulbs had clear glass, and their glare was limited to the area just around the filament. The later gas-filled bulbs were brighter and had a frosted interior to prevent reflections, but their diffused light was more difficult to shield. The only solution PH saw was to conceal the light source with a closed system of shades to prevent glare. The PH 5 lamp concealed the light bulb completely, filtering the light through three – later two – smaller interior shades in a reddish-orange and a reddish blue. Thus, PH had, once and for all, succeeded in transforming electric light into a warm, muted and soothing evening glow and 'making (...) the evening restful'.[1] In 1958, PH argued that artificial light ought to 'contain the many red rays of the evening and morning'.[2]

In the PH 5 lamp, which was named after the 50-cm diameter of the upper shade, PH combined his accumulated experience with lighting. With four reflecting shades and smaller, coloured interior shades, the lamp could hang low over a dining table. It emitted a subtle, sideways light and a more focused, but soft and warm, downwards light.[3] In 1966, PH said about the PH 5: 'It modifies the overly bright light of the incandescent bulb by means of an inserted, almost horizontal coloured shade. (...) Thus, increasingly, the average consumer of light began to notice the PH lamp.'[4] However, the PH 5 lamp was too dim when fitted with an ordinary incandescent light bulb. Hence, the vertical metal shade was later replaced with a semi-transparent, frosted base plate that lets out more light while still preventing glare.

The Danish architect Viggo Sten Møller concluded in 1980 that the PH lamp was 'one of the very finest functionalist designs in the Nordic countries'.[5] The PH lamps were the tangible manifestation of the efforts of the functionalist period. Form followed function, in accordance with the functionalist credo, and part of this function was to bring warm, soft evening lighting into Danish homes, a demand that the PH 5 lamp met. The lamp was a commercial success and took over the title and reputation of 'the actual PH lamp'.[6] The PH 5 model has for years been the Louis Poulsen company's top seller, and allegedly a PH lamp is found in one out of five Danish homes.[7] The PH lamp set a new standard for the design of luminaires that provide pleasant, glare-free lighting regardless of the light source. In 1958, PH pointed out that the model was capable of concealing any light source and that one could 'put anything in it', from a 100-watt bulb to glow worms and Christmas lights, but, he added, 'a strip light in its current form would be too long'.[8]

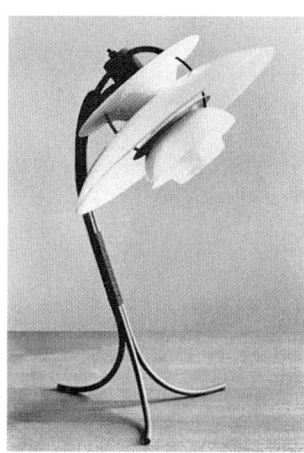

The PH 5 was made in rugged aluminium sheeting that could handle a tumble, but the shades on this rickety frame were made of Plexiglas. The variant shown here never made it onto the retail market, however.

Later, when the strip light was twisted and folded up to provide energy-efficient lighting, it was a challenge for energy-conscious consumers to fit the unusually shaped light bulb into their PH lamps. Soon, however, the new light sources came to be shaped like the old light bulbs, and today most of the many PH 5 lamps in public and private settings are fitted with LED lights.

'With a closed system of shades, the luminaire can be turned in any direction without producing glare. It is my hope that the new PH lamp will bring others the same pleasure as it brings me when I see its reflection in my coffee cup.'
—Poul Henningsen, 1958[9]

Poul Henningsen: Artichoke lamp

Louis Poulsen—1958

PH explained in 1958 that the Artichoke lamp was the first construction where he had employed sight lines in a design that concealed the entire incandescent light bulb.

The PH 5 lamps soon found widespread use, as PH had hoped, not least in private homes. However, that was not the intention behind his large, expensive Artichoke lamp. It was designed on commission for the fashionable Langelinie Pavilion restaurant.

When the architects Eva and Nils Koppel (1916–2006 and 1914–2009) asked PH to design the lighting for the restaurant, in 1957, he created the main attraction, the Artichoke lamp, in just three months. This feat was possible because he based the design on the Septima lamp, also known as the seven-shade chandelier, where the bulb was covered by glass shades (developed in 1927–1931), with a staggered pattern of frosted and clear fields (see page 170). PH found a direct source of inspiration for the new construction in an unrealized version of the lamp where the staggered design had been translated into rows of individual metal panels or 'leaves': 'individual leaves, as in a pine cone'.[1] Hence the lamp's Danish name, the Pine Cone lamp.

The same 1958 issue of *NYT* that presented the PH 5 pendant also included an article about the lighting at the Langelinie Pavilion. Here, Nils Koppel explained how the restaurateur had wanted to make the restaurant 'festive and cosy' and that it would have been 'an admission of defeat if this essential "function" could not be accommodated in the functionalist building'.[2] Koppel pointed out that light from the Artichoke was both embellishing and festive — essential qualities in restaurant lighting. The brief also called for it to be warm and glare-free, requirements that PH also delivered on.

The Artichoke lamp was constructed of 72 bent and angled copper scales individually mounted on a nickel-plated steel frame in a logarithmic spiral with twelve rows of six scales, like 'twelve staggered picket fences'.[3] The lattices that carry the 'leaves' come together under the bulb, and just as artichoke leaves envelop the heart of the vegetable, the copper leaves envelop the luminous core. Without blocking the light completely, they conceal the light source, and the light illuminates the luminaire itself and is emitted in a round, symmetrical pattern, glare-free from every angle. The outward-facing side of the copper leaves was brushed and lacquered, while the inside had the same hue as the rose-coloured Septima.

PH designed the Artichoke lamp in three sizes: an impressive luminaire with a diameter of 84 cm, a slightly smaller version of 72 cm and a 60-cm version, the latter still an imposing lamp. For the Langelinie Pavilion, PH also designed the smaller Langelinie pendant, later named the Plate lamp due to its form. These pendants were used over the tables in the restaurant. The Plate lamp's horizontal shades, spreading out like rings in water with an outer diameter of 44 cm, were made in solid copper. Given the same surface finish as the copper in the Artichoke lamp, it too cast a warm, golden light on the tables and diners. The Plate lamp was also designed in larger versions, with a diameter of 60 or 80 cm. Production was discontinued in 1984.

In the 1958 book *Brugskunst: møbler, textiler, lamper* (Applied Art: Furniture, Textiles, Lamps), the interior designers Birgit and Christian Enevoldsen present 'the finest Danish applied art of ensuring worth'. Alongside a full-page photo of the new Artichoke lamp, the authors describe exemplary lamps that are both 'functional luminaires and atmospheric elements'.[4] In *History of Modern Design*, the American art historian David Raizman sees the Artichoke lamp as a principal example of modernist Danish design after the Second World War. With his retrospective outsider's gaze, Raizman describes how PH's post-war expression developed into more intricate and sculptural designs. He considers the 'Artichoke hanging lamp' exemplary of Scandinavian, organic design, where 'an increasing freedom and esthetic dimension' is promoted by the cold climate and the resulting focus on comfortable indoor living.[5] Most Danes encountered the large Artichoke lamps in the public realm, but in 2006 it was launched in a smaller version of 48 cm for smaller rooms, which made it appropriate for low-ceilinged modern homes. Artichoke lamps are also made in other materials besides copper and have remained in continuous production since their launch.

'When you look out over the rooms in the evening, the Artichoke lamp dominates and creates a festive light. (...) And when you sit at one of the tables, they cast their gentle, golden, embellishing light on patrons and tables.' —Nils Koppel, 1958[6]

Jørgen Bo and Vilhelm Wohlert: Louisiana pendant

Louis Poulsen—1958

In 1958, the Louisiana Museum of Modern Art opened in Humlebæk, north of Copenhagen. Its founder, Knud W. Jensen, had commissioned the architects Jørgen Bo (1919–1999) and Vilhelm Wohlert (1920–2007) to create the architectural setting for the artworks.[1] The museum was built as an expansion on a large detached house, named Louisiana. The new, modernist section extended from the original house through the park, subjecting itself to the magnificent landscape. The project included furnishings and lighting designed to unify the sections and create a homely atmosphere, a key goal for Jensen, as Bo and Wohlert explained in 1958:

The attempt was to extend the homely atmosphere of the old house into the new section in a contemporary interpretation by means of simple dispositions, such as maintaining low ceiling heights and bringing in ample daylight from the side, the latter bringing the interior into contact with the outdoors, as in a normal living room. (...) In terms of lighting, too, the building aims for the same conditions under which a work of art is viewed in a private home.[2]

The quote is from an article by the architects in *Mobilia*, which dedicated an issue to the new art museum. Interior photos show a hemispherical copper lamp in two sizes hung high in all the galleries to provide general lighting, angled to highlight the most important surfaces in the museum: the walls.[3] The lamps were also used as pendants in what was then, in 1958, the library, which later became the cafeteria.

The lamp was designed by Wohlert, with inspiration from the old lamps in the sculptors' studio at the Royal Danish Academy of Fine Arts.[4] The interior of the hemispherical shade was painted white for optimal reflection. The only other features in the simple lamp were a socket and an incandescent light bulb, shielded by slightly recessed white metal grating to avoid dazzling the museum-goers. For the long glazed connecting walkway, Wohlert had designed a discreet bracket lamp that was mounted on the wooden bars between the window panes: a cylinder and truncated cone made of bent sheet copper that provided atmospheric orientation lighting in the dusk and dark.[5] All the copper lamps had a clear lacquer finish to prevent verdigris. Their simple expression matched the subtle architecture and colour scheme, designed to provide the optimal setting for the art on display. Louis Poulsen produced the hemispherical pendant and also launched it in shops as the Louisiana pendant.[6] Bo and Wohlert subsequently used it in their interior design of a dispatch hall for the publishing house Gyldendal, for which they also designed a small spherical lamp.[7]

In 1957, the year before Louisiana opened, Wohlert had designed the geometric bracket lamp Model 204 for Le Klint, later nicknamed the Toadstool. The lampshade was pleated in white paper in a fairly simple but striking construction. The shade is pulled together around a metal frame that also holds the socket. The hand-pleated shade was placed in a wall-mounted bracket made of Oregon pine, which gave rise to an interplay between the grain of the wood and the dense pleats. The cord ran through the lower part of the bracket and became an integral part of the visual form. The lamp was presented at the Landsforeningen Dansk Kunsthaandværk's Annual Exhibition in 1957 and was used in two interior designs that same year commissioned by the nuclear physicist Niels Bohr (1885–1962).[8]

Jensen wrote in 1986 of Wohlert that his particular strength was 'his grasp of interiors, space, materials; refined and meticulously finished details'.[9] During the early 1940s, Wohlert had studied under Kaare Klint at the Royal Danish Academy of Fine Arts, School of Architecture, and also assisted him in his work, and this experience had significantly shaped his approach to design and architecture. Like Bo, he passed on this approach at the Academy, where they both had long tenures as professors of architecture.[10]

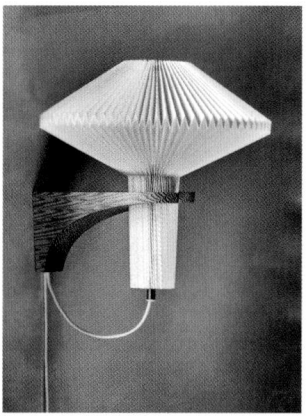

Vilhelm Wohlert's Model 204 for Le Klint from 1957 was nicknamed the Toadstool.
→ In connection with Louisiana's 60th anniversary in 2018, the museum cafe was redesigned with a bespoke collection of new chairs and lamps based on Wohlert's original designs specially produced for Louisiana by the international design brand Stellar Works.

'In proportioning the building, we have aimed for simple dimensions and primary forms, in the whole as in the detail. The motivation for this architectural asceticism lies in the rich content and the lush surroundings.'
—Jørgen Bo and Wilhelm Wohlert, 1958[11]

Verner Panton: Topan

Louis Poulsen—1959

Panton's first lamps were exhibited at Landsforeningen Dansk Kunsthaandværk's annual exhibition in 1955.
→ Verner Panton's interior design of the Astoria restaurant in Trondheim was a Gesamtkunstwerk with Topan lamps, Cone chairs and op-art textiles.

After attending technical college, Verner Panton (1926–1998) enrolled at the Royal Danish Academy of Fine Arts, School of Architecture, graduating in 1951. During these early years, Panton met two important mentors outside the Academy. The first was PH, who for a brief time was Panton's father-in-law and with whom Panton developed a close friendship, which also had him learning from the master lighting designer and developing an interest in lighting theory.[1] The other was Arne Jacobsen, who employed Panton from 1950 to 1952. At Jacobsen's studio, Panton was involved in the design of the three-legged moulded veneer Ant chair. Along with his other work for Jacobsen, the Ant project taught Panton valuable lessons about experimenting with materials and production techniques, pushing both to the limit in collaboration with knowledgeable manufacturers. After two years with Jacobsen, Panton bought a VW van, which was his home for a few years and which he used to tour Europe and build a professional network.[2]

In the summer of 1955, the mobile home was back on Danish soil, parked in front of his friend and design retailer Torben Ørskov's (1928–2008) flat. Ørskov was already distributing some metal candlesticks designed by Panton, and now Panton wanted to try his hand at lamp design.[3] The result was nine different pendant lamps, which were presented at the annual exhibition of the National Association of Danish Crafts in 1955.[4] All the pendants had between three and nine floating reflecting shades with differently shaped cross-sections and one coloured shade above and around the bulb. They were intended to be used in varying constellations. Kirsten Ørskov, who was Ørskov's girlfriend in 1955, said in 2019:

Verner's many aluminium shades were inspired by PH's, something he never tried to hide. They had little holes drilled into them, and then Verner, Torben and I tied knots in circular-knitted nylon string connecting one shade to the next. We were working like mad, because they had to be ready for the exhibition, and everything was done by eye. At the exhibition they hung in a corner, looking interesting, if a little crooked. Afterwards, they were sold to a restaurant in the Tivoli Gardens, where they were in use for a few years. We couldn't stand how crooked they looked, so we talked about adding some metal spacers, but nothing ever came of it.[5]

Panton later developed the deconstructed multi-shade pendants into elongated ones where the reflecting shades floated like UFOs around a cylindrical core over the bulb, the lower part covered by a hemispherical interior shade. In 1958, they were included in Panton's interior design of a new-built annex for his father's inn, Kom-Igen (Come Again), on the Danish island of Funen. This was Panton's first total interior design, which led to the task of designing the restaurant at Hotel Astoria in Trondheim, Norway. While the room at Kom-Igen had daylight coming in, Panton wrapped the restaurant at the Norwegian hotel in fabric, so the lighting was crucial. It came from countless shiny, spherical Topan pendants, which had been presented at the furniture fair in Cologne in 1959.[6] The bottom of the 21-cm spherical shell was cut off to produce a smaller opening that gave out a fairly focused beam of light on the restaurant tables and the musical performers in the atmospheric room. The round shape was echoed in the Cone chairs in the restaurant and in the op-art fabric, with its circles and squares on various scales, that covered the floors, walls and ceilings. The interior of the pendant was painted white to reflect the light optimally, while a metal mesh, lacquered white, prevented glare. In 1961, PH wrote that in technical terms, the lighting in the restaurant did not break any new ground:

But of course, Panton is not a lighting engineer. He does not construct intricate luminaires. The key is that he has a real instinct for lighting in a room. Part of this instinct is a most precious sense, which most modern human beings have just about lost: the sense of the dark. This sense may be compared to a sense for the pause, which is the condition of all music.[7]

Topan was Panton's first luminaire to be put into industrial production. It was also his simplest. Panton was only getting started.[8] Topan provided direct lighting, but Panton returned to the spherical shape and also continued to develop the concept of coordinated shades to provide both reflected and diffused light.

'He has a real instinct for lighting in a room. Part of this instinct is a most precious sense, which most modern human beings have just about lost: the sense of the dark.'
—PH about Verner Panton, 1961⁹

Lars Eiler Schiøler: Pearlshade

P.J. Høyrup—1960

When the Butterfly lamp is lit, the overlapping plastic elements produce a ribbon of rhomboid shadows ringing the middle of the shade.

The lighting company P.J. Høyrup was one of the first in Denmark to sell flat-pack lamps to be assembled by people in their own living room. However, the company's beginnings lay somewhere else entirely, as one of its first endeavours was a relaunch of the 19th-century Heiberg lamp[1] (see page 16). Later, it made a big leap to lamps made in vacuum-formed plastic.

The lighting company was founded in the early 1950s by Preben Johan Høyrup (1918–2005). Lars Eiler Schiøler (1913–1982), who had trained as a shop clerk, joined as a partner with responsibility for design and production.[2] Around 1955, Schiøler began to experiment with making lamps in vacuum-formed plastic. The technology was sound, but it was difficult to find plastic of sufficient quality.[3] Regular production was not established until 1960, when the company purchased a large vacuum-forming machine and the quality of plastic had improved.[4] The machine was also used to experiment with different textures. One such experiment with a metal ventilation grille produced an attractive waffle pattern and proved that the plastic stayed completely pliable: 'It could be bent and folded this way and that along the lines of the pattern.'[5]

This waffle plastic was then pleated and folded into a volume, resulting in the most successful outcome of the new technique: the Pearlshade pendant, which was patented in 1961.[6] Inside the lamp was a clear, transparent plastic cylinder mounted on cast plastic rings at the top and bottom. The rings defined the ends of the cylinder and gave the pleated waffle plastic its shape. At the top of the cylinder was another ring, this one in metal, that held the socket and cord, positioning the bulb in the middle of the interior cylinder. Made in transparent plastic, the cylinder did not produce a shadow, unlike the traditional metal mount. Pearlshade came in several sizes and in a range of colours that filtered and toned the light; however, the white shades proved the most popular. Pearlshade was a big success and enabled the company to invest in new machines, says Uffe Schiøler (b. 1946), Lars Eiler Schiøler's son, who joined the company in 1966.

The many vacuum-formed lamps were sold to department stores and shops all over Denmark and its neighbouring countries.[7] The Swedish company IKEA carried several lamps from P.J. Høyrup. Since 1956, IKEA had been a pioneer in self-assembly furniture, and now the lighting company offered IKEA the first flat-pack lamp.[8] In 1968, Lars Eiler Schiøler designed the Butterfly pendant, which consisted of 15 coloured plastic leaves to be assembled at home, based on simple step-by-step instructions. First, the leaves were folded and joined together; next, the form was mounted on a round plastic ring that also held a metal mount for the socket. Socket and cord were bought separately. The thin plastic leaves were translucent, and the rose-coloured edition emitted a soft, reddish light. In the middle of the lamp, the leaves overlapped, which reduced the translucency and gave rise to a rhomboid shadow band. Butterfly came in a variety of colours, but in this case too, white was the most popular option.

IKEA opened its first Danish shop in 1969, where Danish shoppers could now buy P.J. Høyrup's very affordable flat-pack lamps. The flat boxes took up less storage space and made delivery simpler and cheaper. That was also an advantage for P.J. Høyrup, since IKEA did not have exclusive rights to the lamps: 'IKEA was a good client, but we sold to many department stores and retailers around the world: from the UK to Australia, to Singapore, Japan, Canada and large shipments to the United States; we were present in more than 40 countries.'[9] Most of the lamps were flat-packed and unassembled, but Pearlshade was also available in its assembled form. Lars Eiler Schiøler stopped designing lamps in the mid 1970s, but his concept of affordable and simple lamp designs lived on.

'They placed a metal ventilation grille in the vacuum machine with a sheet of plastic over it. The result was a plastic sheet with a nice pattern – and that was the beginning of Pearlshade.'
—Uffe Schiøler, 2019[10]

Hans J. Wegner: Wegner pendant, Model JH604

Johannes Hansen—1962

Hans J. Wegner (1914–2007) has justly been called the king of chairs. He designed some 500 of them, several of them gaining world renown. The Round Chair, JH501 (1949) – later dubbed The Chair on the American market – exemplifies the trained cabinetmaker's exceptional grasp of wood and his dogged persistence to keep at a design until he got it right: 'You can always improve on a thing.'[1] Wegner applied the same persistence to the two rise-and-fall pendants that he created ten years apart: JH1 and the Wegner pendant JH604, now named The Pendant – of course!

Wegner's JH1 (Johannes Hansen, 1952) and Frits Schlegel's P295 (Lyfa, 1956).

Wegner turned his hand to lamp design for several reasons. One was his annual presentations of new furniture designs, including at the Copenhagen Cabinetmakers' Guild exhibition.[2] Here the furniture was presented in realistic interiors, including lamps above the dining and coffee tables. Instead of using somebody else's lamps, Wegner chose to design his own. He had begun to collaborate with the progressive cabinetmaker Johannes Hansen in 1940, and in the 1952 guild exhibition, when Wegner presented his wooden furniture at a joint stand with Hansen's company, Johannes Hansens Møbelsnedkeri, he hung a simple, geometric rise-and-fall brass pendant above the table.[3] 'My dad didn't like it when things got too complicated, so he based his design on a simple, conical pendant,' says the architect Marianne Wegner (b. 1947), who began working with her father in 1973.[4] The JH1 brass pendant has a 52-cm conical lampshade with a collar. The shade is mounted on an interior brass bracket bent into a trapezoid with the long side facing down and the short side facing up. Like the luminaire itself, the standard pulley system is made of brass. The interior of the lampshade is painted white for optimal reflection. As lighting lay outside the expertise of Hansen's firm, the lamp was produced on commission by a hollowware factory.

In 1956, the big Danish lighting company Lyfa put a rise-and-fall pendant into production, designed by the architect Frits Schlegel, that is quite similar to Wegner's. This smaller pendant (with a shade diameter of 44 cm) was much more successful in retail than Wegner's lamp, probably due to both pricing and an intense marketing campaign.[5] However, Wegner continued to use his own pendant in exhibitions and also installed the practical luminaire in his own home.[6] At the time, there were several rise-and-fall pendants on the market. The flexible solution is practical because a large open lampshade casts good light on a dining table; however, if the light bulb is not covered, the lamp has to be low enough to conceal the light source but not so low that it blocks the view of the person across the table. Wegner was well aware of the dilemma, and in 1962, again in cooperation with Johannes Hansen, he presented a replacement for the JH1 with updated functionality and a more modern form.

Like its predecessor, the JH604, is based on a conical lampshade but in an even simpler, softly rounded form. The curvature of the steel bracket that holds the socket and also serves as a handle matches the oval steel ball containing the pulley system. The bracket is pleasant to grip and makes it easy to adjust the height. Wegner also added a feature for adjusting the position of the bulb inside the shade at the turn of a screw. Thus, if the pendant was moved up or down, the position of the bulb could be adjusted to prevent glare. A small but revolutionizing feature. The original 1962 version was painted white; later, other colours and a brass version were added, all with a white interior for optimal lighting.[7] At 50 cm in diameter, the shade casts most of the light on the tabletop, but some light escapes through the open top to contribute to the general lighting in the room. This second rise-and-fall pendant was commercially successful and has remained in continual production. Production was taken over by Louis Poulsen and later by Pandul,[8] which produces the versatile height-adjustable pendant today.

'Of course, we never know when
we're done with a thing.'
—Hans J. Wegner, 1964[9]

Poul Henningsen: Contrast lamp

Louis Poulsen—1962

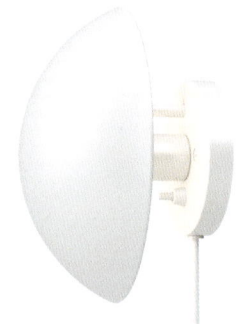

In 1926, PH had found his design solution for providing pleasant shaded electrical lighting: glare-free, warm light that created sufficient, but not hard, shadows to define a form. For the rest of his life, PH continued to develop variations on this original principle, just as he continued to share his thoughts on proper lighting with the world, in speech and writing. In November 1966, PH summarized his insights in an interview in *Bo Bedre*: 'Proper lighting simply means having as much – or as little – light as you need and are comfortable with, and having it in the right places. There should be many lamps in a house, and each lamp should provide a new lighting experience. Lamps should be exciting.'[1]

His Contrast lamp, launched four years prior after a lengthy development process, was certainly exciting. It was a complex design that was really three lamps in one. The core design principle was ten shades with four different finishes: red, blue and white paint and high-gloss lacquer. The bulb is placed in the centre of the luminaire, but an annular feature at the top of the pendant tube makes it possible to move the bulb up and down inside the lamp housing, which alters the quality of the lighting. Each shade has a kink, resulting in the assembled luminaire having three conical sections – and thus, in essence, three lamps. The edges of the shades form the first section ('the screening lamp'). They have a matt white top side and a shiny underside, and the light is evenly distributed without shifts in luminance.[2] The next conical section, the actual light source ('the luminous lamp'), has white undersides and shiny top sides. The third conical section ('the colour lamp') has a red exterior and a blue interior.[3] Lowering and raising the bulb varies the amount of light that strikes the exterior versus the interior. When the bulb is raised, the blue sides are illuminated more, the light gets colder, and more light is directed into the room. When it is lowered, the red sides are illuminated more, and the downwards light becomes warmer and more intense. Thus, the light can be varied between cold and warm by means of a simple mechanical principle. The colour temperature can be adjusted seamlessly without any changes in light intensity. This option of modifying the colour contrasts of the light is the lamp's unique characteristic and the source of its name.[4]

To PH, these were the kinds of qualities that made a lamp exciting; it was not about form. In *Mobilia* magazine in 1961, PH addressed the complicated construction of the upcoming Contrast lamp, crisply concluding that it would have been 'easier to stick a light bulb in a lady's hat. However, burgundy requires an effort'.[5] In 1966, PH rebuked the architects who placed form over good lighting: 'Unfortunately, some architects design ladies' hats instead of lampshades. (...) I wish architects would pay more attention to function rather than the design of "interesting" shapes.'[6] For years, 'lady's hat' had been PH's term for a lamp that was more form than function (see page 92).

In 1961, PH had, with poorly concealed irony, named a new and very simple wall lamp P Hat. The shade, a spherical section, is attached to a cylindrical base. Thus, tipping the hat (the shade) produces a more intense, unshielded downwards light. The luminaire was simple and painted white, while the shade had a lightly rose-coloured lacquer on the inside to give the light a slightly reddish tint. Unlike the Contrast lamp, the P Hat is still in production today – albeit under the less quirky and more systems-oriented name PH Hat.

While PH was designing P Hat and the Contrast lamp, a PH 5 table lamp was also in the works. Launched in 1965, it made the cover of *Bo Bedre*'s 1966 special issue on (better) lighting. In the table model, the PH 5 shade was mounted on a three-legged brass frame that was reminiscent of the frame of PH's Model 1 from the 1925 Paris exhibition (see page 25).[7] The design had come full circle.

↑ Under the name PH Hat, the lamp is now only in production in the smaller version with a diameter of 22.5 cm.
← The frame for the PH 5 table lamp from 1962 has similarities to the one used in PH's Model 1, which was presented at the Paris exhibition in 1925.

'Finally, after many attempts and models, the new ten-shade lamp has been launched. (...) P.S.: by the way, this construction, which has been a dream of mine for many years, has become bloody expensive. The gross price is 735 good Danish kroner. Converted to other metrics, it is probably about a quarter of the cost for a silver-wedding party (and only if you go easy on the wine). I possess no means to bring down the price, so we have to put the whole thing down to the notion of quality labour. Sincerely, and sorry, PH.'
—Poul Henningsen, 1962[8]

Simon P. Henningsen: Divan 2

Lyfa—1962

Simon Henningsen behind the Tivoli lamp, which are no longer in production but continue to illuminate flower beds in the Tivoli Gardens.

The architect Simon P. Henningsen (1920–1974) had yet to graduate from the Royal Danish Academy of Fine Arts, School of Architecture, when he was employed, in 1942, by his father, Poul Henningsen, who had just been appointed Tivoli's chief architect. The two men worked together on design tasks in the amusement park until 1948, when Simon Henningsen succeeded his father as chief architect. Simon Henningsen did not set out to follow in PH's footsteps, but in hindsight, on his 50th birthday, in 1970, he explained why that had become his path:

As a young man I helped my dad investigate the impact of different kinds of lighting on the colour balance in a Lundstrøm painting and thus learnt about the impact of lighting quality. I never really intended to work with lighting, but in my work for Tivoli I returned to these challenges.[1]

In 1962, Simon Henningsen designed the Divan 2 lamp for the new elegant function rooms facing the Tivoli lake in the former restaurant Divan 2. Throughout, both the general layout and the lighting were designed for maximum flexibility. The architect Louis Weisdorf, who worked in Tivoli's design studio at the time, has described how he and Simon Henningsen designed the partitions between the individual rooms as wall sections that could be lowered into the basement through a groove in the floor. The rooms also had flexible table arrangements for dinner and coffee. As the design brief called for lamps above the individual tables rather than general room lighting, the lamps could be lowered and raised to match every conceivable table arrangement: 'The staff simply pushed the "coffee" button or, if it was time for fireworks, the "fireworks" button, and then all the lamps would be raised out of the way, up to the ceiling, and dimmed, so the guests could take in the fireworks on the lake. So they weren't novelty lamps; they had important built-in functionality.'[2] Unfortunately, no one had considered it might be risky to have the lampshade end in a sharp edge, so occasionally, guests had to visit the emergency room after bumping their head on the lamp.[3]

In the Divan 2 lamp, the light bulb is unshielded downwards but encircled by 20 rectangular steel slats cut off at an oblique angle to shield the bulb from lateral view. The light hits the slats, which reflect it into the room. The slats have shiny chromium plating on the outside, while the inside is lacquered in six different colours, leading to a fascinating display of colour – quite in the Tivoli spirit.[4]

Poul and Simon had designed a plan for Tivoli's development and set up guidelines for the lighting; strip lighting was banned, and all light had to be indirect and reflected. Half the magic of Tivoli stems from the light. And even if we often heard complaints about the cap on the number of stalls in the gardens, as there was a lot of empty space, Poul and Simon always insisted that it was necessary to include pauses, as in a piece of music. Pauses and lights create variation and ambience.[5]

Simon Henningsen also designed an outdoor lamp on a spike that could be used to create spatial effects in Tivoli's flower beds. The steel-slat shades directed the light down towards the ground. The upper side of the outer ring of the slats was painted green, while the staggered lower ring was painted yellow or red, and when seen from above, the lamp resembled a stylized harebell. In 1962, this Tivoli lamp too became available in retail as an outdoor lamp for private homeowners. At a time when many people were moving out of the city into the leafy suburbs, a Lyfa ad for the lamp read, 'The latest trend is to underscore the garden's soothing character with light effects that add a touch of magic after dark and extends your enjoyment of the garden. A piece of advice: be cautious; avoid dramatic effects. Your garden should be a source of quiet pleasure, not an amusement park.'[6] Food for thought, not least today, when more and more homeowners illuminate their gardens during the dark months of the year – most in moderation, others, quite deliberately, not so.

'I never really intended to work with lighting.' —Simon P. Henningsen, 1970[7]

Henning Koppel: Petronella

Louis Poulsen—1962

'Petronella was born little over a year ago to Henning Koppel and is already much courted and widely admired. In the cradle, she was endowed with all the gifts to make her desirable.'—Advertisement, 1963[1]

The silver jug nicknamed the Pregnant Duck (Georg Jensen, 1952) has the same rounded, organic form as the Petronella lamp.

From the latter part of the 19th century, the kerosene lamp led to a marked improvement in lighting in many Danish homes. However, it was gradually replaced by electric lighting as the new power source became widely accessible. The transition did not happen overnight. World wars and rationing gave kerosene lamps renewed relevance, but soon after, these remnants from a time before modernity and modernism were put away and largely forgotten. As late as the 1960s, however, there were still areas without electricity and thus a continued demand for alternative lamps.[2] The monthly home design magazine *Bo Bedre* (Better Living) released its first issue in March 1961. The first editor-in-chief, the architect Anker Tiedemann, reluctantly had to include antiques in the stylish modern magazine every time it had a feature on summer cottages. Kerosene lamps remained the best form of lighting for the many cottages without electricity. In a conversation with Louis Poulsen's then CEO, Jens Kaastrup-Olsen, Tiedemann lamented the lack of modern kerosene lamps and suggested that Jens Kaastrup-Olsen ask Henning Koppel (1918–1981) to take on the task.[3] And so he did.

Henning Koppel is perhaps best known for his renewal of modern silver design. He trained as a sculptor at the Royal Danish Academy of Fine Arts, and after the Second World War he joined the Georg Jensen company. Koppel's sculpted silver hollowware had a distinctly organic expression, as did his utilitarian designs in steel, glass, textile, plastic, wood and porcelain. Naturally, when Koppel was asked to design a modern kerosene lamp, he chose a gentle, supple form for the brass base and glass globe that enveloped the kerosene, the classic Argand burner, the wick, the wick tube and the live flame. The chubby shiny lacquered brass base, which narrows in at the waist, combines with the opal-glass globe – its curvature the typical Koppel arc – in an organic, new-look redesign of the classic lamp. The ads promised that the lamp would provide a gentle, flattering light. As indeed it does.

The name of the lamp with the appealing hourglass figure says it all: a feminized kerosene lamp, echoing the Danish word for kerosene, 'petroleum'. Perhaps it also references the lovely maiden Petronella, the spiritual daughter of Saint Peter. The feminine reference was underscored in the ads for the 'spiritual daughter' of Koppel:

Petronella is a little beauty, with delicate curves and lines … an ornament in your living room. She stands firmly on her well-shaped, golden base and provides 50 hours of light on a single drink of kerosene. The threaded fitting is flawless, and her 'hat' is perfectly balanced. How many of her worn-out family members could claim the same? Petronella 'clings' to her owner – a bright and cheerful companion at dusk on the balcony, on the patio table, even in the pavilion in the far corner of the garden. Consider her your living shelter – always at the top of her form, whether indoors or out. You have to have her – and she can be yours for only 87 kroner.[4]

In 1975, the architecture critic Henrik Sten Møller commented that Koppel's more exclusive designs showed no concern for the consumer's wallet, but that, indeed, it made no sense to be a '"social" artist when you work with silver, the experience of the material alone is enough to make a social attitude paradoxical'.[5] With a price tag of DKK 87, Petronella was an affordable design. It was immediately featured in *Bo Bedre*.[6] That may have contributed to sales figures of over 10,000 shortly after its launch. Petronella's live flame now matched the mood of the modern living room. It did not emit the bright light consumers had grown accustomed to, as *Bo Bedre* noted, but a cosy light. To this day, the live flame continues to hold our fascination, and both the kerosene lamp and the flame will be revisited in later chapters.

Jo Hammerborg: Orient

Fog & Mørup—1962

Johannes Hammerborg Nielsen's (1920–1982) lamp designs were conditioned by two crucial factors: form and light. His grasp of form was refined through his training as a silversmith, while his understanding of light was honed by his training as a visual artist. The two influences interacted to shape each other and the many lamps produced under his artist's name, Jo Hammerborg.

Johannes Hammerborg Nielsen completed his silversmith's training in 1943. Following this, he spent a year working at the silverware company Hejl & Co. Sølvvarefabrik in his hometown of Randers before enrolling at the Royal Danish Academy of Fine Arts in Copenhagen, where important mentors were Professors Axel Jørgensen (1920–1953) and Vilhelm Lundstrøm (1893–1950).[1] From 1949 until 1957, Nielsen worked at the silver workshop Georg Jensens Sølvsmedie, until he joined the lighting company Fog & Mørup.[2] From that time, his career was entirely dedicated to lamp design, and he changed his name to Jo Hammerborg.[3]

In 1962, Hammerborg designed the Orient lamp with an organic, dome-shaped shade drawing on Eastern inspiration. The shade was made in an aluminium and a copper version, both ending in a teak tip. It is interesting to see this lamp in light of Hammerborg's employment at Georg Jensens during a time when Henning Koppel was creating his organic silver jugs, bowls and lidded serving dishes.[4] However, the lamp was not only defined by form. In 1962, Orient was highlighted in the magazine *Elnyt*, which was delivered door-to-door. The magazine pointed out that contemporary 'hanging lamps' were both better made than previous ones and 'better shielded, thus producing cosier and better lighting. Several of them also emit both upwards and downwards light'.[5] Hammerborg had aimed for good downwards lighting, in part by giving the lampshade a white interior for optimal reflection of the light from the bulb and in part by adding plastic grating at the bottom to prevent glare.[6] Moreover, the top of the metal dome had an array of narrow vertical stamped-out slits that filtered the light. This allowed the heat from the light bulb to escape, thus preventing overheating, and also cast light on the milled wooden component on top of the shade.

Jo Hammerborg's use of shiny metals and rounded, often hand-spun shapes is repeated in several models, including the hemispherical Milieu (1975) and the bell-shaped Silhuet (Silhouette) (1977). His silversmith's sense of form is evident, as is his attention to detail. In several designs, Hammerborg also used the slits in the shades not to prevent overheating but simply for the visual effect of the light illuminating the exterior of the luminaire. A striking example of his use of light effects is the Kastor pendant (1969), which emits both upwards and downwards light. In Kastor, eight tapered oval, gently curved and slight overlapping brass or copper shells are mounted in a star-shaped formation on metal tubes around the light source. The star shape is repeated in the shadow cast on the ceiling and table when the lamp is lit.[7]

Like many others at the time, Hammerborg was fascinated by the sky and outer space, something that is reflected in the names of several of his lamps. When Hammerborg was not designing, he not only gazed into the sky above but also conquered it, as a pilot and parachutist.[8] The latter, sadly, cost him his life at only 62 years of age.[9] In his lifetime, however, Hammerborg managed to create an impressive lamp production, a theme that is revisited on page 102.

Since 2013, the Orient pendant has been relaunched, and the metal shade is still hand-spun. The new editions do not have a the glare-preventing grating, so the bulb is in direct view to anyone right beneath the lamp; however, the incurving lip prevents the reflections from the bulb in the white interior from bouncing off the edge and thus producing glare.

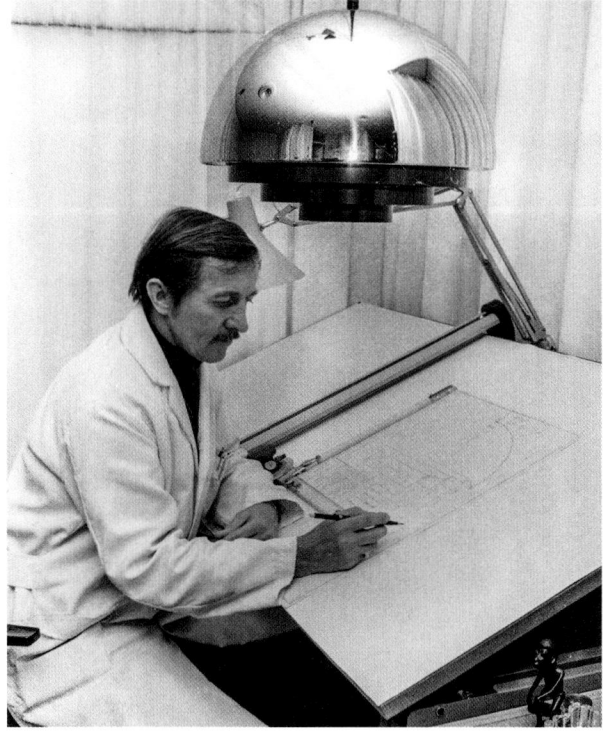

Jo Hammerborg underneath the Milieu Maxi pendant (1975), which has a diameter of 44 cm. The golden shade had a white lacquered interior, and the plastic grating at the bottom almost completely eliminated glare. The photo was taken in the studio at the Fog & Mørup factory.
→ Orient in a contemporary version by Fritz Hansen.

'Hammerborg Nielsen has prospects of becoming an accomplished artist.'
—Randers Amtsavis, 1946[10]

Jens Møller-Jensen: Albertslund Post

Louis Poulsen—1963

Today, the Albertslund Post and Wall lamps illuminate buildings and streets all over the world.

The Albertslund lamp is named after the city it was designed to illuminate – specifically, the low-rise, high-density housing development Albertslund South, west of Copenhagen, which was one of the biggest new developments in Denmark during the construction boom of the 1960s.[1] The lead architects for Albertslund South were Tyge Arnfred (b. 1919) and Viggo Møller-Jensen (1907–2003), the duo behind the architecture firm Fællestegnestuen. In 1963, Møller-Jensen's son, Jens Møller-Jensen (b. 1938), was brought in to design a new outdoor light to provide quality lighting for the labyrinthine development, with footpaths, open squares and a canal. Stark fluorescent lighting would not do; the light had to be softer.[2]

Another key goal was to find a cheaper solution than the one the architects had originally intended to use.[3]

At the time, Jens Møller-Jensen (1938–2024) was still a student at the Royal Danish Academy of Fine Arts, School of Architecture. He graduated the following year from the architect Erik Herløv's (1913–1991) newly established Department of Industrial Design.[4] From the time Jens Møller-Jensen was handed the assignment at the weekly site meeting, it took only one week (which he took off from his studies but certainly not from work) before he was ready to present a model: 'A post from a street sign, a few bits of plywood, some stays in specific dimensions, which were only available from one supplier, and a lamp chimney from Struer placed over a socket and an incandescent light bulb.'[5] The design concept was in place.

The architecture writer Henrik Sten Møller saw the lamp as 'an improvement on the so-called Slotsholm light.'[6] The lamp can be viewed as a refinement of PH's streetlight, which was not glare-free (see page 34). Jens Møller-Jensen achieved that by placing a wide galvanized-steel ring around the lamp chimney to cover the light source. The light from the bulb struck the large top shade, which radiated it downwards, while the steel ring shielded the light source from view. Some light was reflected outwards in between the ring and the top plate, while most of it was radiated downwards in a circular form. It was a 360-degree glare-free, well-proportioned lamp.

Glare-free light was one demand; simplicity and, thus, low cost was another. Jens Møller-Jensen once criticized the fact that many architects set out to design 'a new lamp of brand-new components' for every new building or development, ignoring the fact that there were good, standard products on the market.[7] The houses in Albertslund South were pre-fab modular concrete structures. Similarly, the lamp was industrially made of a small number of glass, aluminium and steel components. By combining low-cost standard components with the all-important anti-glare ring, Jens Møller-Jensen had designed a lamp at about a third of the cost of the originally intended luminaire.[8]

Albertslund South was a large-scale experiment with regard to urban planning, home layout and construction techniques, and comprehensive repairs were soon needed. The specially designed luminaire, however, functioned impeccably as a streetlight along the canal and as a bracket wall lamp on individual buildings. The industrially conceived design solution worked, in terms of both aesthetics and illumination, and also became popular abroad. Outside Denmark it was called the Orbiter in reference to the circular cone of light. Today, the lamp bears the international name Albertslund Post both in Denmark and abroad. The lamp itself is not illuminated, as it is not the intended focus of attention, but emits a gentle and sufficient outwards and downwards light, providing illumination and a sense of security – key qualities of outdoor lighting. Its popularity has led to many copies over the years and, consequently, many lawsuits by the manufacturer that first launched the enduring design. The lamp has remained in continuous production, and in 2000 it was awarded the Danish Design Council's Classics Award. Due to new demands for efficiency, the series was updated with LED lighting in 2012, a development that matched Jens Møller-Jensen's original design concept.[9]

'PH had one in his garden.'
—Henrik Steen Møller, 1975[10]

'PH liked my lamp – both the light and the price!' —Jens Møller-Jensen, 2019[11]

Friis & Moltke: Pendant

Friis & Moltke—1963

Based on the original cylindrical pendant, the expanded Lampas series was created by the architect Ove Rix. The poster was created by the graphic artist Erik Rasmussen, who designed Lampas's graphic style in 1973.

The architects Elmar Moltke Nielsen (1924–1997) and Knud Friis (1926–2010) met at the Royal Danish Academy of Fine Arts, School of Architecture, in Copenhagen. After graduating in 1950, they each founded their own studios. In 1954, they formed a joint firm, Friis & Moltke, although for a few years they could only work on their own projects after hours, before they were finally able to focus full-time on their own firm.[1]

From the outset, the two architects aimed for coherence, simplicity and quality. It can be difficult to maintain complete aesthetic control of an interior when designing single-family homes. However, their 1963 design of Hotel Tre Ege (Three Oaks Hotel) in the city of Brabrand, near Aarhus, provided a first opportunity to create a total design, a regular Gesamtkunstwerk.[2] Friis & Moltke designed all the furnishings, including lamps, creating an interior that was 'permeated by the same idea' throughout.[3]

For Tre Ege, Friis & Moltke designed a pendant lamp in two sizes based on a cylinder with three small holes at the top to accommodate a frame made of three steel rods welded onto a small disc with a hole that was just big enough to feed an electric cord through. Underneath this frame were the porcelain socket and light bulb. The cylinder, which had a black exterior and a white interior, radiated light upwards and downwards. A plumber, 'Blik-Poulsen' (Tinman Poulsen), helped Friis & Moltke make the cylinders with a diameter of either 16 or 35 cm in thin sheets of rolled and bent metal with a visible welding seam.[4] Friis & Moltke's current head of design, Mikkel Bahr, says, 'No doubt they loved the fact that the seam was visible, that the expression was a little raw. It had to be honest and plain.'[5] From 1963, the luminous cylinders were used in many building projects because they matched the architects' robust expression and their gentler version of brutalism.

Shortly after the pendants were launched, the architect Ove Rix (b. 1931) joined the studio. He became a partner in 1968 and later headed the firm's Design Department. Rix was in charge of design in 1973 when the lamps were put into production by the newly founded lighting company Lampas, eventually growing into a family of luminaires, all with the same design DNA of simplicity and functionality.[6] The pendants took on a more substantial expression, with thicker metal, nicer welding seams and lacquer. A 4-cm-wide black band was painted at the top and bottom of the white interior of the shade to prevent the light inside the cylindrical shade from bouncing off the lower rim and producing glare. The band was difficult to paint precisely and illustrates the improved finish.[7] Rix also added a lid at the top of the cylinder that allowed a small ring of light to escape. The white underside of the lid provided a reflective surface that directed even more light downwards.

An important addition to the series was several robust outdoor lamps with the same clear-cut geometric forms. The simple and uncomplicated lamps were easy to integrate on facades and in entrance areas and have inspired other designers. In one variant, a horizontal cylinder was folded down to envelop the socket and bulb and subsequently up again to form a longer wall plate with room for text, which was thus illuminated.[8] Another model featured a simple vertical arc around the bulb. The latter lamp, with its distinctive semi-cylinder made of bent 2-mm sheet steel, has remained in production since the launch.[9]

After a lapse of some years, the pendants designed for Tre Ege were relaunched in 2014, and new sizes were added. To distinguish the old models from the new, the former are called FM1954 – named after the year when Friis & Moltke began their partnership – while the new are called FM2014, the founding year of the new lamp brand Rewired.[10] Bahr managed to draw Rix out of retirement to be part of the project to ensure that the new designs remained true to their roots.[11]

'The individual elements in the house should be children of the same family, so that everything is logical, from the main lines to the smallest items — simply put, it should all be permeated by the same idea.'
—Knud Friis and Elmar Moltke Nielsen, 1976[12]

Finn Juhl: Table lamp

Lyfa—1963

In 1930, a young Finn Juhl (1912–1989) visited the *Stockholm Exhibition* where he witnessed the Nordic breakthrough of functionalism. Here, he saw the architect Gunner Asplund's elegant pavilions firsthand, a key source of inspiration when he began his training at the Royal Danish Academy of Fine Arts, School of Architecture, that autumn.[1] Just after his graduation, in 1934, Juhl joined Vilhelm Lauritzen's architectural firm. At the time, Lauritzen had just begun work on Radiohuset, and Juhl played an important role in the design of furnishings for the new building. He is said to have been particularly pivotal in the design of the brass bracket and table lamps with the organic, obliquely cut-off lamp head. As Juhl was merely an employee, Lauritzen is naturally credited with the design, hence also the name, VL38.[2] Juhl used many of the lamps from Radiohuset in 1947 in his design of the Bing & Grøndahl shop in central Copenhagen (see page 50). Interior and product design came to be Juhl's main areas of work.

Juhl taught at the School of Interior Design during the key period, from 1945 to 1955, that is considered the golden age of Danish design and the culmination of a culture of quality.[3] There was an emphasis on making democratic furniture and other products for the home that suited the small flats and houses of the time and which average families could afford. It was also during this that Denmark, not least thanks to Juhl, became known around the world for organic, modernist design.[4] The same year that Juhl began to teach at the school, he founded his own studio, and his interior design of the Trusteeship Council Chamber in the UN Building on Manhattan in 1950–1952 made him an international name.

Organic modernism reached its zenith during the 1950s, but the round luminaires from 1941 that Juhl helped design for Radiohuset were an early manifestation of the style. The dynamic, fluid and organic lines are echoed in Juhl's furniture design and in the luminaire he created for the Trusteeship Council Chamber. The latter was a dual-direction wall lamp in brushed brass that is really two lamps in one: a smaller downlight and larger uplight, the latter illuminating the ceiling grid and its multicoloured lighting fixtures.[5] The gently curving form of the shade openings aligned with the organic lines of the interior overall. The lamps were made in Denmark, but Juhl's 1963 drafts of an anglepoise lamp were probably intended for an American manufacturer. As it turned out, a modified version of the design was put into production that same year by Lyfa in pendant, table and wall lamps.[6]

From the early 1960s, Juhl's furniture design became more geometric in shape. The same is true of his pendant, table and wall lamps of lacquered metal, which are characterized by production-friendly simplicity and clearly defined components. The lamps were made in two colours: one in two neutral shades of grey and one, Juhl's favourite, in shades of blue. In all three types – pendant, table and wall – the outer, darker lampshade can move in relation to the lighter interior lampshade, which is fixed. Able to adopt a wide range of oblique positions, the lamp can thus be made to vary in both look and form. In the table lamp, the opening of the darker shade is equal in size to the diameter of the circular base,[7] just as the shape of the opening of the shade on the VL38 table lamp from 1941 is echoed in the base of the lamp.

Juhl's pendant and table lamps from 1963 only remained in production for seven years and are now highly sought-after collector's items. In 2011, the Danish manufacturer Onecollection, which holds the rights to several of Juhl's furniture designs, relaunched the lamps in the original design but only in the neutral grey colour scheme.[8]

Table lamp designed for Radiohuset in 1941, shown in Louis Poulsen's relaunched edition, VL38.

'It seems to me there are few good luminaires available in the world today. (...) Most of them handle such simple lighting tasks that the main effort concerns their exterior form.'—Finn Juhl, 1954[9]

Louis Weisdorf: Conch

Lyfa—1964

Weisdorf's Model 177 A for Le Klint.

The architect (MAA) and industrial designer Louis Weisdorf (1932–2021) graduated from the Royal Danish Academy of Fine Arts, School of Architecture, in 1954. Soon after his graduation, Weisdorf realized that architecture was not, in fact, his favourite field: 'At the time, fortunately, the programme was very broad, so my profile was similarly broad.'[1] Industrial design became his primary focus, and 'the main reason why I soon turned to design was that I wound up working for PH'.[2] Weisdorf worked for PH in 1958–1959, after which he spent some time working for Verner Panton.[3] One day in 1961, PH rang Weisdorf on behalf of his son Simon Henningsen, the chief architect of Tivoli, who was looking for a temporary assistant for his design work for Tivoli. The temporary job turned into a ten-year period of employment as Simon Henningsen's principal assistant at Tivoli combined with independent projects in Weisdorf's own design firm.[4]

Weisdorf was inspired by both PH and Panton, and in 1963 he designed his first lamp, mainly with inspiration from Panton – specifically Panton's 1960 Moon pendant (see page 98), which consists of 10 concentric, vertically mounted circular metal bands that can be rotated freely around the light bulb. Weisdorf was particularly interested in the way the bands were mounted but wanted to modify the concept to use identical elements. Weisdorf's lamp thus consists of 12 curved metal bands, each kinked to form a conch-like figure around the bulb when they are vertically interwoven around the axis – hence the name. Weisdorf did not design the Conch for Tivoli, 'but Tivoli's people were excited when they saw the cardboard model and ordered it for use in the gardens. I proposed that a metal version for that setting should be red and orange inside with gold anodization on the outside to emit a warm light that matched the mood of the gardens'.[5]

When the designer Nanna Ditzel (1923–2005), who was a close friend of Panton's, saw Weisdorf's lamp model in the *Politiken* newspaper,[6] she found that it plagiarized Panton's Moon pendant, which according to Weisdorf had merely served as inspiration for the design. Weisdorf contacted the master lamp designer PH personally to determine whether the design was too close to its source of inspiration, in which case he would immediately put a stop to the project. PH showed up at Tivoli and inspected the lamp. In his familiar outspoken style, he concluded, 'Of course, none of them are lamps, but as ladies' hats, they are quite dissimilar!' He added, 'Don't change a thing,' and so Weisdorf continued to work on the lamp as an independent, further development of the original design.[7]

In 1964, the Conch lamps, with their warm, golden glow, were ready to be hung from the tree branches in Tivoli. Next, Lyfa launched retail versions in additional colour combinations. Looking back in 2019, Weisdorf mentions that Panton taught him how 'design can be colourful and exciting'. Weisdorf also underscores that the Conch was mainly an interesting but unpretentious lamp design and that it was actually also 'quite nice in white'.[8] In the all-white version, the form, with its variations and dynamic, stands out clearly, and this dynamic appearance is essential to Weisdorf, because 'that makes it a product you can keep looking at and which doesn't get boring'.[9] When Le Klint later, in 1975, put Weisdorf's Models 177 A and B into production, they were folded in a single rectangular white sheet, like all Le Klint's lamps. The curvilinear pleats in the PVC sheet give rise to a fascinating dynamic. As a 'natural result of the lamp construction' with the deep pleats, the pendant's diffused light produces dramatic shadow effects in the shade itself and in the room.[10]

The Conch lamps still send out their soft evening glow in the trees near the Japanese Pagoda in Tivoli, but neither they nor the Le Klint models are in production today.

'Variation should be a natural result of the lamp's construction; that's the way it is with the Conch. There is no added decoration. It is the construction that makes it decorative.' —Louis Weisdorf, 2019[11]

Jacob E. Bang: Bang pendant

Fog & Mørup and
Holmegaard—ca. 1964

Late in life, Jacob E. Bang (1899–1965) designed the simple, beautifully curved glass pendant Bang. Using a special flash technique, he was able to make the inside of the lamp a different colour than the outside, which produced a particularly beautiful light. Bang graduated as an architect from the Royal Danish Academy of Fine Arts, School of Architecture, but had a significant impact as an industrial designer by expressing functionalism's simplified formal and social aspirations in glass design.[1]

As an employee of Kay Fisker's (1893–1965) architecture firm, Bang was involved in designing the Danish pavilion for the International Exhibition of Modern Decorative and Industrial Arts in Paris in 1925, where PH presented his multi-shade lamps, System PH (see pages 25 and 36).[2] Bang remarked how owning a PH pendant affirmed one's standing as 'an intellectual and an avant-gardist' in his retrospective description of the functionalist endeavour: 'We aimed for synthesis, the pure, unfalsified, clarified type: for example, not just a lamp but simply the lamp – not just a beer glass but simply the beer glass.'[3]

In 1926, Bang designed his first drinking glass for Holmegaard, dedicated to the everyman: 'The glass for Denmark's Hansen! (...) Appropriate, strong, affordable, beautiful.'[4] With this, he referenced functionalism's social idea and manifested it in a form that followed function in the unornamented glass Hogla. It was not a groundbreaking new design but a redesigned 19th-century bar glass.[5] As Kaare Klint stated in 1930, 'The problems are not so new; in many cases they have been addressed before' (see page 56). A shift in industrial art towards clean, simple everyday items was one of the programmatic goals of Kritisk Revy, the liberal leftist magazine edited by PH. In 1928, the magazine featured a photo collage with Bang's beer glasses centrally positioned and a caption saying that Hogla 'represents a beautiful and proper solution to the task'.[6]

Bang redesigned Hogla around 1950, when Holmegaard began to use machines for glass annealing. The new glass did not have a base knop, but the simple tulip form matched the organic design trend that was winning favour at the time. The trend is also reflected in Bang's late glass design, including in his 1964 lamps.[7]

The Bang pendant is almost equally simple in form as in name: a glass shade placed over a bulb. The lamp, which was developed in collaboration with the lighting manufacturer Fog & Mørup, does not break new ground – neither in form nor in lighting engineering terms – the way the PH lamp had. Created at a time when functionalist furniture had found its way into many Danish homes and interest in home design was booming, the Bang pendant reflects the designer's notion that an appropriate form is beautiful, simply because it is 'sober, modest, neutral and anonymous'. And yet, the 41-cm-tall slender shade drawn in a soft organic line in a smooth S-curve – or bottle shape, if you like – has a functional purpose, clasping the cord, widening around the bulb and tapering towards the bottom. The two-layered glass, created using the flash technique, which makes it possible to have a coloured exterior in combination with a white interior (see also page 118), reflects clear, white light from the bulb downwards through the slender form and out through the relatively narrow opening at the bottom, while some light is filtered through the coloured layer, illuminating the pendant itself.

The pendant was also made in opal white. With the coloured variants, Bang was not aiming to create a lamp that offers bright illumination for general lighting purposes; instead, he aimed for a more atmospheric effect. In 'coral, ocean blue or midnight blue', the lamp was certainly neither 'modest' nor 'anonymous'.[8] When the bulb shone through the glass, form and colour stood out clearly, and the sculptural pendant, used singly or in clusters, provided mood lighting for cosy family evenings. And that was the intent.

With his functional and beautiful designs, Bang helped Holmegaard achieve its position as a leading industrial glass manufacturer.[9] Jacob E. Bang's glassware appeared on the dinner table in many homes, while his son, Michael Bang, was instrumental in adding glass lamps to the decor (see page 120).

'An everyday glass must be appropriate, strong, affordable and, ultimately, also beautiful.'
—Jacob E. Bang, 1949[10]

Andreas Hansen: Pine Cone lamp, Model 153

Le Klint—1964

Andreas Hansen experimented with the use of paint to shield the light. Seen here are the Pine Cone lamp and the Fan lamp in special versions with either gold or dark brown paint.

Andreas Hansen (b. 1936) trained as a cabinetmaker and subsequently attended the School of Arts and Crafts. He continued on to the Furniture School at the Royal Danish Academy of Fine Arts, but the foundation had been laid: 'I learnt nothing new, except maybe what is good taste and bad!'[1] Hansen worked for Vilhelm Wohlert and Jørgen Bo for a while but has had his own design firm since 1963. Furniture design has been the predominant theme in a long career, with pleated lamps as a significant sideline.

The Pine Cone lamp has been in the shops since 1964. The first step in the design process occurred in 1962 while Hansen was still attending the School of Arts and Crafts and entered a competition held by the Copenhagen lamp factory Grubert: 'I won second prize, and it wasn't a design they could produce, so I was given free rein to use it. It was a folded paper shade, so I went to Le Klint's shop in Kirkestræde. The sales director, Allan Bock, thought it looked interesting and encouraged me to keep at it.'[2] The resulting lamp was strikingly different from the early cross-pleated Le Klint shades (see pages 56–57). In technical terms, however, the round lamp with the eye-catching zigzag pattern is not so different from Kaare Klint's Fruit Lantern, 'it's simply a new approach to the old design, as Klint's lamp is also based on the repetition of identical triangles',[3] Hansen explains and adds that the surfaces on his own lamp form a rhomboid with two parallel sides: 'All the angles are divisible by 15 degrees; in fact, it's simply two different angles that are staggered, like the identical steps in a spiral staircase. The staggering produces the form – as when you fold a paper garland.'[4]

The new white Le Klint shade, Model 153, was launched as the Pine Cone lamp in 1964.[5] The name contains the same nature reference as Klint's lantern, but there is also a reference to PH's Artichoke lamp, which is called the Pine Cone lamp in Danish. Indeed, PH plays a role in the story about Hansen's lamp: Hansen experimented with colour in his shades, not only for decorative purposes but mainly to modify the lighting: 'I was aiming for the same effect as in a PH lamp that shields the light and directs it downwards. I dimmed the fields facing up, so that the light was directed towards the horizontal surface, while some soft light was still emitted into the room.'[6] In 2019, Hansen describes how PH visited the School of Arts and Crafts around 1960 to give a lecture: 'PH explained his lighting principles, using a board with an incandescent light bulb surrounded by several angled pieces of cardboard, so we could see how each of the pieces could direct the light downwards. The first PH lamp had three shades, subsequent ones had more, but it was the same principle that I used in my colouring of the folded shades.'[7]

The coloured shades remained an experiment, but to the customers' delight Hansen continued to explore the potential of the pleating technique in the 3D geometric figures. The year after the launch of the Pine Cone, his Cactus lamp was launched in 1965, with even deeper and larger zigzag pleats. The following year saw the launch of the Fan lamp, with even more dramatic pleats, possibly making it a little 'too bold and complicated for the customers', according to the designer,[8] who also experimented with dimming this latter model with expressive dark upwards-facing fields.

Hansen continued to develop the pleating technique that Klint used in his faceted Fruit Lantern, and so did the architects Peter Hvidt (1916–1986) and Orla Mølgaard-Nielsen (1907–1993), who created their own, crystalline models.[9] In 1968, Hansen commented, 'The exciting thing about working with stereometric shapes is the rich sculptural expression that can be achieved, despite the strict mathematical regularity.'[10] The rather dramatic pleats, compared to the more disciplined Klintian tradition, inspired Poul Christiansen's curvilinear pleats a few years later (see page 122).

Hansen soon noticed a key difference between the deep horizontal zigzag pattern of his Pine Cone lamp and the vertical facets of Klint's Fruit Lantern: Hansen's model gathered more dust. When he mentioned this to Director Bock, he replied, 'Well, then you know where you've got it!'[11] Fortunately, the shades can simply be rinsed off in the shower.

'If you're holding a sheet of paper, you'll soon discover how hard it is to turn it into a ball. But if you crumple it slightly, the paper begins to take shape, and you can study how it crumpled: a triangle here, another one there. That gives you an ample source of inspiration. You can systematize what happened randomly – repeating a detail to create a controlled three-dimensional shape.'
—Andreas Hansen, 2019[12]

Verner Panton: Shell lamp

J. Lüber—1964

'It attracted a great deal of attention at the fair in Frankfurt!'
—Marianne Panton, 2019[1]

From 1958, stagnation was replaced by renewed momentum thanks to a strong upturn in the international economy.[2] Growth and development, both in industry and in the public sector, sparked the demand for new lighting in industrial and public spaces. Strip lights became widespread but provided flat, uniform illumination without the shadows and variation needed for pleasant and atmospheric lighting. In his design of the Astoria restaurant in 1961, Panton used his first industrially produced lamp, Topan (see page 72). PH was not impressed with the pendant from a technical perspective, but he applauded Panton's ability to incorporate darkness and contrasts into his lighting design. PH wrote in his review of the restaurant that Panton's design was the first proper solution to a problem that had persisted since the breakthrough of functionalism: how to design 'a restaurant that people could stand to be in'.[3]

PH facilitated Panton's introduction to the Louis Poulsen company, which was widely identified with PH's lampshade system. In 1961, Louis Poulsen launched Panton's Visor pendant on the retail market, where it soon became known as the Moon pendant.[4] Unlike PH's horizontal slat constructions and Panton's early, similarly horizontal, floating shade rings (see page 72), Visor consists of ten rings, lacquered white, mounted on a vertical axis and placed around the bulb as a protective, reflecting visor. The rings can be rotated individually to vary both the lamp's appearance and the light. It was an early attempt at activating the user, an invitation to play with the light and interact with space that would become a key characteristic of Panton's design. As Panton put it, 'Even the best planned interior only really comes into its own when people take possession of it and use it.'[5] Interiors should offer a sensory experience, and this was fully accomplished with the 1964 Shell lamp.

In 1961, Panton left Denmark, initially settling in southern France and later in Switzerland, where he worked with European manufacturers, with Basel as his centrally located base. At the 1964 Frankfurt fair, Panton presented the Shell lamp made by the Swiss company J. Lüber. Panton's widow, Marianne Panton, describes that the lamp attracted a great deal of attention.[6] While Topan, as an individual object, was a geometric pendant with modernist roots, the Shell lamp was an organic, spatial formation. It was a dramatic modern chandelier where the centred light bulb was hidden behind numerous round, semi-transparent discs stamped out in shiny mother-of-pearl. The shells, which were less than half a millimetre thick, were connected via tiny steel rings into large clusters suspended from a ceiling plate. The discs would be set in motion by the heat from the incandescent light bulb – and by the air currents from people moving in the room – which produced a softly flickering light and a pleasant jingling sound. Panton explained, 'The sound is like cow bells ringing in the distance. It is very soothing.'[7] Panton's original prototype used discs of tin foil, and when the Shell lamps were developed into a series, some of the models featured shiny aluminium discs rather than mother-of-pearl. The non-transparent aluminium leads to a different, dimmer light. The sound effect is still there, but that too is very different.

PH is said to have loved the lamps.[8] And he was not the only fan. After the exhibition, the Shell lamp received widespread media coverage. It was also featured in the James Bond film *On Her Majesty's Secret Service* (1969) in a scene where the lead female character runs her fingers through the shells, generating the characteristic jingle.[9] With its reflected, diffused light and crisp sound from the many natural shells, the lamp was mainly intended as an atmospheric element. As such, it was more than a luminaire – it was a sensory experience, and Panton often used it in exhibitions.

The Shell lamp was part of the Fun series, which included a range of pendants, table lamps and a floor lamp – all based on large numbers of circles.[10] The name of the series reflects the playful approach to lighting, and along with the emphasis on colours, play and imagination were key ingredients in Panton's universe, which was a far cry from the Danish tradition.

Visir/Moon lamp, Louis Poulsen, 1960, currently in production by Verpan.
→ The dining room in Verner Panton's home in Binningen, Switzerland, doubled as a showroom. The ceiling was decorated with hundreds of thousands of sea shells, like a giant Shell lamp.

Bent Gantzel-Boysen: LamPetit

Louis Poulsen—1966

A gaggle of LamPetits.

'The new Louis Poulsen baby' was the headline when LamPetit was introduced to the world in 1966 in *NYT*.[1] Although the lamp was new and small, the angular, non-organic form sparks no associations to chubby-cheeked infants. 'It is no beauty, but it is practical and handy and stylistically consistent,' wrote the regional newspaper *Fyns Tidende* after the launch.[2] Beautiful or not, that is a matter of taste, but the stylistic consistence is indisputable.

The buyer received the lamp folded up in a small, rectangular lidded box measuring only 5.8 x 6.7 x 22 cm. As the design researcher Lars Dybdahl points out, it will have appeared both 'slightly aloof and a little "odd" in the cut-off monolithic wedge shape of its collapsed state'.[3] However, when the lamp head is pulled away from the base and raised rigidly up, moving freely in a 360-degree circle on the two telescopic rods that keep it in place and power the bulb, the little lamp suddenly comes alive. The luminous head on the long, rigid giraffe neck lends it an animalistic character.

In engineering terms, the design marked a Danish innovation; although the system used in the lamp was known from Japanese and American low-voltage lamps, none of these foreign designs had been approved for use by the Danish authorities. Now, Bent Gantzel-Boysen (1930–2008) had designed a Danish version.

Gantzel-Boysen was trained as an electrician and, subsequently, as an engineer from Aarhus Technical School. Shortly after his graduation, in 1956, the young man came to work for Louis Poulsen, where he learnt about the art of lighting from the renowned lighting designer PH.[4] In the design of LamPetit, the mechanically knowledgeable engineer used a 12-volt car light bulb. Via the conductive neck, the transformer in the base of the lamp powered the bulb, which had an effect matching that of a 40–60-watt light bulb mounted in a reflector. With two lighting levels, LamPetit could provide either a good, concentrated white working light or a cosier, soft, warm light. In 1966, LamPetit was only available in black, but one year later a grey and a fashionable red were added[5] and, later, a bold orange version.

LamPetit was a clever design that was easy to fold up and carry without risk of breaking, providing its own convenient transport case. At the destination, it could be unfolded, hung on a wall or stand on its own, taking up only a tiny space. Handy in every regard. A review in the national newspaper *Ekstrabladet* concluded, 'In technical and practical terms the little lamp is a child genius with an untold potential. The company's advertising slogan "You're going to need that lamp" is not just hot air.'[6]

By basing his design solution on a car light bulb, Gantzel-Boysen had made his luminaire small and handy, a precursor of the halogen lamps that made their way into Danish homes from the early 1980s, which were similarly capable of converting 220 volts to only 12 volts via a transformer. In fact, it was during this decade that the production of LamPetit was discontinued.

In the 1970s, Gantzel-Boysen was appointed head of Louis Poulsen's design team, and he designed several lamps for the lighting company, including spot lights (see page 126). Gantzel-Boysen was a very modest man, who never became a household designer name. That may be the source of the stubborn rumour that LamPetit was in fact designed by Verner Panton. Although Gantzel-Boysen and Panton developed a close friendship, Panton had nothing to do with the design of LamPetit,[7] nor does it resemble a Panton design. However, just a few years after the birth of LamPetit, both Gantzel-Boysen and, not least, Panton presented the lighting company with many new iconic babies.

'It is not often in this country that we are presented with actual lamp innovations, but now the designer Bent Gantzel Boysen has created a so-called low-voltage lamp for use in private homes for Louis Poulsen & Co.' —Fyens Stiftstidende, 1966[8]

Jo Hammerborg: Trombone

Fog & Mørup—1966

Although almost 40 years have passed since Jo Hammerborg passed away, and only one of his lamps is currently in production, Jo Hammerborg lamps are found in many Danish homes. They have gained renewed prominence in recent years as a result of the retro wave, but Hammerborg's lamps are also widespread because so many models were launched and sold. Over the years, more than 100 models have been in production.[1]

In continuation of early functionalist ideas, Hammerborg was a proponent of contemporary and simple interior design. Importantly, he also sought to make the style affordable. Hence, the lamps were not intended for the few but as affordable designs. Henni Hammerborg explains that her husband was frankly 'appalled that not everybody had the necessary skills to create a well-designed interior; he believed that form and colour should be taught to all schoolchildren as a mandatory subject. Johs was extremely style-conscious'.[2]

Style, form and colour naturally varied among the many lamps Hammerborg created over a period of just over two decades. While many luminaires had curvy organic lines (see page 85), Hammerborg also designed strictly geometric lamps. One of the lamps that remains in widespread use, even though it is no longer in production, is the cylindrical Trombone from 1966, which was produced as a floor lamp, a table lamp and a series of single- or multi-shade pendants. Trombone was only one among many lamps using cylindrical shades.

Five years earlier, Hammerborg designed Studio, which was originally made in copper and aluminium. The shade consists of two components: a small, closed cylinder covers the socket, while a wider cylinder shields the bulb. The open cylinder has a white interior with a wide grey band painted on the lower two centimetres. Hammerborg used this feature in several models to prevent the light from being captured by the edge of the shade. Due to the difference in size between the two cylinders, the lamp emits not only a downwards light but also a circle of light in the gap between the two shades that illuminates the outside of the metal shade.[3] The lamp head is mounted on a thin metal arm attached to a thin tubular stem with a 90-degree kink standing on a cylindrical base. At Henni and Jo Hammerborg's wedding in 1965, the staff of Fog & Mørup formed a 'sabre arch' using the lightweight Studio lamps.[4]

The Trombone shade is a simple metal cylinder, and like the Studio shade it has a white interior. However, a ring of narrow vertical slits has been punched into the top and bottom of this cylindrical shade to let the light through and illuminate the lamp itself. This is different from the Orient, which only had slits at the top (see page 85). In the floor lamp Trombone II, the cylinder is suspended in between two slender metal rods connected with a cross bar. The resemblance to a trombone is, of course, the source of the name, and although the rods do not telescope, the adjustable lamp head can be moved up and down.[5] This model has a square grey lacquered base, adding to a clean expression that is somewhat softened by the openwork trim. The table lamp was launched first, while the floor lamp was almost abandoned, because it proved difficult to push the cord all the way through the long, thin tube. For the designer, it was an ultimate demand that the cord be hidden inside the lamp.[6] The pendant versions were sold as individual lamps or assembled, by means of wooden rods, into horizontal compositions with two, three or four shades.

During his long employment at Fog & Mørup, Hammerborg influenced many of the lamps the manufacturer sold for use in private homes. Many of them were his own designs entirely, and Trombone was one of the Hammerborg lamps that made its way into many Danish homes. Hammerborg left the company in 1980.[7]

'Sabre arch' of Studio lamps and tennis rackets at Henni and Jo Hammerborg's wedding.

'Johs had a mission of making more Danes embrace a simple and contemporary interior design style.'
—Henni Hammerborg, 2019[8]

Benny Frandsen: Ball Model 1300

Frandsen—1968

When Benny Frandsen (1941–2021) was 14 years old, he designed his first lamp and stated that one day he wanted to have his own factory. He had his factory by 1968. Prior to this, Frandsen had completed his training as both an electrician and an electrical engineer and had married. The first production was set up in the couple's basement, and Inge Frandsen, who was a schoolteacher, recruited the first employees: a couple of students who helped assemble lamps after school. Thinking back to these early days, Benny Frandsen says that he 'bought all the parts and then we assembled them ourselves. Back then, that's what everybody did. It was a big industry, there were many wholesalers and the lamps were sold from small electrician's shops'.[1]

The first lamps were square: 'My engineer's brain preferred geometric shapes, and I liked the idea of square lamps; there weren't many of them around.'[2] The design developed into a full-fledged series with a pendant, table, floor and wall lamps and a spotlight. 'We had the full range; I was convinced it was just the thing, only it wasn't, not then, but I persisted for a long time.'[3] Meanwhile, Frandsen had examined the market and discovered that round forms were much easier to sell. 'That led to the Ball lamp, initially as a pendant, and later we added the floor lamp.' The spherical form with the cut-off bottom was difficult to make but was eventually accomplished in 1968, with the assistance of a supplier who had a special tool that could remove the finished iron shell from the casting mould: 'A split chuck consisting of a large number of slats that could be folded up once the sphere was finished; it was a brilliant tool.'[4] A ring of circular holes was then punched into the top of the 18-cm-wide shell to provide an outlet for the heat generated by the incandescent light bulb. The weight keeps the iron shell stable when it is hung.[5]

The first round lamp was a pendant, but the Ball series also featured other models, including a floor lamp with two lamp heads. The stem was mounted on a circular base, painted in the same colour as the lamp heads, which were mounted on arms that could be moved to direct the light to where it was needed. The two-shade floor lamp was a popular item during the 1970s. Today it is marketed as the Ball Double, but at the time it was called Model 1300.

Production numbers remained modest until 1970; after that time, the lamps also made it into Danish department stores. In 1973, Frandsen's round pendant and the floor lamp with the two lamp heads appeared for the first time in the autumn catalogue for Daells Varehus.[6] The round lamps also found a receptive audience in Norway, where the Model 1300 was the best-selling floor lamp in 1975.[7] It was produced in a special version for the Norwegian market, since the white shade interior that reflected the light into the room was not enough for the Norwegians: 'They wanted as much light as possible, so we added a mirror reflector to the ball.' In Denmark, Frandsen mainly sold balls with mirror reflectors – an extra shiny shade interior – for shop lighting, because the light was much too bright for Danish living rooms: 'In Denmark we have always preferred a warm light, while the light in southern countries and especially in the East always had to be bright and completely white. Now that the Scandinavian style is so popular around the world, we are selling the cosy soft, golden Danish light everywhere, because it is a natural aspect of

The Ball magnet lamp was redesigned in the early 1990s.

Scandinavian design.'[8]

The light emitted by the small magnet lamps that were so popular in Denmark during the 1970s was cosy too. A wall magnet lamp was added to the Ball series in the late 1970s. It had a slightly smaller iron globe placed on a wall plate equipped with 'a large core magnet, an iron magnet with a hole in it. At the time, there were several such lamps. In the early 1990s, I designed the version that's still around today, which has a magnet that is both much stronger and much smaller. The smaller magnet made for a much more attractive lamp design'.[9] The story illustrates how Frandsen continued to develop the Ball lamps. The same is true of his company, which now has 85 employees. Many designs are sent into the world from the Frandsen Group's large factory in Horsens, eastern Jutland, including the Ball lamps – both the Model 1300 (Ball Double) and the magnet lamp – and many others, and soon, the square lamps will be coming back, too.[10]

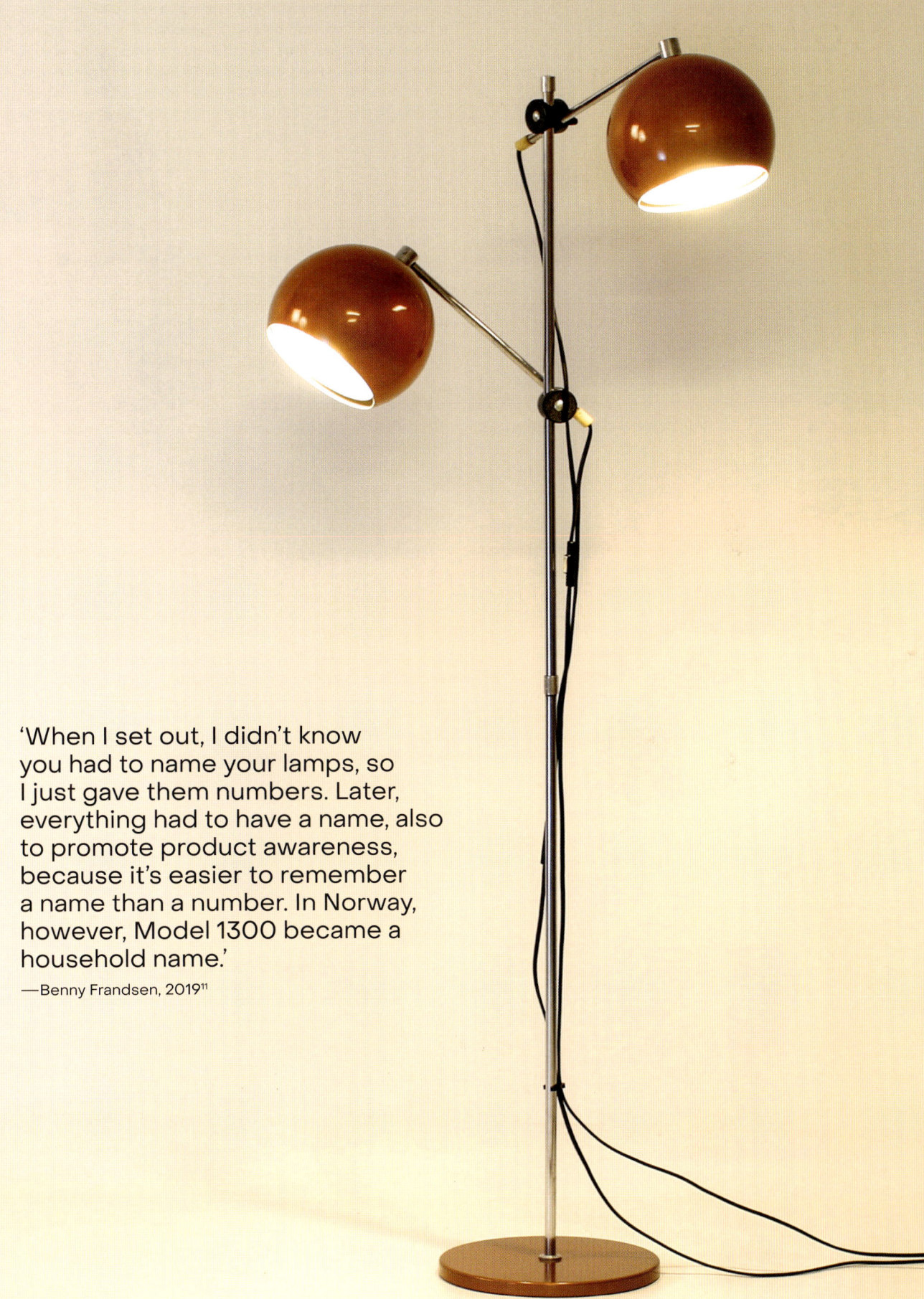

'When I set out, I didn't know you had to name your lamps, so I just gave them numbers. Later, everything had to have a name, also to promote product awareness, because it's easier to remember a name than a number. In Norway, however, Model 1300 became a household name.'
—Benny Frandsen, 2019[11]

Verner Panton: Flowerpot

Louis Poulsen—1968

'The most wonderful thing for our home: A FLOWER POT!
The lines are playful and light, a fresh and beautiful sight!
It soothes the nerves. And it sends out a light that we LIKE A LOT!'
—Olaf Gynt, 1971[1]

In 1968, nine years after Verner Panton designed Topan, and eight years after the Visor, or Moon, pendant (see pages 72–73 and 98), Panton had another pendant put into production by Louis Poulsen. Flowerpot was a simple, geometric form consisting of two hemispherical enamelled metal shades, in 2:1 proportions: a large upper shade and a smaller lower shade with half the diameter of the upper one. The upper shade directed the light downwards, while the lower one shielded the bulb and reflected the light upwards, so that it was radiated downwards without glare. The Flowerpot lamp had high-gloss enamel exteriors in orange, red, turquoise, violet, white and black, complete with matching plastic cords.[2] The interior of the upper shade was white, while the interior of the lower shade was lacquered orange or rose-coloured to achieve a warm reflected light. This was in accordance with PH's ideas about glare-free light in a warm, reddish tone, directed to where it was needed, as a 'supplement to the room's otherwise localized and defining lighting'.[3]

Panton mostly used the Flowerpot lamps for localized lighting in large clusters. That was also the case when he was commissioned by the German chemical company Bayer, in spring 1968, to design the interior of an excursion boat on the Rhine in connection with the furniture fair in Cologne. The focus of this first Visiona exhibition was on showcasing Bayer's new Dralon fabric, but in Panton's total design, lighting also played a crucial role, particularly with the use of Flowerpot lamps. The exhibition was reviewed in both Mobilia and, naturally, in Louis Poulsen's magazine LP & Co. NYT. The latter wrote, 'Everywhere, Verner Panton used the Flowerpot in clusters, and although the lamp can of course be used on its own, clusters are likely to become the more common approach.'[4]

As far as private homes were concerned, that prediction did not hold, but while the expensive Shell lamp (see pages 98–99) was out of reach for all but the most affluent flower children, most youth rebels could afford a Flowerpot. The simple lamp was fairly cheap to make, and the reasonable price tag made it affordable for large consumer segments, who, instead of a total design in psychedelic colours and patterns, were more easily seduced into acquiring just a single little lamp. As many as 240,000 small Flowerpots were sold in 1968 alone.[5] Many issues of Bo Bedre ran Flowerpot ads, the earliest of them aimed mainly at the readers' teenage children.[6] Even during the day, when they were not lit, the pendants with the brightly coloured monochrome shades added a dash of colour to the light Danish home interiors.

Panton preferred to use the lamps in systematically designed groups.[7] The Visiona exhibition ship on the Rhine in 1968 and the display at the Frankfurt Fair that same spring featured hundreds of Flowerpots in different colours, like huge bouquets of luminous flowers. According to Panton, the name refers to this flower theme. Later, the association to flower power culture and pot smoking seemed natural, in light of prominent cultural trends at the time when the lamp was created.[8] In 1970, in a more fashion-oriented representation of the contemporary context, a series of big Flowerpot lamps with a two-tone op art-inspired pattern in black/white, pale yellow/yellow, pale orange/orange and pale blue/blue was produced.[9] Despite the 'wild' pattern, the colour selection was as systematic as the lamp's lighting properties and the award-winning harmonious form.[10] Panton offered the following insight into his approach to colour:

I have mainly worked with parallel colours, colours that are close to each other on the colour spectrum. However, you could also work with complementary colours, colours that are opposite to each other on the spectrum. In that case, however, one of the colours has to be dominant, while the others are used for accentuation. Colour planning is an underrated aspect of modern design; we need more research in this area.[11]

↑ Advertisement for Flowerpot lamps in Bo Bedre, April 1969.
← Verner Panton in a photo for Louis Poulsen's magazine LP & Co. NYT, 1971.
→ Flowerpot lamps in Panton's design of the canteen in Der Spiegel's offices in Hamburg, Germany. Today, the canteen has been reproduced in an exhibition hall at the Museum für Kunst und Gewerbe (Museum for Arts and Crafts), also in Hamburg.

Sven Middelboe: Verona

Nordisk Solar Compagni—1968

Sven Middelboe (1910–2002) had a business degree, but design became his chosen path, and lighting his specialty.[1] From 1949 to 1955, he had his own company as a lighting manufacturer, which produced the architect Jørn Utzon's lamps (see page 60) as well as, probably, some of Middelboe's own lamps. Both Utzon and Middelboe have described the very basic production set-up they relied on at the time: after receiving a large delivery of specially designed lampshades, stamped out in aluminium, the two men now had to lacquer the shades in different colours and assemble the lamps. They assembled the lamps in the sports and event venue K.B. Hallen in Frederiksberg, thanks to the intervention of Middelboe's father, who was the chairman of the tennis club. Understandably, they had been asked to take the paintwork outdoors, and so set up on the pavement in front of the hall. Here they cautiously paused every time a tram drove by, lest someone suspect them of painting graffiti and call the police.[2]

In 1955, Nordisk Solar Compagni hired Middelboe as their in-house designer as part of a larger effort to expand the company's involvement in lamp production.[3] In addition to designing luminaires, Middelboe was also responsible for the design of the company's many exhibition stands. The former CEO Thorkild Thage Jørgensen said in 2019: 'Every year we presented our lamps at the Hannover fair. Sven was our exhibition architect from day one, and he was good at it. When you walked through the halls, his stands were always among the most beautiful; they were always very harmonious, and he had a great sense of colour.'[4]

A large catalogue from 1958 shows many of Middelboe's luminaires. Few of them have a name, but the Pagode (Pagoda) pendant does.[5] The dome-shaped metal shade, with a coloured exterior and a white interior, had a pointy pagoda-shaped top in teak leading up to the cord – a simple, organic pendant matching contemporary interior design styles. Middelboe designed lamps for several decades, and his expression and choice of materials evolved with the changing trends in home design. His early luminaires were made of either glass or metal or a combination of the two. From around 1970, Middelboe designed several plastic lamps, including the Nite-cap wall lamp and the Nord-Lys (Northern Light) pendant.[6] The lamps were cast in trendy colours, including yellow, orange and purple.

In 1968, Middelboe's continued experimentation with shade constructions and combinations resulted in his best-selling series Verona,[7] which included ceiling fittings, pendant lamps and a table lamp. Originally, the pendant came in two variants with either six or eight shades in trendy colour combinations of white/yellow, brass-coloured/orange and lacquered aluminium/purple.[8] The shades were mounted around the bulb on three metal rods, held apart by spacers. The light from the bulb was reflected and emitted between the shades, all of which had a white lacquer interior, in some cases with additional colour – for example, orange on the top shades. The lower shade had a grey interior to reduce glare from the bottom of the lamp. In the pendant version, the luminaire is open on top, so that some of the light is emitted upwards, adding indirect light reflected from the ceiling.

This multi-shade luminaire is one of the many designs created with inspiration from PH's technically innovative lamp designs.[9] Verona was accused of being too close to PH's lamps – see, for example, PH's ten-shade Contrast lamp (1958–1962, see page 79). The Verona lamps have ring-shaped shades and a coloured interior in common with PH's more structurally complicated and expensive pendant. The Verona lamps in the different variants with different numbers of shades had a simpler construction and were thus more affordable. According to Jørgensen, the series sold in large numbers both to private customers and on the contract market.[10]

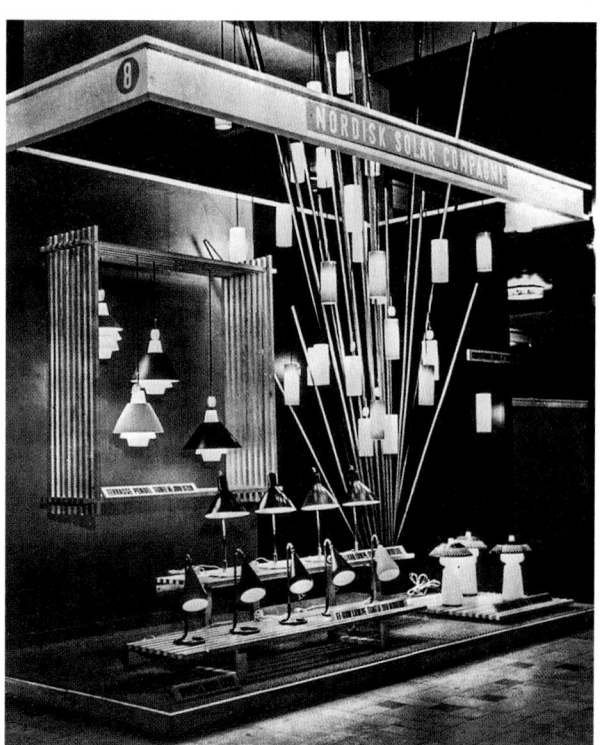

Exhibition stand for Nordisk Solar Compagni in 1956, designed by Sven Middelboe.

'That is proper design in connection with a good lighting effect.'—Nordisk Solar Compagni, 1978[11]

Torsten Thorup and Claus Bonderup: Semi

Fog & Mørup—1969

The architects Torsten Thorup (b. 1944) and Claus Bonderup (1943–2022) first met in connection with the entrance exam to the Royal Danish Academy of Fine Arts, School of Architecture, in 1965. They enrolled in separate departments, but both spent their final year of studies in Professor Henning Larsen's department, where drawings and model photos of their jointly developed Semi pendant lamp were among the projects they presented for evaluation that year, alongside individual design, urban planning and building projects.

When the two architects graduated in spring 1969, Semi was already in production, as the lighting firm Fog & Mørup included the pendant in their lamp collection that year.

Fog & Mørup saw commercial potential in the clean lines of the form: a lamp 'designed for a chrome-cap bulb as a simple geometric form that begins as a direct extension of the cord and expands over the bulb, the curved surfaces reflecting the rays from the filament'.[1] Thus, the form is in direct dialogue with the light source, a chrome-cap bulb with a highly reflective coating on top. The chrome-cap bulb was positioned so it was perfectly flush with the horizontal tangent on the shade form as an integral part of the lamp design. This created a flawless pendant lamp that efficiently utilized the reflected light. By blocking the light, the cap prevents glare and the light is instead emitted from the remaining part of the bulb and reflected by the shade, the inside of the cap adding to the reflection inside the shade.

Thorup explains the rationale behind the name of the lamp: 'The name refers to the elevation of the lamp, which is formed by two quarter circles that together form a semi-circle.'[2] The pendant was launched at the annual lighting exhibition *Salone del Mobile Euroluce* in Milan in 1969 and was subsequently sold in several sizes and colours, initially white, black, chrome and a special edition with 24-carat gold plating. In bespoke projects, it further appeared in a wide range of colours. A few years later came the Semi floor lamp, an uplight where the lampshade was turned upside down.

Designed during the time of the youth rebellion, with its general rejection of the prevailing tastes of the parental generation, the two young men's Semi lamp was simultaneously pure geometric form and verging on the psychedelic. With the accentuating chrome-cap bulb, the floating pendant lamp also flirted with the still-current international space look.[3] Semi quickly became a commercial success abroad, and in 1973 it received the (West) German design award Die gute Industrieform (Good Industrial Form). Owing to its harmonious form, based on two quarter-circle arcs in cross section put together back to back, the pendant, which is typically used above a table, has maintained its currency over the years and in many different interiors.

When Lyfa took over Fog & Mørup in 1978, production and sales of the Semi lamp in the Far East was outsourced to the Japanese company Yamagiva. Throughout the 1980s and 1990s, Semi was one of the best-selling Danish industrial design products, helped along by IKEA's inclusion of the original Semi lamp in their lighting collection. This success naturally inspired a wide range of copies of the appealing geometric shade that emerged in a smooth and seamless transition from the line formed by the cord.

The simple geometry was also a characteristic of the duo's subsequent lamp designs: 'We wanted to make something simple, recognizably geometric, and, equally important, plain good lighting. A lamp can be sculptural, but not for the sake of being sculptural, only for the sake of function.'[4]

Since 2012, the Semi pendant has been produced by the design company Gubi and continues to enjoy international success.

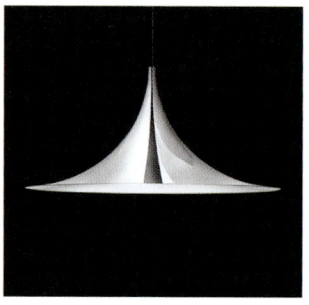 

Semi has been in production by Gubi since 2012.
↗ LED version of a chrome-capped light bulb.

'A lamp should be designed for a purpose and be sculptural; it can't just be an illuminating sculpture.'
—Torsten Thorup, 2019[5]

Verner Panton: Spiegel Fittings

Louis Poulsen—1969

Ring lamps in the corridor in the Pantons' mansion in Binningen.
→ The Varna restaurant in Aarhus in 1971, enveloped in pop music and warm lighting from a mix of Spiegel Fittings and Ring lamps.

In 1969, Verner Panton participated in the Paris exhibition *Qu'est ce que Le Design?* (What Is Design?), which also featured Joe Colombo (1930–1971), Roger Tallon (1929–2011) and Charles Eames (1907–1978), among others. Panton's answer was to cover the walls and ceilings in a classical room at the Louvre's Pavillon de Marsan with square luminous bricks in shades of orange, red and purple as an integrating background for his large multi-tiered sitting sculpture Living Tower.[1] In response to a growing demand for compact interior solutions, Living Tower utilized the height of the room. In fact, with the tower and the illuminated wall and ceiling surfaces Panton reinterpreted the very concept of being in a room. His colour-saturated and intense use of materials and the all-encompassing lighting design, as opposed to individual lamps here and there, created a holistic experience that invited people to rethink interior design. The luminous bricks, each measuring 62.5 x 62.2 cm, were stamped out in sheet iron and lacquered in different colours. They had a round hollow for the light bulb, which was hidden from view by a hemispherical shade, while the concave ring that emerged in the gap reflected the light.[2] Originally designed for the weekly German magazine *Der Spiegel*'s offices in Hamburg, completed in 1969, they were named Spiegel Fittings when they were put into production by Louis Poulsen. In the Spiegel building, the bricks were placed side by side on the ceilings and walls, their luminous colour play blurring the dimensions of the buildings rectangular lobby and canteens.[3]

Panton immediately developed these luminaires into the similarly square Ring lamp in clear and coloured acrylic. Panton used these acrylic tiles with the luminous rings in 1970 in his third design of Bayer's exhibition ship on the Rhine as part of the annual furniture fair in Cologne.[4] At *Visiona II*, Panton took both total design and the above-mentioned lighting philosophy a step further. In the central, 48-m² exhibition hall, which had no incoming daylight, he created a fantasy landscape where foam rubber and padded furniture with fabric upholstery in flowing, wavy shapes seemed to grow out of the floor and spread over the walls and ceiling. The colourful flowing form ranged from the cooler blue end of the spectrum on the periphery to a glowing red and yellow area in the centre. The lighting came from light sources built into the large textile construction (see page 30).[5]

Panton's large, almost body-like combined furniture installation and light source reinterpreted both the concept of the total work of art and the use of coloured lampshades. In 1927, PH commented that people exaggerated the use of red and yellow silk shades in their cluttered, Victorian-style living rooms in order to achieve a warm light.[6] Now, Panton not only reintroduced padded furniture but deliberately used intense colours to achieve both a warmer light and a more challenging spatial experience. Panton's lighting was intended not to be functional but spectacular!

The three-dimensional furniture landscapes and spatially defining lighting marked a clear shift from functionalism's 'sitting machines' to an experiential, body-oriented approach to home design. Panton's inspiration came not only from his Danish training and Danish design traditions but also from the international pop movement, a direction in art and design that emerged during the 1960s in response to general economic and technological optimism. Designers found inspiration in mass consumerism and popular culture, and in a rejection of modernism they sought to express the democratic spirit of the time by replacing modernist values and functionalist requirements with aspirations of fun, wit, variety and, not least, an alternative.[7]

At the time, Panton was the only Danish lighting designer who had radically moved on since PH, in the sense of flouting contemporary rules and notions. While the functionalists had sought to make rooms as bright as possible, Panton went in the opposite direction in his use of lighting engineering and material properties to construct warm lighting. In Paris, Hamburg and Cologne, he represented a colourful concept of pervasive lighting rather than the use of lamps here and there. This put him ahead of his time, but, naturally, the light source behind the shades was still the incandescent light bulb.

'In an almost magical effect, the luminous walls render the boundaries of the rooms indeterminate; the fairly limited rooms expand.' —Svend Erik Møller, 1969[8]

Verner Panton: Ilumesa

Louis Poulsen—1970

Spiral lamps at the Varna restaurant in Aarhus, 1971.

After the successful Fun series from 1964 (see page 98), Verner Panton used the same frame concept in his Ball lamp and Spiral lamp series for J. Lüber. Instead of sea shells and aluminium discs, these new lamps featured plastic balls and spiral ribbons combined into spherical volumes around the bulb. The meditative look and sound of the jingling Shell lamp, where the light is diffused through the thin shells and reflected in the mother-of-pearl surface, is quite different from the Ball lamp with its plastic balls in the parallel colours of pink and red. However, the effect of the Spiral lamp's spiral ribbons in varying lengths is almost as hypnotic as that of the Shell lamp when air currents make the spirals spin around their axis. The effect is particularly mesmerizing and dizzying when the light flickers in the chrome-plated version and the surrounding room is reflected in countless shattered fragments.[1] These shiny Spiral lamps played a key role in the interior when Panton hung them above the tables in the Varna restaurant near Aarhus. The architect Svend Erik Møller wrote in a review of the interior in Louis Poulsen's magazine *LP & Co. NYT*, 'Although the plastic spiral lamps are not made by Louis Poulsen & Co. but by Lüber in Switzerland, I have been granted permission to find them wonderful. With an effect reminiscent of crystal chandeliers in motion, if you can imagine such a thing.'[2]

Both the Ball and Spiral lamps were launched in connection with the annual furniture fair in Cologne in January 1970, when Panton created a third exhibition ship for Bayer. In this futuristic vision, Panton presented several new lamp models, including three that he had developed in cooperation with Louis Poulsen and which were launched over the following months: the large (monochrome or patterned) version of Flowerpot (see page 106), the acrylic Ring bricks, which were a further development of the sheet iron elements from the interior at the Spiegel building (see pages 107 and 112) and, finally, the all-new Ilumesa, which was both lamp and table or pouffe. It was a round, luminous, sturdy cylinder in acrylic with a diameter of 72 cm and a height that was half of that, constructed of two sections with the socket and bulb centred in the lower one.

LP & Co. NYT first mentioned Ilumesa in a report from the exhibition: 'We expect that the table will become the luminous centrepiece of many living rooms.'[3] Regarded as a table, Ilumesa was not intended to be a high-luminance interior element but merely a mood light. That is borne out by the colour selection of orange or red. It was also available in white, but the manufacturer underscored that Ilumesa was 'most beautiful with a 15–25-watt bulb'.[4]

The multipurpose combined luminaire and furniture piece in plastic was a far cry from the Danish cabinetmaking tradition and was instead aligned with contemporary international pop aesthetic. In a Danish context, it was an invitation to rethink, exactly as the PH lamp had been. However, while PH's lamp was a design solution aimed at providing the right electric lighting, Ilumesa was not a solution to a specific problem. Like the wavy, luminous fantasy landscape that was the core of the same *Visiona II* exhibition (see page 30), only in a much simpler form, Ilumesa was a manifestation of Panton's idea that people should not spend their time in rooms where their mutual interaction was restricted by rigid social conventions. Panton said:

Although many of my experiments may seem utopian, they are important because they can expand our experience base. Nowhere is it written into law that a living room must forever be furnished with a sofa and two easy chairs around a low table. There must be others, perhaps better, approaches to a home environment dedicated to relaxation and leisure.[5]

Ilumesa never did become 'the luminous centrepiece in many living rooms'[6] – it was easier and much cheaper to integrate a single little colourful Flowerpot (see page 106). In late 1970, however, a creative *Bo Bedre* writer followed up on Panton's idea of a multipurpose object and suggested, without referencing the designer, that the readers invest some of their free time into making a 'similar' but low-cost DIY lamp out of two plastic bowls: 'A plastic wash basin – 30 cm in diameter – costs about 2.50 kroner. Two cost 5 kroner.'[7] Plastic fantastic for dedicated followers of fashion!

'Red-orange is welcoming.'
—Verner Panton, 1991[8]

Verner Panton: VP Globe

Louis Poulsen—1970

'It's brilliant, it's over the top cool, and at the same time it's a homage to PH.' —Louise Campbell[1]

When Verner Panton designed Bayer's exhibition Visiona II in Cologne in January 1970, he included a range of new lamps, both Swiss- and Danish-made. Three Louis Poulsen lamps were ready for launch, and in addition there were several 'prototypes requiring further development'.[2] However, as Louis Poulsen's report from the exhibition in *NYT* pointed out: 'A common quality in all of them was a festive and unconventional form that makes them interesting to develop further.'[3] One of the prototypes was the Globe lamp, subsequently named VP Globe.[4]

It certainly had an unconventional form for a pendant — at least on the surface: a 60-cm floating, luminous bubble. However, the interior shade principle rests on PH's technical achievements, including his PH 5 and Contrast lamps (see pages 66–67 and 78–79). The design of the VP Globe aims to shield the incandescent light bulb to radiate glare-free light into the room and uses coloured reflectors to control the colour of the light, giving the upwards light a blueish tint and the downwards light a reddish tint — exactly as in PH's lamps.

The spherical luminaire has links to the earliest pendants Panton designed in 1955 in collaboration with Torben Ørskov (see page 72). From the outset, Panton openly acknowledged that his inspiration for the shade design came from PH. In 1955, he deconstructed PH's lamps, and the VP Globe with five concave or convex shades can similarly be seen as a deconstruction. The pendant, which was launched in 1970, consists of an exterior globe in transparent acrylic put together of two hemispheres. The bulb is centrally positioned inside the globe, concealed behind a hollow, inward-curving shade that directs the light down and up, where it is captured by the two large, curved shades placed above and below the bulb. With their white lacquer interior, the reflectors radiate some of the light towards the shiny exterior of the shade around the bulb, which in turn reflects it into the room. In addition, the large shades emit light through the gap in between them, which hits the small, curvy, outer shades — a blue one on top and a red one below. They in turn reflect some of the light back to the shiny chromed exteriors of the large shades, which thus reflect a colour-tinted light into the room through the acrylic globe — most of it downwards.[5]

In contrast to PH's lamps, Panton wanted to make it possible to rotate the aluminium shades to modify the lighting. Panton had pursued the same idea in his earliest lamps, but while the differently shaped floating reflectors in the 1955 pendants were slightly crooked, being assembled by hand using nylon string, the shades in the floating, industrially made VP Globe were professionally assembled with chains made of tiny steel balls. The acrylic glass forms a halo-like spherical display case around the essential interior. PH had passed away a few years earlier, and the globe might well be seen as a homage to Panton's mentor and friend.[6]

In 1975, Louis Poulsen launched 'a little brother, although it's not that much smaller than the big brother' on the retail market.[7] This new VP Globe was merely 10 cm smaller, but it made a difference that it was now available with a 50-cm diameter, because it was easier to fit into low-ceilinged rooms.

Panton's exploration of spheres and hemispheres led to additional lamp designs, and the year after Panton had presented the VP Globe, he split another sphere in two to create the hugely successful Panthella lamp (see pages 124–125).

In 1977, Panton designed the Panto pendant, which has some superficial similarity to the VP Globe in the sense that the actual luminaire — socket, bulb and, in this case, four white aluminium shades — again, like a ship in a bottle, is encapsulated in a transparent acrylic sphere. However, the light emitted from the sphere is different and even more downwardly radiated. In fact, it is closer to the light from a Flowerpot, here achieved via a lower reflector that shields the bulb and radiates the light upwards and three upper shades that radiate most of the light downwards. A simple red stripe on the inside right above the bulb gives the light a faint reddish tone.[8]

Big and small VP Globes featured in Louis Poulsen's magazine *LP & Co. NYT* in September 1975.

Bent Karlby: Pantre

Lyfa—1970

'You could probably safely say that lighting must be suitable – only to be caught up in a wild debate about what is the right definition of that term. For me, it would have to include an attractive appearance, and I would argue that an object does not deserve the designation if it isn't also decorative.'

—Bent Karlby, 1949[1]

The versatile architect Bent Karlby created numerous lamp designs, covering a wide expressive range. During the 1940s, his lamps were often softly rounded and had a romantic or nostalgic touch; towards the end of the decade in particular, some of his chandeliers had shades resembling the chimneys from kerosene or gas lamps. Karlby also had a keen grasp of what people wanted. As the design scholar Vibeke Andersson Møller points out in her monograph on Karlby, his lamp design changed dramatically during the 1950s. Like many of the other modernist architects, he now went for pure geometric shapes: cone, cylinder and arc.[2] Karlby designed several conical pendant lamps, including the simple Mosaik (Mosaic) from 1959 – a small, pointy conical pendant that 'thanks to its slatted bottom, shaped with the graceful expression of a ballet skirt, provides the right light', thus the romantic assessment of the design in a Lyfa advertisement in connection with the launch.[3] A photograph shows Karlby sitting at his desk underneath the 1967 Toledo pendant, which is shaped like a larger, wider truncated cone and has a similar 'ballet skirt'. The translucent acrylic shade was either yellow, red or green and thus emitted a diffused coloured light into the room and a brighter, white light on to the tabletop.

In the 1942 home design book *Bo for To*, Karlby wrote, 'The raw light from the incandescent light bulb is rather cold and may seem harsh and clinical; in an attempt to alleviate this, lamps are designed with coloured glass or coloured metal shades.'[4] However, Karlby cautions against 'using coloured light for anything other than "mood lighting"; it is less suitable as a working light'.[5] From 1968, Karlby designed the Pan lamp series, which had polished metal cylinders with coloured interiors as its main motif. The Pantre (Panthree) pendant, launched by Lyfa in 1970, is one of several hanging lamps in the series, which features luminous tubes mounted together in rings or as wall-mounted reliefs. In the latter, the reference to the pan flute is particularly obvious.

All the Pan models are based on the same concept: a tube bisected vertically to produce a back section, upon which a shorter front section is mounted, forming a hollow space that holds a socket and light bulb. The front section can be moved up and down to alter the distribution of downwards and upwards light. The name Pantre indicates that this version features three pan (flute) metal elements. The three tubular sections are assembled, back to back, to form a luminous sculpture that mainly illuminates itself but also emits light from each of the three light sources downwards and upwards into the room. The back halves have a coloured inside – yellow in the photo – which contributes to the lamp's decorative effect when it is switched off. Pop design and bright colours were trending, and the yellow colour in particular ensures a warm golden light when the bulbs are lit. Verner Panton wrote that yellow 'with its warm luminosity (...) has a liberating and heartening effect'.[6] The pendant demonstrates this uplifting influence.

Using the tubular Pan system, Karlby also created impressive reliefs that had an even more pronounced decorative effect. The same is true of his wall lamp Påfuglen (The Peacock), constructed of seven metal rings in descending size. The base is a 27-cm white lacquered metal bowl, which forms the lamp's wall mount and contains its E14 socket. Five discs mounted with spacers in between surround the bulb and allow the light to shine through, while a seventh disc-shaped element forms a front cover. Lacquered in seven different colours, the circular elements make the lamp a striking wall-mounted decoration, also in daylight. After dark, when it is switched on, it really comes to life, as the light is reflected by the coloured shades.[7] Karlby describes how it gives rise to 'beautiful soft shadow effects that add character to the room and make it pleasant and cosy'.[8]

Karlby designed a wide and diverse range of luminaires[9] that reflected changing times and fashions. An experienced lighting engineer, he always took a pragmatic approach. As his grandson concluded in 2019, 'He just made the stuff. There wasn't a lot of talk about it.'[10]

The Peacock: wall lamp and decorative relief.
→ Pantre – a lamp from the Pan series. Here with a warm yellow interior. H: 36 cm, W: 19 cm.

Michael Bang: Parasol

Holmegaard—1970

Michael Bang (1942–2013) called himself a glass draughtsman.[1] He trained as a model maker at the Royal Porcelain Factory (now Royal Copenhagen) and subsequently worked as a designer at the Swedish glassworks Ekenäs Bruk. In 1968, he joined the Odense plant of Holmegaard glassworks. As the son of Jacob E. Bang, Michael Bang grew up surrounded by glass, and he shared his father's passion.[2] However, he belonged to the new generation and did not share his father's functionalist dictum that a suitable form is beautiful because it is 'sober, modest, neutral and anonymous' (see page 94). By contrast, Michael Bang said, 'When some people regard function as a thing of beauty in itself, I'm not sure they are right,'[3] adding,

There should be a sensory experience involved in using an object. There is nothing worse than seeing everything boiled down to functional analysis. (…) Naturally, lighting should be glare-free, a vase should hold water, and a glass should be suitable for drinking from. Once that is in place, I think functionalism has been given its due.[4]

In 1968 (the year of anti-authoritarian rebellion), Michael Bang developed a new way of working with glass in the Odense plant, where the glassmaker stood on a raised platform and blew the glass into a mould that was placed on the floor. The method was well suited for luminaires, he explained in 1980, because it was possible to blow 'large bodies, and the flash technique, which these glassblowers also master, is great for lighting, because it produces a coloured secondary light, a colourless primary light and a milky white interior that produces excellent reflection'.[5] Bang's Parasol table lamp and his small wall-mounted Astronaut lamp, both from 1970, were based on this new technique.

The year after the two American astronauts Neil Armstrong and Buzz Aldrin walked on the moon, Bang's lamp, shaped like an astronaut's helmet, touched down in Denmark. The glassblowers blew the white interior shape in a single piece and subsequently added an exterior (the flash) in yellow, orange, red, green, black or white. The socket was concealed inside in the base, while the light from the rounded top of the bulb was emitted through the circular opening of the shade. The Parasol table lamp stood on a similar but taller base. Made in two parts, it was available with a differently coloured base and shade: all the models had a white base and an opal white shade with a coloured flash exterior in green, yellow, red or brown and radiated a bright light on the parasol stand as well as a coloured light through the shade.[6]

Bang was Holmegaard's first own lamp designer.[7] His particular ambition was to create lamps that held an appeal whether they were on or off, and with these humorous space travel and pop lamps he accomplished this goal. Two years later, Bang designed a seemingly fairly conventional kerosene lamp with a traditional burner, lamp globe and shade, named Victoria. In Bang's version, however, the lower part was made in bright colours, such as yellow or turquoise, or in clear glass, the latter offering a view of the fuel and wick. The flame was hidden inside the opal white glass globe, which emitted a traditional diffused light. The base resembles that used in Parasol and Astronaut: stout, simple and modern, in contrast to the top part of Victoria. However, the form relates to this part and thus becomes a modern reflection of an old form – also in the field of lighting. If it strikes a nostalgic, Victorian note, with its primary-yellow base it does so with a twinkle in its eye.[8]

In step with the times, these lamps were followed up by far less pop-inspired table lamps and many pendants, not least in white opal glass.[9] Bang was Holmegaard's most prolific lamp draughtsman, and his view of functional form is clearly expressed in this statement from 1980: 'Although I don't care for the overly ornamented, and I like to keep things simple and functional, I still can't resist adding some sort of twist.'[10]

Michael Bang's small helmet-shaped Astronaut lamp with a green exterior and white interior.

'I like to give my things something beyond the functional. They should have a little zest, some vivacity … I guess I'll never be a puritan.'
—Michael Bang, 1980[11]

Poul Christiansen: SinusLine Model 172A

Le Klint—1971

Model 167A from 1967 was the first model in the SinusLine series.

Cross-pleated Le Klint lampshades in various shapes had adorned Danish interiors for more than two decades when in 1967 an architecture student stepped into the Le Klint shop in Store Kirkestræde in central Copenhagen with a game-changing innovation: a lampshade folded along geometric curves. This was not the young man's first visit to the shop: as one of the assignments for his entrance exam to the architecture programme in 1967, Poul Christiansen (b. 1947) had to design an alternative to the egg tray:

I passed the Le Klint shop every day on my way from my home in Knabrostræde to the Academy, which was at Kongens Nytorv at the time. That day I went into the shop and wound up speaking with the sales director, Allan Bock, about pleating techniques. At the time, I didn't know that all Le Klint's lamps were made of a single rectangular sheet that is folded, so there's only one seam. That was their concept, and no notches were allowed. Wiser now, I kept folding, although I never did manage to make an egg tray[1]

With his interest in paper folding sparked, Christiansen embarked on his studies with a goal of designing buildings inspired by 'Pier Luigi Nervi's folded concrete constructions and Jørn Utzon's latest shell constructions in the Sydney Opera House. The shapes were geometrically defined and were absurdly beautiful, because their basis was pure maths'.[2] Christiansen continued to explore paper folding with this goal in mind: 'One day I was scoring a sheet of paper with a pair of dividers and folding along the scores. If you fold along an arc rather than a straight line, the paper comes along and gives rise to convex and concave surfaces that flow into each other and meet around the pleat. I found that fascinating.'[3] Christiansen scored more arcs into the paper, folding along them, and then added mathematical curves: sinusoid, parable, hyperbola, ellipsis. What emerged was a system of wavy, psychedelic curves in tune with the spirit of the late 1960s.

Christiansen set out with large-scale, architectural sketches in mind but ended up with a form resembling a lamp. So he returned to the Le Klint shop and Allan Bock. Bock took the model to the factory in Odense, where the innovative lamp was well received: a form folded in a single sheet but with curved pleats! It seemed realistic for the pleating girls to master the design. What seemed more in doubt was what the customers would make of the novel design: 'When the finished lamps, folded in Le Klint's washable PVC foil, were launched, they were a success, but people thought Le Klint had begun to cast lamps.'[4]

Although this was not initially a story about a fascination with light, it turned into one: 'When the first model, the 167a, was lit for the first time, something magical happened; it was transformed. It had a completely different form when it was lit, as the shadows on the lamp made it more facetted and sculptural.'[5] The 167A from 1967 was followed up by a series of lamps based on pleats that with four, five or six repetitions turned into cubic or cylindrical shapes, a closed volume when the top and bottom were folded in. However, Christiansen also wanted 'a regular sphere'.[6] The sinusoid was the answer, and around 1970, in the middle of the space age, the undulating spherical shape reflected the young architecture student's fascination with the 'luminous phenomena in space'. The pendant suggested a radiant moon with deep craters. By then, the Moon had been conquered and, with the planting of the flag, brought closer to earth.[7]

The luminous sphere, SinusLine Model 172, was put in the window when the series was presented in the design shop and showroom Den Permanente, in Copenhagen, in 1971. The exhibition was a success, and over time the 172 became the top-seller of the SinusLine series. Christiansen created the many different models while he was still a student. In 1973, he graduated and chose for a time to concentrate on architecture.[8] However, in 1987 he founded Komplot Design together with the designer Boris Berlin, choosing design over architecture. The smaller scale ultimately won out – or maybe not: in 2003 SinusLine added a Model 172 Giant, with a diameter of 85 cm.

'Initially, it was the folding that captured my interest, but then light came into the picture: it is the light that gives the folded volume form.'
—Poul Christiansen, 2019[9]

Verner Panton: Panthella

Louis Poulsen—1971

After the Flowerpot lamps and the Spiegel Fittings, Verner Panton's exploration of the hemispherical shape continued in his 1971 design hit Panthella.

The luminous bricks that Panton had designed for the Spiegel office building in Hamburg had a round hollow for the light bulb, which was shielded by a hemispherical shade, while the concave ring between the hollow and the shade reflected the light (see pages 112–113). The same principle was repeated in the new sculptural lamp. In Panthella, the bulb was placed as an uplight at the top of the stem, the light captured by the large hemispherical acrylic shade. In the opal-white variant, the shade then emitted the same diffused light into the room as the Japanese rice-paper lamps that were so popular at the time. The light was also reflected downwards onto the shiny, flared base, adding an extra facet to the lighting experience. According to *LP & Co. NYT*'s editors in 1972, Panthella's immediate success was attributable in part to 'Verner Panton's excellent design and in part to the special incandescent light bulb with three filaments for three different light intensities'.[1] The special tri-light bulb made it possible to change from white light to a softer, warmer light at a push of the round switch at the base of the lamp. To replace the light bulb, one simply unscrewed the small shiny ball on top of the lamp to lift off the shade. Any spare cord could be rolled up inside the base to avoid cluttering up the floor.

According to the design researcher Penny Sparke, Panton intended the lamp to look like 'a single "space-age" form'.[2] This certainly resonated with the time and with one aspect of Panton's design. However, the lamp with the opal-white acrylic shade that emitted a soft light into the room and down onto the base and allowed for modulating the intensity of the light also shows a keen grasp of lighting theory and material usage, and the result emphasizes both function and down-to-earth usability.

PH noted in 1961 that Panton's lamps did not contain any technical advances, which should come as no surprise, since Panton was, of course, not a lighting engineer (see page 72). Since then, Panton had designed many luminaires and learnt a great deal about lighting, but he remained at heart a designer, not an engineer. However, he worked closely with technical experts.[3] The importance of collaborating with technically insightful manufacturers was a lesson Panton had learnt from an early stage during his time at Arne Jacobsen's studio. Given Panton's constant search for new materials to enable new expressions, this technical insight was paramount.

Initially, Panthella also came with a chrome finish and in variants with a chrome base and a coloured shade in either grey, red or green. These were, however, discontinued due to technical complications.[4] The white lamps remained in production and found their way into many Danish homes; they were easy to fit into the bright interiors and offered excellent functionality.

Panton continued developing new lighting designs until his death in 1998, but today it is the lamps from the 1960s and 1970s that are most closely associated with his name.[5] In 2000, the Danish modern art museum Louisiana showed the exhibition *Vision and Reality. Conceptions of the 20th Century*, which included a smaller replica of Panton's luminous, polychrome total design *Visiona II* from 1970 (see page 30).[6] The exhibition offered a review of 20th-century design styles via a presentation of the visual legacy from the avant-garde movements, including Panton's 1970 vision of future spatial design: a total work of art in colours and light. Panton's conceptual space remained an all-encompassing and coherent vision that was never realized on a wider scale – unlike his now iconic lamps, not least the best-selling Flowerpot and Panthella. They were the closest Panton's design came to shaping the home design preferences of a generation, although, in fact, only the white Panthella has remained in continuous production.[7]

Today, Panthella is once again available with a shiny exterior in high-gloss polished steel in the Panthella Mini version that Louis Poulsen added to the collection in 2018

'White is pure and clear, neutral, weightless, without tension. White permits the highest degree of human development. Mediates between all shades of colour.'
—Verner Panton, 1991[8]

Bent Gantzel-Boysen: Unispot

Louis Poulsen—1971

Black Louis with the red switch can swivel in any direction on its long, flexible arm to meet the need for close-up lighting – for example, as a convenient bedside lamp. The lamp is not currently in production.

Naturally, not just private homes needed lighting; growing prosperity had led to a significant growth in the consumption of material goods, and the consumer society called for more expressive illumination to highlight the items on display in shops and department stores as well as in galleries and exhibition halls. It made no sense simply to install strip lights. What was needed was lighting that could create shadow effects and bring the displayed items to life – in short, more dramatic lighting that helped shape the experience. Originally, theatres had used large, heavy spotlights, but new lightweight alloy metals and knock-proof plastics made it possible to produce new spotlights, wall lamps and ceiling lamps. This innovative field was a high priority for the lighting companies Nordisk Solar Compagni and Fog & Mørup as well as for Louis Poulsen & Co., which sold a growing number of spotlights during the 1960s and which put the spotlight Unispot into production in 1971.[1]

The compact Unispot, which elegantly combines a cube and a cylinder, was designed for Louis Poulsen by Bent Gantzel-Boysen. Designed with a reflective lining, the lamp only needed a standard clear light bulb to produce a concentrated beam without unpleasant glare. Unispot was available in three versions: as a built-in ceiling light, mounted on a Lytespan conductor rail (1967) and with a mounting plate for installation on the wall or ceiling.[2] Weighing in at 900 g, Unispot was a featherweight for its size, which was symbolized by a picture of a feather on the cover of the brochure that came with the earliest spots – highlighted with a Unispot, of course! Because of its low weight, the lamp could be screwed directly into walls and ceilings made of lightweight materials. The first Unispot was black, but as early as the following year white, yellow and red versions were added to the line. It was exhibited at the Hannover Fair in 1973, where it was presented as the 'only plastic spotlight on the international market'.[3]

The trendy and handy Unispot soon showed up virtually everywhere, including the Copenhagen fashion shop Nørgaard På Strøget, both inside the shop itself and in the large display window facing the busy pedestrian street. The owner, Jørgen Nørgaard, had a real feel for what was hot in the world of design and fashion, and the new spot was hot indeed!

The spotlight, which was ideal for shop windows and exhibitions, also found its way into Danish home interiors. In 1981, the new stylish Danish home design magazine *Skønne Hjem* (Beautiful Homes) described Unispot as one of the trendy and popular lamps at the time and stated that 'the Uni-spot from Louis Poulsen was the first spotlight to really enter private home interiors'.[4] The successful Unispot was later followed up by a smaller version named Lillebror (Little Brother) intended mainly for private homes, as was SorteLouis (BlackLouis), which was launched in 1974.[5] Gantzel-Boysen gave the latter lamp a long, movable neck and a red switch thus deliberately highlighting the on-off function. Bent Gantzel-Boysen's widow, Dorit Gantzel-Boysen, explains, 'Bent often created designs in black, and there *always* had to be a red detail. One day he showed me a new design, which I applauded, but then I asked, isn't there something missing? Something red? The next time I saw it, it had a red feature.'[6] The architect and architecture writer Hakon Stephensen wrote an homage to the lamp, 'SorteLouis er min ven' (BlackLouis Is My Friend), about a friendship that was destined to last, as Stephensen had already bought six lamps but was ready to buy more.[7]

Gantzel-Boysen also designed the anglepoise lamp IT from 1972 and the floor lamp Butler from 1974.[8] Before he left Louis Poulsen to found his own design firm, he designed the smaller LouiSpot for halogen lights under his own name.[9] His name had never been mentioned in connection with the launch of the other lamps. After leaving Louis Poulsen, Gantzel-Boysen designed many lamps for IKEA between 1979 and 1987, including the DUETT pendant from 1983.[10] DUETT and the many Louis Poulsen models are no longer in production but have become sought-after items in recent years.

'At Louis Poulsen we are just a little bit proud to, once again, launch a Danish product that is also going to reach the global market.' —Unispot, 1971[11]

Jørgen Gammelgaard: Tip Top pendant

Design Forum—1972

The six-shade Tip Top luminaire was supplemented with a series of single-shade pendants, all of which remain in production.

When the 19-year-old Jørgen Gammelgaard (1938–1991) had completed his cabinetmaker's training, he enrolled in the Furniture Department of the School of Arts and Crafts. After his graduation in 1962, he applied for a place as a visiting student in the Department of Furniture and Spatial Art at the Royal Danish Academy of Fine Arts, School of Architecture. At the time, Ole Wanscher was the professor of the department, and Poul Kjærholm was one of the teachers. Concurrent with his two years at the Academy, Gammelgaard worked for Grete Jalk, Steen Eiler Rasmussen and Mogens Koch. Before founding his own firm in 1973, Gammelgaard also worked briefly for Arne Jacobsen. Gammelgaard's training as a craftsman is important to mention, but so is his connection to these designers. Gammelgaard's furniture design continued the analytical functionalist tradition, first analysing the function in depth and then the aesthetic, because the aesthetic always had to be informed by function.[1]

The story behind the Tip Top lamp, which was finished in 1971, begins with a specific lighting need far from Denmark. In 1965–1967, Jørgen Gammelgaard and his wife, the weaver Karin Gammelgaard, were stationed in West Samoa to teach furniture design and cabinetmaking, a stay that was arranged by the Danish Ministry of Foreign Affairs on behalf of the United Nations. The couple were not happy with lighting in the home they had been assigned: 'We covered the light bulbs with wicker baskets; they made the most beautiful baskets,'[2] says Karin Gammelgaard and adds:

One day we were in a hardware shop, a real jumble. In a corner, Jørgen discovered a long electric light bulb – not a strip light, it was an incandescent bulb, but in a shape we'd never seen – and when he found some curved, white plastic shades in another corner, he had an idea. He strung six white shades together with fishing line and hung them around the bulb; it was a very nice and useful lamp, and it was put together because we needed the light.[3]

In 1971, Jørgen Gammelgaard turned the initial idea into a fully fledged design solution for a tubular incandescent light bulb, and the following year the six-shade Tip Top lamp was launched by the newly founded company Design Forum, which marketed experimental designs by young designers.[4] Tip Top was a detailed metal lamp based on six identical conical shades attached to a socket shell and held together with metal spacers, so that the light was both reflected outwards in between the individual shades and directed downwards at the horizontal surface.[5] Just after the launch, the six-shade luminaire was bought by the Danish Arts Foundation, and in 1980 *Bo Bedre* wrote that Tip Top had become 'one of the Danes' favourite lamps'.[6] The appeal of the unusual form was affirmed by the appearance of similar pendants from other companies. Lyfa was quick to follow up with a six-shade model of their own, and Bent Gantzel-Boysen's DUETT was launched in the 1983 IKEA catalogue. Both the latter examples had shades of a different shape, and IKEA's luminaire further stood out with a graded colour scale.

Gammelgaard's monochrome, six-shade luminaire came as a pendant and as a wall light mounted on a metal bracket. A series of single-shade pendants was also launched for use with a standard light bulb. The exterior form of this pendant is near-identical to a classic shoemaker's lamp, where the light source is covered with a conical shade to direct the light towards the work surface. Gammelgaard's pendant also emits a small amount of light from a gap where the shade is connected to the socket shell, which softens the contrast between light and dark. The larger variants were made with a second, detachable interior shade that makes for a narrower beam than a large, open cone and thus helps prevent glare. In 1988, production was taken over by Pandul. Since 2023, the lamps have been produced for Carl Hansen & Søn.

'Jørgen Gammelgaard, cabinetmaker, architect and professor, continues in the great tradition of his Danish mentors.'
—Jens Nielsen, 1988[7]

Henning Koppel: Bubi

Louis Poulsen—1972

Henning Koppel's bust of his grandson Adam wearing a sun hat formed the inspiration for Bubi. Here, the hat is in brass, plated with 24-carat gold, because gold does not tarnish when the lamp is handled.

With Petronella, the sculptor and designer Henning Koppel in 1962 enveloped the flame of a kerosene burner in a modern form (see page 82). Exactly ten years later, he designed a form for the electric light bulb, wrapping it up soft and warm in a chubby figure. The inspiration for the small organic lamp from Koppel's hand was a young child.

On a summer's day in 1968, Koppel drew his daughter Hannah Koppel's nearly two-year-old son, who was sitting in the garden wearing a sun hat. Initially, the drawing was used as a sketch for a bust, but later the little head with the hat served as inspiration for a lamp.[1] The lamp shows a kinship with Koppel's three-dimensional silver hollowware for Georg Jensen and, not least, appeared as a unique personality in its own right, just like Petronella, which preceded Bubi by ten years and was consistently portrayed as a female figure in ads. Here, an example from 1963: 'Petronella was born little over a year ago to Henning Koppel and is already much courted and widely admired. In the cradle, she was endowed with all the gifts to make her desirable.'[2] In 1972, the new little Koppel with the charming name Bubi – an informal German term for lad or little boy – was brought to life at Louis Poulsen.

Petronella's base was 'gracefully curved in the shiniest brass' topped with a globe in matt opal glass. Similarly, Bubi's closed 'hat', which concealed the socket, was made in brass, while the light from the incandescent bulb was filtered and diffused through opalized polycarbonate.

Despite Bubi's appealing form, the lamp was discontinued after just five years.[3] Claus Juhlin, the owner of the lighting company Pandul, which relaunched the lamp in 2010, explains why its initial run was so brief: 'It didn't live up to Henning Koppel's intentions for the design. It was not only intended as a pendant but was also supposed to be able to simply lie on a shelf, but that was impossible; it overheated – even with just a 40-watt bulb.'[4] In fact, the lamp could get so hot that it destroyed both the socket and the cord, and the heat discoloured the knock-proof polycarbonate, which had been chosen for its heat-resistant properties.[5] When a TV reporter in the 1970s asked Koppel about the design process behind his large silver hollowware works, Koppel replied, 'In my opinion, everything should, above all, be beautiful. Making an object functionalistic and practical is not as hard as some would have it.'[6] The key was to persist.[7] In the case of Bubi, development persisted even after Koppel's death, as Claus Juhlin explains:

In 2010, low-energy light bulbs had emerged that did not produce nearly as much heat. I also got permission to make the lamp 10% bigger, so now the lamp lived up to all Henning Koppel's demands, as it no longer overheated. That also meant that the blueish lower shade, made in outdated polycarbonate, could be replaced with more attractive white knock-proof acrylic. Thus, it is still a robust lamp, and it can be placed directly on a shelf or on the floor. With the latest LED bulbs, which can be used with a dimmer switch, the lamp is now exactly as Koppel envisioned it long before it was possible.[8]

Juhlin further describes the production: 'Henning Koppel is known as the master of silver, but the lamp was made in brass. It still is, in fact, but the exterior is chromium-plated because we wanted the association to silver.'[9] Bubi also comes in a version with 24-carat gold plating that is superior to brass when it comes to handling fingerprints.

The current version of the chubby-cheeked Bubi – including the sun hat in shiny chrome or brass – is 16 cm in height and has a diameter of 22 cm. The Koppel family placed their own Bubi lamp on a small base on a shelf, but now it can safely be laid down directly on the floor, a shelf or a table.

'You can always make an object beautiful, even if it is functional; it's a matter of persistence.'
—Henning Koppel, 1968[10]

Hans Due: Optima

Fog & Mørup—1972

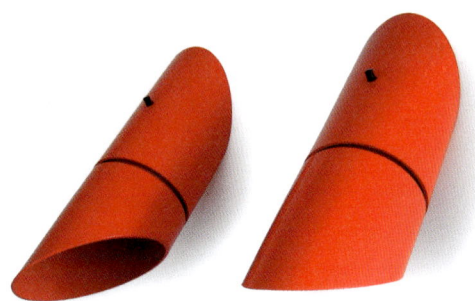

Phister: pop art and practical lamp in one.

The floating, UFO-like luminous discs were designed during the year of the last human lunar landing. At the time, many were predicting that moon bases and expeditions to Mars would follow soon. The continued ability of space exploration to capture the imagination is evident in Optima, created by the graphic designer Hans Due (b. 1941). Due graduated from the Graphic Arts Institute of Denmark in 1964 and has since worked with both 2D and 3D design.[1] In 2019, Due described how he contacted Fog & Mørup in 1972 with a specific idea for a pendant lamp:

Many of the lamps designed to hang above a dining table were very voluminous; it bothered me when there was one of these big blobs in the way, preventing you from seeing who was sitting across the table. The development of the chrome-capped bulb allowed for a flat design, where the entire bulb did not have to be concealed but could be a visible, integrated part of the design. But it still had to be properly shielded, so that the light was optimally distributed over the table without creating glare.[2]

Due had the graphically linear but gently rounded design in place: a vertical cylinder that concealed the socket and transitioned into a horizontally floating disc. The disc was bent to make a wide, rounded edge that matched the chrome-capped bulb's visible hemispherical form underneath the shade. The cylinder also had a rounded top and bottom: 'The form should have a friendly appearance, also when the lamp was not in use.'[3] Head of Design Jo Hammerborg liked the design, and with input from professional lighting engineers, the Optima design was finished. The main feature was the large aluminium shade, white on the inside, supplemented with a smaller white interior shade with a hole in the middle. The hole let the light from the bulb through to be reflected onto the large white shade, which in turn reflected the light into the exterior and interior of the inner shade enveloping the bulb. Because the light around the bulb's focal point was so intense, the inside of the shade had a red rim to dampen contrast glare. The red band also gave the light a slightly warmer tone.

The shades for the floating spaceship-like Optima pendants came in three sizes and were also used for wall, table and floor lamps.[4] All the shades had white lacquer and a shiny metal frame to match the chrome-capped bulb – producing the proper white-and-silver space look. To boost sales, the trendy colours of the time, yellow and brown, were added, and 'suddenly the white ones flew off the shelf. When people saw the three colours together, they went for the white version'.[5]

In 1977 came the bracket lamp Phister, which had a graphic and geometric look: a cylinder with the ends cut off at opposite 45-degree angles. The lamp is constructed in two parts. The top part, which is attached to the wall, contains the socket and a cylindrical switch that stands out on the top of the cylinder as a decorative element. It is placed at the top to make it easy to switch the lamp on and off, 'so that if you were using it as a bedside lamp, you wouldn't have to search for an inline switch'.[6] The bottom section shields the light bulb and swivels 360 degrees, 'so you can have the light coming in from the side or turn it away from you'.[7] The gap between the two components illustrates that they are two separate parts and not a single tube; it further stands out as a luminous ring when the lamp is switched on.

Due originally intended for Phister to be made of metal. However, Fog & Mørup did not see the lamp as a high-tech design; they felt the form had a greater commercial potential as a young, trendy pop design in coloured plastic.[8] In the red version, the sharply cut-off form sparked associations to a perfectly shaped, oversize lipstick, a functional pop-art design. However, the plastic was difficult to work with:

At first, it was hard to make the plastic behave and to mix the pigments to get the 'right' colours and avoid darker colouration along the edges. Today, it's hard to understand how that would pose a problem. Some designs you could only dream of back then, because they weren't physically feasible. Today, the possibilities are much greater – now, virtually any form is possible.[9]

'The lamp design arose by chance, at the same time as my graphic design work developed with very varying projects, from concept development to graphic design and product design.'—Hans Due, 2019[10]

Hans Jørgen Berthel and Hans Erik Vestergård Schmidt: Abo Mag, Model H 63

Abo—1973

This is a story about a 12-cm wall bracket lamp that is not an inherently Danish design but which became a huge commercial success in Denmark and thus a lamp that many Danes will remember and relate to.

In Denmark, Panton had created the ball-shaped Topan pendant lamp in 1959, Bo and Wohlert had created a ball-shaped spotlight in 1962 and Frandsen had mounted Ball lamps on stems in 1968 (see pages 70, 72 and 104). In 1962, the Italian designer Angelo Lelli (1911–1979) launched the spherical spotlight Lexio mounted on a variety of magnetic bases.[1] The ball-shaped lamp head from Abo was Italian, but the rest of the lamp was Danish.

In the early 1970s, Director Hans Jørgen Berthel (1940-2023) and his partner Hans Erik Vestergård Schmidt (1922–1993) of the, at that time still small, company Abo had the idea of making a fun, affordable lamp: a ball-shaped shade attached to a base by magnetism that could rotate freely in all directions.[2] Berthel says in 2019, 'In late 1972, Hans finds this strange lamp. What it resembles most of all is a car's headlight, but it can move like an eye within an exterior shell. When we take it apart, we see that the "eye" sits on a magnet inside the body.'[3] The two men wanted to develop a similar design, seeing a potential in 'a cheap, simple lamp with a single shade – never more than a single shade, to keep the cost down – that could never cost more than a packet of washing powder'.[4] They acquired some magnets and milled a model in wood that was subsequently stamped out in steel, and two weeks later they had a prototype ready. Now they set out to produce the lamps in time for the Gothenburg lighting fair in January 1973: 'I got hold of everything we needed for 100 lamps; we needed 100 to provide a proper impression of the lamp.'[5] A local company was commissioned to make the magnetic housing designed by Vestergård Schmidt, while 100 round spherical shells, intended for car headlights, were ordered from Italy, since 'we couldn't find a Danish manufacturer'.[6] Next, the shells had to be painted: 'Ten different colours and some in chrome and gold.'[7] For optimal lighting, the interior of the lamps was lacquered white. Finally, a label was designed to be placed over the magnet to prevent scratches on the back of the sphere.

The lamp was ready in time for the fair, complete with a child-safe plug and an inline cord switch. Only the mandatory certification, the D-label, was lacking. The advertising folder also had to wait, since 'the cover showed a table with a bottle of wine and a pipe. We wanted to strike a warm, cosy mood, but Sweden had a ban on wine and tobacco in advertising'.[8] Berthel explains how their stand at the fair featured a tall pillar with the lamps, their bulbs covered with shiny caps.[9] The eye-catching pillar proved effective: 'It was the most talked-about lamp at the 1973 fair.' Many of the visitors showed a real interest in the lamp, among them a buyer from the Copenhagen department store Daells Varehus, who wanted the lamp delivered as soon as possible: 'The order was 60,000, with the first delivery due in May. It was the single biggest order in the company's history!'[10]

At the fair, the ball-shaped shade of the magnetic lamps had provided an open view of the bulb, but as part of the process to acquire the D-label, a ring-shaped grate was added to make the lamps glare-free. The designers also found a paint shop that was able to handle the large order more efficiently.[11] Abo's lamp premiered in the autumn 1974 catalogue from Daells Varehus, which was distributed door-to-door. It was featured in brown, the top-trending colour of the time.[12] Later, Abo developed a wide range of models, all based on the spherical shade, but the initial H63 model was the best-seller, for some time turned out at a rate of 1,200 a day.[13]

Berthel's story is one of entrepreneurship and truly democratic lamp design, as the low retail price made large production numbers possible. Daells Varehus was the first to distribute photos of the lamp all over Denmark, but subsequently the H63 was available from 'virtually all the country's electrician's shops and department stores, including Magasin, Salling and Bilka'.[14] When Berthel left Abo in 1982, the company had sold two million magnetic lamps.[15]

The Abo magnet lamp was first included in the Daells Varehus catalogue in 1974. These photos are from the 1978 spring catalogue. Price: DKK 51.

134

'Design is often for the few. We made something for everybody, without ever compromising. It had to be up to par – but we were the cheap boys!'
—Hans Jørgen Berthel, 2019[16]

Louis Weisdorf: Multi-Lite

Lyfa—1973

The Turbo pendant from 1967 is Louis Weisdof's personal favourite because it consists of basic elements that come to life when they are combined and because the lamp's expression varies with the viewer's vantage point.

In 1965, the architect and industrial designer Louis Weisdorf designed the Turbo pendant lamp, which was put into production by Lyfa in 1967. The pendant is made of 12 identical aluminium slats pulled together into a spiralling globe that emits glare-free lighting, based on the principles articulated by the lighting designer PH. Weisdorf, who remembers his childhood street being lit by gaslights, says about his veneration for PH:

The lamps that preceded PH's were not adapted to electric light at all; what he did was a big leap forward. Turbo is based on PH's principles for lighting. I received the NYT magazine and read everything PH wrote, although I never discussed lighting theory with him. We spoke about many other things, including opinions on a great many topics, but I think he might have balked if I, as a young architect, would have tried to discuss lighting theory with him. What PH had said about lighting was then, as it is today, in the back of my mind every time I work with lamp design.[1]

Turbo looks like a turbine. The resemblance is most striking when it is seen from beneath, an angle that really brings out the beauty of the lamp: 'I definitely intended it for industrial production, and I like it when very simple elements are combined and come to life.'[2] Weisdorf is particularly fond of this lamp because of its light distribution and form, and in 1973 the pendant received the coveted German product design award Die gute Industrieform. Meanwhile, in 1972 Weisdorf had completed a lamp that differed markedly from Turbo and, in fact, all his other luminaires. 'The great benefit of being trained as an architect is the tools one has acquired for dealing with tasks and improving on things, whatever the specific area. Indeed, my motto is, "Versatility, my specialty!"'[3] Despite this versatility, several of Weisdorf's lamps rest on common principles, as, for example, the uniform slats he uses in Conch (1963, see page 92), Turbo, Facet (1966) and Ekko (Echo) (1968):

People were surprised when I made Multi-Lite, which consists of fewer parts but which is in fact more complicated. It is not that dissimilar from many other lamps – some interior shades and a round exterior shade – but to me, the fact that the user can take it apart and pick different set-ups was the key quality.[4]

Weisdorf points out that he has never designed a lamp for a specific purpose or need: like other designs, the lamps emerged when he had an idea that seemed interesting to pursue: 'Multi-Lite was an idea that suddenly came to me, and from the outset I wanted to involve the users by enabling them to vary the form, so they wouldn't have to look at the same lamp all the time. This was about the ability to vary the look of the lamp and modify the light.'[5]

The principle behind Multi-Lite is that the light source is encircled by two cylindrical shades, a larger shade around a smaller one. This basic element directs the light downwards, but the luminaire additionally has two adjustable quarter-spherical shades. The components are assembled and attached to a metal ring. Within this circular form, the user can move the two adjustable shades – for example, pulling them together to form a hemispherical upper shade that directs all the light downwards or staggering them to make a step formation that emits light both upwards and downwards. It actually invites people to play with the light.

The lamp was designed in 1972, and like Turbo it was a good match for the playful home interiors of the 1970s with their wealth of colours and patterns. Production of the two luminaires was discontinued in the late 1970s but was later resumed by the design company Gubi. In its second incarnation, Multi-Lite also comes as a floor lamp and a table lamp.[6] These later models were designed by Weisdorf in collaboration with Gubi. Weisdorf continues to develop brand-new design solutions – including lamps – and with the use of 3D computer-aided design and 3D printers, his ideas are now translated into tangible lamp prototypes designed for the latest in diode technology.

'The Multi-Lite was a design I just had to draw when the idea came to me. It is the versatility that makes it special. Otherwise, it all gets so dull and uniform.'—Louis Weisdorf, 2019[7]

Hans J. Wegner: Opala

Louis Poulsen—1973

Hans J. Wegner designed his first lamps while still a student at the School of Arts and Crafts. They were competition entries and exist only as coloured sketches, but they are testimony that lighting had a place in Wegner's world of form as early as the 1930s. In 1938, Wegner left the school in Copenhagen and moved to Aarhus. He had been employed by Arne Jacobsen and Erik Møller to assist in the interior design of Aarhus City Hall, a task that included lamps: 'I designed all the furnishings for the City Hall. Naturally, it was discussed with Erik Møller, who was responsible for the hall,' Wegner explained, underscoring that 'it's Erik Møller and Arne Jacobsen's furniture in the City Hall'.[1]

After this, Wegner created lamps under his own name for exhibitions and on commission. For exhibition use, Wegner designed lamps to match and, not least, illuminate the furniture on display. Some of his designs were one-offs, while others had a much longer lifespan. Opala is an example of the latter.

Opala was designed for the Hotel Scandinavia in Copenhagen in 1973. Wegner was tasked with designing the furniture but also created rugs and bedspreads, and as this began to approach a total design of the hotel rooms, 'he figured he ought to include a lamp as well'.[2] He thus drew a table lamp, a floor lamp with a larger shade, and a pendant in three sizes. The starting point was the table lamp, which was positioned asymmetrically on its base so that it could stand close to the wall on a small side table and take up very little room. To direct the light where it was needed, the conical shade was also cut off at an asymmetrical angle. As suggested by the name, the shade was made in knock-proof opalized acrylic, while the rod, the circular base and the rounded cap covering the socket were lacquered metal.

Working with the weaver Vibeke Klint (b. 1927), Wegner designed green rugs and striped bedspreads in four colourways: yellow, red, green and blue. To match all four colour schemes, the lamps were lacquered in a brownish grey-green that contained all the different shades of colour, says the architect Marianne Wegner (b. 1947), who had joined the studio, and the project, that same year.[3] When the hotel manager saw the lamps, he immediately rejected them, stating that they were not in the process of building a spaceship! Instead, he chose lamps from Bing & Grøndahl made of substantial porcelain bases with large, white fabric shades. 'He preferred a "classic hotel style". The lamps were too modern!'[4]

Louis Poulsen produced the Opala lamps in 1973, but they were not available for sale until a couple of years later in connection with a production of streetlights by Wegner.[5] In December 1975, Louis Poulsen had announced a competition for luminaires for special urban environments, and four months later Wegner's streetlight was picked as the winner. In *LP & Co. NYT*, the winning project is described as

Wegner with the street lamp that won a competition for lighting in architectural heritage settings in 1976. Today, the lamps are installed, among other places, near Wegner's childhood home on the square in front of the church in Tønder.

an 'elegant and accomplished renewal of a familiar theme'.[6] Before the streetlight was put into production, some of its features were modified, but not the tilted lamp head or the concept of shedding soft light on buildings listed as worthy of preservation while making the most efficient use of the light without causing glare for passers-by or the occupants of the historical houses. Wegner's streetlight is still in use in his hometown of Tønder, among other places. Since 2017, it has been produced by Okholm Lighting, located in Southern Jutland, and recently 14 new LED streetlights were installed at Kirkepladsen in Tønder, the site of Wegner's childhood home.[7] The Opala lamps also remain in production, with minor modifications carried out in consultation with the Wegner family, who were also involved in adaptations of the Wegner streetlight.[8]

'Wegner is very industrious person. He is constantly at work, always seeking new experiences in the world of form that he has established around him.'
—Henrik Sten Møller, 1975[9]

When Pandul acquired the rights and relaunched the Opala table lamp in 2006, the design was updated in some regards. Among other changes, the base was made thinner.

Torsten Thorup and Claus Bonderup: Pendant No. 1, Calot and Confetti

Focus—1975

Quarto was also produced as a tall and a low park lamp on free-standing stems.

Torsten Thorup and Claus Bonderup both graduated from Professor Henning Larsen's department at the Royal Danish Academy of Fine Arts, School of Architecture, in 1969. Before and after their graduation, they worked in different parts of Denmark, at Henning Larsen Architects in Copenhagen and Jacob Blegvad's architecture firm in Aalborg. At these firms, they both worked on large-scale urban planning and construction projects, competing against each other and thus unable to discuss ideas related to the competition projects: 'The studio bosses let us work on joint design projects but prohibited us from doing building and planning projects while we worked in their respective firms.'[1]

The two architects regularly collaborated on design solutions in dialogue across the country and during holidays. The three 1970 lamps Pendant No. 1, Calot and Confetti are the result of such a successful collaboration, all based on simple geometric shapes with an interplay of light and shadow and the use of reflected light. Pendant No. 1 has a wide, conical silhouette that has its counterpoint in the visible rounded top of the chrome-cap light bulb peeking out below the horizontal axis of the lampshade. Calot's rounded shade, on the other hand, is a narrow section of a large sphere. The shape is mirrored in the chrome-cap bulb that is also visible in this model. The small Confetti pendants combine the cone, the cube and the hemisphere in an effort to find the smallest possible form that achieves the right reflected light with a chrome-cap light bulb.

The chrome-cap bulb is thus an integrated component in the design of all three luminaires, and in each case the basic concept is that 'the white interior of the shade reflects the light from the filament of the bulb and the interior of the chrome cap. The reflected light creates soft, beautiful shadows of the objects it strikes and a distribution of light that is most intense just underneath the lamp with an evenly diminishing horizontal distribution without stark contrasts'.[2]

The three lamps were put into production in 1975 by the newly founded lighting company Focus, and the following year Calot received the French Forme Utile, one of the most prestigious design awards in Europe.[3] By then, Thorup and Bonderup had designed yet another geometric lamp:

The Quarto wall lamp was designed in 1974 for a gym in Greenland that called for a robust knock-proof and weather-resistant lamp for indoor and outdoor use. The luminaire consists of a shade shaped like a quarter sphere, initially made in steel, and a semicircular base of knock-proof opalized acrylic. For indoor use, the lamp can be used as either a downlight or an uplight.[4]

The lighting company Focus was commissioned to produce the lamps, but it was not until 1980, when Focus included the lamp in their collection, that the quarter-spherical lamp was named Quarto. Apropos of name and form: 'In order to make the form appear as an actual quarter sphere, we designed the shade as a quarter sphere with 5-mm horizontal and vertical optical extensions, which creates the visual perception of a proper quarter sphere.'[5]

Thorup and Bonderup's use of geometric shapes 'was not about some "architecty" aesthetic emphasis on form for form's sake', the two architects emphasized in 1980.[6] Nevertheless, when the Confetti lamps were launched, in 1981, in pastel pink and blue, their shape and colour made them a match for the somewhat toned-down Danish variant of postmodernist interior design.

Quarto has remained in continuous production with Focus, while the two architects have recently collaborated with the furniture manufacturer Carl Hansen & Søn on a relaunch of Pendant No. 1, Calot and Confetti. And so, the 1970 trio shines on, now with updated LED lights — still chrome-capped, of course.

'We think along the same lines, so we don't need many words to understand one another. We are excited by the same things.'
—Torsten Thorup and Claus Bonderup, 1991[7]

Alfred Homann: Nyhavn Wall

Louis Poulsen—1976

Nyhavn Post (1992) alongside Homann's Kipp Bollard light (1999).

To celebrate the European Architectural Heritage Year in 1975, the Louis Poulsen company held a design competition for lighting in historically and architecturally valuable urban settings. The brief said, in part,

Our surroundings are rapidly changing. (...) Even those urban spaces whose particular architectural and historical qualities deserve special attention and protective measures are often subjected to disfiguring and misguided interventions, including the installation of luminaires designed for other scales and functional requirements.[1]

Hence a competition for contemporary but thoughtful lighting for architectural heritage settings. The luminaires were to be designed for incandescent light bulbs.

Only four months later, the winners were announced. The luminaire that was later named Nyhavn, after one of Copenhagen's atmospheric canal streets, won praise and a prize for showing sensitivity to the importance of the size of a luminaire intended for a historical urban environment – a thoughtful and user-friendly public lighting design.[2] 'The point was that the luminaire had to have a simple, delicate form and, not least, be smaller than the existing products on the market,' said the architect and industrial designer Alfred Homann (1948–2022) 43 years after the competition in a comment on the project, which was completed in a hectic race with time colliding with his graduation from the Royal Danish Academy of Fine Arts, School of Architecture. He went on to say, 'I had the design concept, sketches and models, but I was running out of time. To meet the competition deadline, I asked the architect Ole Kjær (b. 1947) to help me finish the working drawings; we spent five hectic days on that.'[3]

Conceptually, the shade system was based on familiar geometric shapes: 'A hemispherical top and a shade form that was familiar to everyone'.[4] A downward-facing incandescent light bulb is placed in an E27 socket, which is concealed inside a truncated gunmetal cone.[5] The bulb is placed inside a closed, clear glass tube with three anti-glare rings and a conical shade. The result is a broad beam of light towards the terrain below. The light also strikes and is reflected off both the shade and the three rings, while no direct light is emitted: 'When the lamp is mounted on a building, one perceives the form of the lamp, whether it is on or off. Thus, the lamp shapes the light, but the light also shapes the lamp.'[6] The anti-glare rings also protect the lamp against vandalism, sadly a necessary concern for anyone designing for urban space: 'Even if someone throws a rock at the lamp, they are unlikely to break the glass behind the rings.'[7]

Nyhavn was very different from Jens Møller-Jensen's 13-year-older Albertslund Post, which was also designed for a very different setting (see page 86). While the Albertslund Post, compared to Nyhavn, sends a relatively bright light onto the building wall, the Nyhavn wall lamp radiates its brightest light onto the ground and only casts soft light on the wall via the light on the shade and the anti-glare rings. The two lamps thus represent two very different approaches to lighting design. Møller-Jensen's lamp aimed to reduce glare, while Homann 'modifies and shapes the light'.[8]

Homann later developed the luminaire further, and today there are seven Nyhavn variants.[9] In 1978, the same year that the first lamps were going into retail, Homann had a studio in Nyhavn 31 – virtually a stone's throw from Louis Poulsen's then head office in Nyhavn 11.

'When the lamp is lit, the lamp shapes the light, but the light also shapes the lamp.'—Alfred Homann, 2019[10]

Torsten Thorup and Claus Bonderup: Floor Lamp and Table Lamp

Focus—1978

Torsten Thorup and Claus Bonderup's Floor Lamp and Table Lamp, two luminous lines drawn in the air, are early Danish examples of luminaires created specifically for halogen lights. This small variant of an incandescent light bulb was exciting for designers because it was so small and thus afforded a range of new options for lamp designers. In 1982, *Bo Bedre* wrote:

If PH had seen what the incandescent light bulb has become today, he would surely have been delighted with the many new options for designing luminaires. Others are already designing for the new bulb types, and the new halogen light, compared to other steam lamps, offers an exciting challenge for designers. Every day, new advanced lamps appear, not least from Italy, which is the modern-day Mecca of lamps.[1]

The Italians had been quick to embrace the little bi-pin light bulb, and in fact Floor Lamp and Table Lamp were initially produced in Italy. In 1972, the duo, now as Torsten Thorup and Claus Bonderup Architects, had a studio in Milan, arranged via the Italian couple behind the design firm MUUD: 'The lamps were developed, by mail, in Denmark in the early 1970s. MUUD had them manufactured in Padova, and they were presented at the fair in Milan in 1973. Here, people from the Museum of Modern Art (MoMA) saw the lamps and wanted to include them in their design collection.'[2]

The diminutive size of the halogen light bulb had allowed for a very lightweight construction: 'The result was a highly international form that was only possible because of the new halogen bulbs, which allowed for a very small lamp head.'[3] The base, on the other hand, had to be big, because it contained the transformer needed to reduce the voltage drastically (to 12 V/50 W). As with Thorup and Bonderup's previous luminaires, these too used familiar geometric shapes: 'Circular tubes, a hemisphere and a cube with rounded edges'.[4] The heavy cubic base also serves to stabilize the lamp. From the base, both the Floor Lamp and the smaller Table Lamp rise up on a slender tube, and at the end of the arced neck, the tiny bi-pin bulb emits an intense bright spotlight. The white light is also distributed through tiny openings on the sides of the lamp head.

MoMA had to wait five years before the lamps reached Manhattan, because the Italian design adventure ended abruptly when the Italian company was closed. Back in Denmark, the design was put into production in 1978 by the lighting company Focus, which finally sent two lamps to MoMA along with Stool, a small seat designed as part of the same series as Floor Lamp and Table Lamp.

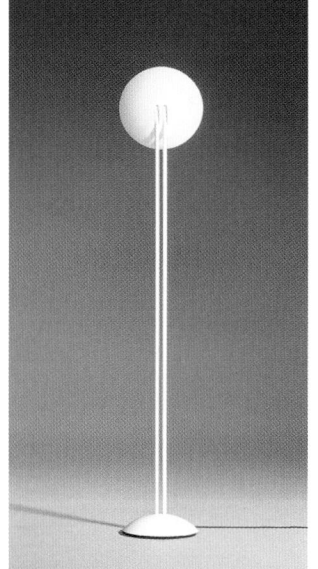

The tall Olympos floor lamp with the adjustable bowl-shaped lamp head.

In 1984, Thorup and Bonderup established a joint design studio in Havnegade 47 in Copenhagen, and in 1985 the two architects designed another halogen luminaire: a tall floor lamp in metal. The lamp was produced in a bronze-anodized version for Georg Jensen's new shop interiors to match the similarly specially designed display cases.[5] The luminaire provided indirect lighting. The bowl-shaped lamp head can be put into a horizontal position, turning the lamp into an uplight, or pushed down into a vertical position to direct the light onto the wall, the lamp in either case reflecting the light that bounces off the ceiling or the wall. The luminaire was named Olympos after the uplight position's direct reference to an Olympic flame in a bowl. In Thorup and Bonderup's bowl, the halogen light takes the place of the ancient flame.[6]

Thorup and Bonderup's geometrically shaped luminaires and, not least, Olympos have clear features of postmodernism's use of simplified classic images from ancient Rome and Greece. The last luminaire the two architects created together, in 1991–1992, is named Pharos, after the lighthouse in Alexandria whose flame guided ancient ships. Pharos is a stylized postmodernist bollard lamp that burns brightly to this day, in continuous production by Focus.[7]

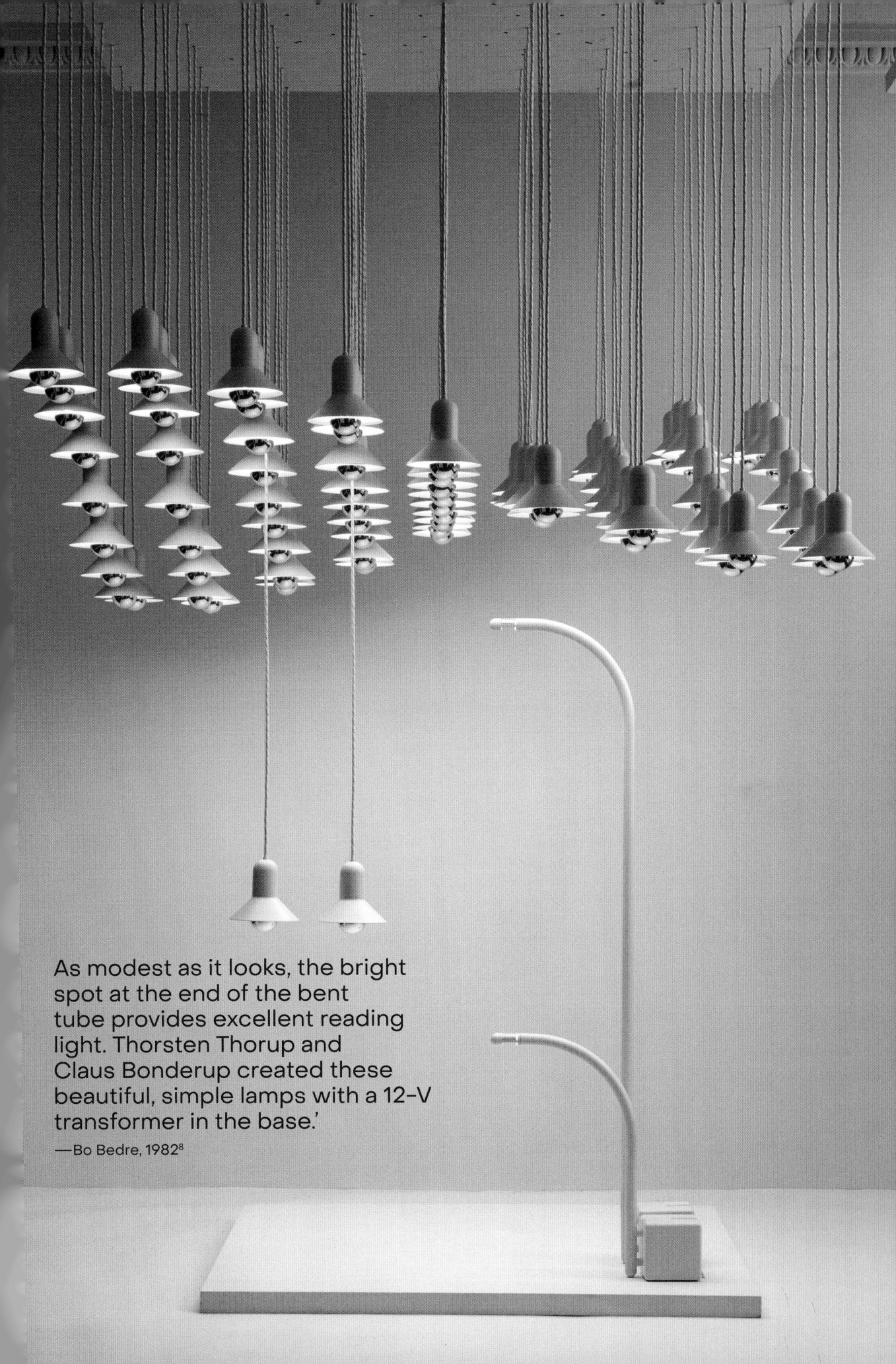

As modest as it looks, the bright spot at the end of the bent tube provides excellent reading light. Thorsten Thorup and Claus Bonderup created these beautiful, simple lamps with a 12-V transformer in the base.'
—Bo Bedre, 1982[8]

Ebbe Christensen and Sophus Frandsen after PH: Charlottenborg 6½–6

Louis Poulsen—1979

Sophus Frandsen's Fibonacci pendant from ca. 1962.
→ Today, the Charlottenborg pendants are used in the Danish Prime Minister's office.

In two articles in *Kritisk Revy,* from 1926 and 1927, PH had published his manifesto on interior lighting. The two most important principles were that light should be glare-free and have a warm colour. Another important concern was shadows: shadows were needed to define form, but they should have soft contours, and there should be smooth transitions from light to dark surfaces. As discussed previously, PH continued to base his many design variants on these general principles (pages 66–69 and 78–79). Although PH had passed away in 1967, a new PH model was created in 1979, based on his early theories. The 6½–6 adhered closely to PH's original four-shade lamp from 1931.[1]

PH's four-shade lamp was intended to be hung high, as an alternative to the chandelier that most people at the time, around 1930, still preferred in the centre of their living room. Thus, it should emit a downwards light as well as a more intense but soft light towards the upper part of the walls. To that end, the hole in the centre of the three ordinary PH shades had been enlarged to allow the light to strike the fourth, upper shade. This fourth shade had a trumpet form comprising several geometric curves, causing it to differ from – and clash slightly with – the logarithmic principle defining the lower shades. The lamp was available both with bronzed metal shades and with glass shades. Although PH preferred the former, because it best lived up to his lighting principles, most people bought the glass versions.[2]

For a redesign of the Charlottenborg exhibition building, near Kongens Nytorv in central Copenhagen, the architects Sophus Frandsen (1927–2013) and Ebbe Christensen (b. 1936) created the larger successor to PH's four-shade lamp, named 6½–6. As indicated by the name, a large shade, measuring 65 cm in diameter, is placed above a 60-cm three-shade lamp.[3] When the interior redesign was unveiled in autumn 1980, the architecture critic Henrik Sten Møller wrote in a review in *Politiken*, 'The true splendour of the room is a new PH lamp that has been used for lighting throughout the exhibition building. (…) It is in fact the most beautiful lamp I have ever seen, and it provides perfect light.'[4] Møller also wrote that the lamp had no 'previous history, because it has never existed before'.[5] Indeed, it had not; not in that form. But of course it had antecedents, and with profound respect for this source of inspiration, Frandsen and Christensen had created a more harmonious relationship between the fourth shade and the others, simultaneously achieving a higher coefficient of utilization. Not least, the two architects had added a blue reflector shade in between the third and second shades, which in combination with the base plate prevented glare from all angles. That was not fully accomplished in PH's version.[6] Due to the white metal shades and the reflector, the Charlottenborg pendant was able to illuminate the exhibition walls and the floor without producing glare.[7]

The two architects who had successfully taken on the four-shade challenge were far from novices when it came to lighting. Frandsen had graduated from the Royal Danish Academy of Fine Arts, School of Architecture, in 1953, Christensen in 1964, and they led the courses in lighting engineering at the School of Architecture after the founder of the course, Mogens Voltelen, retired in 1978 (see page 50).[8] Frandsen's interest in lighting in general and PH's principles in particular was expressed in the former's early pendant lamp Fibonacci, launched by Fog & Mørup in 1960.[9]

The PH lamp utilized the reflected light from the underside of the shade and could thus also be made in a non-translucent material. Frandsen's pendant was made in metal, either copper or aluminium. It consists of six horizontal rings of descending size that are held in place around the bulb by three V-shaped metal rods. The rods are attached to the outside shade and pass through the construction to a centred cylinder that hides the socket.[10] The rings rest alternately on the upper and lower arm of the V, which produces a spiral effect in the shade's distribution of light. This effect is further underscored by the truncated-cone shape of the lowest shade.[11] A base interior disc is attached beneath the bulb to allow glare-free light to be reflected into the luminaire itself and into the room. Like the Charlottenborg pendant, the lighting engineering in the Fibonacci lamp matches PH's work.[12]

'A design effort that is remarkable. That lamp is worth the visit in itself.'
—Henrik Sten Møller, 1980[13]

Erik Magnussen: Porcelight

Louis Poulsen—1982

Coaee cup from the award-winning tableware Hank, Bing & Grøndahl, 1970.
→ Made By Hand has been producing the Porcelight lamp series since 2013.

Erik Magnussen (1940–2014) graduated from the ceramics line at the School of Arts and Crafts in 1960, and throughout his professional career he referred to himself as a ceramicist, although he was best known for his industrial designs.[1] Magnussen founded his own studio, but after his graduation he was immediately attached to the porcelain factory Bing & Grøndahl. Magnussen's graduation project had been a cylindrical teapot, which laid the groundwork for his Form 679 service (1965) for Bing & Grøndahl. Five years later came Magnussen's own favourite service, Hank (Handle), a service that huge numbers of Danes would come into contact with over the years, as it was used in the cafeteria on the ferries that carried trains and cars across the Great Belt strait until the bridge was opened in 1998. For this functional service, Magnussen was awarded the Danish ID Prize in 1972 and the Knud V. Engelhardt Memorial Grant in 1975. Magnussen thus had extensive knowledge of porcelain production and of the particular possibilities and properties of porcelain when he designed a lampshade in the white clay in 1982. Later, in 1986, he spoke about the role of the material in a given design solution:

I define the function first, because to me good design is an honest approach to function; next, I choose the material. It's not that I am determined to make things in a particular material whatever it takes. Once I have determined the functional aspects, it is important for me to choose the ideal material for that particular function. Because, in fact, the material is as important as anything else.[2]

Magnussen's first lamp, Porcelight, was named after its material. In 1982, the pendant was launched by Louis Poulsen, but it was produced in cooperation with the porcelain factory. Magnussen knew all about the translucence of porcelain and was well aware that the light would not only be radiated downwards from the pendant but would also be emitted softly through the thin white shade. In his own words, his goal was to achieve a warmer light than would be possible with opal glass, the material used by many other lamp designers. In his design of the small pendants, Magnussen had drawn on inspiration from the classic white porcelain socket, and in the final form the socket is vaguely visible when the lamp is lit. Characteristically for Magnussen, the shade design is simple and has a clean, functionalist expression. It was well suited for serial production as it could be made on an existing machine that the porcelain factory normally used for making large mugs! Magnussen had deliberately considered how to combine the most functional form, from the user's perspective, with the most efficient form, from an industrial production perspective.[3]

The form of the white pendant was suitable for virtually all interiors. When it was lit over the breakfast or dinner table, sending its warm light into the room, the small size – 12 cm in height and 11 cm in diameter – also ensured that it did not block the view of the people at the table.

After a number of years, Louis Poulsen discontinued production of the pendant, but it was reintroduced in 2007. In connection with the relaunch, Magnussen expanded the series from the original pendant in two sizes to include a wall lamp and a floor lamp.

Magnussen has explained how most of his designs were inspired by needs he encountered in his own everyday life or by shortcomings in existing designs.[4] His luminaires, whether they were intended for use in the home or outside it, were all carefully designed for their particular use. The year after Magnussen designed the tactile Porcelight, he created an outdoor lamp in a very different material, because that was the optimal choice for the function of that particular lamp.

'To me, function is paramount – making things that really work and are usable.' —Erik Magnussen, 1986⁵

Erik Magnussen: Ship's lamp and EM oil lamp

Stelton—1982 and 1983

EM oil lamp from 2001 side by side with Magnussen's iconic vacuum jug from 1977.

Erik Magnussen said, 'You begin with Adam and Eve every time you take on a new material. You need to know things as well as you possibly can. If you know a material well, you can take it to the limit. If you don't, you wind up with something that's just a vague fantasy.'[1]

Stainless steel is difficult to work with; the architect Arne Jacobsen had discovered that when he developed his Cylinda-Line series for Stelton. It took three years before the first products were ready to launch in 1967. Just under ten years later, Stelton's CEO wanted to add a vacuum jug to the series. Magnussen naturally looked to Jacobsen's expression but designed his cylinder around an existing vacuum glass insert, which helped reduce the cost of the jug.[2] The vacuum jug became yet another classic in Stelton's product range; it continued the existing line but was a perfect match for the modern high-tech era. As an innovative feature, it could be operated with one hand, automatically opening when the user tipped it to pour and closing when it was put down on the table. The same year that the EM77 vacuum jug was launched, it was awarded the Danish ID Prize.

In 1982, Magnussen designed the Ship's lamp for Stelton. The light came from a live flame fuelled by kerosene or lamp oil. Twenty years earlier, when Henning Koppel designed the kerosene lamp Petronella, the then new home design magazine *Bo Bedre* had lamented the difficulty of 'finding a beautiful, contemporary oil lamp'. Only at the ship chandler's could one hope to find 'well-made lamps without frills and ornamentation, sturdy and simple, like most of the items that are used at sea'.[3] However, these traditional models were a far cry from the exclusive streamlined version Magnussen launched based on a need he had experienced in his own life as an avid yachtsman.[4] With Magnussen's typical focus on function, the Ship's lamp not only provided a beautiful light but was also designed to serve as a source of heat and a dehumidifier – good properties in a ship's cabin or a summer cottage in the Scandinavian climate. The lamp, which can be used hanging or standing, has a geometric shade in steel at the vertical middle of the lamp to optimize the downwards light from the flame.

In 1983, the smaller and much simpler EM oil lamp was added to the Stelton range. Launching yet another kerosene lamp might seem to be a retrospective move, but the rational and geometric lantern had a modern expression and was designed to meet a lasting need for a lamp that did not require electricity – no longer to cover areas without electricity but to make it possible to use the lamp outdoors. The lamp has clean lines with a lower section in maintenance-free, satin-polished stainless steel that complements the matt cylindrical glass chimney. Like the Cylinda-Line range, it exemplified simple, functional no-frills design. Magnussen's underlying ambition of optimizing existing designs is at play here too. And, most importantly, when the oil lamp is lit, a soft, diffused light is emitted through the frosted glass chimney. At the threshold to the new millennium, two smaller versions of the lamp were launched, one with frosted glass and one with clear glass, like the Ship's lamp, the latter offering a direct view of the mesmerizing live flame.[5]

As modern versions of traditional oil or kerosene lamps, Magnussen's lamps were successors to Henning Koppel's Petronella from 1962.[6] In 1983, Magnussen received the Danish Design Council's Annual Award for 'his carefully thought-out and well-functioning design'.[7]

'In most cases, my point of departure has been something I found lacking in my everyday life or lacking qualities in existing products.'—Erik Magnussen, 1986[8]

Jørgen Gammelgaard: VIP

Design Forum—1983

Jørgen Gammelgaard appeared under many job titles: joiner, cabinetmaker, industrial designer and, from 1988, professor. Throughout his life, he preferred 'tool drafter'.[1] He was a perfectionist and found this to be a more apt term than 'designer', which he felt had a hollow ring to it in Danish. To be a 'tool drafter', on the other hand, suggested an uncompromising approach that characterized Gammelgaard's design in every respect. 'When a result was good enough, that didn't mean it would be put to use; instead it would be improved or discarded. The goal was perfection,' wrote Professor of Design Per Mollerup in 1995.[2]

The Swing VIP table lamp swivels and is height-adjustable.

Ten years after Gammelgaard had completed Tip Top (see page 128), he designed the working lamp JoGa. Mounted on a stationary vertical stem is an arm that can be moved up or folded into the stem, carrying a shallow circular shade.[3]

Two years later, Gammelgaard presented the first lamps in the VIP series created for Design Forum. This was a perfected and even more flexible luminaire, where the same shade – a softly rounded cone, stamped out in aluminium – was used on lamps for virtually any conceivable purpose. The series included a floor lamp, wall lamps and a variety of table lamps. With a specially designed mount, the shade was used at an oblique angle as gallery lighting in 1983 when Gammelgaard designed permanent exhibition lighting for Marienlyst Palace in Elsinore, north of Copenhagen. The series was also expanded with the ½ VIP – a shade cut in half, as the name suggests. This non-adjustable lamp is mounted directly on the wall and can also be used outdoors. All the other shades can be adjusted to produce a direct or an indirect light, as needed. Due to the many adjustment options, each lamp has a wide range of possible expressions.

The floor lamp has a very high degree of flexibility. It is height-adjustable, the arm swivels, and the shade rotates 360 degrees. The horizontal arc of the shade is echoed in the large flat, circular base. By contrast, the Swing VIP table lamp has a small compact, cylindrical base and a swivel arm. In this lamp too, the shade is fully adjustable.

The multipurpose and multi-adjustable VIP series was the last lamp design Gammelgaard created for the retail market. In 1987, he was appointed professor at the Royal Danish Academy of Fine Arts, School of Architecture, Department of Furniture and Spatial Design, but continued his design practice concurrently. In 1989, for example, he designed the lighting for a renovation of the lobby at Frederiksborg Castle in Hillerød, north of Copenhagen.

Gammelgaard died in 1991, only 53 years old. In 1995, the Danish Museum of Art & Design showed a retrospective exhibition of his work. In connection with the exhibition, the architect Grete Jalk (1920–2006) spoke about her first meeting with Gammelgaard while she was a teacher at the School of Arts and Crafts. She remembered Gammelgaard as a student who not only completed all his assignments but perfected every single one.[4] In 1988, *Bo Bedre* wrote about Gammelgaard that he 'creates industrial designs that are so carefully finished that they receive awards as if they were artistic craft objects'.[5] Upon their launch in 1983, the VIP lamps were widely covered in architecture magazines, and like the Tip Top pendant they were purchased by the Danish Arts Foundation. Luminaire design was not the tool drafter Gammelgaard's main field, but the VIP series was a functional and thoroughly perfected contribution to Danish industrial design. Most of the models in the series were in production at Pandul until 2023. In 2024, the VIP series is in production at Carl Hansen & Søn.[6]

'The word "compromise" did not exist in Jørgen Gammelgaard's dictionary.' —Per Mollerup, 1995[7]

Stig Gerlach: String Light

Sirius—1984

'The DNA of Sirius is light decorations, which I began to make in the mid 1980s. Today, we are the market leader for light decorations, which were brought into Danish homes by Sirius, no doubt about it.'
—Stig Gerlach, 2019[1]

In November 1984, the home design magazine *Bo Bedre* proclaimed the advent of 'the white look', showing a completely white home interior with a string light, complete with a white cord, as a luminous feature. While string lights had previously been reserved for Christmas trees, they were now being used as a festive home decoration.[2] That innovation marked the beginning of a new, viable trend pioneered by Stig Gerlach (b. 1952). Gerlach, who is the CEO of the Sirius company, has a business degree, but as a designer he is self-taught. A passion for design and, not least, lighting caused him to take the leap to create his own light decorations.

It all began with the traditional Christmas tree lights, but in the 1980s I replaced the green cord with transparent and white cords that matched contemporary home design trends, where everything was painted white. That marked a transition; the lights were no longer just for the tree but could be integrated into the home as a decorative element. I envisioned a luminous decoration that could be hung around a mirror, put in a glass vase, essentially integrated into all sorts of things – a creative lamp, you could say, that people could shape as they liked. That is what string lights offer: a potential for creating a unique, creative universe.[3]

A string light is an electric cord with light bulbs on it. During the mid 1980s, the light sources were tiny incandescent bulbs, and because the filament was porous, individual bulbs would often burn out. The problem was that an entire row of lights would be out of use until the one defective bulb was replaced, because the bulbs were installed as a parallel circuit: 'The first serially connected string lights were sold for Christmas 1989. I added a so-called light bridge to the filament, so that the power would simply bypass it if it burned out, rather than switching everything off. That was revolutionizing; it gave people a much more satisfactory product.'[4]

In Denmark, Gerlach was also a pioneer when he began to use LEDs (light-emitting diodes) in 2000. LEDs were first produced in 1962, but it would take many years before they made it into Danish homes. It was not until 2007 that LEDs became a common light source in Denmark, and for many years they were mainly used in public buildings.[5] Sirius initially made decorations using two different kinds of light bulbs in parallel circuits, but as LED lighting became more affordable and the colour of the light was improved, LED became the standard option in string lights.[6]

The use of LEDs made light decorations much more versatile. Because the diodes use so little power, they could be efficiently powered by batteries, thus eliminating the need for an outlet and expanding the range of applications. New tiny diodes could be mounted on thin conductive wires to make very delicate string lights that could be integrated into other objects – for example a glass ball. Trio from 2004 consists of three glass balls in different sizes seemingly floating in air mounted on ultrathin steel tubes. The stems vary in length, and each one is mounted on a metal base that contains a battery. From the base, a conductive wire winds its way around the stem and inside the glass ball, where the diodes sparkle when the luminaire is switched on. The patented glass balls also exist in a hanging version with a decorative battery case specially developed by Gerlach: 'It's the "motor" that makes the ball light up and also acts as a suspension or weight to hold it stable as it floats above a branch.'[7] The decoration is formed by the object as a whole. Gerlach emphasizes that the company not only uses glass spheres but has 'several different glass bodies enclosing the light. The key is that it is the light that drives the decoration'.[8] In a comment on the quality of this light, Gerlach adds:

We recently introduced a remote control for our decorations, so you can switch them on and off as you like. We could add a dimmer switch, but there is no need, because we have gone for the right colour, which is our DNA. We could also introduce colour switching, based on RGB. But I stay true to my roots, sticking to a warm Nordic light; that's what the Danish audience prefers.[9]

In Gerlach's assessment, the light of the Sirius decorations has exactly the right colour, which eliminates the need to adjust the intensity. The warm Nordic light that is Sirius's DNA is thus a core design quality.

The decoration string light Lucas from 2016 is three metres long and has ten bright, spherical LED bulbs but can be extended to as many as 100 bulbs (30 metres). The lights can be used both indoors and out.

Sidse Werner: Phoenix

Holmegaard—1985

The Bibliotek table lamp from 1981, which has a light source in both the base and the lamp head, was a step on the way to the design of the Phoenix lamp.

The designer Sidse Werner (1931–1989) was born and raised during a time when few women attained higher education, and even fewer worked professionally with industrial lighting design – despite the fact that women were often responsible for interior home design, including lighting and lamps.

Werner originally trained as an interior decorator.[1] Later, she took courses at the Danish Technological Institute, while the remainder of her professional development was practice-based, initially as an assistant to the designer Nanna Ditzel (1923–2005) and later in a joint design firm with the designer Leif Alring (1936–1987).[2] Together, Werner and Alring designed both furniture and lamps. In 1970, the duo created the pop- and space-age-inspired lamp family Formland for Fog & Mørup. The series included pendants, table lamps, a wall lamp and a floor lamp, all combining high-gloss metal in the bright primary colours of red, yellow and blue with opalized CAB plastic.[3] The table lamp combines a cylindrical base with a spherical top. While the base and the lower hemisphere are in lacquered metal, the top hemisphere is made of translucent CAB plastic, which lets the light pass through and diffuse into the room.[4]

Also in 1970, Werner went solo, designed the stylized tubular-steel Coat Tree for Fritz Hansens Eftf., which has since become an evergreen, and was attached to the Holmegaard glassworks.[5] Werner was employed as a lamp designer and convinced Holmegaard to make them in metal.[6] When she designed the Skibslampen (Ship's Lamp) in 1973, she said, 'Things should be reliable; they have to work under all conditions.'[7] Skibslampen was mainly metal with only a small amount of glass, but Werner learnt everything about the properties and making of glass, and in 1981 she was able to present several opal white glass lamps that matched the white trend in interior design. This included the Apoteker (Apothecary) pendant and table lamps, with a simple expression inspired by old apothecary jars, and the Bibliotek (Library) pendant, which had a more playful and swelling form. In 1981, Werner said, 'Atmosphere and beauty are key terms for what I aim for in glass pendants.'[8] The following year, she developed the latter design into a larger lamp family, which also included a smaller pendant and a table lamp in two sizes. The unique feature of these table lamps was that they had two light sources that could be switched on and off independently. One was conventionally placed on top of the base, while the other was placed inside the glass base, turning the base itself into a luminous object. 'It is beautiful when the base becomes a luminaire,' Werner said in 1982 and added, 'You can choose between a diffuse atmospheric light, only turning on the light source inside the base, and a brighter general light when both light sources are on.'[9]

Werner explained that her interest lay with the interplay between glass and light and that she would like to go even further, 'using the more advanced interior light source. Maybe they will cause us to revise our habits and ideas in relation to lighting'.[10] Werner continued exploring light in glass forms, and in 1985 she designed the table lamp Phoenix. It too was made in white drawn opal glass, but in this toadstool-shaped lamp, the conical base and slightly conical shade are one form. With clear reference to a phoenix, the bird, the chrome-capped bulb was visible above the open base and thus placed in the hollow of the open shade, so that the light was distributed upwards and evenly over the wide shade and down into and around the base. Yet another way to use the combination of light and glass.[11]

Werner had a keen curiosity about new materials and production techniques. In the late 1960s, she travelled to the United States, in part to study new materials and production methods.[12] At Holmegaard, she was the first to work with spun glass, and today she is known for glass series in clear spun glass. Above all, however, her name is associated with the white opal glass lamps for 'harmonious lighting in a room'.[13] Besides Michael Bang, she was the most prolific lamp designer for Holmegaard.[14]

'With a lamp family whose members have different lighting functions but are characterized by a shared attitude to form and materials, you can achieve harmonious lighting in a room.'
—Sidse Werner, 1982[15]

Alfred Homann: Rappe Louis

Louis Poulsen—1989

During his studies at the Royal Danish Academy of Fine Arts, School of Architecture, Alfred Homann worked at Vilhelm Wohlert's architecture firm,[1] and after graduating in 1976 he was assigned to the project of expanding the Louisiana Museum of Modern Art. These early years were key in shaping Homann's respect for good collaboration and good process dialogues. In a comment on his collaboration with Knud W. Jensen, the founder of Louisiana, he says, 'It was inspiring for me, as a young architect, to experience his open-minded approach in striving for optimal solutions.'[2]

In 1976, Homann designed his first lamp for Louis Poulsen (see page 142), and although the projects from the design and architecture firm that he founded in 1978 covered a wide and diverse range, he has continued to create design solutions for the lighting manufacturer.[3] Thus, Homann has continually adapted his design to new needs and light sources: 'There's no point in resisting development, you have to address it head-on and make the most of it, with the benefits and drawbacks it entails; that's what makes every new task so challenging and exciting,' Homann said in 2019.[4]

During the 1980s, personal computers came to desks in every office throughout the land, and towards the end of the decade the, still fairly large, 'home computers' also began to make their way into Danish homes:

I was given a free assignment of designing a table lamp at a time when people began to have computers with keyboards, and when you put that on a desk there was little room for anything else. Thus, the lamp had to be compact, and it had to provide asymmetrical light that hit the keyboard, not the screen.[5]

Rappe Louis (a pun on 'rap' in Danish, which is both the adjective 'nimble' and 'quack', the sound made by a duck) was cast in a synthetic material. It had an oblique angle, and the fixed height was ideal for a desktop keyboard. It was also a streamlined luminaire without the many movable segments known from the traditional anglepoise lamp. The light source was the popular halogen bulb, its tiny size allowing for a smaller lamp head, which had a reflector that cast bright white light onto the keyboard. The transformer was contained inside the base, the weight keeping the lamp stable: 'It took a certain amount of material to ensure stability, hence the added curve to its back and belly.'[6]

That home computers were not yet ubiquitous is evident from the fact that Louis Poulsen does not mention them but points to several other uses in its advertisement for the new lamp:

Rappe Louis is a new, lightweight lamp for your table, your shelf or anywhere you can find room for the tiny base. (…) Rappe Louis is a small featherweight, as easy to move around as it is to operate. With its beautiful, simple form, the lamp fits in anywhere. All you need to do is check where it's needed. You can do that tonight, after dark. Tomorrow, you can go see Rappe Louis in your local lamp shop.[7]

Rappe Louis was intended for both office and home use, while most of the 50 products that Homann designed for Louis Poulsen are intended for the professional market. Many of the lamps are found in the outdoor public realm.[8] The latest new addition is on a very different scale than Rappe Louis. The up to 4-metre-tall Homann Park from 2017 uses LEDs and is intended for public squares and

Homann Park from 2017 directs the light at the terrain below but also reflects a ring of light up, over the lamp head. Seen from a tall building, the latter light outlines both the form of the individual lamps and the course of the streets and paths they line.

paths in many different types of architecture. It comes in two variants. One emits a downwards light onto the road or path, the other also has a slightly luminous top, as some of the light is reflected upwards into the lamp housing:

This means that people living on the third floor, for example, can look down at the round circles of light at night. This light feature helps outline the course of the road and the shape of the luminaire. In all my lighting, the lamp shapes the light, but the light also shapes the lamp. Lamps, too, should be simple, clear and logical.[9]

'Simple, clear and logical, that is the philosophy behind all my work.'
—Alfred Homann, 2019[10]

Piet Hein: Sinus lamp

Uniline—1996

Super-Eggs aglow.

As a young man, the designer and poet Piet Hein studied art at the Royal Institute of Art in Stockholm followed by theoretical physics at the University of Copenhagen. His insight into physics and mathematics is combined with an artistic expression in his many design solutions, almost all of which were driven by mathematical calculations. Hein's first two lamps, the Ra lamp (see page 48) and Funco, were developed in the early 1930s.[1] Over the years, Hein created a wide and diverse range of artistic projects, but light remained a passion throughout.

During the Second World War, Hein and his family lived in Argentina, and in the South American night sky he missed the constellations he remembered from the northern hemisphere. This inspired him to design a candelabrum 'that brought back the Great Bear', the flames of the seven candles 'forming the big, simple constellation of the Great Bear'.[2] While his Ra lamp was based on associations to the sun and sun god, a decade later he thus turned stars into flames.[3] His subsequent luminaires, like all lamps, were substitutes for the sun, but above all they were mathematically derived geometric forms enveloping a light source.

Today, Hein's name is inextricably linked with the 'superellipse', a form he developed in 1959 for the design of Sergels Torg, a square in central Stockholm. The superellipse is Hein's name for a mathematical figure based on a formula that combines the ellipse and the rectangle. The first use for the mathematically and aesthetically concise form was thus to handle the challenges of a busy traffic junction in the Swedish capital. Later, on a smaller scale, it was used to seat people around a dining table. Hein mounted a superellipse tabletop on span legs to create the now world-famous Super-Elliptical table. In 1964, the table was put into production by the Swedish furniture manufacturer Bruno Mathsson, and since 1968 it has been in continuous production with the Danish manufacturer Fritz Hansen. In 1965, Hein spun the 2D figure on its longitudinal axis to create a 3D volume that he named the Super-Egg. In 1965, it was put into production as 'the first deliberate attempt to create a necessity of life without any practical purpose'.[4] The form was applied to virtually all conceivable objects, including lamps, some of which remained sketches for a number of years. Among them is a 'super-egg' pendant lamp in opal glass with a cut-out in the bottom, a form reminiscent of the open glass globe that was common in 1940s luminaires (see pages 50–51 and 58). A metal lampshade shaped as a 'super-egg' cut in half was used for a table and pendant lamp that was put into production by Lyfa.[5] The lampshade was later named Super.

Hein's mathematically derived cross between a rectangle and an ellipse inspired his later fusion of a straight line and a sinusoid into the more angular 'super-sinusoid'. Based on this curve, Hein began, in 1967, to work on the design he presented as the Flying Saucer lamp in 1975, and which he referred to in a 1991 sketch as the '"Galaxy lamp", temporary name'.[6] In 1993, it was launched as the Sinusoid lamp. For a brief period, it was made in light, strong polycarbonate, but Hein was not fully satisfied with the result until he saw it in glass, shortly before his death. In connection with Hein's 90th birthday, in 1995, *Bo Bedre* wrote, 'Over the coming years, new lamps that are not yet in production will see the light of day — based on Piet Hein's old drawings.'[7] The prediction proved true. Already the following year, which was also the year of Hein's death, the Sinusoid lamp was relaunched, now in frosted, mouth-blown glass. The curvy shape of the Sinusoid lamp combined with the opening in the base concentrates the light in the centre of the form on the illuminated surface while diffusing glare-free light into the room. The Super pendant, the half 'super-egg', was also relaunched, now in five sizes, also in frosted glass.[8] Today, the wavy curves that envelop the light source are produced by the Piet Hein company.

'That the straight line is straight
— Is its nature and fate,
But for my taste a bit of a minus.
I should welcome a World
With the straight lines more curled
Designed in the sign of the Sinus.'
—Piet Hein[9]

Peter Bysted: Rubbie

Peter Bysted—2000

'We wanted to create a small oasis among the many pavilions, offering a sense of intimacy and a calm, pleasant space. It's rare to find a calm space at a world exposition. We placed the building in a large terraced pool. Around the pool we laid a wooden pavement, and here we placed Rubbie. As a source of light, a lamp is only interesting at night, so why not use it for something else during the daytime?'—Peter Bysted, 2019[1]

In the summer of 2000, EXPO 2000 in Hannover marked the beginning of a new millennium. The Danish EXPO pavilion, designed by the architect and industrial designer Peter Bysted (b. 1951), attracted a total of 1.5 million visitors – an average of 10,000 daily people who stopped by to see Bysted's orchestration of Danish architecture, design and art.[2] Here, they could take a break seated on Bysted's bollard, Rubbie, or, at night, enjoy the area around the pavilion bathed in its glare-free light. As a component of the exhibition, the bollard was a new versatile Danish urban furniture design.

A distinction is drawn between road lighting, which primarily serves to light up the road surface while preventing reflection, and the lighting of streets of squares with a variety of buildings and planting. Bollard lamps are used for orientation lighting, defining the boundaries of the space from a low height and aiding wayfinding. The latter is illustrated by Rubbie's maritime lighthouse reference. Bysted designed it in raw rubber, which adds a tactile quality to the lamp and the environment it is placed in. In addition to providing a wide horizontal distribution of light with effective, glare-free illumination of the nearby surroundings, Rubbie was designed 'with a soft, round top, so you can sit on it, and children can leap-frog over it. Rubber is warm and pleasant to the touch, inviting this sort of interaction, but it is also robust, and the design aimed to signal that',[3] Bysted explained in 2019, adding that he was surprised that rubber is not used more for luminaires: 'It's a strong material; just think of car tyres and what they are put through!'[4] However, the untraditional choice of material was one of the reasons why it took ten years before Louis Poulsen put Rubbie into production.[5] Six months later, Rubbie received the British Lighting Design Award for best outdoor product in 2011.

Rubbie's inviting surface and good lighting qualities were owed in part to Bysted's experience from the design of a similar type of lighting several years earlier. He graduated from the Aarhus School of Architecture in 1978. Industrial design was the core focus of his studies, and in 1976 he took part in a competition held by Louis Poulsen to design a luminaire for historical urban settings with heritage architecture. Bysted designed a steel bollard, which won second prize. The bollard, named Bysted, consists of a low tubular post with four shades designed as low truncated cones. The top of the unit is closed, so that only downwards light is emitted. The interior of the shades is

Bysted was designed for a 200-watt incandescent light bulb in 1976. Today, it uses an LED light source.
→ Originally designed for Expo 2000, Rubbie was put into production by Louis Poulsen in 2010. Here, Rubbie is used at the St George Shipwreck Museum in Thorsminde.

painted white to provide an optimal distribution of light on the exterior of the bollard, which was designed to weather and take on a rusty appearance. The comments from the jury, which were quoted in Louis Poulsen's magazine *LP & Co. NYT*, included the observation that 'the sandblasted shades will lend the light a "smouldering" appearance, not least when they develop rust'.[6] Bysted added in 2019, 'Even then, I was very interested in tactile surfaces, but furniture for streets and urban spaces should also have a coarse texture that matches the outdoor setting.'[7] He explained that the shades are cast iron, while the post is Corten steel, which oxidizes quickly and develops a raw, rusty look that protects it from further corrosion.[8] 'But that was not why I wanted the rust; it was in order to achieve the beautiful "fuzzy" surface that glows when the light strikes it.'[9]

In 2000, Rubbie was introduced to the world in Hannover, and over the years the Bysted bollard has found its way into projects around the world as orientation lighting in the landscape: 'If you go outside on a starry night and look up, you need very little light to navigate. Today, our environment is awash in light; I have sought to create soft, beautiful light and imbue the lamps with warm and human dimensions.'[10]

Sofie Refer: Bulb

Unique Interior
Copenhagen—2000

Ice Blue from 2006 with a cluster of mouth-blown glass orbs. Ice is currently produced by &Tradition.
→ Mega Bulb was launched in 2006. H: 18.5 cm, Ø: 23 cm. Today, the glass forms its halo-like effect around an LED bulb.

Bulb is the name of Sofie Refer's first lamp and the first chapter in the story of a lighting designer who has maintained a focus on lighting ever since her student days. Refer (b. 1974) enrolled at The Danish Design School in 1998, and only two years later Unique Interior Copenhagen put her first luminaire into production: a naked bulb in a porcelain socket behind a transparent glass shade that both follows and enhances the shape of the socket and bulb as a composite object.

My first lamp was a romantic take on the old porcelain socket and the naked incandescent light bulb. In 1999, we were introduced to a variety of light bulbs and sockets as part of a student project. I was really fascinated with the increasingly rare porcelain socket and the carbon-filament bulb, which was also becoming obsolete. Both were beautiful in themselves and reminded me that when the incandescent bulb was first introduced, it was often used without a shade. Eventually, everything was covered. I was the first Danish designer to undress the light bulb again and present it in the socket, everything fully visible, covered only by a clear mouth-blown glass sphere that echoed the shape.[1]

The design students' prototypes were exhibited at Bella Center: 'The businessman Klaus Kastbjerg stopped by. He saw an innovative quality in my pendant, and it was soon put into production by Unique.'[2] Bulb quickly proved a success. The pendant received the 2001 GOOD DESIGN Award from the Museum of Architecture and Design in Chicago. In 2019, sales figures are still showing a slight upward trend. A sure sign of the lamp's success is the many knock-offs as well as closely related and further developed designs that followed in the wake of the incandescent light bulb pendant.

To Refer, Bulb was both a revelation and the beginning of a career in lighting design. After her graduation in 2003, she founded her own company, and in 2005 she brought in a partner, Jakob Stær, to form the lighting company Refer+Staer. With assistance from a manufacturer on the Danish island of Funen, Refer launched the Ice chandelier in London that same year. Ice consists of transparent mouth-blown glass orbs that are dyed, sanded and polished. Next, they are assembled into a cluster and hung from a canopy made of colour-anodized aluminium.[3] 'I wanted to make an attractive, exclusive whole; a chandelier in beautiful materials and with colours as a key aspect. It was particularly important for me to match the colour of the glass to the colour of the aluminium.'[4] The chandelier appeared in a variety of colours, but the blue was particularly successful. Ice Blue received *Wallpaper** magazine's 2006 Design Award for best lighting. It was seen as unique:

No one had ever done this before, clustering all these orbs and with a coloured canopy. Other lamps at the time all used either white glass or anodized aluminium without colour, and the canopy never matched the rest of the lamp. I wanted to reinterpret the classic chandelier, bringing its multiple light sources and shapes together in a beautiful and sensuous whole.[5]

Refer constantly challenges her Scandinavian functionalist background in her lighting design, where inspiration from nature adds a sense of generosity and extravagance to her expression. In 2006, Refer explained in the newspaper *Berlingske Tidende* how her designs incorporated traditional lavish and extravagant crystal chandeliers, only in a contemporary interpretation.[6] In 2019, she described how the shiny glass orbs give rise to an interplay of light that is akin to the effect of crystal chandeliers but with a simpler expression. Since Ice, she has continued on the same path: 'That has become my signature.'[7]

Bulb's transparent glass shade was designed to envelop a traditional bulb shape. Bulb and Mega Bulb are currently in production by &Tradition.

'I am trained in a functionalist tradition and have become known for simplicity and respect for the materials, but I also challenge the very functional approach. I and many in my generation were longing for a more sensuous quality. Not that the old Danish masters didn't make sensuous things, but there was a tendency for highly functional and minimalist design. A very puritanical approach that I didn't care for. It also wasn't what I saw in nature, which is overwhelming and full of joy and generosity. That shouldn't be removed, and in my lamps I want to bring that out.'—Sofie Refer, 2019[8]

Simon Karkov: Norm 69

Normann Copenhagen—2001

Throughout his long, prolific career, the architect Simon Karkov (1932–2017) worked in both others' and his own firms, specializing in building design and construction management. For a time, he also worked as a teacher at the Royal Danish Academy of Fine Arts, School of Architecture, under Vilhelm Wohlert.[1] In 2001, when Simon Karkov was 69 years old and in retirement, he suddenly became a household name when an old lamp design of his was pulled out of the archives and put into production by the newly founded company Normann Copenhagen. The pendant was named Norm 69, because buyers assemble the lamp themselves from 69 components, and because the design was completed in 1969.[2]

Jan Andersen (b. 1970) and Poul Madsen (b. 1971) had recently founded the design shop Normann Copenhagen on Strandboulevarden in Copenhagen's Østerbro district, 'and we had one lamp in the window', said Madsen in 2019:

One day, a sports car pulls up with screeching tyres, and an elderly gentleman with a long, white beard jumps out. He says, 'I have a friend who made a lamp that's much nicer than the one you have in the window. Are you interested?' Of course we are. He drives off and returns with a lamp that is yellow with age and full of pigeon droppings, because it has come straight from his attic. However, we recognize immediately that it has something – in fact, everything a Scandinavian lamp needs.[3]

Subsequently, Madsen and Andersen met the lamp's maker, Karkov, and began the process of putting it into production, drawing on Karkov's initial experiences.[4] The transparent plastic shade is flat-packed and comes with 12-point assembly instructions. When assembled, it forms a large, spherical body with 66 stylized cone-like scales. Experienced LEGO builders would be in their element, as the assembly requires no tools or glue. PH's exclusive Artichoke lamp conceals the light bulb behind 72 bent and angled individual shades in twelve vertical rows with six shades on each, mounted on a steel frame (see page 68). In Karkov's unpretentious DIY lamp, a 12-sided interior cylinder is clicked together and scales are mounted on top, which bends them into angular shapes in 11 different sizes, six of each, to end up with a rather robust sphere. Finally, the light bulb and socket are lowered into the interior cylinder and attached with two conical pieces, which are the last pieces to be folded and put into place. The socket is purchased separately. Thus, in principle, it is simply a lampshade, which was an advantage for the manufacturer: 'The box only contains the plastic components, so we didn't have to worry about whether the lamp was being sold in Japan, the United States or other countries with different standards than we have in Denmark.'[5]

Norm 69 was featured in *Bo Bedre* in 2001 under the heading 'Jigsaw Puzzle That Lights Up'.[6] That was exactly what it was, and the concept struck a chord: a home design object with a story that people could feel a sense of ownership with and thus make the story even more personal. The award-winning lamp was an instant success: 'It was out of control. We would pack as many lamps as we could every night – 300–400 pieces – and by the end of the next day, they would be gone.'[7] Madsen explains that the lamp provided the new business with important revenue and, equally importantly, a direction: 'We realized that this was the right track and put together a collection of simple quality designs by established designers that we could sell at an affordable price.'[8]

After the 1969 lamp was put into production, Karkov began to develop new self-assembly lamps. In 2006, Norm 06 was launched after a three-to-four-year development process. In Karkov's own words, 'When I get an idea, I first make a drawing, which is then turned into a model. I adapt the model over time, until the finished prototype is ready.'[9] For the smaller Norm 06, which is in 34 parts, Karkov also drew inspiration from nature, this time from lilies and water lilies, but Karkov, ever the architect, also wanted to work on a bigger scale: 'I dream of developing new ways to design furniture and large objects based on the self-assembly concept. The concept has to work on a large scale; that's what fascinates me.'[10] Karkov never realized that dream, but for Normann Copenhagen, Norm 69 had a large-scale impact indeed.

Medium-sized Norm 06 lamp. H: 30 x Ø: 62 cm.

'The construction of the lamp is so exact that a deviation of just a few millimetres in the stamping makes it difficult to assemble. It's very precisely calculated. I asked Simon how he had possibly managed to calculate all the different shade sizes. He just looked at me, puzzled, and asked me what I meant, since they were just simple mathematical calculations.'
—Poul Madsen, Normann Copenhagen, 2019[11]

Olafur Eliasson: Opera House Chandeliers

Olafur Eliasson—2004

In July 2019, a retrospective exhibition on the work of the Danish-Icelandic artist Olafur Eliasson (b. 1967) opened at Tate Modern in London. The exhibition presented works from the past three decades, going all the way back to Eliasson's early student days at the Royal Danish Academy of Fine Arts. Since graduating from the Academy in 1995, he has created numerous works where light plays a key role.

I have been working with light ever since my student days at the Royal Danish Academy of Fine Arts, working with daylight, LEDs and mono-frequency light and the way light is diffused, reflected and refracted. Several of my early works with electric light are actually on display at Tate Modern right now, including Window Projection *(1990), where I projected the silhouette of a window onto a wall,* Wannabe *(1991), a spotlight that forms a circle of light on the floor, and* Room for One Colour *(1997), which was one of my first works to use mono-frequency light, a light that reduces all the colours in a given room to shades of black and yellow. I used the same light when I did* The Weather Project *(2003).*[1]

Eliasson created the atmospheric art installation *The Weather Project* specifically for the converted former power plant on the Thames that houses Tate Modern. Eliasson filled the museum's large turbine hall with a light mist and installed a semicircular sun, made of yellow light bulbs, in the ceiling along with a mirror that completed the circle and thus brought the sun inside. Eliasson explains that the artificial sun was created by 'a semicircular form with more than 200 mono-frequency lamps that were reflected and doubled by an overhead mirror foil that covered the entire ceiling, doubling the size of the room. It was actually a fairly simple construction, which was part of the concept. I wanted people to be able to understand how the illusion was achieved'.[2] What most fascinated Eliasson about the project was how much the audience embraced it and made it their own: 'They spent a long time in the installation, sat on the floor and lay in the light of the artificial sun, looking at themselves in the mirror. People also began to collaborate to do things in this space, writing or drawing images.'[3] The artificial sun only illuminated the museum space in London for a limited time, but the following year three faceted spheres were installed in Copenhagen as decoration and lighting.

In late 2004, the prestige project of the new Opera House on the island of Holmen, in Copenhagen, was completed. As requested by the client, the shipping tycoon Mærsk Mc-Kinney Møller, the building was designed by Henning Larsen Architects; Møller wanted a world-class opera house, which called for world-class art. Thus, when the Opera welcomed the audience for its premiere show in 2005, three giant luminous and glittering works of art were suspended from the ceiling in the foyer.[4] Each luminous sphere measures just under three metres in diameter and is mounted in the ceiling on a long copper tube, the round shapes and straight lines matching the building's interior structure.[5]

Eliasson explains that he was contacted personally by Møller, who requested a work of art that integrated light. Echoing the globe-like form of the auditorium, the three luminous spheres bring a representation of the central, rounded space into the more stringent foyer: 'I did some sketches based on patterns you can find in nature, such as sea urchins and conches, which we then elaborated. The geometry is based on two sets of overlapping spirals, which in turn are overlaid with a three-dimensional pattern of triangular pieces of glass with dichromatic properties.'[6] Each sphere has 330 halogen light bulbs mounted on the inside of a spiralling copper construction that also holds 1,430 pieces of colour-effect glass. The glass varies in appearance with the angle of the light striking it, ranging from opaque to translucent, and filters the light, emitting mainly blue light into the room and warm yellow light onto the foyer floor. Thus, 'the colours of the glass vary with your vantage point'.[7] Due to the reflections from the glass, the orbs also sparkle in daylight, but it is when they are lit that they really come into their own. Illumination and art installations in one, the lamps went on to inspire new art projects.[8]

The Weather Project at Tate Modern in London, 2003.

'Since then, I have continued to experiment with different geometries and different types of glass, but the Opera House Chandeliers were actually the first of their type!'—Olafur Eliasson, 2019[9]

Louise Campbell: Campbell

Louis Poulsen—2004

PH's Septima, where the light bulb is shielded by a segmented, staggered pattern of matt and clear sections on the glass shades.

Although PH's main ambition was to design lighting for private homes, at the turn of the millennium the Louis Poulsen company, which was – and is – known primarily for PH's lamp system, mainly sold lighting solutions for public settings. To address this, in 2000 the company decided to develop a concept targeted at private homes, and to that end they contacted the young designer Louise Campbell (b. 1970). Campbell, who is now an acclaimed designer, was virtually a novice when it came to lighting, but she had a successful career, and in interviews she had expressed clear views on lighting design. That, and the fact that she was a woman, was the direct reason why Louis Poulsen chose to reach out to her.[1] From 2000, Campbell thus worked in Louis Poulsen's workshop, where her many ideas were refined through regular training in lighting engineering. Campbell describes the process:

Louis Poulsen has so many rules for what constitutes good lighting, because PH, the genius, worked for them: lamps must be glare-free, so the light source can't be in direct view. The shade should illuminate itself and must, of course, above all, produce excellent light: functional light as well as quality mood lighting.[2]

The previous pages have presented one lamp after another mostly designed by men. Hence, it should be pointed out that Louis Poulsen now deliberately went for a female designer. Campbell says that Louis Poulsen 'from an early stage had assigned me to the category of home design and showpieces intended to sell their other products'.[3] In 2004, the collaboration between designer and manufacturer had resulted in a number of showpieces, in the form of lighting studies, that were presented at the Danish furniture fair at Bella Center in 2004. The so-called Fatso prototypes were featured in the invitation to the exhibition. The ten lamps all consisted of two polyester bowls, a large exterior bowl enclosing a smaller interior one with a 2-cm gap in between. Campbell has inserted branches, leaves and other items into this gap to filter the light:

I had a thousand ideas but only one core thought in relation to Louis Poulsen: at an early stage, I decided that I would work with layers. Soft filtering of the light through multiple layers, that would be my approach. The task was all about respecting the spirit of the company, which is defined by PH's philosophies, but I was able to soften it.[4]

One lamp was ready for production, in Campbell's description the subtlest and most sober of the lot: the Campbell pendant. This lavish Fatso edition consists of two shades in clear mouth-blown glass. From 1927 to 1931, PH had developed the seven-shade pendant Septima, where the bulb is shielded by a staggered sectional pattern of matt and clear fields on the glass shade. Now, in 2004, Campbell was using wide, matt sandblasted stripes on the shades; by staggering the pattern on the two shades, she was able to shield the bulb and prevent glare. In this version, the gap between the shades is empty, as the light is broken up sufficiently by passing through them. The matt stripes add an interplay of shadows to produce a soft diffused light. The press release in connection with the launch pointed out that the lamp could be fitted with either a 60-watt incandescent light bulb or, as an alternative as early as 2004, a 16-watt energy-efficient bulb. The latter bulb, which is really a strip light, bent, with the two ends coming together in the socket, did not live up to the designer's criteria. Instead, she emphasized the importance of using an incandescent bulb to imitate filtered daylight:

The lamp was designed to hang centrally in a room to produce soft, diffuse shadows. The shadows on the lamp itself are more important than the shadows cast into the room, which are merely a pleasant side effect. The upwards and direct downwards light, however, remains completely undisturbed.[5]

For 11 years, the pendant remained available in shops to light up private living rooms. It was discontinued in early 2015.

'I will do whatever it takes to shield the naked light bulb. You never look directly into the sun; that's why I want to create filters.' —Louise Campbell[6]

Philip Bro Ludvigsen: UnderCover

Le Klint—2004

Sunflower, Model 190, Le Klint 2003.
→ The UnderCover pendant in the foreground, featuring the Isfahan interior shade designed by Philip Bro Ludvigsen in collaboration with Anne Tejg Holm.

In the early 1970s, the young architect Poul Christiansen had revolutionized existing perceptions of what a pleated Le Klint shade could look like; in 2004, the designer Philip Bro Ludvigsen (b. 1962) similarly challenged expectations of lamps from the renowned Danish design company.

Ludvigsen's path to lighting design began after his graduation, in 1989, from the School of Decorative Art.[1] A few months later, the Berlin Wall came down, the world was opening up, and three designer friends travelled to Czechoslovakia. There, at a chandelier factory in Bohemia, they created innovative lamps that combined modern halogen bulbs with classic crystal prisms.[2] After his return to Denmark, Ludvigsen also used the halogen bulb in the Le Klint table and floor lamps Model 395 and Model 396, which he created together with the designer Thomas Krause (b. 1959). The lamps, which were launched in 1995, were the first halogen lamps from Le Klint, but the shades were Espen Klint's simplification of the Fruit Lantern from 1949.

During the late 1990s, Ludvigsen designed several lamps for Le Klint using existing shades, but in 2003 he created an entirely new lamp design: Sunflower.[3] The Sunflower clearly references the characteristic pleated Le Klint shade, but the form was entirely new: a folded, horizontally floating flower that produces an indirect light because the pleats come together around an opalized acrylic disc. 'It was successful, but it was fitted with a round strip light that is not nearly energy-efficient enough for today's standards, so it has since been discontinued.'[4] However, the lamp itself is not obsolete, and perhaps new LED technology might make the sunflower blossom once more.

After a generational shift in 2001, Le Klint considered focusing more on the contract market: 'For the contract market, the pleated shades were too delicate; they simply weren't sturdy enough for high-volume public settings.'[5] The new CEO, Kim Weckstrøm Jensen, therefore welcomed Ludvigsen's idea for a new lamp where the pleated shade was enclosed in a strong acrylic exterior shade. Replicating the conical shape of the classic pleated design, the transparent shell had a folded-in lip that was just wide enough to enclose the pleated interior form. The biggest leap for the CEO was to approve the designer's innovative idea of also adding a collection of smooth interior shades in a variety of patterns and colours. Up to four interior shades could be added, combining the different colours and patterns. Kaare Klint had experimented with coloured pleated shades in 1944, but they never made it into retail, and since then the product line had been *entirely* white. Ludvigsen designed some of the interior shades himself: 'I am particularly pleased with the Isfahan cover. I drew on inspiration from Islamic ornamentation. The direct view of the bulb via the shiny fields gives rise to delicate, filigree shadows.'[6] Two textile designers were also involved in the project, and later the Finnish design brand Marimekko was commissioned to create interior shades based on Maija Isola's iconic poppy-print fabric.[7]

'When the lamps were launched, in 2004, they were very well received. They were not actually sold on the contract market but to private buyers, and the patterned and coloured foils proved very successful.'[8] In 2007, UnderCover received the prestigious Red Dot Design Award. The new design thus had both the blue stamp of approval from design critics and commercial success. The lamps provided sorely needed renewal for Le Klint without completely transforming the image of the esteemed purveyor to the Royal Danish Court. The pleated shades are still the hallmark of Le Klint, but UnderCover opened a parallel track of innovative lamp designs and matched millennial consumers' demands for interactive and personalized designs.

'The desire to design lighting also stems from a desire to create poetic designs. Something unique happens in the design process when you work with lighting. At some point, you switch on the light, and what happens is always a little unpredictable. If it is successful, the outcome is poetic. It inevitably brings out emotions, and that appeals to me.'—Philip Bro Ludvigsen, 2019

Cecilie Manz: Caravaggio

Lightyears—2005

In 2005, the new lighting manufacturer Lightyears presented 30 brand-new lamps at the Copenhagen International Furniture Fair at Bella Center. The large black pendant Caravaggio with the red cord attracted attention from day one and secured the company's bottom line. Today, as the lamp approaches its 15th anniversary, Caravaggio is considered a modern lamp icon.[1] It was created by the designer Cecilie Manz (b. 1972), who graduated in 1997 from The Danish Design School and founded her own design firm the following year. In 2004, she was contacted by a team that was rethinking and preparing to relaunch an existing lighting company.[2] The company's head of design had seen Manz's sketches and invited her to develop her first luminaires. The brief called for lamps for private homes that would also have a potential on the contract market.

'Good lighting involves a whole range of requirements, which I naturally had to consider. Functionality is an important aspect of design. Perhaps because these were my first lighting designs, I needed to start from scratch, with the light source at the centre, creating something very simple,' said Manz in 2019.[3] While PH hid the light bulb behind multiple shades to achieve glare-free lighting, Manz concealed it inside a deep but open shade: 'My design was based on the idea of leaving the small number of components that make up a lamp fully visible: the light source hanging from its cord, a shade wrapped around it, a visible mount. I wanted to integrate the cord into the lamp, so that the cord itself it illuminated. The shape of the shade was determined by what it needed to cover.'[4] Thus, the shade was shaped as a large cone that is wide enough to give the bulb ample space and deep enough to conceal it completely. At the top, the shade narrows to close in around the socket and mount, and 'I wanted a regular cover around the light source with a hole at the top and bottom'.[5] Most of the light is downwards, with a smaller amount escaping into the room at the top, reducing the contrast between light and dark areas. Just as the shade envelops the bulb, the light envelops the cord and mount. The mount is attached to both the socket and the shade and consists of three quarter-arc braces in matt metal that meet around the cord, serving as a sophisticated, illuminated pendant tube that keeps the lamp plumb.

Caravaggio came in two high-gloss-lacquer combinations: a white shade with a grey fabric cord and a black shade with a red fabric cord. At a time when many luminaires were white, the black-and-red variant in particular drew attention. Both versions had a white interior for optimal reflection, contrasting sharply with the shiny black exterior and the red cord, which further stood out because it was illuminated. After Manz and Lightyears had introduced this coloured fabric cord in Denmark, others quickly followed suit, creating a regular trend. Today, it is difficult to imagine just how striking the cord was at the fair in 2005.[6]

Manz pursues a minimalistic expression, and for the 2005 fair she had also designed the table lamp Mondrian, which consists simply of four thin metal tubes that form the base, stem and arm with an integrated lamp head.[7] The lamp was deliberately made in the thinnest tubes possible, fitted with the smallest bipin halogen bulb available and lacquered white to be almost invisible against a white wall. Unsurprisingly, it was overshadowed by the 70-cm-tall distinctive pendant lamp – named after the baroque painter Caravaggio (1571–1610), who was known for brightly lit figures on a dark background[8] – and with the Caravaggio lamp, Manz introduced a new style in Danish lighting design. The series, which featured pendants in five sizes, was popular both in Denmark and abroad.[9] Since 2008, Caravaggio has also been available with a white opal glass shade, which emits a diffuse light through the enveloping shade and makes the lamp itself a luminous object.[10] The series originally included a table and a floor lamp as well, but in 2016, in collaboration with Fritz Hansen, the Caravaggio series was expanded to include the Read series in matt grey lacquer: a new table lamp, floor lamp and wall lamp.[11] Read is a successful extension of Caravaggio, which, based on simple aesthetic form elements, was conceived from the outset as a functional solution.

Mondrian, which is constructed in the thinnest possible tubing, has a cast collar around the small bipin bulb that controls the direction of the light and prevents glare.

'When you design the components of a pendant lamp, you have a cord, a socket, a bulb and, last but not least, a shade that is fastened around the bulb. In Caravaggio, I wanted all the components to be visible, except for the bulb.'
—Cecilie Manz, 2019[12]

Jørn Utzon: Opera

Lightyears—2005

'The architect must have an ability to imagine and to create, an ability that is sometimes called fantasy, sometimes dreams.'—Jørn Utzon, 1948[1]

After graduating in 1942 from the Royal Danish Academy of Fine Arts, Jørn Utzon moved to Stockholm, where he connected with other Danish expats, among them PH, the master of lighting. When Utzon returned to Denmark after the war, he supplemented his income by making lamps. While PH's glare-free solution was achieved by means of shades that controlled and reflected the light, Utzon allowed for direct downwards light, upwards light and, not least, light cast onto the luminaire itself, bringing out its form (see also pages 60–61).

Before Utzon established his own firm in 1957, when he won the international competition for the Sydney Opera House, he had a joint studio with the brothers Erik and Henry Andersson in Helsingborg, Sweden. This involved many ferry trips across the narrow strait between Denmark and Sweden, and during the crossing Utzon would often stand on the deck, looking at the train carriages on the lower deck. He was fascinated by the ventilation cowls on the train-car roofs spinning in the wind as the vertical slats caught the wind.[2] In the lamp, Utzon paraphrased the effect with a series of slats or shades arranged to emit downwards light through the opening, while light emitted through the gaps in between the shades illuminates the lamp itself. At the bottom, the slats were joined together and joined to a rib at the lower edge of the lamp with visible mounting screws that revealed the construction. The luminaire, which was given the obvious name Visir (Visor) is an example of Utzon's lamp design experiments, some of which were put into production, while others remained as prototypes or were only made in small series.[3] The latter was the case with Visir, which was briefly included in Nordisk Solar Compagni's catalogue during the late 1950s.[4]

Another lamp experiment that never reached retail can be seen in Utzon's *Gesamtkunstwerk* Bagsværd Church, which was built in 1973–1976. Ten years earlier, Utzon had come up with the idea of placing a series of clear, unshielded incandescent light bulbs side by side in a long perforated aluminium tube. Because the bulbs were connected in pairs, the voltage was only 110, rather than the standard 220. The dimmer light was pleasant to the eyes, and the design created 'a poetic garland effect'.[5] Showing a bare light bulb ran counter to the idea behind PH's shade systems, but Utzon wanted to achieve a candle-like effect that works perfectly in the church. Here, the aluminium tubes, each with 18 bulbs, are placed in rows lining the aisles, and the staff refer to them as 'runner lights'.[6] Like everything else in the building, they are not built into the wall but mounted on it, providing full transparency of construction.

Most of Utzon's lamp production took place during the early years of his career, but in connection with the launch of the new lighting company Lightyears in 2005, two of his older experiments were revisited, with Utzon's approval. One was Visir, which was recreated as close to the original design form as possible, based on photos.[7] In 2005, the lamp was renamed Opera. Also in 2005, another of Utzon's early experiments was relaunched in a revised version under the name Concert. The reference is obvious, and the lamps may be seen to reflect a dynamic, architectural shell principle.[8]

The Concert lamp is also interesting in another comparison with PH's designs. PH often used rods or stays to connect the shades in his multi-shade lamps, but Utzon wanted to do without these. Instead, he mounted the shades on an experimental glass core, which could be turned upside down if needed. Mounted directly on the glass core, the shades seemed to float when the lamp was lit. Utzon's original model was intended for CFLs, compact fluorescent lamps. The 2005 version was based on Jørn Utzon's ideas but redesigned by Jan Utzon, in collaboration with Lightyears, to match an ordinary bulb shape in an E27 socket. Thus, the Concert pendant is constructed on a conical glass core with steps that the four aluminium shades rest on. The glass core is connected to a base plate in frosted glass that diffuses the light, preventing glare even if the pendant is hung high. In 1948, Jørn Utzon declared, 'It is necessary to be in tune with the age and with the surroundings.'[9] Today, the floating shades thus form an updated, contemporary Utzon pendant.[10]

The Concert pendant from 2005 is a further development of an older prototype.

Stig Gerlach: LED candle

Sirius—2005

Increasingly, the paraffin-coated LED lights are finding their way into Danish homes.

Danish lamp design has emerged in a dialogue with international trends and developments, but one particular challenge and motivation for Danish designers is the demand for a cosy atmosphere, known in Danish as *hygge*, in the home. The *hygge* expert Jeppe Trolle Linnet points out that the candle is the one item most commonly mentioned by Danes as a component of *hygge*; he mentions that Denmark has the world's highest per capita consumption of candles, with the average Dane buying 3.5 kg of candles a year.[1] Candles *do* make for a cosy atmosphere, but the live flame is a fire hazard, and candles emit particles with harmful effects on indoor climate and health. One alternative in particular has become increasingly widespread in recent years: battery-operated flameless candles. They emit no harmful substances, and they can be used in places where a live flame would be reckless or is not allowed, for example in nurseries or nursing homes.

The flameless candle was created by Stig Gerlach. He did not design a new form but used the classic shapes that Danes are familiar with; the innovation lies in the combination: 'I integrated the gently flickering diode flame into the form of the classic candle, and I own that patent.'[2]

The candle – or lamp – is shaped like a pillar candle and has a plastic core and a battery chamber at the bottom. From the battery chamber, wires lead up to the diode flame at the top. Everything is encased in paraffin, even the 'flame' is embedded in the wax. It is half concealed behind an uneven, translucent rim of paraffin that resembles the way a classic pillar candle burns. The rim shields the diode, which is further encapsulated in the flame-like moving component. When the candle is lit, the flame moves gently back and forth. Seen from a distance, the illusion is almost perfect. 'We put an extreme amount of effort into perfecting the way the light strikes the flame component, so the shadows seem authentic.'[3]

Authenticity is a key term. When the diode goes from being inside a lamp to creating the effect of a candle, dressed with a layer of paraffin, and the LED bulb is shaped and presented as a flickering flame in an attempt to optimize the cosy atmosphere, opinion is sharply divided. Has it become an inauthentic kitsch object? Gerlach's key point is that his design solution is an adaptation to the possibilities of a new era: 'It actually *is* a wax candle where the wick has been replaced with contemporary lighting technology.'[4]

The sale of flameless LED candles has increased sharply in recent years. The main reason is that the 'flames' have become very life-like, and the colour of the light has become warmer. Gerlach explains that increased awareness of climate issues has also played a part: 'We sell 1.7 million of these candles in Europe annually, the vast majority of them in Denmark, so after a period of adaptation the Danes have definitely embraced them.'[5]

Today, the product range includes pillar candles, taper candles, tealights and small Christmas-tree candles. The tealight came first, while the Christmas-tree candle is the latest addition. The small, slender Christmas-tree candles, which fit into people's existing collections of candle holders, is switched on with a remote control, as are many of the other models: 'The first thing I do in the morning is to light a couple of candles with the remote. It's easy, and it has an integrated timer, so the candles switch themselves off. With a quality battery they can go on for months.'[6]

LEDs have many advantages, not least the elimination of harmful particles and the need to worry about whether one remembered to blow out the candle. They also eliminate the need to constantly buy new candles: 'The LED wick lasts for ever, so it's really an everlasting candle – except, in the long term, the paraffin will become porous, so the candle itself will probably perish long before the flame. A completely inverted situation!'[7]

'Diodes can go into anything. I put them and the wire into paraffin to replace the wick and created a candle that is a lamp. The battery lets you take the candle with you and place it anywhere you like.'
—Stig Gerlach, 2019[8]

Louise Campbell: Collage

Louis Poulsen—2005

Ornamentation is making a comeback in the 21st century: the pattern for the Collage lamps was carved out using a high-precision laser technique that was also used to make Louise Campbell's Prince chair (Hay 2002). The circular openwork pattern on the three staggered shades gives rise to a complex interplay of motifs and glare-free light.

Louise Campbell's earliest lamp designs were inspired by natural light and memories of the carefree days of childhood, lounging on her back on soft moss, looking up at the interplay of light and shade in the foliage of the tree crowns: 'This ever-changing pattern is perfect, because it cannot be controlled, and complete, because it is in constant, gentle motion – it is virtually impossible for a design to match that.'[1] It was these flickering effects that the impressionists sought to capture in their paintings during the latter half of the 19th century. They also served as the challenging basis of Campbell's design of the Collage pendant.

The initial prototypes for Collage were presented at the furniture exhibition at Bella Center in 2004, where they were so well received that Louis Poulsen decided to put them into production immediately. However, the path from the prototype to a version suited for mass production proved long. It required the rapid development of a brand-new technology for laser-cutting patterns in three sizes of acrylic sheets that could subsequently be bent into a circular form, staggered precisely in relation to each other and assembled. Another challenge lay in making the simple pattern, which consists of elliptical formations, to generate captivating shadow effects while also ensuring glare-free light.

While the Campbell pendant (see page 170) features a two-layered glass shade, the Collage pendant, like the classic PH lamp, had a triple-shade structure. However, the interactions between the three staggered openwork acrylic shades give rise to a complex pattern. When the lamp is switched on, the luminous pattern resembles the effect of sunlight being filtered through the foliage. The project was a success, and the investment into the development of new technology paid off, as the lamp with the beautiful interplay of light and shade was also commercially successful.

In 2005, *Bo Bedre* selected Louise Campbell as Designer of the Year, and the Collage pendant was launched in white, pink, blue, green and smoke-coloured. In 2007, a further two colours were added: yellow and orange. With the brightly coloured monochrome shades – three on each pendant – Collage seemed to bring the PH lamp and Panton's Flowerpot together in a lamp for the 2000s. It further reintroduced the use of ornamentation, which had been virtually banned from 20th-century industrial product design, in order to add an element of storytelling that matched the philosophy behind modern home design for the new millennium. In a comment on ornamentation, Campbell argued that although it had returned, it had become fleeting and fragmented. She also underscored that it always served a functional purpose in her design:

A point that I often struggle to get across is that there is always a reason for any ornamentation in my designs. It adds a function, in one way or another. I don't dress things up. But I also can't stand the completely pared-down look. I want light that's alive, full stop; that's my secret recipe: light that is alive and atmospheric.[2]

That is Campbell's definition of the main purpose of lighting. And that does not change whether the lamps aim to reproduce the soft, warm light filtering through the foliage in a summer forest or the winter light among the snowflakes. And it was in fact winter light that provided the inspiration for Campbell's next lamp, Snow (see pages 186–187).

In 2009, Collage 600, which has a diameter of 60 cm and also came as a floor lamp, was supplemented with a smaller version, Collage 450. The floor lamp is no longer in production, while the pendant, in two sizes, is still available, but only in white.

'I'm fascinated by designing with shadow effects. The shadows are at least as important as the light in a lamp design; the two are inseparable. Still, shadows are a completely neglected aspect of lamp design.'—Louise Campbell, 2005[3]

Tom Rossau: TR7

Tom Rossau—2005

In the TR36 table lamp from 2019, the light bulb is enclosed behind overlapping strips of polycarbonate, creating an interplay of light and shadow similar to the eaect in the veneer lamps.

Tom Rossau (b. 1970) is a self-taught designer. 'Originally, I wanted to be an engineer, but then I bought a motorcycle and travelled the world.'[1] In 1997, Rossau opened a shop on Istedgade in central Copenhagen, mainly selling leather clothes of his own design as well as the shop furnishings, which he also designed. Since 2004, Rossau has mainly designed lamps in veneer. His first collection, which included four veneer lamps, was finished in 2005. In 2006, it was launched at the annual Copenhagen International Furniture Fair at Bella Center, where the TR7 model was voted the Årets Publikumsfavorit (Audience's Favourite).[2] At the time, birch-veneer lamps were a novelty, but contemporary trends favoured the design: natural materials were coming into focus, Scandinavian design was again attracting attention around the world and Rossau's Danish lamps made of Finnish birch wood were also appealing to an international audience.[3]

Rossau's veneer pendants are a physical triumph in terms of utilizing the properties of this natural material, challenging the limitations and potential of the thin strips of wood. The material was central in defining both the design and the light: 'My main focus was not on the light; my initial focus was on material and form, a desire to create a sculptural expression and get the proportions right.'[4] TR7 is made up of 20 long three-ply slats of birch veneer that come together around two round cores. 'First, they are attached to one of the cores, then the whole thing is turned around and they are attached to the other core. When it is stood on end, they displace and a spiral form emerges.'[5] The form is mounted on a long steel tube that keeps the two ends of the shade in place. The tube runs through the centre of the form and is bent to make room for a socket and light source in the middle, creating a symmetrical distribution of light:

I think there's a beauty to simple forms, since anyone who sees the lamp will recognize what it is. It's very honest: 20 strips of veneer curved in an S-shape and, when you see the form as a whole, an hourglass form. Thanks to the geometry and the number and width of the slats, the light source is properly shielded. The translucent veneer produces a soft, golden light. The light is emitted both through the gaps between the slats and, not least, through the slats themselves. The TR7 is not a reading lamp; it provides a cosy atmospheric light.[6]

Rossau designed the TR7 at a time when people were struggling to filter the cold light from the energy-efficient light bulbs: 'The birch veneer softens the blueish light. The effect is amazing. So are the textural quality and the inherent lightness and strength of the material.'[7]

Rossau's many lamps, mainly in veneer, are produced and displayed in Rossau's premises on Frederiksberg Allé.[8] There is a magical quality to Rossau's sculptural lamp universe – in his own words, something 'slightly infantile, because my approach to the design process is playful. I capture my ideas in a quick sketch, and then I work with the veneer strips to build the prototypes'.[9] This playful expression is particularly pronounced in his Model 747, a pendant with an aeronautical theme, as indicated by the name, and a nod to Ingo Maurer. In the lamp, which has a total circumference of 80 cm, 32 birch-veneer planes – folded like paper aeroplanes – mounted on thin metal rods circle a free-hanging light source, which is thus part of the object and the experience. The bulb becomes a sphere, encircled by the planes, casting light and shadows into the room.[10]

At *Salone del Mobile Euroluce* in Milan in April 2019, Rossau presented the table lamp TR36. Its cylindrical shade floats on a rectangle made of bent metal tubing welded onto a square made of the same type of tube. The geometric forms contrast the light. The shade is made of overlapping strips of polycarbonate, whose coarse polyethylene fibres diffuse soft light into the room. As in the veneer lamps, the overlap creates an interplay of light and shadow that contributes to defining the luminous form.[11] Anyone buying a TR36, a TR7 or a TR747 will take home a design made at Rossau's workshop on Frederiksberg Allé: 'It's a small company, the logistics make sense and I think we tell a good story. The label "Handmade in Denmark" is not just a cliché; you can see it for yourself if you look in the window.'[12]

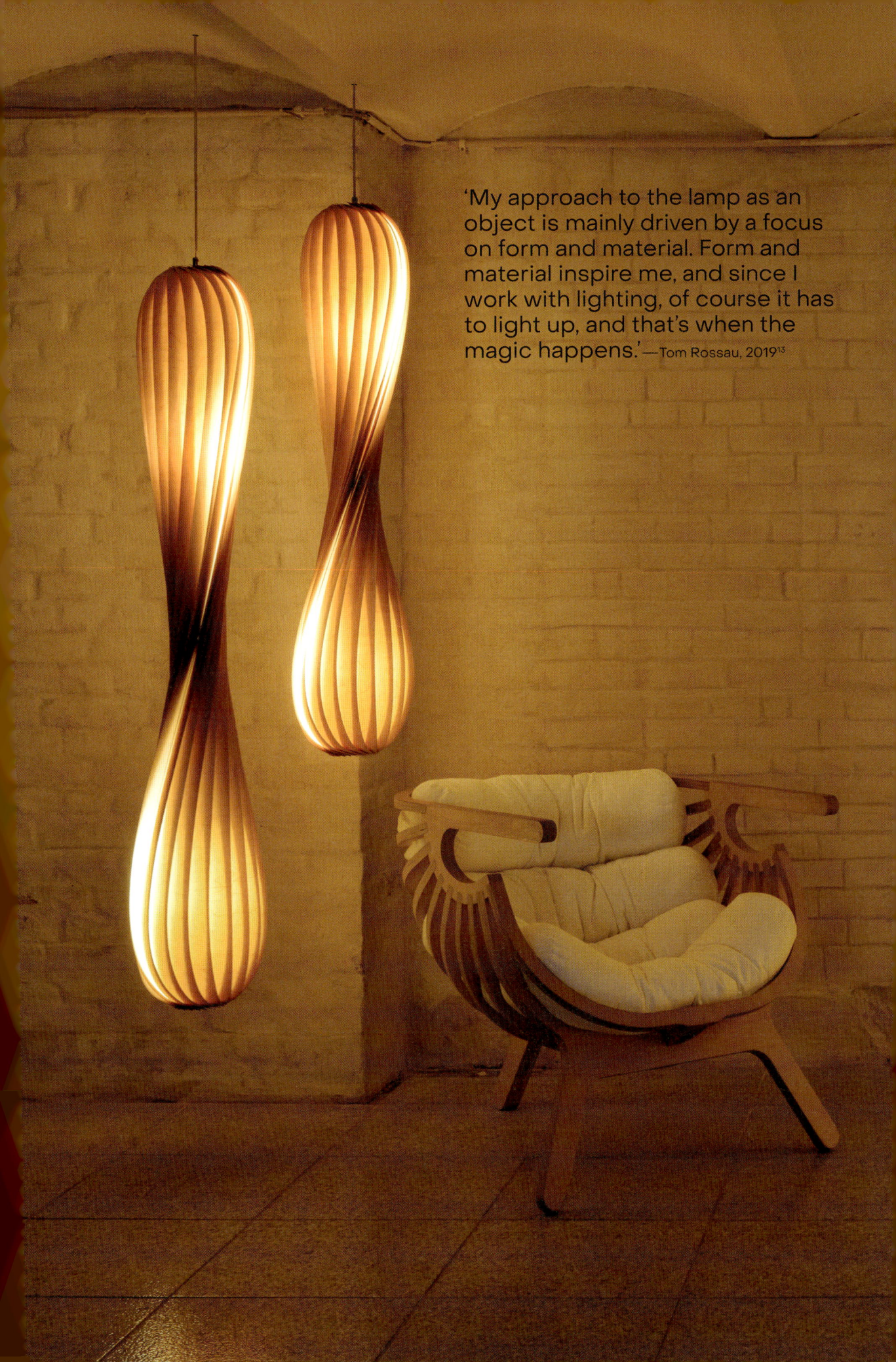

'My approach to the lamp as an object is mainly driven by a focus on form and material. Form and material inspire me, and since I work with lighting, of course it has to light up, and that's when the magic happens.'—Tom Rossau, 2019[13]

Poul Christiansen: Elysion

Le Klint—2006

The architect Poul Christiansen designed his first lamp for Le Klint in 1967, and up to 1975 he created several additional SinusLine lamps. For a number of years after that, Christiansen focused on architecture, but he never quite ended his design collaboration with Le Klint. In 2003, the popular Model 172 came out in a 'Giant' edition, and Christiansen also designed the drop-shaped Model 181, his first to reference Kaare Klint's cross-pleated Fruit Lantern (see page 56). 'Apart from that, I deliberately held back, because I didn't want to repeat myself. I didn't want to water down the design.'[1]

It was pleating, not lighting, that had been the architect's main focus, and in terms of lighting engineering the lamps were not revolutionary. The SinusLine lamps emit a softly diffused light with few shadows, but the shadow play on the lamps themselves makes them intriguing. Over time, the light itself became more of a priority. In 2006, Christiansen created an architectural lighting sculpture with an almost cultish expression. It was named Elysion – the name of the mythological Islands of the Blessed, where the Greek gods would send deserving departed souls, as well as a play on the Danish word 'lys' for light.[2] The lamp sparks associations to the human figure, to elegantly sculpted minarets and to new computer-generated organic architecture.[3]

The first Elysion lamps were created as one-off models for a special exhibition in the large lobby at Bella Center, in Copenhagen. Christiansen now used 'computer programs to generate the wavy lines and curves'.[4] One of the models was put into production just under two years later, challenging Le Klint's concept as well as the company's production method by emphasizing sculptural expression over functional considerations and by being cut into shape. This violated the rule that all Le Klint lamps had to be folded from a single rectangular sheet. The floor lamp is made of the same sheet plastic as Le Klint's other lamps, only in a slightly heavier quality. Like the other lamps, it is hand-folded. The four sides are joined together to close the form, generating an overlap that had to be glued. The joint was turned into a decorative element: a curvy line that is invisible until the lamp is switched on. The light from the lamp proved a major challenge:

I wanted to use LEDs, but it was difficult to distribute the light properly, and at the time, it was also a costly light source. Ultimately, we used a strip light in a clear acrylic tube that is attached to the bottom and held in place by a thin, clear acrylic halo at the top. The tube stands apart inside the lamp, but of course the light is brighter where the lamp is narrowest.[5]

The large shade and the strip light socket are attached to a metal plate that has an on/off switch with a dimmer. In 2008, an outdoor version of Elysion was launched. Again, it necessitated technological innovation, as it was rotation-moulded in plastic. The outdoor lamp too can be dimmed, by remote control. 'An outdoor lamp should always have a dimmer function.'[6]

The latest lamp to date is Calabash from 2010, a co-design in collaboration with Christiansen's business partner Boris Berlin for the Lightyears company. The lamp has a shiny, open shade but the same curves as the many Le Klint lamps: 'A lamp shade should enclose and shield the light, but it is still present in the room after the light has been switched off. Calabash has an organic, convex double-curvature form and a shiny, mirror-like surface that reflects the entire room.'[7] Christiansen continuously creates new designs, and a new lamp is due to launch soon, from another manufacturer.

'Light is one of the most important factors. A completely uniform grey sky still provides light but no shadows. Everything looks flat, and that's where the light from a lamp comes in; it should cast shadows, it should bring variation to the lighting and the lamp should be nice to look at.'—Poul Christiansen, 2019[8]

The Calabash pendants from 2010 were developed in collaboration with Boris Berlin.
→ The Elysion floor lamp was launched in a version for outdoor use in 2008.

Louise Campbell: Snow

Louis Poulsen—2008

The cover of Bo Bedre's November 2008 edition announced 'Spotlighting home design trend number 1: new lamps with attitude'. Inside, the magazine wrote that while lamps had for some time been, and still were, 'sculptural and dominant, another theme waiting just around the corner is lamps with a poetic and personal manifesto'.[1] One of the new lamp designs featured in the article represents both attitude and poetry: Louise Campbell's floor lamp Snow.

In 2013, Louise Campbell was photographed for *Wallpaper** magazine under the almost two-metre-tall chandelier Nervous Zénith.

The inspiration for the 150-cm-tall floor lamp was the bright light on a snowy day in Denmark. The lamp consists of two conical forms put together, the larger cone acting as the lamp base and the smaller one the lamp head. The two conical elements are made of vacuum-formed clear acrylic with added silk-screen prints of snowflakes that shield the light bulb. A heavy circular counterweight — shaped like a snow ball! — hangs freely suspended, centred inside the larger cone, stabilizing the lamp and enabling a minimal use of materials.

Campbell describes the technical aspects of the solution as sublime, for which she credits the skilled engineers involved in the project. Of the process of finding the right design to shield the light bulb, she says, 'I glued every single one of the many snowflakes on by hand very precisely'.[2] While Campbell took an almost impressionist approach in her design of Collage (see page 180), she now followed in the footsteps of the pointillists. Shielded by the snowflakes, the resulting light had prominent shadow effects: the two aspects of lighting that are inseparable in Campbell's design.

Campbell mentions that all her design solutions are handmade at some point in the process. She had prior experience with hand-crafting lamps from a series of bowl-shaped lamps, MyMoon, that she created together with the designer Malene Reitzel for an exhibition in 1998. The lamps, which were made of fibreglass and latex, drew inspiration from the light of the moon, their uneven surface intended to resemble the craters in the lunar surface and to break the light and reproduce the unique shadow effects of moonlight.

Snow was launched in 2009, coinciding with the onset of the finance crisis and the resulting economic pessimism and reduction in consumer spending, and sales of the exclusive lamp to private buyers never really took off. The form is debatable, and the 'sculptural and dominant' lamp has both its fans and its detractors. Although this is the one of Campbell's lamps for Louis Poulsen that has the least in common with PH's lamp system, it clearly does shield the bulb. Thus it lives up to the general lighting principles that PH formulated when he constructed a rationally determined multi-shade lamp. There is also no doubt that the dance of the many snowflakes on the acrylic shades represents, if not a 'poetic manifesto', certainly a poetic story. It is not a modest design, and as a design solution the functional purpose of the lamp is combined with a very clear, almost dominant, element of storytelling.

In 2013, Campbell designed another extravagant lamp: the two-metre-tall crystal chandelier Nervous Zénith for the French manufacturer of crystal glassware Baccarat.[3] In 2019, it is still Campbell's most recent lamp. The huge showpiece features 48 light bulbs hidden behind silk shades and, at the very top, a single traditional wax candle as a direct reference to traditional chandeliers. Thus, while daylight and moonlight provided the inspiration for Campbell's earlier lamp designs, the chandelier is a reference to lighting from earlier times. Without any hint of functionalist ideology, it is also anything but democratic but instead a lavish and non-rational lighting design. A foreign-made, priceless showpiece, far removed from the PH lamp system and other Danish lamp designs.

'Sometimes it's nice to be able to make a big gesture.'—Louise Campbell[4]

Salto & Sigsgaard: Nosy

Lightyears—2008

When the architect Thomas Sigsgaard (b. 1966) and the designer Kasper Salto (b. 1967) began what would become a successful and award-winning partnership, their objective was to develop a working lamp: 'It began back in 2001 – our first joint project.'[1] The lamp arose from a specific need for good lighting that it would be a pleasure to work with and in. An additional motivation was a common desire to offer an alternative to the traditional anglepoise lamp, which had remained largely unchanged since it first appeared.

Nosy sprang from our immediate need for a working lamp that you could simply grip and intuitively adjust. The Luxo lamp was an image of the types we wanted to move past: it's a little old-fashioned, with its crane function, and consists of about 50 components. We felt it had to be possible to renew the anglepoise lamp. We wanted a completely no-nonsense lamp, simple and in one piece.[2]

The lamp head and base are made of polycarbonate, a strong lightweight and heat-resistant synthetic material. The two ends of the lamp are connected by a long, slender, flexible body that appears to be nothing more than a lamp cord, simply and elegantly twisting and bending. Inside is a steel (cannula) tube that extends from the base to the lamp's highest point, where it connects with a flex tube. This construction lets the user move the cord and the lamp head in any direction. Flex tubes are common in lamps; the new feature was that the cord that has to extend from the base to the socket actually looked like a cord:

What does it take to make a bulb light up? An electric cord. Full stop. That was the task and the simplification in relation to the anglepoise lamp. That's why the flex tube had to be as thin as possible, so it wouldn't look like a water hose but as a cord. That effect was crucial for the design.[3]

The body has a rubberized exterior to imitate the expression of the cord and to tie the head, body and base into a simple, organic whole, an effect that is underscored by the ability of the flexible body to bend and turn in any direction. The lamp looks virtually alive, an impression that is heightened by the name, Nosy – almost creating the impression that the lamp is curiously searching for something on the desk that needs lighting. The slender, lightweight funnel-shaped shade that encloses the bulb and directs the light has two rectangular heat-regulating 'eye sockets', which further adds to the lamp's animal appearance. The light can be adjusted by a ring-shaped touch-control dimmer switch placed centrally on the lamp base.

The path to a no-nonsense design proved complicated and long; Nosy was not finished until 2008, when it was launched by Lightyears. As for the light source, the light from LEDs was 'still lousy' at the time, so the lamp was fitted with a 35-watt halogen bulb in a GO635 socket, which has since been almost completely phased out. While Nosy still appears 'simple and modern', changes in lighting technology, regrettably, led to it being discontinued. In 2008, Salto & Sigsgaard created the innovative Wet Bell pendant with an LED. Later, Lightyears handed the duo a brief for a pendant with an energy-efficient light bulb. While the development of Nosy was lengthy and arduous and turned into an ongoing endeavour alongside other projects, the new lamp, Juicy, was ready after six months and has remained in production since 2011. A targeted design effort aimed at accommodating a specific light source challenge is the common denominator for all three lamps.

After Juicy, Salto & Sigsgaard turned to other areas of design for a while. At the time of writing, they are once again working on exciting new lighting projects, but it all began with Nosy:

Nosy was our first joint product, and it really helped shape our design philosophy. There has to be a need that we can meet. We never do form for form's sake. Design has to be relevant, and it's important to us, from a design-history point of view, to keep moving forward.[4]

Salto & Sigsgaard compare the principle behind the lamp to the anatomy of a snake: the animal's strong muscles along a flexible skeleton give it the strength and agility to bend and hold itself up, similar to the arm of the Nosy lamp.

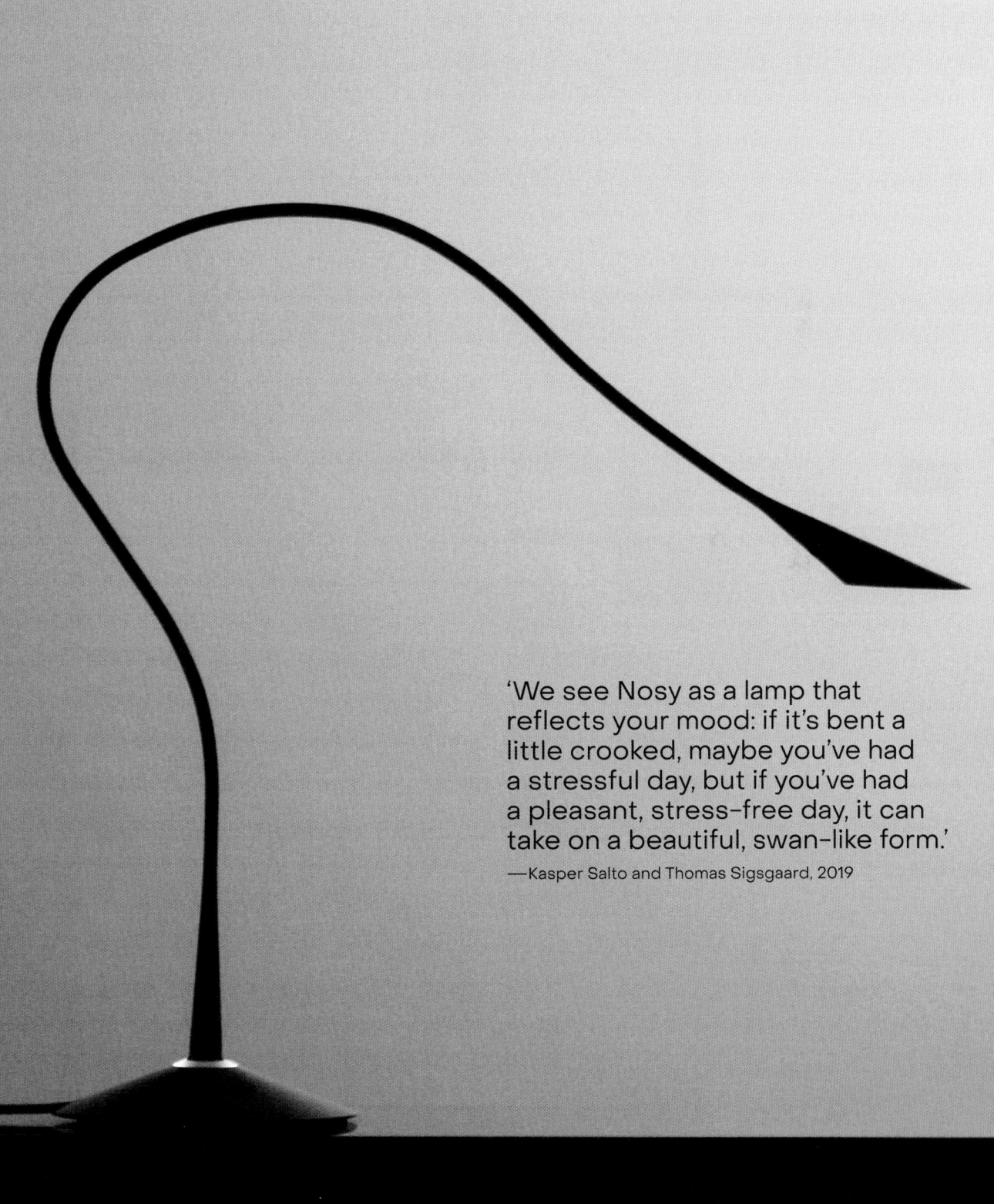

'We see Nosy as a lamp that reflects your mood: if it's bent a little crooked, maybe you've had a stressful day, but if you've had a pleasant, stress-free day, it can take on a beautiful, swan-like form.'
—Kasper Salto and Thomas Sigsgaard, 2019

Salto & Sigsgaard: Wet Bell

Salto & Sigsgaard—2009

Juicy (2008) was originally designed for an energy-eaicient light bulb.

After the launch of Kasper Salto and Thomas Sigsgaard's working lamp Nosy, the duo designed another lamp, where the cord played a central role, now from a position under a large parabolic shade with an LED light source. Wet Bell was presented at the Danish MINDCRAFT exhibition in Milan in 2009.

Danish Crafts asked us to make a piece for MINDCRAFT in 2009. We wanted to create a piece that was also a design solution, and the brief we gave ourselves called for an LED lamp. Unlike the working lamp, it should avoid stark shadows and emit a reflected light. Also, we wanted to avoid the blueish tint that LEDs had at the time. So we decided to have the light source facing up and to construct something around it to reflect the light.[1]

Salto and Sigsgaard therefore used an LED light source which they turned up to face the parabolic shade, which reflected the light into the room. To add a warm tone to the reflected light, the interior of the shade was lacquered a reddish white.

Then we had to get a cord to the light source, and we didn't want to make a hole in the shade; we had created a real obstacle for ourselves with that, but it turned into design, and we love that! That way, when people ask, 'How did you come up with that?' the answer isn't just 'Because we thought it looked neat ...'. No, it is the result of a series of rational decisions during the process. It is extremely important to us that there is a logic behind a product, and there is no aspect of this design that came about by chance.[2]

Salto and Sigsgaard underscore that this is how they always work and that they make all the decisions during the design process together: 'Everything we do has a rational explanation; ultimately, it all has to come together in a coherent story – but never storytelling for the sake of the story. We also never make an important choice without both of us being present, and we keep working in tandem until we reach the stage where it's just about working out the practical details.'[3]

As for the cord, the solution was to have it run on the outside of the lamp rather than through it. Thus, instead of suspending the shade from the cord, they have the cord hold up the shade. The innovative pendant design appealed to the Italian manufacturer CASSINA-Nemo, whose representatives saw Wet Bell in Milan and subsequently put the large pendant into production.

In 2008, the European Union passed a regulation that gradually phased out incandescent light bulbs in favour of either energy-efficient diodes or the energy-efficient light bulb, a small bent strip light. The latter was the preferred solution at the time in industry and public settings. It was also the light source Lightyears had in mind when they followed up on their collaboration with Salto and Sigsgaard on the table lamp Nosy, which used a bipin bulb. This time, the company wanted a pendant for an energy-efficient bulb. Sigsgaard and Salto wanted to make a low-maintenance pendant in every regard because it was intended, in part, for public settings: 'It had to be easy to clean, and it was; it is streamlined, shiny and smooth and easy to wipe down. The shade has a bayonet joint so it can be taken apart in a split second when the light bulb is replaced.' The joint is clearly visible, not least when the lamp is lit, highlighted as a luminous ring. The pendant can be hung high, because the bottom is capped with a honeycomb filter, which concentrates the light, makes it glare-free and gives the cool light from the energy-efficient bulb a softer, warmer tone.[4] The Juicy pendant was launched in 2011 and has remained in continuous production, although it now has a traditional E27 socket for an LED light source.[5]

Nosy, Wet Bell and Juicy were all created as solutions to a light source challenge: 'The only light source we never made a design for was the incandescent light bulb.' It had become obsolete.[6]

'When we began to work on Wet Bell, we said to each other that the incandescent light bulb is dead, so we had to turn to diodes.'
—Kasper Salto and Thomas Sigsgaard, 2019[7]

Ole Jensen: OJ lamp

Louis Poulsen—2010

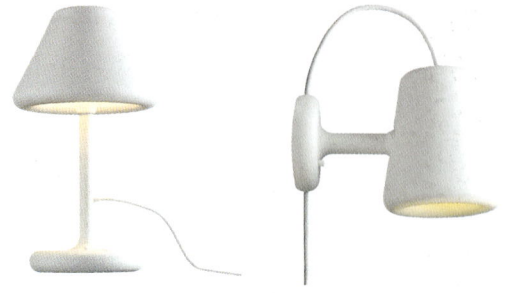

OJ table lamp and OJ wall lamp of white lacquered metal, where both the white fabric cord and the classic, elegant switch on the base are important integrated design features.

The ceramicist and designer Ole Jensen (b. 1958) graduated from Kunsthåndværkerskolen (the School of Arts and Crafts) in Kolding in 1985 and subsequently attended the Royal Danish Academy of Fine Arts, Schools of Visual Art, in Copenhagen: 'In Kolding, I honed my craftsmanship; at the Academy, I developed an awareness of what it means to be an independent maker. Today, I see myself as a ceramicist and a designer and prefer to have my work interpreted through that lens.'[1] Throughout his career, Ole Jensen has challenged form and design with innovative solutions for everyday life. Among his best-known designs are porcelain for Royal Copenhagen and a dustpan and, not least, a rubber washing-up bowl for Normann Copenhagen. The latter was launched in 2002 and became a design icon for the inescapable quality of everyday life.[2]

In 2007, the lighting company Louis Poulsen asked Jensen to design a lamp for private homes: 'My basic idea was that as a lamp for home use, it should have a clearly homely expression. A textural effect that was homely, warm and cosy.'[3] The manufacturer's only requirement was that it accommodate an energy-efficient light bulb; however, the sharp light from this twisted or bent strip light seems virtually incompatible with these qualities. Hence, Jensen's initial models were wrapped in textile, lending them a tactile quality that led to 'a sort of padded lighting'. Even more importantly, however, the 'forms should be easy to decode, and the cord and switch should be revealed, not hidden'.[4] Everything, from the lamp head to the cord, was given the same textile exterior to achieve a monolithic expression, where the shade, stem, base and cord form a functional whole.

The production models were made of steel with a matt white powder-coated finish combined with a matt white textile cord. This made the floor, table and wall lamps stand out even more clearly as unambiguous signs – or pictograms – for lamps. Compared to the initial models, the emphasis was more on pure form than on *hygge*: 'Generally, I may have a slight modernist tendency, for when all is said and done, I don't want more *hygge* than is absolutely necessary. That the lamps were ultimately made in metal makes sense, based on their technical aspect; the end result was a straightforward industrial design.'[5] Still, everything is rounded and pleasant to touch, including the delicate switch that responds with a classic click when the lamp is switched on or off. The gently rounded forms add an element of *hygge* that softens their symbolic character and almost makes them come alive. 'A child might draw a lamp this way but would probably make it less rounded. That comes from my ceramic affinity for soft forms. It made sense to give the shade some volume.'[6]

Jensen explains that when he makes a jug, for example, he always strives to have 'the liquid come out of the jug in a fascinating, beautiful way'. When the three OJ lamps were launched in 2010, they all enclosed the intended energy-efficient bulb in a non-transparent conical shade. The downwards light falls softly over the lip of the chubby shade, just as upwards light slips out from the top, where it is partially reflected and fades out over the exterior of the shade. Jensen described the light and its functional aspects as follows:

The light flows out of the heavy shade in rounded shapes, almost like a malleable mass. The table lamp spreads the light, while the floor lamp has a moderate concentrating effect. Both are easy to pick up and move to where you need the light. The wall lamp concentrates the light, which can be directed outwards, downwards or towards the sides.[7]

Mission accomplished. Ten years after Jensen was working on the OJ lamps, which have since been discontinued, he reflects: 'There is nothing as seductive as light. If you switch on a light source in a dark room, the light source is everything. In these lamps, the light is really understated, and so is the storytelling; I probably have too much faith in the object itself. I still think they're well made and recognizable.'[8]

At first glance, the OJ table, floor and wall lamps are archetypes of these objects. Upon closer inspection, they are unique lamps with a form that reveals the ceramicist's touch.[9]

'A soft and organic light is emitted from the consistently rounded forms of the voluminous shade. The light almost seems to slip into the surrounding space. All the elements – the base, the stem, the shade, the cord and the switch – are combined into a condensed and functional whole.' —Ole Jensen, 2010[10]

Norm Architects: Milk

&Tradition—2010

Stone lamp (Menu, 2017) with a frosted glass shade and sand-coloured base.

A norm is a set of principles that shape human behaviour. For more than a decade, award-winning Norm Architects has created numerous architectural and design solutions aimed at meeting a need and based on seeing mass-produced designs as tools intended to simplify everyday life.[1] The result is design stripped of all superfluous elements but rich in character, as exemplified by their lamp designs.

Norm Architects was founded in 2008 by Kasper Rønn (b. 1976) and Jonas Bjerre-Poulsen (b. 1976), both graduates of the Royal Danish Academy of Fine Arts, School of Architecture, in 2002 and 2004, respectively. While they were still students, they both worked for the designer Ole Palsby (1935–2010): 'He was a modernist to the core, so the design was super-rational and simple, stripped of all ornamentation. And we came to embrace that same approach.'[2]

Milk, which was put into production by &Tradition in 2010, was the Norm team's first lamp. It sprang from a specific need for a small lamp: 'In our interior design projects we kept encountering the need for a small lamp that would fit on a window sill or a small table to provide general lighting. Every corner has to be lit in order to define the space. However, most lamps were too big, so we saw a gap in the market.'[3] Milk is a small lamp with a diameter of 20 cm and a height of 25 cm. It provides the intended soft, broadly emitted light from a bipin bulb shining through an opalized glass shade placed on an acrylic plate that holds the G9 porcelain socket and is fitted with three small wooden legs. The legs are made of scraps left over from furniture production. 'The wood is cheap, even though it's quality oak, because the pieces are scraps that have no other use. So there is a sustainability aspect to it too.'[4] The wood is not the only furniture reference; Milk actually resembles a small milking stool, which is no accident:

Milk began as a lamp made entirely of glass, constructed of a glass base and top holding an incandescent light bulb. However, the lamp got intensely hot, so we needed ventilation. We considered several solutions for the two-part design. In the studio we had this old wooden stool, so just for fun, we set the glass top on it and began to play with the idea of approaching the lamp as a small piece of furniture. We worked on the shape of the legs and the glass orb, aiming for an aesthetic where things were small and round, and we ended up with a very biomorphic form.[5]

Bjerre-Poulsen describes the lamp with the Japanese adjective *kawaii*, which is typically translated as cute. It appeals to our instinct to care for anything that bears resemblance to an animal or a human baby and draws on our tendency to read ourselves into objects, speaking of a bottle 'neck' and a lamp 'head'. 'The same is true in architecture, where we understand everything from the point of view of our own scale, form and symmetry. Our work is based on the architect's analytical approach, which also includes geometry, but we softened it with rounded forms and proportions that made the lamp more human or animalistic.'[6]

In 2017, the team produced another small, chubby lamp, Stone lamp, which was put into production by the design company Menu. Like Milk, it has a diameter of 20 cm, and it meets similar needs. Stone lamp is 6 cm shorter and placed on a circular ceramic base, which makes it a little less animalistic; however, it is even softer and rounder, as is the light. It has a standard E27 socket, so behind the rounded glass shade, the small table lamp has a classic bulb shape. 'It is more robust than Milk and is closer in form to the lamp we were initially working on before it turned into Milk.'[7] The base has a matt glaze to achieve a soft texture reminiscent of natural stone. It is available in sand and black, while the glass orb is either frosted glass or transparent smoke-coloured glass, making the bulb visible. Animalistic or not, both Milk and Stone reflect a desire for a small lamp that fits in anywhere and contributes a soft, broadly emitted light with the same ability as candlelight to light up the darkest corners in a room.

'In Japan, they have the term kawaii, which means cute. The term applies to Milk, which has a highly biomorphic form: small, chubby, cute.' —Jonas Bjerre-Poulsen, 2019[8]

Maria Berntsen: Design with Light lantern

Holmegaard—2011

'We are fascinated by the movement of the flickering flame, it's like gazing into a fire, and I don't think we'll ever lose that fascination. New lighting technology will lead to entirely different lamps, but the live flame retains its exclusive and natural feel.'—Maria Berntsen, 2019[1]

The designer Maria Berntsen (b. 1961) attended the Royal Danish Academy of Fine Arts, School of Architecture, from 1987. After three years, she chose to continue her studies at the architecture school l'École d'Architecture de Bordeaux in France. When Berntsen returned to Denmark in 1992, she founded her own studio, focusing on product design from day one.

For the past 20 years, the Holmegaard glassworks has been one of the designer's regular collaboration partners. In 2005, Berntsen created the lamp series One for Holmegaard, including a particularly distinctive clear-glass table lamp. Normally, a table lamp consists of multiple components, but this one had a base and shade in one piece: 'It's called One because I sketched it in a single, continuous line. An object that could be inflated, and it was so neat the way the glass was able to accommodate that.'[2] The lamp with the rounded shapes is blown in a wooden mould and is a very sensuous body to see and touch. The socket shell is an aluminium bowl that floats in the transition between the shade and the base. From here, a bright red cord extends that takes on a life of its own as it descends from the socket through the base and on to the table. The light bulb is not shielded but showcased. When the lamp is switched on, the bulb and the cord stand out as the essence of a lamp, while the glass forms a clear halo around them.[3]

When Holmegaard discontinued its years-long production of electric lighting in 2008, Berntsen continued to design lamps, only now with non-electric light sources.[4] In 2011, she created the lantern Design with Light, which became Holmegaard's best-selling product ever.[5] The lantern in glass and butt leather was so successful because it is a very accomplished design solution. The lantern is both beautiful and carefully thought out:

It sprang from a desire to make it possible to take the light with you, indoors and out. Hence the leather strap. The strap communicates portability and also adds an elegant detail by bringing in a second natural material. The hole in the glass serves a dual purpose: it provides easy access to handling the pillar candle, including lighting and extinguishing it, and it provides important air circulation for an optimal burn. The lantern is topped by a metal lid with a hole in the middle, which further helps to regulate the circulation of air. When it is placed on top of the glass, the lid adds a nice detail and introduces a third material. The lid also makes the flame less susceptible to wind when it is used outdoors; it can even sustain a light drizzle without being extinguished.[6]

A lantern with a live flame is pleasant and cosy, but to prevent indoor particle pollution, it is a good idea to take the lantern outside. In a time when Danes increasingly move the functions of the home outdoors during the summer months, a lantern variant was launched, in 2016, where the pillar candle was replaced by lamp oil and a wick. The oil lantern was more robust, designed for patio living. Again, the leather strap invites the user to take the

The oil lantern Design With Light was designed to make it possible to bring the light outdoors.

lamp along, put it down or hang it where it is needed and thus create a cosy illuminated space. It has a traditional flame-spreader burner, and the development process emphasized fire safety.[7] The technical requirements for an oil lantern are high, while there are none for a lantern for pillar candles: 'It was a challenging process, but in cooperation with the skilled technical team we managed to meet all the requirements, including that no oil can leak out if the lamp is knocked over. The end result is fully optimized for all kinds of weather.'[8]

Thus, during a time with growing awareness of particle pollution as well as a persistent desire to be able to enjoy the sight of open fires and other live flames, Danish consumers now once again have access to an oil lamp in a contemporary design. Maria Berntsen concludes: 'I see it as a successful extension of the candle lantern series Design with Light. It is extremely functional!'[9]

Louise Campbell: LC Shutters

Louis Poulsen—2012

Louise Campbell followed in Poul Henningsen's footsteps at Louis Poulsen, creating an optimized modernist lamp where the ornamentation serves the functional purpose of improving the distribution of the light.

When Louise Campbell's fourth lamp for the lighting company Louis Poulsen was presented in 2012, it summarized a 12-year-long collaboration on lighting design. The white-lacquered lampshade is made of a thin sheet of aluminium turned into a dome-shaped form. A pattern is cut and stamped into the shade, forming two interacting layers that filter and soften the light inside the shade and give rise to a light effect on the outside as the light shines through the perforated pattern. The bottom of the cut and stamped shade is finished with a lace-like trim.

As a lighting designer, Campbell is influenced by the legacy of PH but also by the two opposite poles in her own background: a Danish father, 'a proper engineer', and an English mother who loves antiques: 'I love the old heirloom silk lampshades in her home; they give out the softest light.'[1] Campbell points to her English, feminine side as a counterbalance to the functional and rational approach that was taught at the Design School in Copenhagen. The LC Shutters pendant brings these two sides together. On the one hand, it does not seem that far removed from the silk shades with their lace trim, while, on the other hand, the material and the machine-based industrial production of the pendant could hardly be farther away. This latest lamp model to follow in PH's footsteps at Louis Poulsen thus reflects Campbell's ambition of bringing out the best qualities of the material and achieving a certain degree of fragility in the expression. The lamp also deserves to be highlighted as a perfect example of a design process resulting in a purely factory-made product, which reduces production costs. Campbell summarizes the process:

It began in 2008; the financial crisis was just about to take full effect, and the assignment was, 'Make something cheap and uncomplicated that can be made in our factory in Vejen'. My brief was 'no sh*t', but it turned out to be much more complicated, so for a long time, it was 'oh, sh*t'. Eventually they had to build a machine that would stamp out, polish and paint an aluminium sheet in less than 25 minutes, completely 'no sh*t'. Even if the resulting expression is not quite simple, the production is totally straightforward.[2]

Campbell explains that she knew from a fairly early point in the process what she was aiming for, also because she had, by now, accumulated enough experience with lighting engineering to know that the idea ought to work:

I wanted to turn one layer into two, and I wanted the shade itself to bring the light outside of the lamp. I developed a perforation principle that has to be finished with a lace trim at the bottom to be fully consistent. I think Louis Poulsen would have preferred a straight edge. But if I am to be uncompromising in my design and do what my principle calls for, it has to look this way. I'm really pleased with the lamp, because the very hard, cold material produces a very soft light. It is gentle. Remembering PH's words about the evening being a restful time, I realized how important that is, because we also need to take it down a notch. Consideration for the diurnal cycle is an extremely important aspect of lighting philosophy.[3]

LC Shutters highlights Campbell's kinship with PH. Her design solution shields the light bulb perfectly. Moreover, with a fairly affordable price tag, it was also a democratic lamp – true to the spirit of functionalism. The pendant is the only one of Campbell's lamps that reaches back to the social aspects of functionalism. Campbell has helped update Danish luminaire design with a focus on the importance of shadows, and she has received many accolades. Most recently, she received the 2019 Knud V. Engelhardt Memorial Grant for 'the courage to create things differently and thus help renew the design profession'.[4]

'My other lamps require care, and you can't knock into them without needing to straighten them afterwards. I wanted a "robust little devil" that still reflected the sense of fragility that I aim for in light.'
—Louise Campbell about LC Shutters, 2015[5]

Olafur Eliasson and Frederik Ottesen: Little Sun

Little Sun—2012

While the artist Olafur Eliasson's large sun in Tate Modern's turbine hall in London and the three luminous spheres at the Copenhagen Opera were out of reach for their audience (see pages 168–169), Little Sun is intended to be within reach in every sense of the word. The story about the small solar-powered lamp begins with a conversation between Eliasson and the solar energy engineer Frederik Ottesen (b. 1967) about the idea of holding sunlight in one's hands – even in the dark.[1] The conversation led the two men in 2012 to found the social business Little Sun, which makes the Little Sun lamp, the subsequent addition Little Sun Diamond and the mobile phone charger Little Sun Charge and distributes the products among the 1.6 billion people who live with no or inadequate access to electricity.

Olafur Eliasson with the solar-cell lamp Little Sun Diamond (2017), which can be worn on a piece of string around the neck or be placed on a stand. The lamp stores daylight to provide lighting for reading or working after dark.

When I first met Frederik, he was developing a solar-powered aeroplane. I had travelled in Ethiopia and was concerned about the lack of electricity in several parts of the country, which makes people use kerosene to light their homes after dark, a dangerous practice that is also a health hazard. Frederik and I discussed what we could do to help. We looked at the other solar-cell lamps that were on the market and decided to make one in a design inspired by the Ethiopian meskel *flower, which symbolizes positivity. We believe if people like a design, it is more likely to reach them.*[2]

The yellow flower sun is so small and light that it can be worn as a piece of jewellery on a strap or a piece of string around the neck. It weighs only 96 g and has a diameter of 12 cm and a depth of 2.9 cm. The solar panel is mounted in the middle of the flower, ringed by sturdy, weather-resistant and, not least, recyclable yellow ABS plastic petals. On one of the petals is a discreet on-off switch. One push provides a bright light, but because the lamp has a built-in dimmer, the user can also hold the switch down for a more muted light. Five hours of charging in the sun enables the lamp to provide many hours of light: four hours of bright light and many more with a dimmer light. The battery lifetime is five years with daily use. All in all, it is a quality lamp that is both product design and art. It was not presented at a lighting fair but in an art context at Tate Modern, under the seemingly controversial concept of 'trade not aid' – an explanation follows. Eliasson had approached the task from an artist's perspective on the world and our actions in it, and in his own description he regards the lamp as a contribution to the important discussion of the inequitable distribution of energy from an artistic perspective:

To me, Little Sun is very much about the feeling of holding the energy of the sun – your own little power plant – in your hand and seeing what the improved lighting quality makes possible: that children can do their homework, or shops can stay open after dark, without the use of kerosene lamps, which are harmful to people's health.[3]

In 2017, the first solar-cell lamp was followed up by Little Sun Diamond, which is only 7.9 x 7.9 x 2.7 cm. According to Eliasson, the main differences between the two lamps is that 'the size has been reduced to the size of the panel on the back, the entire front is a faceted lens that provides high-quality light and it has a stand, which is something many people had suggested for Little Sun'.[4] Eliasson underscores that like Little Sun, it can be worn around one's neck, and that 'both lamps have an iconic design that is recognizable and has a positive connotations'.[5]

In Denmark and other developed countries, Little Sun, Little Sun Diamond and Little Sun Charge are sold at a modest surcharge, which helps fund distribution in the areas that the solar-cell lamps and the charger were intended for.[6] People in, for example, Ethiopia, Zimbabwe and Senegal should be able to buy a lamp at a very affordable price, and local retailers should also be able to turn a small profit, in accordance with Eliasson and Ottesen's idea of promoting local shops through 'trade not aid'. The lamps thus light the way in more ways than one. To date, more than one million lamps have been sold, making it 'a work of art that works in life'.[7]

'Your own little power plant – right in your hand.'—Olafur Eliasson, 2019[8]

Anne Qvist: Outfit L905

Lampas—2014

The architect and industrial designer Anne Qvist (b. 1962) does not create timeless designs. It is an important point for her that all her designs spring from and are embedded in their time: 'Nothing is timeless; you always belong in a certain time and create things based on what it affords. The development in light sources in recent years should impact new designs.'[1] Qvist's street lamp Outfit is a design from a time when an increased focus on reducing CO_2 emissions and counteracting climate change has inspired an effort to make energy-consuming products more efficient. Outfit is a big design based on LED driver technology that ensures energy-efficient intelligent light management while making the urban space more comfortable.

Qvist graduated from the Aarhus School of Architecture in 1992. After her graduation, she headed Schmidt Hammer Lassen Architects' design department for ten years followed by eight years as head of design at Arkitema. In 2012, she founded Anne Qvist Design Office, which handles a wide range in product and spatial design. Outfit, which was put into production by Veksø in 2014, covers both fields at once.

Briefly told, the Outfit luminaire is a matt black cylindrical column made of powder-coated hot-dip galvanized steel with one to three added arms, each enclosing a downlight. The light source, an LED, is mounted within an aluminium reflector and covered by an elliptical shield of frosted glass. This lamp head emits a warm white (3,000 Kelvin) light, which is glare-free thanks to the opal glass. The Outfit columns contain a built-in LED driver that makes it possible to control and vary the light. All three lights can be controlled at once, or they can be programmed individually to enable individual dimming.[2]

In a seemingly impossible balance between distinctive, sculptural identity and discreet appearance, the stoic column rises up, most of all resembling a large, naked tree – like a symbol or pictogram for a tree – not least when all three arms are installed. In the dark, it furnishes the space around it and is able to accommodate a variety of lighting needs.

The goal was to make lighting that is simultaneously asymmetrical and rotationally symmetrical. When it only has one arm in the lowest position it provides asymmetrical light; from the edge of a pavement it can light up the pavement and pedestrians. The spatial effect is lost if the light is distributed too far. It has to focus on what is happening. If you add another arm above it, the lamp can also light up the street, and if you add a third, the distribution is rotationally symmetrical. Then you have a full circle, and you can light up a large area.[3]

The latter makes good sense in a large square, and indeed the three-armed Outfit is installed in a public square in Ørestad, in southern Copenhagen, where it enters into a dialogue with both the trees in the square and the new buildings around it.[4] Outfit is easy to furnish a public space with: 'Despite the size, in some ways it's quite subtle, just column + stick + stick + stick. *That's all.* The design should not clamour for attention. Space is a scarce commodity, and the street environment contains a lot of information!'[5] Qvist underscores, 'When you work with spatial design, you have to place people centre stage. You should never make people feel small or insignificant. It's no good if everything shouts, but it's fine if it tells a story.'[6] Outfit has several stories to tell:

The basic function is that Outfit brings light where there is dark, and it does so in an energy-efficient manner. But there is much more to it, because there is always an element of magic in the way light stages and shapes a space; it can make a space vibrant and eventful. It's fascinating when the light from the three arms comes together in a circular light on the ground. It's exciting to create beautiful street lighting – shaping a space and bringing a sense of security.[7]

Back in 1892, the first electric street lamps illuminated streets and squares from a height of 11 metres. The lowest positioned light source in the Outfit lamp illuminates the pavement from a height of just over three metres. Thoughtful technological development has brought the light closer.

'There's a difference between designing an object that is close to the individual person and an object that relates more to a landscape or an urban space.' —Anne Qvist, 2019[8]

Øivind Slaatto: Swirl

Le Klint—2014

'Swirl was the first thing I did after I graduated,' says Øivind Alexander Slaatto (b. 1978), who earned a degree in industrial design from The Danish Design School in 2007.

I have a special relationship with light, because I have always been sensitive to light, and after I had a concussion, it got worse. Swirl was designed to provide as much light as possible, and the best light possible, without producing glare. Hence it had to be based on PH's principles for glare-free lighting. PH has always been my idol![1]

Swirl can be compared to PH's pendants, but while the latter have overlapping shades in different sizes, Swirl has six identical leaves, arranged in a logarithmic spiral form where each leaf is staggered a sixth of a turn in relation to its neighbours. This overlapping principle keeps the bulb just out of sight.

The pendant is extremely light-efficient, producing a great deal of downwards reflected illumination, as the light bounces off a shade that radiates it downwards – the PH principle in action. Moreover, the thin translucent plastic sheet lets some of the light pass through, as in the other Le Klint shades. Thus, the design combines two principles – reflection and diffusion – to provide optimal light. The combination creates a pleasant light with an emphasis on downwards light and soft shadows that keep the light glare-free and 'make (...) people beautiful'.[2] The construction also minimizes the loss of light from the bulb.

The main source of inspiration for the form was nature: 'The shape of a Swirl was not defined by me but by gravity. Everything in nature grows in spirals, a phenomenon that the Italian mathematician Leonardo Fibonacci translated into a formula.'[3] The Swirl lamps clearly show their source of inspiration – a snail shell, a shape that has always fascinated Slaatto, because it is a mathematically honest shape and a very strong construction and, not least, because every single detail has a reason. That is also true of Swirl, whose sophisticated geometry conceals the bulb from every angle: 'All my lamps are dictated by physics, but the reason why the lamp had to be white is simply that white lamps are more efficient when it comes to emitting light, diffused as well as reflected.'[4]

Slaatto's initial model, made in white paper, resembles the finished lamp, but it still had a long way to go before it was ready for production. It was only when Slaatto was paid for the loudspeaker Beoplay 9A, which he designed for Bang & Olufsen, that he could afford to finish Swirl, which he had begun to work on as early as 2007: 'I made the loudspeaker in 2012, then I spent about six months working exclusively on the lamp before I presented it to Le Klint in the winter of 2013.'[5] However, thanks to the years of preliminary work and the carefully worked-out prototype, actual product development of the first Swirl pendant was completed very quickly: 'Only three months after I presented my prototypes, the finished lamp was ready to be presented to the public – it premiered in Japan – and six months later it was in the shops in Denmark.'[6] Another successful Le Klint design; subsequently, additional models and sizes were added to make an entire collection that met a variety of different needs.

While adhering to the lighting principles formulated by PH, Swirl is also a new and improved lamp. For Le Klint, it also marked an innovation, as the company had to introduce a new production method, although costs were limited because it did not require new tools, only a cutting machine to cut the six leaves from a single sheet of plastic. The shade is assembled by hand by Le Klint's 'pleating girls' in Odense: 'I designed the lamp to require as little labour as possible; that's a condition for my lamps being produced in a country where labour is as relatively expensive as it is in Denmark.'[7]

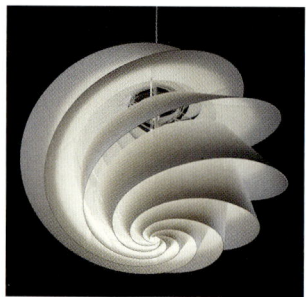

Swirl is made as a wall lamp, a ceiling lamp and a pendant lamp. All the Swirl models have the same elegant closure at the bottom, which makes the lamps suitable for being seen from below without producing glare.

'My lamp design is fully guided by lighting principles, but it's also driven by curiosity and wonder!'

—Øivind Slaatto, 2019[8]

Øivind Slaatto: Patera

Louis Poulsen—2015

'Not a single detail in the lamps is there by chance; there are no random shadows, no light that falls in the wrong direction. Many lamps have interior shadows; I work hard to eliminate that and to get all the details just right. In lighting engineering terms, I got it right.'
—Øivind Slaatto, 2019[1]

Patera Silver (2019) in reflective silver-coloured foil is a sparkling reinterpretation of a chandelier.

The year after the launch of Øivind Slaatto's Swirl, the designer was ready to present Patera in collaboration with Louis Poulsen. His ambition in this case was to design a modern chandelier. Seen from a distance, the lamp looks like an orb: 'The same shape as the condition of all life and the most important light source in our solar system: the sun. The use of such a basic form means the lamp can fit in virtually anywhere, because the orb can handle being repeated – in a canteen or in a ballroom – without the lighting dominating the architecture.'[2]

Up close, the lamp reveals a mathematical geometry that is simultaneously regular and unpredictable. The geometry is based on PH's lighting principles, which means that most of the light is directed downwards, where it is most needed, while the surroundings are bathed in a gentle light with no stark shifts between light and dark – and always without a direct view of the light source. In Patera, the latter consideration has been set aside directly underneath the lamp in order to increase the light efficiency, as the reflected and diffused light is supplemented with direct light above a table or the floor. The design prevents glare by minimizing contrast and by keeping the light source out of view except from a point directly underneath the orb. The natural appearance of the spherical Patera, whether on or off, is no accident. 'Patera also sprang from my fascination with the Fibonacci sequence. The spiral pattern is found everywhere in nature – for example, in the seed formation of sunflowers and pine cones,' says Slaatto of his inspiration. 'Patera is actually a three-dimensional Fibonacci sequence.'[3] Slaatto also underscores that he sees the lamp as a substitute for the fireplace:

In the old days, we used the fireplace as our primary source of heat and light in the home. No one would do that today, but one of the most beautiful qualities of a fire is that you can keep gazing into the flames without getting bored, because the fire and the flames are predictable and unpredictable at the same time. Just as the fire is constantly changing, Patera too seems to change, depending on the angle you see it from. It's that combination of the magical and unpredictable with the regular and mathematical that sparks fascination and means that you can live with a design like this for a long time. Because you're never quite done with it.[4]

Patera was launched in 2015 as a classic white lamp in translucent plastic that reflected and emphasized the light and its varying effects. However, the initial sketches and prototypes had been made in a very different, sparkling material that made the orbs light up like glittering jewels and made the lamp a modern, timeless crystal chandelier that fragmented the light and bounced it in all directions in bright flashes. Slaatto had discovered the material while he was working on another, unrelated project. He had been asked to design a number of giant lamps to impress TV viewers and the live audience when Denmark hosted the 2014 Eurovision Song Contest. When the event took place, six giant diamond-shaped lamps in colourful polycarbonate brought sparkle and glamour to the musical extravaganza. An exterior rainbow-coloured foil struck a festive note.

Giant Diamonds was a very unusual project: bling-bling, party time, colours. In the Eurovision Song Contest, kitsch is king. It helped me that as a former musician I had learnt that whatever you play – or do – it only works if you go all the way. The same is true of kitsch. If you have a grain of ironic detachment or if you patronize your audience, it becomes awkward and embarrassing; but if you go all in, respect it and love it, the end result can be fantastic.[5]

For a shiny Patera version, it was necessary to tone the material down to make it suitable for mass production and for everyday settings that are not always about glam and glitter.[6] It took a long time to find the right material, but in 2019 Louis Poulsen was able to launch Patera Silver – a modern sparkling chandelier.

Jonas Edvard: Gesso

Jonas Edvard—2015

'We'll never run out of limestone; it's a fossil material that's found all over the world. It makes sense to use the materials we have to hand, and depending on where we are in the world, they will be unique and different. We need to make better use of resources and use history to confirm how that's been done in the past. Sustainability shouldn't be a burden or a chore but something we do because it's fun – like giving someone a bouquet of flowers.'
—Jonas Edvard, 2019[1]

This is the story of a number of lamps whose form can almost be regarded as coming second while the design process took precedent. The path to the design solutions was based on exploring and experimenting with naturally occurring resources from Danish nature to create new materials that form the basis of new sustainable designs.

Jonas Edvard (b. 1982) graduated from the Royal Danish Academy of Fine Arts, School of Design, in 2013, but as early as 2012 he had designed a lamp in ash veneer. The pendant, Konkret (Concrete), emits a direct light onto the surface as well as a warm, diffuse light through the ash veneer that brings out the distinctive grain of the wood. Konkret was put into production in 2016 by the Swedish lighting company Örsjö.

My awareness of sustainable design only really began to take form while I was working on my graduation project, and I was in traffic accident that almost killed me. Afterwards, I reflected on what was most important to me – and to everyone else. I realized that the essence of Danish design is to create things that have something good in them. That improve the world somehow. Changing the world was an aspiration that the circle around PH was quite good at expressing.[2]

For his graduation project, Edvard grew a mushroom lampshade on a substrate of waste products. After the oyster mushrooms were eaten, what remained was a stable lampshade: 'The mushroom project got me going; material experimentation was my main driver, and I have continued on that path ever since.'[3] In 2015, Edvard developed the Terroir pendant made of seaweed and recycled paper together with his design colleague Nikolaj Steenfatt Thomsen (b. 1987). The simple lampshade is made in an innovative material that is light, hard and durable. The surface is warm and tactile with colours ranging from light green to dark brown, depending on the species of seaweed and where along the Danish coast it was sourced.

That same year, Edvard presented another pendant, this one a solo project, also made of a Danish raw material, limestone, which can be dyed and proved a promising material for lighting:

When you design a lamp, the key is to find a material that has aesthetic value in itself. Limestone consists of tiny crystals. Due to their amorphous surfaces, they are constantly reflecting the light in many different directions, diffusing it into the room in a beautiful and pleasant way.[4]

The Gesso lamp is an opaque, conical shade made of limestone and a bio-based binder. Although it is, in principle, a stone lamp, it is lightweight yet strong: the 5–6-mm shell construction weighs only 800 g. The lamp was created for the Danish Crafts Collection 19 in 2015.[5] That same year, the lamp was also presented at the Maison & Objet fair in Paris, where Edvard received a Rising Talent award. In 2018, the noma restaurant opened on the Refshaleøen island in a new interior with Danish-designed ceramics, furniture, linen and lamps, including the Gesso lamp in a new and bigger version.[6] The limestone lamps shed light on and complement the ingredients on the plate. To complete the sustainable design, Edvard used quality LED bulbs. For the noma project, Edvard worked with David Thulstrup Architects to modify the lamp to accommodate the LED bulbs that the lighting company Anker og Co produced for the restaurant interior. Edvard is the only person who can create the new unique bio-composite and thus the lamps: 'In principle, the form can be varied. Right now I make four basic models; the latest addition is the conical shade for noma. In that sense, the form is less important; instead, the narrative is driven by the material and the history.'[7]

↖ In the Konkret veneer lamp from 2012, the bottom is stained black to provide an edge that blocks the light from spreading through the veneer, thus heightening the contrast between the downwards, direct light and the indirect light.
↑ Terroir from 2015 is made from seaweed and recycled paper.
→ This variant of the Gesso pendant was installed in the Copenhagen restaurant noma in 2018.

Norm Architects: Carrie

Menu—2016

Norm Architects, which was formed in 2008 by Jonas Bjerre-Poulsen and Kasper Rønn, has by now grown into a company with 20 employees, and a few years ago, the designer Frederik Werner (b. 1988) joined the design team.[1] Lamps continue to be part of a wide product line with roots in the functionalist design tradition.

The Danish functionalists took an interest in Japanese simplicity and applied art early on. The Carrie lamp from 2016 reinterprets a traditional Japanese lantern in modern materials using the latest lighting technology: 'Carrie was created specifically to address the need to bring the light with you, including outdoors. When we made it, the quality of LED lighting had improved and used so little power that batteries lasted a long time, which made cordless lamps viable. That gave rise to a whole range of new possibilities.'[2] The design was inspired by traditional Japanese rice-paper lanterns, which have a candle inside and a handle for carrying. The tall handle refers directly to these traditional lights, as the length is needed to provide sufficient distance from the candle to prevent burns from the hot flame.

Carrie is a minimalist steel basket that holds a luminous glass globe. The handle can be removed, leaving the globe to stand alone on the base, which in addition to supporting the globe also contains the technical components and the USB charging port for the lamp. The LED light radiates into the room from the globe – which is not quite spherical, as the bottom is cut off. As the light source cannot be replaced, the designers put intense effort into finding the right colour temperature for the light. The soft and warm light emitted through the sand-blasted glass shade makes the lamp a good substitute for a wax candle.[3] They also included a dimmer, a feature that is just as important as the minimalist look: 'The world is flooded with visual impressions, so our design is also an attempt at creating calm.'[4]

The same year that Carrie went into production at Menu and became available in retail, the even more minimalist Mass Light was put into production at &Tradition.

Mass Light is the essence of an electric light source: a socket with a light bulb. It is, however, also a carefully designed luminaire, based on the idea of combining stone and glass: a G9 socket built into a marble block. A threaded hole is drilled into the marble, matching the thread that is cast into the glass globe. The two are screwed together, and the light from the small bipin bulb is diffused through the opal glass shade.[5] 'As always, we worked with basic geometric shapes, but we modified the geometry slightly in order to soften the expression.'[6] In Mass Light, this is evident from the way in which the stone embraces the glass, but otherwise the lamp is about as simple as it gets.

And yet, while Mass Light is a shade and a small bipin bulb, the Socket Occasional Lamp (Menu, 2017) is merely a regular cylindrical brass base hiding an E27 socket, fitted with any matching bulb. While the Milk and Stone ta-

Socket Occasional Lamp's brass column is an independent object intended to hold a lamp socket, but it can also be used, for example, as a paper weight.

ble lamps were small (see page 194), this base is just 8 cm tall, so the lamp fits into even the smallest spaces. Socket Occasional Lamp is made by metalworkers in Kathmandu, as it was created with the goal of supporting marginalized women in Nepal. The women make and pack the design object, which consists of a brass tube with a slit cut into it. The tube is blackened on the inside and has a brushed exterior. 'It's completely basic; you put the socket into the brass cylinder, which becomes the lamp base. It is really heavy, which means that the luminaire is not easily knocked over. It's a small lamp with a real quality feel!'[7] The sculptural and minimalist lamp provides illumination as well as important support for the women workers.

Norm Architects' design team works in extension of the norm-setting Danish functionalist tradition. The lamps, all of which serve a purpose, or several, are decorative but stripped of superfluous decoration, and each of them is developed for contemporary technology and continues to develop with it.

'We begin every design process by identifying the need; in this case, what function should the lamp serve and what need should it meet? In addition to the light, we also examine how to make it pleasant to carry and how it feels in the hand, and that brings the senses into play. The aesthetic is always the final aspect to fall into place.'
—Jonas Bjerre-Poulsen, 2019[8]

GamFratesi: Suspence

Lightyears—2016

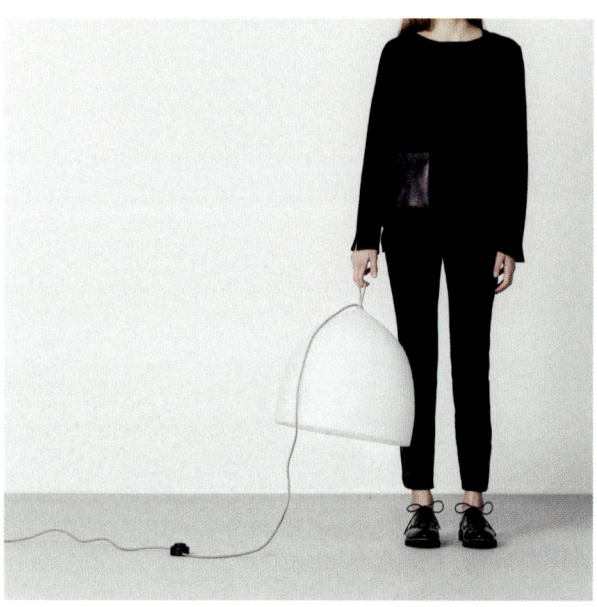

Although most homes have numerous outlets and lamps, people still have a need to bring the light with them. Thanks to the long cord, the large but lightweight Suspence Nomad has a long reach – even to the balcony or patio.

The Danish-Italian design studio GamFratesi was founded in 2006 by the architects Stine Gam (b. 1975) and Enrico Fratesi (b. 1978). They met as architecture students at the university in Ferrara, in northern Italy, in 2004; later they both studied at Aarhus School of Architecture and founded a joint firm in Copenhagen just after graduation. The lamps Suspence and Suspence Nomad, which were designed ten years later, are characteristic of the duo's cross-cultural fusion of tradition and renewal in approach and expression. In Gam and Fratesi's own words, 'We work together every step of the process. Our approach is quite traditional, but sometimes we tweak it a little in relation to a particular function or material. We dedicate a lot of attention to the details, because even a small detail can make a big difference; it can turn everything around.'[1]

Suspence and Suspence Nomad are based on the same shade form and were created in parallel. 'Our focus was on how to create a simple lamp with very few details but plenty of personality.'[2] The most important point was the transition between shade and cord, which was designed to look as if the cord is drawn out of the shade, although it is in fact a fusion of the two very different materials of plastic and aluminium.[3] The cord is thus dyed to match the exact colour of the lampshade. The bulb is hidden behind an opalized polycarbonate shade that diffuses the light gently: 'The light should be gentle, because that is an important aspect of our design expression,' says Fratesi.[4] Thus, it is possible to look directly into the lamp without being dazzled. The curvature of the outer shade creates an illusion of looking into a completely empty lampshade.[5]

Suspence Nomad is based on a different concept. The shade has the same form, but in this variant it is made of white, translucent polyethylene, a robust material that emits a soft, diffuse light. Unlike the pendant, this lamp, as the name suggests, is not intended for a stationary position but is meant to be portable. Instead of fusing shade and cord, the lamp has a contrasting strap in soft silicone that can be carried on a finger. This makes it easy to bring the lamp along and put it down on the floor wherever it is convenient. With a four-metre cord, it has a fairly wide range without the need for a new outlet. The bottom is open, as there is no reason to worry about glare when the lamp is placed directly on the floor. 'Our main goal was to create an informal and robust lamp that you could take with you, and we were able to give it a very beautiful diffused light.'[6] The light is gentle, 'cosy', as the manufacturer puts it, but this is no cosy little lantern; it is a large shade with an eye-catching cord.[7] The luminaire is a striking form in the room, an architectural element with a spatial effect.

When we speak of good light, there are two elements to be considered. One of them is people: how can we enable people to thrive and interact with the light? The other is about the surroundings: how can we make the surroundings beautiful, both when the lamp is off and when it is on? Good light embraces the surroundings and supports an interplay with and between people.[8]

The concept and inspiration for the Suspence lamps spring from a detail. The same is the case with GamFratesi's glass pendant Soffi (for Poltrona Frau, 2018), where a leather strap has become a small but significant element contrasting with the lamp's other main element: a mouth-blown glass bubble. The leather strap is just big enough to hide the lamp's necessary technical components and thus serve the important purpose of enabling a clean, simple look: leather, glass, light.[9] The lamp has edge, but the light is gentle, a hallmark of all the duo's lamps.

'Good lighting is very much about drawing the surroundings – including the right light conditions – into the home – that is, to respect the place in the world where we live and to connect the indoor setting to the outdoors. In Denmark, this is called *hygge*, but essentially, it's about bringing a positive mood – a positive story about light – into our everyday life.'
—Enrico Fratesi, 2019[10]

Anne Qvist: AQ01

Fritz Hansen—2017

A good new design almost always references something familiar, but it should also address its own time, offer improvements on historical models and, if possible, incorporate optimized technology. That is an important point for the architect and industrial designer Anne Qvist, and she underscores the need to understand the references of her working lamp, AQ01: 'In principle, the lamp uses the technology on the same terms as the familiar working lamp; it has arms that can be moved by means of springs, it has a centrally placed light source and a conical shade, it's all very classic.'[1] The AQ01 is a traditional working lamp: it has two arms, springs and a lamp head. However, in comparison to its predecessors, it is light and delicate, the springs are hidden and the lamp head is small, although it is still a distinctive form in a room that makes you want to reach out and touch it.

Qvist had refined every single detail to create a lamp that invites touch and creates an intimate luminous space when it is pulled closer: 'The table lamp is very close to the user, in contrast to a streetlight, which has to be big and strong to sustain all kinds of weather and, not least, is far removed from the body. We don't touch a streetlight. In my work, scale and spatial conditions are always paramount.'[2]

The working lamp was presented three years after Qvist's streetlight Outfit (see page 202) began to show up in the streetscape, but the concept for the lamp had been underway even longer.

The idea had been in my mind for many years, but the lamp looked this way from the first take. The basic principle was that it could only have two arms – two tubes – which had to come together in a point where they could move. At its heart is the idea that you have a tube, and then you pinch it to get a very small contact face. That's a very industrial approach, a holdover from the past, since today everything is cast that way. But it tells the story of connecting the tubular arms with the moving parts. That was the basic principle; next came the detailed effort to make all the moving components work and humanize the technical aspects, because it's something that you grip.[3]

The cord is concealed inside the thin lamp arms but becomes visible in the moving joints, and if the arm is lifted, the cord follows along:

It's part of the story that the cord runs inside the arms and pops out where there is a need for movement and that it can then stretch but also pops back in again. All the many details have been thought out in microscopic detail, because the lamp is so close to its user.[4]

The circular form is found in the moving parts and in the end points of the luminaire: the lamp head (which also moves up and down and to the sides) and the base. The table lamp is mounted on a heavy circular base but is also available with a small circular (of course) wall fitting. Mounted on the wall it can be used, for example, as a reading lamp that can be pulled towards the book or magazine to provide a reading light precisely where it is needed.

The base and the metal components of the frame have a uniform matt lacquer finish. The lamp head's flat top has an integrated touch-control button that switches the light on, turns it up or down and switches it off again at the lightest touch. The LED is hidden behind the diffuser in a white heat-resistant polycarbonate that is thicker towards the rim to prevent glare and direct the light downwards. This part of the lamp head 'becomes the light source that never needs replacing', Qvist explains – a closed unit the user cannot access.

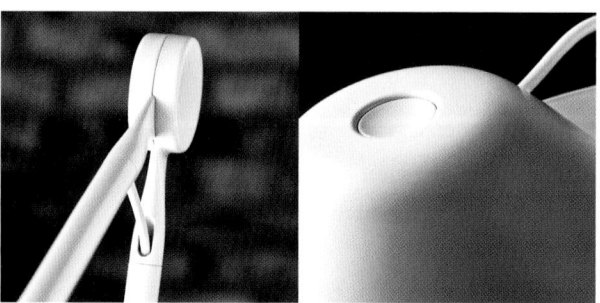

In AQ01, which is currently produced by Lightyears, the cord runs inside the lamp arms but is visible in the movable joints. The control for dimming and switching the light on and off is placed at the top of the lamp head.

I was very involved in the design of the light itself, because it had to be beautiful. The LED technology makes it possible to make a very small lamp, and it is small, but I wanted to have something to grip, touch, interact with, so you can create a space where you are also present. Light should always be as close as possible, I think. It's a matter of scale and of relating to the human user – that must never be lost in the proportioning.[5]

'It turned into a play with geometry, an effort to make everything come together and appear very simple. It was a classic play with the bearing, the borne and mutual proportions, but in this lamp the emphasis had to be on micro-detailing and on humanizing the technical content.'—Anne Qvist, 2019[6]

GamFratesi: Yuh

Louis Poulsen—2017

Stine Gam and Enrico Fratesi call themselves furniture architects: 'Due to our architectural training, we apply an architectural method and approach to the world when we create a design. It's all about one's approach to an issue – in this case, lamp design. To us, it's always about the whole context: people, surroundings, materials and their mutual interaction,'[1] says Fratesi and draws a reference to the time almost a century ago when 'Kaare Klint taught the future furniture architects the importance of going to the core of the task with an understanding of the use of the object. That is something we have channelled in our design, putting it into a contemporary context'.[2]

GamFratesi's lamp series Yuh is a product of the duo's cross-cultural fusion of tradition and renewal.[3] Understanding the tradition and addressing it actively in the design process make it possible to challenge it:

When we designed Yuh, we had two mentors in mind: Arne Jacobsen and PH, both of whom had created lamps for Louis Poulsen. We wanted to bring both of them into the new millennium in a new way with regard to functionality and design. What we liked about Arne Jacobsen's AJ lamps was the very architectural expression and the stringent geometry. We had PH in mind with regard to the light quality, how light affects the room and how it should be reflected outwards to prevent a direct, dazzling light.[4]

Yuh was designed as a compact lamp that could be pointed in as many directions as possible without having too technical an appearance. To achieve this, the lamp design was very simple: 'Essentially, we saw the lamp as a stick with a shade that could move up and down on the stick and which could be rotated and tilted to direct the light in any direction.'[5] The lamp base is circular, as is the opening of the shade, while the shade's slightly pinched and curved conical form stems from following the lines enabled by the movements of the shade.

The conical aluminium shade directs the light onto the tabletop, but an opening in the top of the cone lets the shade move on the stand, which was a new way to approach the movement of a lampshade. The opening at the top of the shade also lets the light escape, illuminating the top of the stand and softening the contrasts in the room – unlike the 60-year-older AJ lamp (see page 64). Yuh has an opalized base plate in polycarbonate that hides the LED light source and diffuses the light softly. It is thus still a directional light but completely glare-free. The switch is placed at the top of the stand; in addition, the lamp has a dimmer and a timer function.[6]

Yuh refers to the phonetic sound of 'you': 'We wanted to let you direct the light exactly where you wanted it to achieve an intimate space between you and the lamp.'[7] Hence, the lamp is designed so it can be regulated on the stand with three movements: height adjustment, swivel and tilt. It was a key point for the two architects to make the lamps flexible in the various usage situations in the home. The name underscores this flexibility.

Gam and Fratesi explain that Yuh was the result of a given assignment: 'Our work unfolds in a variety of ways, sometimes an idea emerges, ends up in the sketch book and is developed from there, but in fact all our lamps have begun with a specific brief from a manufacturer.'[8] In this case, the client was Louis Poulsen, which launched the lamp series in white and black in 2017; it was well received, and in 2019 the series was presented at the lighting fair in Milan in a new version with a marble base in either black or white.[9] A brand-new material in a Louis Poulsen context, but for the GamFratesi duo a logical addition of a detail that, once again, challenges tradition.

Yuh has become a homage to Arne Jacobsen's AJ lamps – a reinterpretation designed with and around modern technology.

'What is good lighting? It is light that promotes a good climate, a good atmosphere and good interactions among people. Yuh is designed to provide the best conceivable light in the room, for the people in the room.'

Stine Gam—2019

Philip Bro Ludvigsen: Hiti

FDB Møbler—2018

Philip Bro Ludvigsen created a table and a floor edition of Hiti together with the Icelandic designer Dögg Guđmundsdóttir.

In 2004, Philip Bro Ludvigsen revolutionized the Le Klint brand with his *non*-pleated lamps, and in 2018 he helped rebrand FDB Møbler (FDB Furniture) with a lamp series.

Ludvigsen had created his first lighting design 18 years earlier, and, ever since, he had challenged the status quo, albeit always with respect for the design legacy he had been given a share in, through his education and through his long-standing collaboration with Le Klint and other design manufacturers. That legacy is Danish functionalism.

When the functionalist ideas were embraced by the Danish public at large, this was due in no small measure to the efforts of FDB's 'people's furniture'. In 1942, the Fællesforeningen for Danmarks Brugsforeninger (Confederation of Danish Manufacturing and Retail Cooperatives; FDB – now Coop) established a design office headed by the furniture designer Børge Mogensen (1914–1972). He initiated a production of contemporary, industrially made quality designs intended to be affordable to everyone. This reflected the functionalist ideal of promoting simple, beautiful and practical interior design as a way of improving the quality of life for individual families and society at large.[1] FDB's design office closed in 1980, but in 2013 Coop relaunched FDB Møbler and some of the now iconic pieces of furniture. Later, new designs were added to the product line, and it was as part of this renewal that the head of FDB Møbler, Ole Kiel, contacted Ludvigsen: 'Ole, who knew my Le Klint products and my designs for Georg Jensen, reached out to me three years ago and asked if I would be interested in making some lamps for FDB.'[2] That became the beginning of a long development process that tested several different directions, until a pendant, a table and a floor lamp were launched in 2018 both in FDB Møbler shops and online at coop.dk.

All three lamps feature a globe that sparks associations to a jellyfish and, in the case of the table and floor lamps, a hot-air balloon. The pendant has the simplest design, with a walnut mount and a shade in mouth-blown clear or frosted glass.

The glass globes referenced hot-air balloons, and that was also the case for my sketches of the pendant, but it turned out looking almost too Oriental. Instead, the pendant globe is cut off just below the point where the curve ends; I was quite pleased with the result. In addition to referring to the FDB furniture, the use of wood also contains a reference to Vilhelm Lauritzen's Radiohus pendant, which also just completes the curve before the glass is cut off in a similar way. In my universe, there's something poetic about that twist.

Ludvigsen explains that the glass globes shaped like hot-air balloons mounted on wooden frames were co-created with the Icelandic designer Dögg Guđmundsdóttir. She was mainly responsible for the wooden frames, which FDB loved: 'That's spot-on – ideally, we'd like even more wood!'[3] The two designers thus engaged in a final sketching phase for the two models in dialogue with FDB, while Ludvigsen designed the pendant series alone. Guđmundsdóttir came up with the name Hiti, which means heat in Icelandic.

In his earlier lamps, Ludvigsen had challenged the potential of new light sources. In 2011, he designed the small, flexible Viper lamp, where the use of an innovative LED light source in turn enabled a new expression among Le Klint's pleated shades. The Hiti series, FDB Møbler's first lamps after the relaunch, were designed with respect for the Danish design tradition, and sustainability was considered in the use of warm Canadian walnut for the frame and mount. The choice of light source was straightforward: the lamps have traditional E27 sockets, which will accommodate high-quality eco-friendly LED bulbs.

'FDB has been amazing to work with; it's a great company with a strong profile and a sense of reverence for our design legacy. A good dialogue with the manufacturer is essential for the development process and for the commitment. We have a common interest in getting the product off to the best possible start.'

—Philip Bro Ludvigsen, 2019[4]

Sofie Refer: Blossi 8

Nuura—2018

The Blossi table lamp emits an indirect golden light as the built-in LED light is reflected in the lamp's metal and glass shades.

Sofie Refer has worked with lighting design for two decades. In 2018, she co-founded the lighting company Nuura together with two partners, and so far she has launched five lamp collections under this brand.[1] All the collections began with a chandelier with the rest of the collection subsequently created around it:

A chandelier is the most beautiful way to honour the light. Whether the chandelier hangs over the table where everybody gathers or high up in the ceiling in a lobby, welcoming people and setting the mood, it should be beautiful and sensuous. Nuura makes large chandeliers in a simple, Scandinavian style: big, sensuous, exclusive but Nordic! The mindset and the values we apply to design in Denmark are appreciated around the world – the fact that there's a reason why things look the way they do.[2]

Blossi 8 is the main piece of the Blossi collection. The chandelier is made up of eight rounded shades in clear glass mounted on a circular gold-coloured metal ring. Each shade is topped by a golden-lacquered metal disc that is linked to a smaller, 'floating' metal disc with integrated LEDs. The light is thus emitted from the small disc at the bottom. The light source itself is hidden, and the light is reflected into the room, bouncing off the golden metallic lacquer above. The clear glass also contributes to the reflection. In the table and floor lamps, that construction is turned on its head. Here, the LED is mounted in the top plate, so that the light hits the small disc and is then reflected up, onto the golden top plate: 'That's the way it has to be to when the light is to be indirect and lamps have to be glare-free.'[3]

Refer underscores that the light in Nordic nature is always an inspiration. Blossi is directly inspired by the golden autumn light when the sunlight hits the fallen leaves on the ground. She wanted to gather in this precious light before the ground turns black and the days turn grey and dark – bring the light indoors to brighten the dark months. As a design student, Refer took an instinctive approach, but over the years her work has become more analytical, and the instinctive responses have been verbalized and turned into technically perfected design solutions, always based on natural light: 'With the developments of LED technology, LEDs now offer high-quality colour reproduction and colour temperatures. When I designed Blossi, I wanted to emphasize the sensuous and atmospheric qualities. A key concern was to give the light the right colour temperature, 2,700 Kelvin.'[4] In Blossi, the light source is integrated to ensure optimal lighting. The light source has a lifetime of up to 50,000 hours. Most importantly, it is not possible to put in an inadequate light source: 'However, the light can be dimmed; light has to be dimmable!'[5] The Blossi collection received the 2019 German Design Award.

Refer's most recent lamp is the Apiales chandelier. An anodized aluminium frame supports 9 or 18 classic opal-glass globes that give out an evenly distributed light. The lamp has a G9 socket – the bipin socket known from the halogen bulbs – and is fitted with the latest G9 LED bulbs, which offer high energy efficiency, long lifetime and high-quality light. This chandelier too draws on inspiration from nature. Apiales is the Latin name for an order of asterids, the chandelier reproducing the way in which the arms of this plant extend to the blossoms: 'The construction works so well because it has no welding joints or screws. After all, with inspiration from a flower, the expression has to be light.'[6] The look is further underscored by the shiny globes that reflect one another:

Shiny opal glass has much more life than matt opal glass, and it's also better for the environment.[7] *A lighting designer has to consider that, just as one has to consider the light sources that are available now. If PH had been alive today, his lamps would likely have looked different.*[8]

'As a lamp designer, I have a responsibility, because the lamp I make is going to influence you when you hang it and switch it on. There is so much happening in lighting these days, so one needs to stay constantly updated. On the other hand, there's no point in making things more complicated than they are. That is what I focus my design on.' —Sofie Refer, 2019[9]

Design by BIG: Gople Lamp RWB

Artemide—2018

'Providing good growing conditions for plants was our focus before we began to consider the issue of form.'—Jakob Lange, 2019[1]

The architecture firm Bjarke Ingels Group, BIG, which was founded in 2005 by the architect Bjarke Ingels (b. 1974), has developed into one of today's most innovative and successful architecture firms in the new Nordic wave. BIG has created high-profile projects both in Denmark and in many countries around the world. The more than 500 employees in the offices in Copenhagen, New York, London and Barcelona are diverse with regard to both nationalities and disciplines; in addition to architects, the firm employs philosophers, culture analysts, anthropologists, engineers, landscape architects and product designers. In an interdisciplinary approach, they all contribute to BIG's boundary-pushing and thought-provoking projects. The architect Jakob Lange (b. 1978) is a partner at BIG. He has spearheaded many of the firm's award-winning projects, and as head of the design team he has also played a key role in the creation of the firm's lighting designs, which are a fairly new initiative.[2]

Just as the Danish firm has become a global phenomenon, the lamp designs too have emerged in an international context. In recent years, BIG has collaborated with the Italian lighting manufacturer Artemide, which in 2018 launched the Gople Lamp RWB pendant. The design sprang from a desire to make a lamp that provided optimal light for indoor plants. Lange reasons in 2019:

At some point, people began to build and live in houses, and since then we have become increasingly removed from nature. We have only really embraced this way of living for a relatively small number of generations; throughout human history until then, we lived in nature, so our bodies have been used to close contact with plants and trees. My personal view is that we need to have more greenery around us. Most houses have limited daylight indoors, so we should promote plant growth through design. We aimed for an attractive design and, naturally, as a lamp, it should also provide good lighting for people.[3]

Through photosynthesis, sunlight drives the biochemical processes that keep plants alive, enabling them to convert carbon dioxide into organic compounds and oxygen. As part of these processes, plants turn green because they form chlorophyll. Chlorophyll absorbs all wavelengths of light, except for green, which is reflected, causing us to perceive stalks and leaves as green. In the absence of photosynthesis, the chlorophyll breaks down; plants turn yellow and eventually die – and without plants, there is no life.[4] Given the relatively low amount of daylight inside our houses, it makes good sense to spoil one's plants with a special lamp. Lange underscores that 'our design was intended to provide good growing conditions; grow lights are not normally designed to have an aesthetic dimension, but ours are.'[5]

Gople Lamp RWB (*gople* being Danish for jellyfish)

Since plants do not need green light, while red and blue light promotes growth, the lamp has diodes for red and blue light, as well as white light, which is also useful for plants as it contains all three wavelengths.

consists of a mouth-blown 41-cm-long rounded glass shade with a diameter of 21 cm, 'a basic pill form, which is a design that supports the function'.[6] The glass shade is opal white at the top, near the light source, with an even graduation towards clear glass at the bottom, where the shade is open. Rather than standard light, the LED light source produces RWB lights (red, white, blue) in order to provide perfect lighting for the plants.[7] In addition to white light, the two colours were chosen because photosynthesis is maximized under blue or red light.[8] The light can be adjusted to the specific colour saturation that matches the plant's growth phase or the time of day – or the desired light in the room. Although good growth conditions for plants was the point of departure, human needs were given equal weight.

The pendant thus also came in a version with the same exterior design but without the special RWB lighting technology. Instead, it has a classic E27 socket to accommodate a wide range of bulbs. In 2018, it was launched in white, silver and bronze versions, which become increasingly transparent towards the bottom to emit a correspondingly brighter light. The lamp was also launched in a smaller version, Gople Mini. In 2019, the series was extended with Gople Table mounted on stands as well as a few new colours

Cecilie Bendixen: Volume Yellow

Cecilie Bendixen—2019

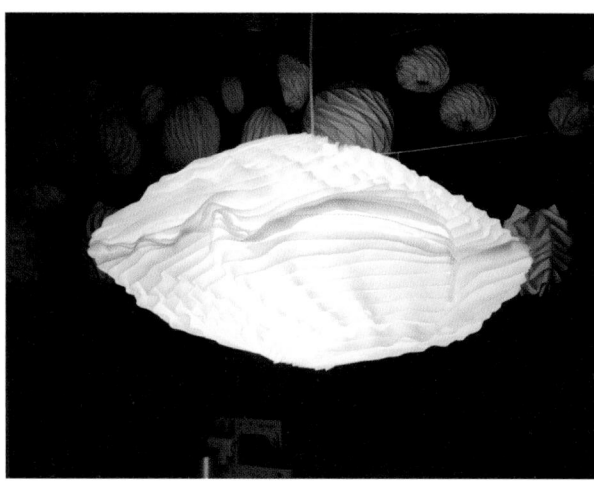

In 2017, Hurricane Eye II was included in Designmuseum Danmark's permanent exhibition collection DANISH DESIGN NOW.

The architect and textile artist Cecilie Bendixen (b. 1975) graduated from the Royal Danish Academy of Fine Arts, School of Architecture, in 2005. In 2013, she earned a PhD from the Academy's School of Design for a thesis on acoustics. The previous year, Bendixen had founded Tegnestuen Tekstile Rum (Textile Spaces Studio). Here she designs lamps whose function goes far beyond what we normally associate with a luminaire and which are more aptly described as sound-absorbing volumes draped over LEDs.

Before Bendixen created her first lamp series, Hurricane Eyes, in 2014, her main focus had been on sound absorption based on three-dimensional pleated forms made of sound-dampening textile. Something new happened when she added a light source to forms made in sound-absorbing and, in this case, translucent textile, which has an effect reminiscent of frosted glass: 'It's woven of a monofilament – a single thread – that contains lots of tiny prisms that disperse the light for a highly diffused effect, as the light is filtered through each of the thin fibres.'[1] The light is broken up by the textile but also by the pleats that shape the lamp. Bendixen underscores the importance of creating objects where 'light, sound and construction fully support each other'.[2] The pleats affect both light and acoustics as well as the spatial experience. They add complexity to the light and heighten sound absorption, because they make it possible to incorporate more textile. In terms of construction, the pleats maintain the lamp's distended form.

The name, Hurricane Eyes, refers to the dynamic movement in the large lamp structure. The eye is the calm centre of a hurricane, and that is exactly where the light source is positioned. Spinning around it is the large, sound-absorbing hurricane formation, consisting only of heavy fabric and thread. 'The threads fixate the pleats, and it seems surprising that the textile can support itself; it's quite amazing. It adds a sense of lightness.'[3]

Bendixen's latest lamp, from 2019, is called Volume (Yellow) and is the 12th lamp in her Volume series. Yellow refers to the yellow thread used to both sew and suspend the volume and which hangs down from it, a natural extension because it is the thread combined with the textile that *is* Volume. The cord, a necessary feature in a lamp, has the same colour as the threads. The lamp uses a standard bulb-shaped light source, an LED bulb with a colour temperature of 2,700 Kelvin that beautifully complements the textile and the refractions that occur in the textile and its pleats.

Bendixen personally produces the lamps, which are sold from Galerie Maria Wettergren in Paris. Bendixen does not regard them as works of art but as architecture, because to her the spatial experience is their primary purpose:

It is the essence of space, defined as what is outside, that I'm trying to bring into the lamp's construction, so that its form suggests a volume: a large spatial volume. In Denmark, indoor climate is a high priority, because we spend so much time inside. But what materials, light sources and acoustic installations does it take to ensure an indoor climate we can stand to be in? Instead of 'the open field', we have sound absorption; instead of the sun, we have the lamp.[4]

The Volume lamps are designed to hang freely in the room to provide optimal acoustics and to allow the light to spread throughout the space. Thus, they would work well as pendants above a table. To Bendixen, the main point is that it is 'a form in an amazing textile that affects sound and light at the same time'.[5] The lamps are very large, as they need to be to have an acoustic effect.[6] The lamps provide effective sound absorption due to the textile itself, the pleated structure and the lamp's placement in the room, with open space around it. The lamp softens the sound in the room – and the light.

'My primary drive is spatial qualities, the sense of space, while acoustic aspects and lighting are a way to achieve that. Sound goes into the form, while light radiates out.'—Cecilie Bendixen, 2019[7]

Maria Berntsen: Stay

Design For The People
by Nordlux—2019

When Maria Berntsen founded her own design firm in 1992, one of her first products was a lamp. The designer and her deliberately affordably priced lamp were featured in *Bo Bedre* under the heading 'Kvindelig PH–afløser' (Female Successor to PH).[1] In a Danish market that was 'flooded with low-quality copies of PH lamps', she explained what she saw as her particular mission: 'To me, the challenge has been to demonstrate that it's possible to design lamps in a contemporary design and in a good quality for the same price that you'd pay for a low-quality copy of a famous design'.[2] The Lumino lamp from 1993 addressed the new technological challenge of its time by incorporating the then new and very differently shaped energy-efficient light bulbs. However, it was mainly driven by an ambition of creating quality design at an affordable price and thus formed an extension of the functionalist endeavour and the FDB furniture with its positive story about design that everybody could afford. Lumino did not become a Berntsen classic; those followed later, and 'today I make a lot of lamps'.[3] In the summer of 2019, new lamps are being launched that address today's technological developments.

The multifunctional wall lamp Stay sprang from a specific need for good lighting and a small table or shelf space by the bed: 'I have a summer house now, and for this house I needed both a bedside lamp and a bedside table. So I began to sketch a solution that was a table and lamp in one, where the lamp could be dimmed and adjusted to provide the right light at the right angle.'[4] The solution was a lamp and a small tabletop held together by a rod with two wall fittings, one next to the lamp head and one next to the table. The two points provide stability, and with the hidden fittings the combined lamp-and-table almost seems to float.

Considering the realities of everyday life in 2019, where we're constantly needing to charge our mobile phones, I included a USB outlet on the side of the table for plugging in your mobile. It makes for good, functional design to add new technology, so that everything is contained in a single design.[5]

The lampshade is conical in shape, and Berntsen 'made an oblique cut into the cone to give the shade a more open, directional form.'[6] There is an LED light source at the top of the shade covered by an opalized acrylic plate to prevent a direct view of the light source. The shade can be rotated and thus set to the desired angle, and the light output can be adjusted to 'three different levels via a touch-control button on the table, so the lamp can provide either bright light or a cosy, softer light'. The on/off switch is incorporated into the tabletop as an elegant, subtle detail.

Stay also exists as a table lamp, which also has both a built-in USB outlet and LED lighting. Here, the circular plate forms the base of the lamp while also serving as a tray and a charging station on the desk, since 'we all keep our mobile close to hand all the time.'[7]

The other luminaire, which was launched during the summer of 2019, is the Angle pendant. As the name suggests, it can be positioned in several different angles for directional lighting. The adjustments are made using a magnet on the cord: 'The idea was to design a flexible lamp that could hang straight down or be positioned in countless oblique angles and where the cord formed a decorative element, so that this functional element also contributed to a more personal expression.'[8] This pendant too has a built-in LED light source shielded by an opalized acrylic plate to make the lamp glare-free, regardless of the angle: 'The goal was to make it possible for people to interact and develop a relationship with the lamp by putting it in just the right position.'[9]

Berntsen's dialogue about the lamps with Design For The People began in 2016. This Nordlux sub-brand produces lamps by acclaimed Danish designers under the motto 'Danish design accessible for all'.[10] Thus, Berntsen has come full circle, returning to where it all began in 1993.

The Angle lamp is a spotlight and pendant in one.

'It was important to find an elegant way to bring in the technology and thus relate to the way we live today.'—Maria Berntsen, 2019[11]

Olafur Eliasson: OE Quasi Light

Louis Poulsen—2019

OE Quasi Light at Tate Modern's Terrace Bar. During the exhibition *Olafur Eliasson: In Real Life* (2019), the bar was redesigned to reflect the ambience of Eliasson's studio and served a vegetarian menu specially developed by SOE Kitchen.

In September 2019, the lighting company Louis Poulsen launched a new pendant lamp. Prior to the launch, it had been presented at the lighting exhibition *Salone del Mobile Euroluce* in Milan. The new pendant, OE Quasi Light, was created by the artist Olafur Eliasson: 'We had initiated a dialogue about me designing a lamp a few years earlier. The design springs from a series of artistic experiments with geometry, light and natural forms I was carrying out together with my studio team.'[1] Note Eliasson's use of the word artistic. He underscores that he always approaches a task as an artist, also when the object is a lamp: 'My works usually begin with a feeling or an idea, which then goes through a process of verbalization, sketching and modelling before it takes concrete form. I try to linger as long as possible in a "pre-language" zone in order to dive into the uncertainty, which I think holds a great creative potential.'[2] Eliasson adds,

What interests me about light is the way it affects our perception of the world and thus how we act in it. My friend Anna Wirz-Justice is a chronobiologist. Among other topics, she studies the difference between the wavelengths in daylight and artificial light and their impact on our sleep pattern and emotional well-being. The varying pattern between day and night across the seasons is part of our biological clock and affects our behaviour and physiology. I find that really fascinating! Cold light contains a lot of blue, which makes us more attentive and awake. Warm light, light with more orange and red, is much more soothing.[3]

When Louis Poulsen began its collaboration with PH, the focus was on addressing the challenge of a new era: shielding the bright electric light bulb to produce a warm, glare-free light. In 2019, Eliasson says of his own work in extension of the PH tradition,

Louis Poulsen's philosophy is very much based on the notion of indirect lighting, and while I strived to be true to that, I also wanted to turn it around. So while PH's lamp designs all have a central light source contained within a shade structure that secures a muted glare-free light, the light source in OE Quasi Light is placed in the frame and reflects the light back to the core of the lamp.[4]

The pendant is constructed of two both contrasting and corresponding geometric forms, one embedded in the other. The exterior form is a fixed, dark aluminium frame shaped as an icosahedron (a geometric figure with 20 triangular sections and 12 corners), while the interior form is a white core in polycarbonate shaped as a dodecahedron (which has 12 pentagonal surfaces and thus 20 corners). The inner core is not a shade containing a light bulb but instead a visible reflector. The LED light source is placed on the inside of the aluminium frame, the diodes placed at the corners and connected via light rails along the interior edges. Thus, the light, as Eliasson explained, is cast back towards the white central reflector, which in turn casts it back and thus into the room.[5]

Eliasson does not regard his LED pendant primarily as a technical solution to our contemporary lighting challenge. His mission is another, in part concerned with promoting sustainability:

My approach to light is aesthetic or political rather than technical: what does light do to the person who experiences it, reads in it or has a drink with someone else in it, and what does it do to our surroundings? When we developed OE Quasi Light, sustainability was a key issue. While Louis Poulsen considers its lamps to be sustainable because they have a long lifetime, I made sure that everything in the lamp could be replaced and that we used as many recycled and recyclable materials as possible to make it. Sustainability is the biggest challenge we are currently facing: how can we create quality lighting that considers the effect the production of a lamp and the consumption of electricity has on our environment?[6]

While the similarly sustainable Little Sun from 2012 was a design intended for the many (see page 200), the light sculpture OE Quasi Light is probably not a pendant that, like the PH 5 lamp, will be in use in many Danish homes: it has a diameter of 90 cm and costs DKK 85,000.[7]

'I regard everything I do as art and approach it as an artist – also when I'm working on a lamp.'
—Olafur Eliasson, 2019[8]

Design by BIG: La Linea

Artemide—2019

La Linea was developed in extension of Alphabet of Light from 2016.

In 2019, the Bjarke Ingels Group presented La Linea at the lighting exhibition *Salone del Mobile Euroluce* in Milan, but the story of the bendable tube – or snake – of light began a few years earlier and was based on the notion of giving people the opportunity to create their own light installations.

La Linea was developed in extension of our first project and collaboration with Artemide, where we talked about giving the contract-market clients their freedom back. We talked about the classic neon signs, which could only be made by specialists, and we wanted to enable the buyers to make their own signs. The result was Alphabet of Light, which was launched in 2016 and is, in principle, two tubes of light: a quarter circle and a straight element as well as some joints and a terminal strip. These very simple elements can be combined in all sorts of ways and, not least, you can write with them.[1]

The above is the description by the head of BIG's Design Department, Jakob Lange, who explains that BIG also developed a font for the letters. Thus, at the furniture fair in Milan in 2016, visitors could write the following sentence in 120-cm-tall luminous letters: 'Quick brown fox jumped over the lazy dog'.[2] The pangram (a sentence containing all the letters in the alphabet) demonstrated how the entire alphabet could be written using the two elements and the terminal strips: 'If you can make an alphabet using so few elements, you can make any conceivable form, create structures to hang from the ceiling or, for example, a giant relief of a person on a facade, where all the lines are placed within a grid; anything is possible – and the light performs pretty well!'[3] The LED light inside the tubes diffuses a warm, white light into the room through the hard, opalized plastic.

While the design of Alphabet of Light is based on strict geometric principles and even a font, La Linea from 2019 is made in silicone, which can be bent and shaped in completely free geometries, and is even more spatially defining.[4] The limber silicone tube has a diameter of 5 cm and comes in a length of either 2.5 or 5 metres but can be extended to any length using the terminal strips. The joint is completely hidden inside the tubes and does not produce a shadow. It also is not possible to tell that the light is produced by a long row of LEDs, because the light is distributed completely evenly, and everything seems to form a luminous optic unity of white, diffused light that is further regulate with a light management system via an app.[5]

La Linea offers infinite lighting possibilities: the silicone snake can be an integrated part of the architecture, following and highlighting the lines of the room, or it can be folded into a figure and become a sculptural element in itself. Similarly, it can become part of a landscape, since it can handle both water and a temperature range from 20 °C below up to 40 °C: 'La Linea can be dropped into a swimming pool or laid out in the Antarctic – it can handle just about anything.'[6]

Regardless of the placement, it forms a thick line of soft, uniform light that gives a sense that the light has almost been poured into the form – a cord turned lamp, a three-dimensional line of light in the air.

'The reason why we, as an architecture firm, take on this sort of design project is that we like to make the stuff we put into our buildings,'[7] says Lange. The flexibility of La Linea makes it possible for the light to interact with the buildings' indoor and outdoor spaces. It is simultaneously good functional lighting and highly conceptual – a work of art that is industrialized but also a volume that creates a room-in-a-room in a very architectural effect.

BIG only began to design lighting a few years ago, but there are more lamps on the way!

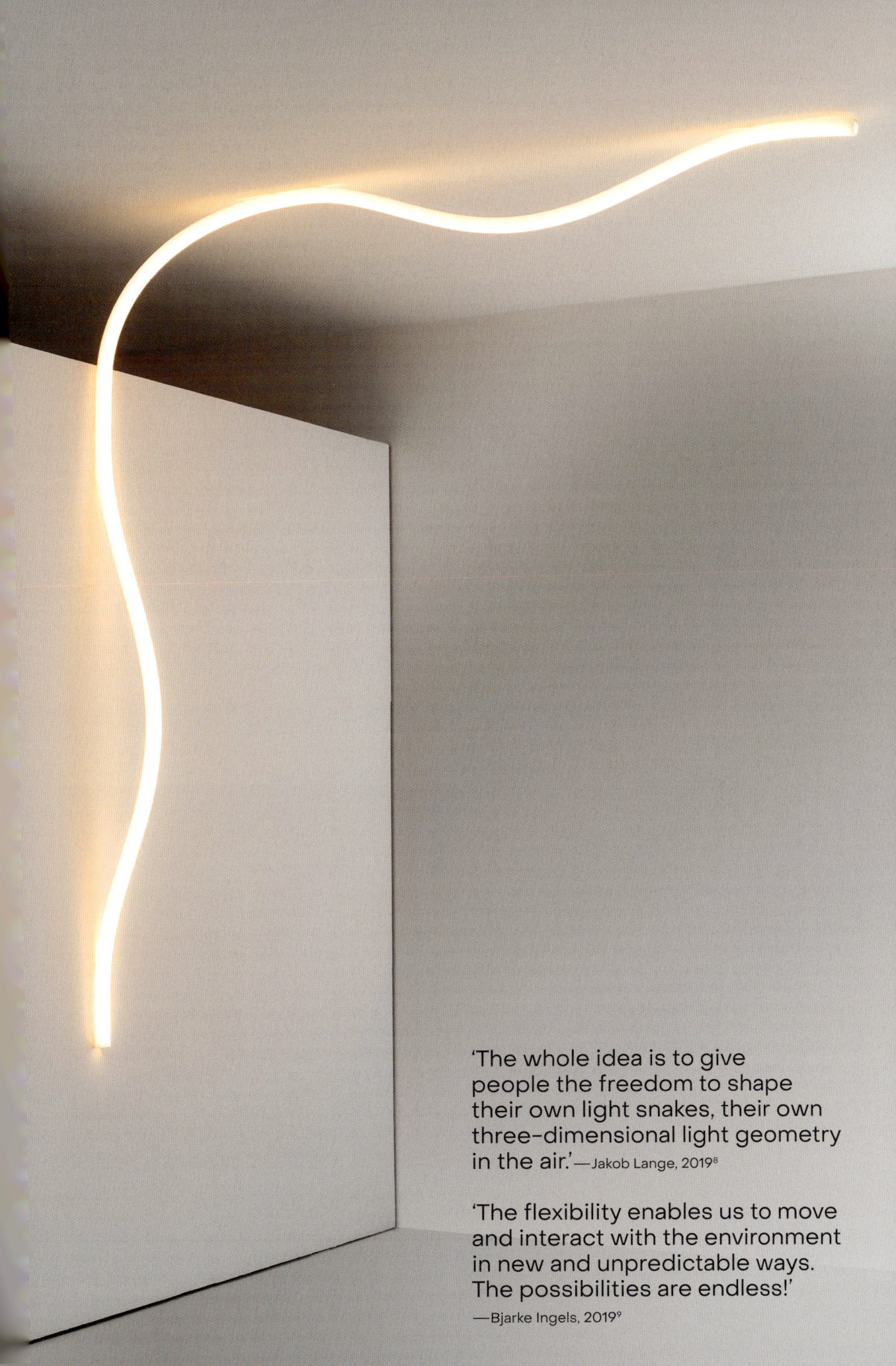

'The whole idea is to give people the freedom to shape their own light snakes, their own three-dimensional light geometry in the air.' —Jakob Lange, 2019[8]

'The flexibility enables us to move and interact with the environment in new and unpredictable ways. The possibilities are endless!'
—Bjarke Ingels, 2019[9]

Øivind Slaatto: Shade Pendant ØS1

Shade—2019

Shade Pendant ØS1 is a very small pendant, but it has a big light source, and it is simultaneously electric and electronic.

For the past century, Danish lighting has been electric. Back then, it seemed a miracle that a modern person only had to push a button before the electric lamp turned night to day as if by magic. As functionalism gained ground in Denmark, with its calls for functional design in bright airy rooms, PH repeatedly lamented modernity's quest for ever brighter, white light. PH poetically stated that 'the goal is to make homes and people beautiful, the evening restful'.[1] In Denmark, the concept of *hygge* has been instrumental in setting the agenda that called for warm light. This has led to high demands for luminaire designs that make the light source emit soft, glare-free light. The designer Øivind Slaatto explains:

You avoid glare by making the transition from light to dark as soft as possible. The eye is not dazzled by light but by the contrast between light and dark. If the transition is sudden, the eye is dazzled, so it is the lamp designer's task to create the conditions for a gentle transition between light and dark.[2]

The light from our lamps also affects our diurnal rhythm. Thus, ideally, lighting should follow the course of the sun, aligning with our biological clock by providing cool, clear light in the morning when we need to wake up, a stronger and more saturated light in the middle of the day and a warmer light in the evening, to help us relax: 'PH's words about making the evening restful are key.'[3]

Slaatto's Shade Pendant ØS1 was designed for the lighting company Shade, which points out that because Denmark has so many hours of dusk or darkness, we have a long tradition for designing and optimizing lighting in the home: 'We are standing on the shoulders of this design tradition, but we combine tradition with the latest new technology.'[4]

While Slaatto's other lighting designs can be described as large, fantastic and carefully executed luminaires, his Shade Pendant ØS1 is a very simple, small circular design with a diameter of only 13 cm and a height of just 4 cm. It is, however, a rather ingenious dynamic lamp aimed at enabling people to create precisely the light they need in a given situation:

What really makes the lamp interesting is that it's not just electric but electronic, so that it can switch on and off just as gently as the dark of the night becomes the clear morning light, and it can change the colour, intensity and direction of the light, as we know it from the way the saturated midday light becomes warmer towards sunset, as the body begins to calm. We sought to make it possible to recreate the full 24-hour cycle of light, from the cold morning light to the clear light of day to the warm, golden evening light.[5]

The pendant is made of frosted polycarbonate, which diffuses the light, and it can be set to three lighting zones: up, down or horizontal. The zones are marked with two rings in polished brass. Shade is controlled with a 'smart switch', Shade Node, which can be mounted on the wall or kept in the user's pocket. The lamp can also be controlled via a smartphone app.[6]

Shade Pendant ØS1 is a design solution that takes advantage of cutting-edge technological developments, but as its most important feature, like all Slaatto's lamps, it has quality light as its top priority.

I have been able to turn the fact that I've always been extremely photosensitive, for better or worse, into a strength, because it enables me to make really good, glare-free lamps. And if you aim to make something that's really good, it automatically has integrity. And high integrity is a characteristic of Danish design and Danish lighting culture.[7]

Øivind Slaatto's latest lamp, Shade ØS1, is available as a pendant, a wall lamp, a floor lamp and – as shown here – a table lamp. The colour, intensity and temperature of the light can be controlled via a smartphone app.

'My lamp design is entirely determined by lighting principles. I am not trying to create something new and innovative; I just want things to be good.'—Øivind Slaatto, 2019[8]

Thanks

Many people have contributed to the making of this book. I am deeply grateful to you all.

First, a special thanks to all the lamp designers I interviewed or was in contact with; I can never thank you enough. You enriched my understanding by sharing your stories and your thoughts on design and light. You not only helped me get the facts straight, including the dates and chronology; you also shed light on all the ideas that go into the making of a design, offering unique insight into the many different steps that constitute the design process. I also thank the many family members of lamp designers, who generously shared their stories from the sidelines and, in many cases, as active participants in the design process.

You are all mentioned in the individual stories, but I wish to take this opportunity to emphasize how rewarding I found working with each and every one of you and how much this dialogue contributed to the accuracy and, not least, the real-life texture of the stories.

I also received much valued help from employees of design firms and lamp manufacturers. No design or lighting manufacturer has any monetary interest in this book, but everyone I reached out to stepped up, without hesitation, to help add substance and new perspectives to the stories. So did people from other areas that I contacted to elucidate specific aspects of a text – from the sexton at Bagsværd Church to the astrophysicist at the Tycho Brahe Planetarium and the associate professor at the Copenhagen Plant Science Center. I am so grateful for your help. It feels wrong to single anyone out, but I do owe special thanks to the extraordinarily dedicated manufacturers Rasmus Markholt and Claus Juhlin, who, in addition to sharing unique insights into the process behind the designs, also facilitated contacts with the family members of deceased designers. Special thanks also go to the retro-lamp vendors who made lamps available for photos, in particular to Houston Wilson, a passionate design enthusiast, a fount of knowledge about design history and a seller of vintage design, who was tremendously helpful throughout the project by facilitating interview appointments and providing photos and specific details about the many historical lamps he has handled over the years.

The publication was made possible by generous grants from private foundations. I was thrilled every time I received another e-mail from Publishing Director Sidsel Kjærulff Rasmussen with the wonderful news of a grant approval. Your faith in the project and your support, which enabled both a Danish and an English edition, have meant the world to me. The same goes for the entire team at Strandberg Publishing, who offered professional assistance and warm support. In addition to the always kind and forthcoming Sidsel Kjærulff Rasmussen, this includes publisher and CEO Lars Erik Strandberg, project coordinator Mille Bjørnstrup, proofreader Sara Kohl, copy editor and proofreader Wendy Brouwer, PR officer Mette Wibeck Olsen and assistant editors Sara Kira Wernberg-Tougaard, Anna Rølle, Sandra Lyngsie Pedersen and Christina Reventlov Petersen. Finally, I thank photographer Brian Buchardt and graphic designer Søren Damstedt, who are responsible for the visual form of this beautiful book. Thank you!

Three people in particular contributed to the editorial process. First, I thank my consultant editor, Lars Dybdahl, who has had an unparalleled influence on the practice and communication of Danish design research. Lars also played a key role in my own professional development. He was my mentor during my art and design history studies the University of Copenhagen, always showing faith in my project ideas and helping to elevate their academic level and, thus, my learning; the same applies to the present publication, where Lars's professional feedback improved my work as well as my confidence in the outcome. My copy editor, Hanne Rask, provided patient and untiring support. Hanne, I cannot thank you enough; you improved my writing and were there for me throughout! Finally, I thank my translator, Dorte Herholdt Silver, who is not only a brilliant translator; at every stage of the process, Dorte generously offered professional feedback, advice and support when things seemed most overwhelming.

Last, but not least, I thank my family and friends for their patience and understanding while the project consumed all my time. Special thanks to my aunt, journalist Birthe Meier, whose help with particularly tricky phrases or passages was always only a phone call away – your steadfast support means the world to me. The same is true of my wise, wonderful mother, Kirsten Lytken, who has offered priceless support and feedback on specific passages when I was in doubt. I also thank my father, Jon Lytken, who was always ready to act as my private chauffeur when an interview appointment was out of reach for public transport.

Countless people assisted my research for the 100 stories and the historical essay. It is impossible to mention all of you by name, but my thanks go, among others, to the librarians at Designmuseum Danmark, the Royal Danish Academy of Fine Arts, the Royal Danish Library and Frederiksberg Library, who tirelessly assisted me in my many literature searches. My sincere thanks to all of you!

My special thanks goes to everyone on the list below for your help throughout the project; you made it possible for me to write this book.

THANKS TO designers: Alfred Homann, architect; Andreas Hansen, architect; Anne Qvist, architect; Benny Frandsen, designer, owner of Frandsen Group; Cecilie Bendixen, architect and textile artist; Cecilie Manz, designer; Enrico Fratesi, architect; Frederik Ottesen, engineer and co-founder of the socioeconomic company Little Sun; Hans Due, graphic designer; Jakob Lange, architect, partner, Design by BIG – Bjarke Ingels Group; Jens Møller-Jensen, architect; Jonas Bjerre-Poulsen, architect, co-owner of Norm Architects; Jonas Edvard Nielsen, designer; Kasper Salto, designer; Louis Weisdorf, architect; Louise Campbell, designer; Maria Berntsen, designer; Olafur Eliasson, artist; Ole Jensen, ceramicist, designer; Peter Bysted, architect; Philip Bro Ludvigsen, architect; Poul Christiansen, architect; Sofie Refer, designer, Nuura; Stig Gerlach, CEO, Sirius Company; Stine Gam, architect; Thomas Sigsgaard, architect; Tom Rossau, designer; Torsten Thorup, architect; Øivind Slaatto, designer.

Family members of designers: Bent Gantzel-Boysen's widow, Dorit Gantzel-Boysen; Bent Gantzel-Boysen's daughters, Gitte and Janne Gantzel-Boysen; Bent Karlby's grandson Hans Schrader; Bent Karlby's grandson's wife, Anne Vibeke Mortensen; Hans J. Wegner's daughter and studio employee, Marianne Wegner; Henning Koppel's daughter Hannah Koppel; Jo Hammerborg's widow, Henni Hammerborg; Jo Hammerborg's daughters, Gry and Marlene Hammerborg; Jørgen Gammelgaard's widow, Karin Gammelgaard; Jørn Utzon's son and studio employee, Jan Utzon; Lars Eiler Schiøler's son Uffe Schiøler; Sven Middelboe's granddaughter Louise Eidemak; Verner Panton's widow, Marianne Panton; Verner Panton's daughter, Carin Panton.

Other contributors: Anne Bay, engineer, director, Danish Lighting Center; Anne-Cathrine Tjørnehøj, PR manager, Signify (formerly Philips Lighting); Anne-Louise Sommer, director, Designmuseum Danmark; Anni Knudsen, secretary, Piet Hein lighting; Bente Riis, marketing manager, Focus Lighting; Berit Lundberg, executive secretary, Royal Danish Academy of Music; Else Rasmussen, Antiquarian and Topographical Archive, National Museum of Denmark; Cecilie Sand Nørholm, astrophysicist, Tycho Brahe Planetarium; Claus Juhlin, owner of Pandul; Frank C. Motzkus, historian; Hanne Thomsen, historian, director, GASmuseet; Hans Jørgen Berthel, founder, former owner of ABO; Henrik Isidor, architect, Vilhelm Lauritzen Architects; Henrik Lund-Larsen, CEO, &Tradition; Houston Wilson, owner of Danish Vintage Design; Jakob Meyling, architect, Vilhelm Lauritzen Architects; Joakim Zacho Weylandt, design archaeologist; Jenny Kjærbo, senior graphic designer, Stelton; Johannes Lundstrøm, writer; Jørgen Ellegård Frederiksen, organist, Bagsværd Church; Karima Andersen, architect, design manager of Lighting, Fritz Hansen; Karin Ørskov, interior designer; Kjeld Kjeldsen, curator, Louisiana Museum of Modern Art; Kjell Berentzen, founder, former owner of Lampas; Klavs Andersen, expert on Thykier lamps in general; Lena McNair, architect, head of Membership Services, Danish Association of Architects; Line Borring, graphic designer; Lisbeth Mansfeldt, lighting expert (former showroom manager, Louis Poulsen); Lone Bødker Pedersen, PR & brand manager, Nordlux – Design for the People; Lone Kudsk, head of marketing, Frandsen Retail, Frandsen Group; Louise Engelbrecht, receptionist, Louis Poulsen; Lærke Rydal Jørgensen, editor, Louisiana Museum of Modern Art; Mathias Bøgeholdt, expert on Arne Jacobsen; Mette Stagsted Larsen, marketing director, Stelton; Mikkel Bahr, architect, partner, head of design, Friis & Moltke; Niels Christiansen, collection curator, Danish Museum of Science and Technology; Nils Zeeberg, senior consultant, co-author of *Byens Nips – om Brandhaner, Lygtepæle og Andet Godt*; Pernille Klemp, photographer, Designmuseum Danmark; Peter Frandsen, CEO, Verpan; Poul Madsen, co-founder, owner of Normann Copenhagen; Rasmus Markholt, co-founder of Lightyears 2004, founder of Lyfa 2020; Sally Ding Lytken; Sebastian Francis Atkins, PR & communications manager, Nuura; Stephan Wenkel, biologist, associate professor, Section for Plant Biochemistry, Copenhagen Plant Science Center, University of Copenhagen; Sune Riishede, owner of Retrogaragen; Susanne Krogh Jensen, collection curator, Danish Museum of Science and Technology; Susanne Outzen, curator, Museum Sydøstdanmark; Søren Andersen, marketing manager, Le Klint; Søren Palsbo, journalist, co-author of *Byens Nips – om Brandhaner, Lygtepæle og Andet Godt*; Søren Lauritsen, head of lighting, Lampas by Veksø; Søren Peter Kristensen, project manager, Rambøll; Thorkild Thage Jørgensen, CEO, Nordisk Solar; Torsten Bløndal, publisher, Edition Bløndal; Ulla Riemer, head of LP Academy, Louis Poulsen; Vicki Hertz, honorary member of and former secretary for the Danish Design Council; Vivi and Erik Sørensen, owners of El-Hjørnet, Godthåbsvej, Frederiksberg; Vivian Etting, senior researcher, National Museum of Denmark.

Notes

Preface

1 Schrøder, 1964, p. 11.
2 Henningsen, P., 1927, p. 72.
3 'Den ideelle Belysning', 1921.

Lamps, lighting and *hygge* in the right light

4 Jonas Edvard, 25 March 2019.
5 Theilgaard, 1915, p. 898.
6 Keiding, 2003.
7 Olafur Eliasson, 12 August 2019.
8 Cecilie Sand Nørholm, 17 September 2019.
9 Paragraph based on personal communication with Cecilie Sand Nørholm, astrophysicist at the Planetarium, 16 September 2019, and engineer Anne Bay, director of the Danish Lighting Center, 20 September 2019.
10 Cecilie Sand Nørholm, 17 September 2019.
11 Hence, people rose with the sun and went to bed at sunset. That made for a long 'day' – and with a little luck, a full moon might even offer additional working hours (Frydensberg, 2019, p. 10).
12 Braae, 1948, p. 566.
13 Linnet, 2010, p. 5.
14 Ibid., p. 98.
15 Henningsen, P., 1974, p. 27.
16 Anne Bay, 20 September 2019. Danish Lighting Center, an association founded in 1948 with the purpose of promoting knowledge of good and appropriate lighting in a Danish context. Knowledge sharing among professionals is one of its main purposes. Bay also considers it an important mission to educate the general Danish public about how to use lighting more thoughtfully in the home.
17 Henningsen, P., 1945, p. 425. The following review of lighting history is largely based on material gathered for Lytken, 2016, Chapters 3 and 4.
18 Jensen, (1908) 1973, p. 75.
19 Øivind Slaatto, 5 April 2019.
20 Baagøe, 1965, p. 9.
21 Troels-Lund, 1914, p. 8. Troels-Lund (1840–1921) authored the multi-volume *Dagligt liv i Norden i det Sekstende Aarhundrede* (Everyday Life in the Nordic Region during the Sixteenth Century), published in 1879–1901. The quote is from the sixth volume, first released in 1884.
22 Ibid.
23 Ibid., p. 10.
24 Ibid., pp. 8–9.
25 Filskov, 1917, p. 881.
26 See, e.g., Kjær, 1923, pp. 300–301, and Schrøder, 1964, pp. 72–73.
27 Finds of wax candles in a Viking tomb in Mammen, Jutland, and in the royal burial chamber in the large Jelling Mound, also in Jutland, show that burning wax candles played a role in the burial rituals of kings and Viking chieftains. Beeswax candles were probably invented by the Phoenicians, and the technology spread north from the Mediterranean. Troels-Lund, 1914, p. 10, Meyer, 1924, p. 176, Baagøe, 1965, pp. 16–17, and Rybczynski, 1986, p. 163.
28 Waagepetersen, 1969, p. 10. Church chandeliers are often associated with bronze, but only wealthier churches could afford bronze. Iron chandeliers were the norm in the many Danish village churches, often made by a local smith (ibid.). The 15th-century chandelier from Gimlinge was donated to the National Museum of Denmark in 1848 by the Rev. Quistgaard (Vivian Etting, senior researcher at the National Museum of Denmark, 20 September 2019).
29 Although farmers could make their own tallow candles, they were still costly. The fat from eight sheep would make 400 candles or 600 of the thinner, longer, often lower-quality tapers, which people used when they moved around the house at night (Thorndahl, 2000, p. 34).
30 Andersen, 1949a. Andersen's personification of the two candles represents the different personality types associated with the candles and also highlights the class distinctions in Andersen's Denmark.
31 Thorndahl, 2000, p. 36. Royals used candles to showcase their status. Frederiksborg Palace had an annual consumption of 30,000 candles during the heyday of courtly life there in the 1620s and 1630s. In the royal chambers, 14 to 16 candles were used every day (Baagøe, 1965, p. 17). In 1770, the Danish King used 22 candles to light his dinner table (ibid.).
32 The paragraph is based on Garrett, 1990, p. 145, Thorndahl, 2000, p. 34, and Rybczynski, 1986, p. 163.
33 Argand shaped the wick into a hollow cylinder, which enhanced the light; however, the more brightly burning wick burnt so much oil that it struggled to absorb it fast enough. Hence, Argand added a higher-placed oil reservoir, so that the heavy, sticky oil only had to rise a few millimetres into the wick to burn. Around the flame he placed a short tubular metal chimney, later replaced with heat-resistant flint glass. This simple solution shielded the flame from irregular air currents, leading to a stronger and more regular air flow around the wick and thus better combustion. See Holst and la Cour, 1904, p. 164, Schrøder, 1964, pp. 94–96, Schrøder, 1968, p. 110, and Garnert, 1993, p. 55.
34 Jacobsen, 1912, p. 18.
35 Schrøder, 1964, p. 112. The first newspaper quote is from Schrøder, 1968, p. 62. Schrøder offers no additional references for the quotes.
36 See Schivelbusch, 1995, p. 168, and Rybczynski, 1986, p. 163.
37 Benjamin Thompson, Count of Rumford, studied thermology, among other topics: heat radiation, heat conductivity and their practical applications. He described his studies in the four-volume publication *Essays, Political, Economical and Philosophical* written 1796–1806.
38 'Moderating the too powerful brightness of Argand's beautiful lamp' (Rumford, 1875, p. 106).
39 Ibid, p. 110.
40 Ibid.
41 Schrøder, 1964, p. 152.
42 Added information comes from Glashistorisk Selskab (Society for Glass History): http://www.glashistoriskselskab.dk/index.php/joomgallery/Belysning/Lamper/Skomagerkugle-1880-457.
43 Stearin for candles is often made of a mixture of palmitic acid and stearic acid.

Both are saturated fatty acids (insoluble in water). The acids are extracted from plant and animal fat, respectively. The pure stearin candle burnt with a cleaner flame than even the expensive wax candles – also because the wick was braided. Unlike the softer wax, the hard, smooth stearin lent itself to mechanized candle making. Ever since the snow-white stearin candles were introduced, straight, white candles became the ideal (Zalewski, 2000, p. 53, and Crowley, 2001, p. 194).

44   Holst and la Cour, 1904, p. 163.
45   All the oil lamps mentioned here, from the Argand lamp to the moderator lamp, were fuelled almost exclusively with refined rape-seed oil in Denmark. Once kerosene became widely available, rape farming was drastically reduced (Theilgaard, 1923, p. 299, and Høst, 1982, p. 93).
46   Garnert, 1993, p. 59. The residual product existed in two forms: heavy and light distillates. The heavy ones were used in part for lubrication, while the lighter ones had what seems, from a 2019 perspective, as a curious fate: petrol was a byproduct of kerosene production, which there was initially no real demand for. Around 1900, cars became more common, and petrol was no longer a chemist's item used mainly for cleaning gloves.
47   There were three different kinds of kerosene lamps, based on three different burners. The earliest model was a flat-flame burner – here, the wick is pushed up and out through an aperture, producing a flat or two-sided flame. This type of kerosene lamp always had a bulbous chimney. In the Argand burner, which was the most common, the wick is pulled together into a tube, and the flame burns in a ring. The chimney was tall and narrow, because that optimized both light and combustion. The third type, which was also a very popular model, is called a flame-spreader burner. Here, the air flow is forced through a series of holes to direct the flame outwards. This results in a large light surface. These lamps always have spherical globes.
48   Theilgaard, 1923, p. 299.
49   Ibid. The earliest kerosene was dangerous because it contained large amounts of volatile substances, particularly naphtha, which has such a low fire point that the fumes can be ignited by a spark at several centimetres' distance. In high-grade kerosene, the naphtha was removed, but during the early years the kerosene trade was quite chaotic, and it was not until the formation of Det Danske Petroleums Aktieselskab (The Danish Kerosene Limited Company) in 1889 that consumers could be sure to buy kerosene with a regular, high fire point. See Schrøder, 1964, p. 180.
50   Aakjær, 1953, p. 12.
51   Paragraph based in part on Garnert, 1993, pp. 59–63, and Schrøder, 1964, pp. 179–196.
52   Schrøder, 1964, p. 196.
53   Voltelen, 1948, p. 193.
54   Schrøder, 1964, p. 199.
55   Filskov, 1917, p. 882.
56   Thomsen, 2011, p. 26.
57   Hanne Thomsen (20 September 2019), director of GASmuseet, says that one side of the Pall Mall in London was gaslit as early as 1807. The first public utility was established in 1812 and began to supply gas for street lighting in 1814 .
58   Paris had its first gasworks in 1815, Berlin in 1826. The Nordic capitals were a little later: Oslo in 1848 and Stockholm and Copenhagen in 1857. Gothenburg, Sweden, was the first Nordic city to install gas, in 1846. Odense was the first Danish city to have its own gasworks, in 1853; Elsinore followed suit in 1854. See Garnert, 1993, p. 69, and Thomsen, 2011, p. 32. Before the public gasworks were established in Denmark, there were a number of small private gasworks, so there were experiments with gaslighting in Copenhagen before 1857. The plumber Johannes experimented with gaslighting in a Copenhagen shop in 1815 and, probably, in the Danish cities of Aalborg and Randers in 1819 (Hanne Thomsen, 20 September 2019).
59   A contributing reason why the construction of gasworks stopped was the competition from kerosene. Gaslighting came to Denmark just a few years before kerosene was introduced in 1861. Since the American production of crude oil increased steadily throughout the 1860s, refined kerosene could be sold cheaply in Europe (Thomsen, 2011, pp. 48–49).
60   The construction of gasworks picked up during 1880–1916; however, the last gasworks was built in 1927, as number 112 in Denmark. While the first major competition was kerosene, from the 1890s it was electricity (Thomsen, 2011, pp. 49–50). The first public power plant was established in Odense in 1891, the second in Copenhagen in 1892.
61   In 1904, the physicists Helge Holst and Poul la Cour wrote about the early stages in the popular-science publication *Menneskeaandens Sejre*, 'People feared the flammability of gas and its foul smell, which was very bothersome at the time because the proper purification processes had not been developed. However, the technical difficulties were eventually overcome in a more satisfactory manner' (Holst and la Cour, 1904, p. 165). It was the sulphur content of the carbon gas which gave the burning gas a smell of rotten eggs (Thomsen, 2011, p. 49).
62   Paragraph and thus dates based on Rybczynski, 1986, p. 167, and Schivelbusch, 1995, p. 176.
63   During the 1830s and 1840s, many European countries held national industrial exhibitions, but an important new era began with the first international exhibition in London in 1851, where 17,000 exhibitors from all over the world presented their finest crafts and industrial products under one roof. However, it was a national French industrial exhibition, held in Paris in 1798, that had heralded the great exhibition era. The French exhibition was part of the mobilization of French industry against cheap British merchandise that was flooding Europe (Stoklund, 2003, p. 171).
64   *The Great Exhibition*, 1851. Text and etchings are reproduced from the 1851 original. The catalogue text identifies the light source used in the designs.
65   Semper, 2006, p. 542.
66   The chemist Carl Auer, Freiherr von Welsbach's (1858–1929) invention of the Welsbach gas mantle in 1885 led to a brighter light. It was a ceramic net with metal impregnation. When heated with a Bunsen burner, it glowed more brightly than the flame itself. The mantle was an important innovation for the gas industry when it had to compete with electricity because lamps with the mantle had a brighter and more stable light than the flames (Hanne Thomsen, 20 September 2019). The patented Welsbach gas mantles, or Welsbach lamps, were up to ten times brighter with the same consumption of gas, so all the old gaslights were quickly replaced. After improving gaslighting, Welsbach also improved the incandescent light bulb by replacing the carbon filament with a metal one. He founded the company that later became Osram (Thomsen, 2011, p. 53).
67   Thomsen, 2011, p. 48–49.
68   Ibid., p. 28, and Garnert, 1993, p. 71.
69   Holst and la Cour, 1904, pp. 165 and 172.
70   Filskov, 1917, p. 882. The English chemist Humphry Davy discovered carbon-arc lighting in 1810, which in the 1840s was developed into an electric light source. It could only be used outdoors, but in 1877 the Russian electrician Jablochkoff invented an arc light that could be used indoors and which was used, for example, in 1879 when the Danish shipyard Burmeister & Wain installed electric light. However, it could not be used in small rooms where people were close to the light source. During the following years, several inventors worked simultaneously to develop incandescent light bulbs, among them the German inventor Heinrich Goebel (1818–1893) and the English physicist Sir Joseph Wilson Swan (1828–1914), who created a functioning light bulb. Swan did not acquire a patent for his solution until after Edison had patented his, but Swan's home in Gateshead, England, was supposedly the first private home in the world to be illuminated by electric ligh. Based on Hansen, Petersen and Wistoft, 1991, pp. 22–24.
71   Filskov, 1917, p. 882.
72   Wistoft, 1991, p. 2.
73   Baldwin, 1995, p. 107. Baldwin writes that Edison was aware of at least Swan's earlier experiments. Through studies of various written sources, Baldwin tried to determine who of the two men was first to develop the incandescent light bulb. He quotes the French periodical *La Lumière Electrique* (Electric Light), which wrote in December 1880 that Swan's lamp seems to have preceded Edison's, but that nothing so far seemed to indicate it was superior to it (ibid.).
74   Bernhard Olsen in *Illustreret Tidende*, 1878. When Edison began his effort to develop electric light, as Olsen indicated in the quote, people knew of the intense electric carbon-arc light, which was far too bright and dazzling to be used in the home. In an article in the *New York Sun*, Edison promised that electricity would replace the gas system that at the time lit the streets of New York at night,

that he would have up to 10,000 lamps light up at the same time, that the power would be led to lower Manhattan through underground cables and that meters would ensure that people only paid for what they actually used ('Edison's Newest Marvel', *New York Sun*, 16 September 1878, quoted in Baldwin, 1995, p. 443). When the first Danish power plant began production in Odense in 1891, it powered a few thousand incandescent light bulbs at once (Kristensen, 2006, p. 6).
75   Baldwin, 1995, p. 131. The exhibition opened on 10 August 1881. A professional conference was also held, where issues related to norms, safety, future training and metering systems were among the topics on the agenda (ibid.).
76   Woaz, 1881, p. 648.
77   Crone, 1892, pp. 124–127.
78   Woaz, 1881, p. 650.
79   Perhaps as a result of this reluctance, several private initiatives aimed to establish electric light powered by block stations without underground cables, which did not require a permit from the city. From the beginning, the main purpose of the gasworks had been to generate gas for lighting in streets, companies and homes, but gradually electricity took over, both indoors and out.
80   Wistoft, 1991, p. 12.
81   Thorndahl, 2000, p. 37.
82   Theilgaard pointed out in *Salmonsens Konversationsleksikon* in 1923 that Danish streetlights 'used train-oil, since [other] oil would freeze, even at modest temperatures below freezing' (Theilgaard, 1923, p. 299). The first Copenhagen streetlights were installed in Købmagergade, along Gammel Strand and along the southern part of what is now the public square Højbro Plads (Palsbo and Zeeberg, 1974, unpaginated [p. 13]).
83   Ibid. and Søren Palsbo and Niels-Kristian Zeeberg, 10 September 2019.
84   Gad, E., grammophone recording, September 1913 (Royal Danish Library, Aarhus, Denmark).
85   Andersen, 1949b, p. 8.
86   Ibid.
87   See Palsbo and Zeeberg, 1974, unpaginated [p. 14]. The first Danish gaslights, which were made in cast iron, were designed in the late 19th century by the architect Ludvig Clausen in the City Architect's office and were intended for the superior Welsbach burners. These lamps were later converted to electricity (ibid.).
88   The first gaslights had an ascending, wide flame, so-called fish-tail burners; later, they were equipped with Welsbach burners, where a much smaller flame burnt inside a Welsbach gas mantle, which in turn emitted a much clearer, whiter light at a significantly lower gas consumption (Nils Zeeberg, 15 September 2019).
89   Ibid. That the train-oil lamp in Andersen's fairy tale is convinced that future streetlights will be fuelled by seawater was – and, at the time of writing, remains – a rather fanciful idea.
90   As early as 1857, even before the gaslights were lit, a demonstration of electric light had been conducted at the riding ground outside the Danish Parliament, Christiansborg, and on cold February days in 1871, electric carbon-arc lamps had illuminated the intrepid skaters gliding along the ice on Sortedam lake in Copenhagen (Palsbo and Zeeberg, 1974, unpaginated [pp. 14–15]). The carbon-arc lamps were imported (Nils Zeeberg, 15 September 2019). In street lighting, gas was not quite a brief intermezzo; in fact, it took just over 100 years before the electric light illuminated all city streets. The last gaslights did not disappear until 1959.
91   Nils Kristian Zeeberg, 15 September 2019. Zeeberg thus corrects information in Palsbo and Zeeberg, 1974, unpaginated [p. 15].
92   J.V. Dahlerup's lamps were subsequently also installed in other central Copenhagen squares: Amagertorv, Gammeltorv/Nytorv and City Hall Square. In 1930, eight lamps were placed on the dam across Copenhagen's Sankt Jørgens Lake. Originally, the lamps had used carbon-arc lighting. In 1998, the first metal-filament lamps, so-called Nernst lamps, were placed in the streets, but it was not until 1910–1915 that the carbon-arc lights in Dahlerup's lamps were replaced by modern incandescent light bulbs (ibid.).
93   Even before electric lamps were installed in Kongens Nytorv, it was possible to have downwards gaslights by means of the Welsbach gas mantle from 1885. Hanne Thomsen explains that as late as the 1920s, 'the bright so-called Sugg lights with several smaller, hanging gas mantles were installed in Denmark. The first downwards (Welsbach) lamps had only one or two mantles, and to ensure a steady combustion, a gas cylinder was placed around the light. The cylinder was not necessary in the Sugg lights, as they used much smaller gas mantles than those previously used. The brighter light necessitated higher posts, which led to a more evenly lit street and a more stable and cheaper operation' (Hanne Thomsen, 20 September 2019).
94   Woaz, 1881, p. 648.
95   'Da folk græd i Gothersgade' (When People Wept in Gothersgade), 1982, pp. 12–13.
96   Palsbo and Zeeberg, 1974, unpaginated [pp. 15–16].
97   In the United Kingdom and the United States,'Victorian style' is often used to describe the many different historical styles characterizing the stuffy and lavishly decorated interiors and furnishings in the homes throughout the reign of Queen Victoria, 1837–1901. In Denmark, this historicist style is often referred to as 'tassel style', with specific reference to the tassels, fringes and trims that became a fashionable adornment to just about any element of home decor from the 1880s. However, while the Victorians from the 1860s began to embrace a simpler style with inspiration from the Arts and Crafts Movement, the Danish 'tassel style' lasted throughout the Victorian era, and in some homes even longer. See, e.g., Vorre, 2008, p. 25.
98   Vorre, 2008, p. 25. In Denmark the Industrial Revolution gave rise to a new social structure. With new job functions in and around the factories, industrialization also led to the emergence of new consumer groups. Increasing urbanization and a growing number of factories and companies thus gave rise to both a new affluent middle class and a petit bourgeoisie who wished to decorate their homes with furniture and utilitarian objects that had until then been the reserve of the upper class (ibid.).
99   Gad, 1949, pp. 13–14. Peter Urban Gad was the son of Rear Admiral Nicolaus Urban Gad and writer Emma Gad.
100   Crone, 1892, pp. 41 and 97.
101   Clemmensen, 1965, p. 70. The art historian Tove Clemmensen mentioned that when the National Museum took over the flat from Mr Christensen's daughters, the decor was guided by the recommendations in the book *Kunsten at Møblere sin Lejlighed*, which had just been released then, in 1892. See ibid., p. 74.
102   Vorre, 2008, p. 24.
103   Information from Tove Clemmensen's original registration cards from 1965 (National Museum of Denmark).
104   Ibid.
105   As mentioned above, gaslight could be directed downwards, but naturally the flame could not, and indeed all the earliest gaslights had upwards light, with fish-tail flames or otherwise. However, in 1885 the Welsbach gas mantle was invented, and the mantle could be turned downwards.
106   'Farvernes Hemmelighed' (The Secret of Colours), 1913. PH was well aware of the issue outlined in the article, and he did have a focus on modifying the new electric lighting to make sure it enhanced a woman's beauty. PH explained that he designed his first lamp for his mother, Agnes Henningsen, to give her a light that brought out her beauty: 'She wanted to look good, and she was always messing with the light in order to look sufficiently pretty.' *Store Danskere. Poul Henningsen*, 2012.
107   'Lampeskærme – Modeller fra Magasin du Nord' (Lampshades – Models from Magasin du Nord), 1913, unpaginated [p. 24].
108   Ibid.
109   'Originale Elektriske Lamper', 1921, unpaginated [p. 38].
110   Bang in Tiedemann and Karlsen, 1961, p. 15.
111   Klint in Henningsen, P., 1927, no. 2, p. 70.
112   Heiberg, 1927, p. 34.
113   Ibid.
114   In the summer of 1923, Bauhaus held an exhibition where the painter Georg Muche had constructed a model for a modern single-family house. The model formed the basis for Heiberg's house on I. H. Mundts Vej 16 in Virum, north of Copenhagen. In 1930, Heiberg taught at the Bauhaus school, which in 1925 had relocated to Dessau, Germany. Heiberg, who was a communist, was enthusiastic about functionalism's social project and was the most direct proponent of the Bauhaus's architectural doctrine in a Danish context. See Sørensen, 2000, pp. 7 and 130–143.
115   Also in Germany, Ludwig Mies van der Rohe (1886–1969) was the chief driver behind the 1927 exhibition *Die Wohnung* (The Dwelling) in Stuttgart, which inspired

Ernst May's (1886–1970) exhibition *Die Wohnung für das Existenzminimum* (The Dwelling for Minimal Existence) in Frankfurt in 1929. These exhibitions marked the culmination of the first functionalist era. Here, a particular influence from the United States should be mentioned. The American home economics teacher Christine Fredericks's (1883–1970) book *Household Enginering. Scientific Management in the Home* (1919) had been published in German as early as 1922 and acquired cult-like status, both among the avant-garde and home economics ideologists, and it had an important impact on both theoretical and practical manifestations (Dybdahl, 2008, p. 33). The American interior rationalization experiments were later continued, not least in Bruno Taut (1880–1938): *Die neue Wohnung. Die Frau als Schöpferin* from 1928, culminating with Ernst May's (1886–1970) 1929 exhibition *Die Wohnung für das Existenzminimum* in Frankfurt, which, among other exhibits, presented Margarete Schütte-Lihotsky's (1997–2000) Frankfurt kitchen. These functionalist ideals spread from Germany throughout the European continent, including Scandinavia. See ibid., pp. 30–37, and Freeman, 2004, pp. 29–42.
116   Lytken, 2013, pp. 2–3. It was the Swedish art historian Gregor Paulsson (1889–1977) who initiated and managed the *Stockholm Exhibition*, where some 400 exhibitors promoted their wares to the citizens of Stockholm as well as all visitors from abroad and from the rest of Sweden. The exhibition was open from 16 May until 29 September 1930. See Rudberg, 1999, pp. 35 and 203.
117   Henningsen, P., in Møller, V.S., 1980, p. 53.
118   Le Corbusier, 1986, p. 107.
119   Rudberg, 1999, p. 116.
120   Ibid.
121   Hansen, 1930, p. 147.
122   Wanscher, 1930, p. 142; see also p. 140.
123   Henningsen, P., 1960.
124   The book *Towards a New Architecture* is based on essays written by Le Corbusier for the magazine *L'Esprit Nouveau* (The New Spirit).
125   Heiberg's review of the Paris exhibition in the Norwegian magazine *Byggekunst* (Architecture) only had praise for a Japanese pavilion, Le Corbusier's pavilion and PH's lamps, the latter being described as 'a light in a swamp of stupidity' (Heiberg, 1925, p. 181).
126   Heiberg in Sommer, 1929, unpaginated [p. 8]. The article places the house in Lyngby, but municipal lines and street names have changed since then. When Heiberg built the house, it was situated on Frederiksdalsvej in Lyngby; today, the address is I. H. Mundts Vej 16, 2830 Virum. On Heiberg's house, see Lundqvist and Brænne, 2009.
127   Lytken, 2008, p. 13.
128   'We thus insist that the discussion pertain strictly to facts' (PH in *Kritisk Revy*, 1926). Although *Kritisk Revy* was only published for a period of three years, it was the most influential cultural periodical in Denmark during the interwar years.

129   Dybdahl underscores that critical points dominated when *Kritisk Revy* covered trends abroad. Criticism was aimed at the neglect of the social dimensions of the task, a one-sided enthusiasm with modern technology and the new fixed parameters that would be the result of this effort to define a modern style (Dybdahl, 2016a, pp. 63–65).
130   Henningsen, P., 1926a, p. 55. PH wrote this in a review of Le Corbusier's book in *Kritisk Revy* in 1926 after *Vers une Architecture* from 1923 was published in a German translation (*Kommende Baukunst*, Stuttgart: Deutsche Verlags-Anstalt) in 1926, which made it more accessible to the Danish architects.
131   'Lampereklame', 1926.
132   Bauhaus was founded in 1919 in Weimar under the leadership of Gropius. According to Gropius's Bauhaus manifesto, education at the school had to rest on a strong basis of craft training. With craft and craftsmanship as the foundation, the students – that is, the artists and architects – should together create a holistic solution for the ideal dwelling of the future. This first period was brief, however, and soon the goal was the production of prototypes for clear, rational and aesthetically enhancing design for mass production – meaning, products adapted to living conditions in the modern industrial society. In 1925, the school relocated to Dessau, and in 1928 the architect Hannes Meyer (1889–1954) took over as leader.
133   Henningsen, P., 1926b.
134   Henningsen, P., 1927.
135   Henningsen, P., 1926b.
136   Henningsen, P., 1927, p. 82.
137   Henningsen, P., 1926b, p. 68.
138   Henningsen, P., 1927. In the article, PH uses a smaller font in the long passages that describe lighting measurements, spectral curves and the shadow effects in various luminaires, while summaries are printed in a bigger font. The long passages add gravity and credibility, and after presenting these facts he could thus more convincingly present passages outlining more personal views on lighting.
139   Drawing and text: Carl Jensen, *Blæksprutten*, Gyldendal, 1943.
140   Respectively, Henningsen, P., 1928, and Henningsen, P., 1974, p. 16.
141   Henningsen, P., in Bundgaard, 1966, pp. 16 and 18.
142   The term 'the functional tradition' is attributed to Kaj Fisker, who first used it in 1950 – thus also applying it retrospectively. The term is the title of a feature article by Fisker in *Arkitekten*: 'Den Functionelle Tradition: Spredte Indtryk af Amerikansk Arkitektur' (The Functional Tradition: Scattered Impressions of American Architecture) (Fisker, 1950, p. 69).
143   Juhl, 1954, pp. 140–141.
144   Maria Berntsen, 25 April 2018.
145   Hansen, 1994, p. 300. In addition to direct glare, it is also important to consider reflex glare, which occurs if the light is reflected in the lampshades. That was a challenge in the shiny luminaires that were PH presented in Paris in 1925 (see p. 36). Similarly, it is a problem if reflected light from a shiny tabletop strikes the eye. Another issue is contrast glare, which occurs if the transitions between light and dark are too stark. Many designers therefore let light escape to light up the luminaire itself to ensure a pleasant contrast balance between the luminous lamp and the dark room around it.
146   Karlby, 1942, p. 77.
147   Henningsen, P., 1958b, p. 24.
148   Ibid.
149   Bay explains that the GU10 and other sockets used for the bipin halogen bulb are included in IEC 60061, the International Electrotechnical Commission's standard for lamp caps and holders, from 1969. Vivi and Erik Sørensen, who have run the lamp and electrician's shop El-Hjørnet on Godthåbsvej in Frederiksberg since 1974, say that they began to carry the halogen bulb a few years later but that it only became popular after 1980 (Vivi and Erik Sørensen, 3 May 2019).
150   The energy-efficient light bulb was invented by General Electric in the 1970s.
151   Henningsen, P., 1941, back cover.
152   LED is an abbreviation for light-emitting diode. The first effective red LEDs were produced as early as 1962, so the LED technology is not new, but it would take many years before it made a real breakthrough as a light source in Danish homes. Red LEDs were mainly used in TVs, radios, pocket calculators, digital watches and cars. It was not until 2007 that LEDs became available as ordinary white light sources, initially used in offices and hotels (Jensen, 2014, p. 147). After LEDs began to be used in lamps, the market has developed rapidly, and for a number of years it was difficult for consumers to navigate among the new options and to tell good products from poor ones. Since then, the quality has improved, as prices have dropped. In 2012, a high-quality LED bulb cost DKK 599/€80 – and could not be used with a dimmer switch.
153   In the LED universe, the Ra index is called CRI, Colour Rendering Index (Anne Bay, 20 September 2019).
154   These paragraphs on light sources were written with expert assistance from Anne Bay, 20 September 2019.
155   Sofie Refer, 6 March 2019.
156   Filskov, 1917, p. 881.

Poul Henningsen: Slotsholmen lamp

1   PH in Wanscher, 1921, p. 293. PH explained how he split the parable structure up into the six shades, whose only formal kinship was the shared focus: 'The reflectors are rotary figures with a parable contour. The focus of the parables is in the light ring and the axis in a ratio of 4/15. With the two lamps being placed 30 metres apart in an 18-metre-wide street, this maximizes the amount of light reaching what are normally the darkest areas.' Ibid.
2   PH in *Politiken* 7 (October 1921), quoted from Jørgensen in Jørstian and Nielsen, 1994, pp. 90–91.
3   Including at Ved Stranden, Højbro Plads, Gyldenløvesgade, Blågaards Plads, Christianshavns Gymnasium, Copenhagen Municipal Hospital, Sundby Hospital and

Frederiksberg City Hall. Here it was used on a post and in a wall version (Joakim Zacho Weylandt, 20 August 2019).
4   PH in Roos, 1964 (short film). The design archaeologist Joakim Zacho Weylandt and Søren Peter Kristensen, project manager at Rambøll, have initiated a registration project with the ultimate aim of restoring and installing seven of the original lamp heads at Slotsholmen as part of a joint effort with Louis Poulsen to explore the possibilities of putting PH's Slotsholmen lamp back into production. Thanks to new LED technology, the light source itself now achieves what PH's original lamp could not: emitting glare-free light (Weistrup, 2018, pp. 20–22, and Joakim Zacho Weylandt and Søren Peter Kristensen, 20 August 2019).
5   Wanscher, 1921, p. 293.

Poul Henningsen: System PH

1   Henningsen, P., 1966, p. 2453.
2   Henningsen, P., 1926b, p. 74.
3   Based on Jørgensen, Jørstian and Nielsen, 1994, p. 76, and Dybdahl, 2012, p. 65. In a detailed review of PH's lamps, the book *Light Years Ahead*, published to mark the centenary of PH's birth, it says that PH's first lamp, created for an interior design assignment in 1915–1916, was an Empire-style crystal chandelier.
4   Jørgensen, Jørstian and Nielsen, 1994, pp. 76–79.
5   Henningsen, P., 1963, p. 2067.
6   Henningsen, P., 1927, p. 68.

Poul Henningsen: PH lamp

1   Henningsen, P., 1927, p. 87.
2   Ibid., p. 83. See also Jørstian, 1994a, p. 4, Raizman, 2003, p. 264, and Dybdahl, 2012, p. 69.
3   See Jørgensen and Jørstian, 1994, pp. 121–122.
4   Henningsen, P., 1966, p. 2456. Louis Poulsen and PH won the contract for lighting in the new 'Kæmpehallen' (the Giant Hall). They had three months to finish the designs and rapidly produce numerous luminaires with a shade diameter of 85 cm, 60 with a diameter of 60 cm and a smaller number with a diameter of 40 cm, for the restaurant. Lundstrøm (2016, p. 83).
5   Jørstian, 1994a, pp. 4–5. The first table lamp was presented in 1927 at an exhibition in Industribygningen (House of Industry), in Copenhagen. The first pendant to be marketed had a diameter of 50 cm. PH explained in 1966 that while the pendants in the Forum building had had a diameter of 30 cm, from 1927 even smaller lamps were made, with a diameter of '25–20 – even as small as 16 cm'. The table lamps were launched in three sizes (Henningsen, P., 1966, pp. 2455–2456). The three shades were normally proportioned in a 3:2:1 ratio. In the 5/5 lamp, the first 5 refers to the large shade size of 50 cm, while the second 5 indicates whether the other shades were the 'standard' sizes, in this case a middle shade of 31 cm and a lower shade of 16.5 cm. When PH used a smaller lower shade, this was reflected in the numbers too, as all upper shades could be combined with middle and lower shades from smaller lamps, which produced 'odd' number combinations, such as 4/3, 3/2 and 2/1 (Ulla Riemer, head of LP Academy, 7 August 2019).
6   *Kritisk Revy* was an early medium for the promotion of PH lamps, and PH's two longest articles in the magazine deal with the topic of electric lighting. The first issue of *Kritisk Revy*, from 1926, contains the 22-page article 'Moderne belysning af rum' (Modern Lighting of Rooms) (Henningsen, P., 1926b, pp. 60–82). Although the PH lamp is not mentioned in the title, an ad for the lamp is featured at the bottom of almost every single page. The focus of the article was PH's effort to design his own lamp system, and it is illustrated with photos of the lamps from the Danish section of the Paris exhibition. In his even longer follow-up article one year later, the title is more explicit: 'Rummets belysning – med særligt Henblik paa Anvendelsen af P.H.-Lampen' (Room Lighting – With Particular Reference to the Use of the P.H. Lamp) (Henningsen, P., 1927, pp. 67–102). Both articles are thus, in fact, dedicated to an in-depth discussion of the PH lamps.
7   Henningsen, P., 1926b, p. 68.
8   Henningsen, P., 1927, p. 82.
9   Nielsen and de Waal, 1994, p. 215.
10   Henningsen, P., 1927, p. 82.

Frits Schlegel and Vilhelm Lauritzen: Fritzsche's Universal lamp

1   Vilhelm Lauritzen enrolled in the Perspective School at the Royal Danish Academy of Fine Arts in 1912, and from here he advanced in 1916 to the School of Architecture. He graduated in 1921 and the following year founded an architectural firm under his own name, where he remained active until 1969. Frits Schlegel began as a bricklayer's apprentice in 1912 and completed his training in 1915. He then attended Polytechnic College and graduated in 1916. That same year, in autumn, Schlegel enrolled at the Royal Danish Academy of Fine Arts, School of Architecture, which he attended until 1922 without graduating, like many others at the time. While Schlegel was a student at the Academy's School of Architecture, he was also employed at Edvard Thomsen's architectural firm, where he remained until 1934. From 1920, he also worked for the landscape architect G.N. Brandt, and along with his work for Edvard Thomsen, this provided important training. Frits Schlegel worked out of his own firm from 1934 until his death in 1965. See Jørgensen, 1994, p. 9, and Møller, 2004, pp. 10–20.
2   See Møller, 2004, pp. 26–28. There were 37 competition entries in total. From 1928, the two architects took on other renovation projects, and in 1933 the functionalist department store opened. In 1936 and during the 1950s, Vilhelm Lauritzen was responsible for additional, major renovations of the department store in a modern, functionalist expression. Daells Varehus closed in 1999 and was subsequently converted into the Hotel Sankt Petri. The building is listed as worthy of preservation.
3   See Møller, 2004, p. 186. See also the review of the lighting exhibition in O.W., 1930, pp. 184–186.
4   Henningsen, P., 1946, p. 488. See also Dybdahl, 1987, p. 96, and Møller, 2004, p. 186.
5   The architect and lighting expert Mogens Voltelen voiced his critique of the light in 'Belysningen paa Elektricitetsudstillingen. Det psykologiske Lys', *Elektroteknikeren*, no. 19, 7 October 1930, p. 375. See Møller, 2004, p. 186. For the counter claims, see Jørgensen, 1994, p. 32.
6   Paragraph based on Dybdahl, 1987, pp. 96–97, Jørgensen, 1994, p. 32, and Møller, 2004, pp. 186–187.
7   O.W., 1930, pp. 184–186.
8   Lauritzen and Schlegel, 1930, p. 191. The article is a response to a comment on the lamp in a review of the exhibition in the previous issue of *Arkitekten*; see O.W., 1930, pp. 184–186.
9   O.W., 1930, pp. 184–186.

Arne Jacobsen: AJ reading lamp

1   In Denmark, Christian Dell's contemporary Goethe lamp (Bünte & Remmler) was marketed in 1930 by Aage Havemanns Efterfølger, which presented it in the big lighting exhibition in Tivoli, in Copenhagen, that same year. See von Holstein-Rathlou, 1930, p. 186. The lamp head itself may also be seen as a paraphrase on the French engineer and designer Bernard-Albin's working lamp Gras from 1921, which Jacobsen undoubtedly knew.
2   Documentation for the design year is lacking, but in their comprehensive book on Arne Jacobsen, the architects Carsten Thau and Kjeld Vindum write that the floor lamp, along with a table lamp version, was shown in interior photos in 1929–1930 of Rothenborgs Hus, a private home designed by Jacobsen in Klampenborg, north of Copenhagen. The floor lamp was also included in an interior design of a study that Arne Jacobsen presented, together with the architect Mogens Lassen, at the Copenhagen Cabinetmakers' Guild exhibition in 1932. The table lamp is not included in the catalogues from Louis Poulsen, and the AJ reading lamp was not included until 1951. It was discontinued in 1970. Mathias Bøgeholdt, 30 December 2022. For some time a variant was available with a partially perforated reflector. See Thau and Vindum, 1998, p. 268.
3   The name Bellevue was introduced when &Tradition relaunched the reading lamp in 2016. It was mainly chosen as a name that sounded well and which would be understood in both a Danish and an international context (Henrik Lund Larsen, &Tradition, 21 May 2019).
4   Møller, 2003, p. 76. Arne Jacobsen used a similarly obliquely cut-off shade in a smaller version on a table lamp when he designed the interior of a branch office for the Danish bank Landmandsbanken in Copenhagen in 1936.

5   Although it was called the Stelling pendant, Jacobsen had used it as early as 1936 in the Landmandsbanken interior (see previous note); Møller, 2003, p. 76. The Stelling pendant was not put into full-scale production until 1965 and was discontinued in 1970. It was briefly relaunched in a limited edition in 2002. Mathias Bøgeholdt, 30 December 2022. In her book *Stellings Hus*, Vibeke Andersson Møller writes that the pendants above the counters back in the 1930s must have attracted attention, because the cords were used as a decorative element in their own right. Going from the lamps to a suspended rail, the cords were both physically and functionally separated from the suspension of the lamps (ibid.). The pendant was used in two sizes, a smaller one above the counters and a bigger one in the display windows. Ibid.
6   Heiberg, 1929, unpaginated [p. 14].
7   Arne Jacobsen's statement in a newspaper from 1930, quoted in Thau and Vindum, 1998, p. 87.

Poul Henningsen: Chandelier with PH lamps

1   For example, the PH lamps were presented at the housing exhibitions *Dit Hjem* (Your Home) and *Bohu – om Boligen og Huset* (Hoho – on Homes and Housing), held at Forum in 1931 and 1934, respectively. See Nørregaard et al., 1994, p. 240, and Nielsen and de Waal, 1994, pp. 215–219. After its opening in Copenhagen in 1931, Den Permanente had a significant impact on middle-class views on modern home design. However, as early as 1928, Copenhageners had been able to buy quality furniture that tended towards the new functionalist style in Boligmagasinet BO (Home Design Shop LIVE). The selection included not only Danish design but also other Nordic and German functionalism with Bauhaus as one source of inspiration. BO closed in 1941, and the current Illums Bolighus took over the building on Amagertorv in the heart of Copenhagen. PH reviewed Den Permanente in *LP & Co. NYT* in the summer of 1943. The many illustrations of interiors in the article feature a large number of PH lamps. See Henningsen, P., 1943, pp. 171–173.
2   Henningsen, P., 1963, p. 2158.
3   PH around 1930, in Jørstian and Nielsen, 1994, p. 162.
4   Kaiser, 1992, p. 74.
5   The architect Anton Rosen (1859–1928) wanted to use PH lamps in his design of the Palace Hotel in Copenhagen's City Hall square and persuaded PH to 'soften the impression' (ibid.) by adding glass prisms to the rim of the upper shades. In early 1928, he installed them in the hotel's marble garden, a large hall with a glass roof that formed the setting for lavish parties. PH's Star chandeliers with glass prisms were available in 1931–1937 featuring three to ten PH triple-shade lamps (Henningsen, P., 1963, p. 2158). Ironically, PH wrote of the chandeliers with prisms, 'Oddly, the type has completely disappeared from the market' (ibid.).
6   See PH in Bundgaard, 1966, p. 18.
7   The large selection of frames and shades diminished with the outbreak of the Second World War and the resulting rationing and shortages. The Bombardment chandelier was the only chandelier included after the war; it remained in Louis Poulsen's catalogue until the mid 1960s (Nielsen and de Waal, 1994, p. 200).
8   Henningsen, P., 1927, p. 82. It was a widespread implicit assumption that indoor lighting should be muted; so much so that the lamps, as PH put it, even 'when switched off gave an impression of a cosy, muted mood' (ibid., p. 82).
9   These models and the willingness to accommodate the preferences of the affluent upper middle class in the product range show an acceptance of *hygge*, which the modernists generally associate with the dark, cluttered rooms they wanted to leave behind. However, PH did not reject *hygge*; he simply insisted that the term should be properly understood: '*Hygge* is character, rest, comfort, but *not superficial style*' (Henningsen, P., 1928, p. 68). From an early time, PH realized that for *hygge*, a golden, reddish evening light was desirable. See, e.g., Jørstian and de Waal, 1994, p. 62. The furniture and lamp designer Andreas Hansen has described how PH, around 1960, gave presentations at the School of Arts and Crafts: 'I still remember PH saying that when the day is over, and the sun begins to set, the light turns redder, and that is when our early ancestors lit a fire, and it too gave out a warm, reddish glow, so the reddish light was preferable in the evening – that was one of his key tenets' (Andreas Hansen, 17 July 2019). PH offers a similar explanation in Bundgaard, 1966, p. 16.
10   Henningsen, P., 1928, p. 68.
11   Catalogue page from 1931 reproduced in Jørstian, 1994b, p. 170.
12   The lamps were now also made in less costly materials, and to enable efficient industrial production and assembly, the frames were simplified. See Jørstian, 1994a, p. 6, and Littrup, 2016, p. 61.
13   Henningsen, P., 1928, p. 68. In 1931, a Danish newspaper wrote that the number of PH lamps sold now exceeded 30,000 – in the Copenhagen area alone! (Nielsen and de Waal, 1994, p. 220).
14   See, e.g., Boesdal, 1931, Boesdal, 1934, and Karlby, 1942.
15   See Dybdahl, 2012, p. 71. The large lighting manufacturer Kjøbenhavns Lampe- og Lysekronefabrik had been founded in 1903, and around 1930 it was a major rival to Louis Poulsen.
16   Henningsen, P., 1926b, pp. 60–82. The title of the 1927 article was 'Rummets belysning – med særligt Henblik paa Anvendelsen af P.H.-Lampen' (Henningsen, P., 1927, pp. 67–102). Subsequently, PH wrote about lighting in Louis Poulsen's magazine *LP & Co. NYT* from the first issue in 1941 until his death in 1967. PH also wrote for and was interviewed by newspapers and magazines and was interviewed on film.
17   Henningsen, P., 1928, p. 68.

Niels Rasmussen Thykier: T3

1   Thykier's full name and dates are confirmed by a death notice in the Weilbach Archive at the Danish National Art Library. *Samlerens Kunstnerleksikon* from 1932 mentions Thykier in vol. II, page 261: 'THYKIER, NIELS RASMUSSEN, Painter, born 23 September 1883 (...) A student of G. Vermehren, the Academy. However, as is evident from the text above, Thykier must have moved in the same circles as the painter and ceramicist Jais Nielsen (1885–1961) and the sculptor Einar Utzon-Frank (1888–1955), who were close to his own age. Nielsen studied under Kristian Zahrtmann (1864–1868) at Kunstnernes Studieskole (the Artists' Study School), later renamed Zahrtmanns Skole (Zahrtmann's School). Thykier may have attended the same school.
2   Boesdal, 1931, p. 7. Boesdal underscored that the aim of the book was to promote interest in practical home design by offering concise and practical guidelines in Danish to the general public (ibid.).
3   Boesdal, 1931, p. 61.
4   Ibid., p. 63.
5   In 1931, Boesdal briefly writes about the lamps, 'Good light and beautiful, calm lines. (Constructed by the sculptor Tykjær. Wholesale Holger Grum, Copenhagen. Decor. Jais Nielsen et al., [DKK] 48.50, without decor. [DKK] 39.50). PH lamp on a stem. (Louis Poulsen & Co. Copenhagen. [DKK] 78)' (Boesdal, 1931, p. 63). Grum was Thykier's first wholesaler, but as turnover grew, the account outgrew his small company, and Thykier switched to Fog & Mørup.
6   The paper shade was available with a floral decoration and with an 'artistic decoration by Professor E. Utzon Frank' (ibid.). The catalogue shows the T3 lamp in three variants and two sizes: Baby (height 40 cm, diameter 29.5 cm), Minor (height 46.5 cm, diameter 37 cm) and Minor N. N stands for 'new' and was introduced by Thykier as a more affordable model, just as Louis Poulsen also began to cheaper, more production-friendly PH lamps. However, Minor N was not a big seller. All models were available with decorated shades.
7   'Moderne Belysning', 1936, pp. 20–21. *Bygge og Bo, Tidsskrift for Moderne Hjem*, which premiered in 1934, had a functionalist outlook but without the political angle of *Kritisk Revy*. The focus was on home design, and many shops advertised in the magazine. However, it never gained broad appeal; it offered little visual guidance in how to create a dream home for the majority of people who had yet to embrace the functionalist ideals and were still living with heavy furnishings, many decorative items and – according to the functionalist architects – unsuitable lighting.
8   The Kongelys lamp appears for the first time in a Fog & Mørup catalogue from October 1940. At the time, material shortages were widespread, and Thykier could not source enough brass to meet demand and had to let his staff go. Prob-

ably to avoid missing out on turnover, Fog & Mørup made a cheaper version based on available materials. Thykier despised the Kongelys lamp as a cheap copy he had to live with because he could not afford suing for plagiarism. In the late 1930s, the T3 lamp was so popular that both Lyfa and Louis Poulsen had made their own copies of it. According to his son, however, Thykier did receive a modest sum as compensation from Fog & Mørup. In spring 1940, Fog & Mørup issued the catalogue *Den blaa Bog* (The Blue Book). An enclosed letter to the retailers mentions that although this was a time when the focus was more on blackouts than on light, life behind the darkened windows still called for lighting. The catalogue does not include the Kongelys lamp but two models of the T3 lamp in its 'original rendition': T3 Baby and T3 Minor. For a surcharge, the lamp is available with a shade decorated by 'Professor E. Utzon Frank'. Fog & Mørup, April 1940, p. 61. There is no mention of Niels Rasmussen Thykier.

9   The closing paragraph is based on the 2004 article https://nordjyske.dk/nyheder/lysgave-fra-aalestrup-til-kronprinsparret/d8c11683-6081-4fe9-b5cf-b4b8e6b694e9 and on Rasmus Markholt, 12 June 2019. In 1991, Horn Belysning took over Lyskær Belysning, including Fog & Mørup, Lyfa and ABO, as all three companies has previously been taken over by Lyskær. In 2005, Horn Belysning was renamed Lightyears. In 2010, Lightyears sold the rights for the Kongelys lamp along with one 2004 lamp to serve as a model for a relaunch that has yet to materialize. This according to Rasmus Markholt, who was a product developer and head of design at Horn Belysning. Rasmus Markholt also explained that he was only aware of the Kongelys lamp and had never heard about T3 or Thykier. Ibid.

10   *Bygge og Bo*, 1936, pp. 6, 20–21.

Piet Hein:
Ra lamp

1   In his youth, Piet Hein studied art at the Royal Institute of Art in Stockholm and later theoretical physics at the University of Copenhagen but never graduated. In the 1934 article in *Arkitekten. Ugehæfte*, he described himself as an engineer.

2   The exhibition opened on 4 February 1933. Piet Hein also presented the simpler Funco lamp with a conical shade, but the Ra lamp stole the limelight. *Politiken* (5 February 1933) described how Piet Hein presented his sensational Ra lamp. It was also mentioned in two other newspapers, *Socialdemokraten* and *Berlingske Tidende*.

3   The paragraph is based on Hein, 1936, pp. 10–11, and Dybdahl, 2006, p. 205.

4   Hein, 1936, p. 11.

5   von Holstein-Rathlou, 1934, p. IX. The article mentions that Ra lamps were also installed in the Department of Mathematics at the University of Copenhagen.

6   Piet Hein in Kristiansen, 2015, p. 81. Quote from the 1939–1940 lighting catalogue from the wholesale company Aage Havemanns Efterfølger. The Piet Hein company archive contains brochures from Kjøbenhavns Lampe- og Lysekronefabrik dating back to 1934, when the Ra lamp became available from retailers.

7   Hein, 1936, p. 11.

8   The Piet Hein company was founded and is run by Piet Hein's son Hugo Piet Hein (b. 1963).

9   Hein, 1936, p. 9.

Vilhelm Lauritzen:
Radiohus pendant

1   Paragraph based on Lund, 1994b, p. 292.

2   Lauritzen, 1954, p. 1185. The Studio lamp had an elliptical mirror installed inside the glass shade above the interior shade centred on the light source. The mirror reflected the light downwards and through the opening in the globe. Although the interior shade was not used in the Radiohus pendant, the lamp, as described by Lauritzen (1954), could be supplemented with the elliptical mirror inside the shade in an almost identical principle. See also Lund, 1994a, pp. 16 and 292. When Mogens Voltelen, as 'Lauritzen's lighting designer', described the lighting at Radiohuset in October 1941, he referred to the Radiohus pendant as 'the office lamp' (Voltelen, 1941).

3   Lauritzen, 1954, p. 1185.

4   Henningsen, P., 1954a, p. 1185.

5   Both China and Japan had a long tradition for paper lanterns, and their simple form appealed to many Danish functionalists – for example, a string of traditional Chinese lanterns hung over Kaare Klint's furniture at Rud. Rasmussen's stand at the 1933 Copenhagen Cabinetmakers' Guild exhibition. See photo from the display in Holmsted Olesen, 2014, p. 23.

6   Lauritzen, 1954, p. 1185.

Vilhelm Lauritzen:
B&G pendant

1   Vilhelm Lauritzen, *LP & Co. NYT*, no. 149, 1954 p. 1185.

2   Juhl, 1947a, p. 559. For the design of Bing & Grøndahl's showrooms, Finn Juhl received an Eckersbergs Medal, an award for outstanding artistic quality. In the article in *LP & Co. NYT*, Juhl (ibid.) mentioned that he had benefited from good advice from the architect Mogens Voltelen in the design of the lighting.

3   Ibid. A later article on Juhl (p. 90) returns to the topic of the B&G pendant, the VL38 table lamp and thus the role Juhl played by designing lamps to Radiohuset.

4   The same magnificent chandelier is found in the lobby of the Danish Royal Theatre, on Kongens Nytorv in Copenhagen, which is open to the public.

5   Like Lauritzen and Schlegel's reading lamp from 1928, it came in both an adjustable and a fixed version. In some models the shade could be tilted up and down and moved sideways. That was the case, for example, with the record-player bracket lamps. See Voltelen, 1941. Lund in LP & Co. NYT, 1994, p. 14. Text mainly based on this source. (husk kursiv)

6   In 1983, the Radio Council Chamber was redecorated. The redesign included a new chandelier to match the new rectangular table. The angular brass frame of the new chandelier features B&G pendant shades, like the ones used on the ring chandeliers Vilhelm Lauritzen created for the Danish Parliament, Christiansborg, in 1951. The new shades were shiny, like the other lampshades in Radiohuset (see Lund, 2008, p. 71).

Tage Klint:
Model 1

1   Benjamin Thompson, Count of Rumford (1875, p. 134), offered the following explanation: 'A hoop, made of strong white writing paper, of about $2^{1}/_{2}$ inches in width, is so fitted to the outside of the dome of the table illuminator below as to embrace it exactly, and in such a manner as to be supported by it.'

2   Klint, 1943, quoted from Harkær, 2010, p. 587.

3   Ibid. In 1905, Tage Klint had become a chartered surveyor, and from his graduation until 1916, he had his own surveyor's business. In 1938, when he patented the collar, he was a sales director for Munke Mølle, a position he held for nine years, until he founded the Le Klint company. Tage Klint's daughter Le was initially in charge of the shop in Copenhagen; see Klint, 1943.

4   See Dybdahl, 2016a, p. 270. Le Klint's professional 'pleating girls' undergo extensive training to master the difficult cross pleats. The text is based mainly on Dalby, 2008, pp. 9–34, Harkær, 2010, pp. 587–590, and Dybdahl, 2016a, pp. 270–273.

5   Quoted from the first catalogue for the Le Klint company in 1943, reproduced in Harkær, 2010, p. 587.

Kaare Klint:
Fruit Lantern, Model 101

1   In 1924, Kaare Klint was appointed the first head of the newly established School of Furniture Design at the Royal Danish Academy of Fine Arts, School of Architecture; in 1944, he was appointed professor of architecture.

2   Kaare Klint, 1930, p. 203. Klint was interested in both Japanese and Chinese paper folding and paper lanterns, and in 1933 traditional Chinese lanterns decorated with Chinese characters hung over his furniture at Rud. Rasmussen's stand at the Copenhagen Cabinetmakers' Guild exhibition. See photo in Holmsted Olesen, 2014, p. 23. In 1937, Klint did a trial hanging of Japanese lamps in the Bethlehem Church due to the good light produced by rice-paper lamps. Klint had had two 170-cm-tall lamps specially made in Japan, decorated with a traditional Japanese design of a simple circle. He had also commissioned a number of smaller lamps. Although he was very pleased with the result, the building committee rejected the idea, and instead he used the lamps for exhibition purposes. Gelfer-Jørgensen, 2013, p. 371. See photo in ibid., p. 370.

3   Kaare Klint, October 1943. Quoted from Harkær, 2010, p. 587.

4   Henningsen, P., 1946, p. 503. PH later explained, 'The cross-pleating method I invented, however, has no connection whatsoever to Le Klint's pleat, which is evident from the very fact that I was able to patent it' (Henningsen, P., 1947, p. 536). Kaare Klint retorted, and the result was a drawn-out lawsuit.
5   Ultimately, the parties agreed that the first to develop the cross-pleating technique was the architect Hans Henrik Koch. He had never patented it but had presented cross-pleated Christmas baskets at the 1925 World's Fair in Paris, where the PH lamp adventure had also begun. See Harkær, 2010, p. 592, and Nørregaard et al., 1994, pp. 262–263.
6   Juhl, 1946, p. 517.
7   Ibid., pp. 515–518.

Bent Karlby:
Peanut lamp, Model P162

1   Like PH, Karlby was not trained at the Royal Danish Academy of Fine Arts, School of Architecture, but from 1936 he called himself an architect, and in 1945 he was accepted into the Danish Architects' Association. See Møller, 2014, pp. 9–10. Karlby was an employee of Vilhelm Lauritzen's architecture firm from 1937 until 1939 according to Jørgensen, 1994, p. 333.
2   Karlby in Lyfa, 1949, p. 1. Reproduced in full in Møller, 2014, p. 84.
3   Karlby quoted in newspaper cuttings from 1949 under the headline 'En ny klunketid?' (A Return of Victorian Style?), reproduced in Møller, 2014, pp. 85–86.
4   Henningsen, P., 1974, p. 27.
5   Henningsen, P., 1949a.
6   In spring 1947, Christian Dior presented the New Look collection that transformed women's fashion and also had an impact on interiors and design. Karlby too must have been inspired by the new style. In 1954, he used the narrow New Look waist in his pendant lamp Ninotchka. See Møller, 2014, pp. 89–90.
7   Møller, 2014, p. 89, and Lund, 1994a, pp. 12–13.
8   Karlby, 1942, p. 78.

Jørn Utzon:
Sundowner and Tivoli pendants

1   Utzon in Tøjner, 2004, p. 15. This is confirmed by Jan Utzon, 7 June 2019.
2   From 1949, Middelboe had his own business as a lamp manufacturer until he joined Nordisk Solar Compagni as a designer in 1955 (Bruun et al., 1979, p. 410). It was after this time that lamp production began to be a significant activity for the company.
3   Described by Torsten Bløndal, who published the 2002 biography Utzon. Inspiration, Vision, Architecture, which was put together in collaboration with Utzon. In connection with this project, he thus heard both Utzon's and Middelboe's stories. See also Weston, 2002, pp. 347 and 422–410, and Jakobsen, 2012, pp. 5–7.
4   Utzon described the trip in Tøjner, 2004, p. 8, and told Bløndal about giving Lloyd Wright a lamp. See Weston, 2002, p. 347. That it was a Sundowner was verified by Jan Utzon (7 June 2019).
5   Jakobsen, 2012, p. 6, and Jan Utzon, 7 June 2019. In 1952–1953, Jørn Utzon designed a house for Middelboe by the Furesøen lake in Holte, north of Copenhagen, and interior photos from both Utzon's house in Hellebæk and Middelboe's house in Holte show Tivoli and Sundowner pendants in both the new houses. See Weston, 2002, pp. 63–64 (Utzon's house) and 73 (Middelboe's house).
6   Solar explains that a young Harald Jørgensen during the late 1940s wanted to put together an appealing collection of lighting for Nordisk Solar Compagni. To that end, he commissioned a lamp from Jørn Utzon in 1949, which became the popular Tivoli pendant (https://www.solar.eu/100-years/june-2019/). Kemp & Lauritzen also carried the Tivoli pendant, and a 1954 brochure from Kemp & Lauritzen shows a drawing of it. It is presented as one of four lamps (three pendants and a wall lamp) designed by Jørn Utzon that the company carried at the time. Neither the Tivoli pendant nor the Sundowner pendant is visible in a photo from Nordisk Solar Compagni's stand at the fair in Hannover in 1956, although other Utzon lamps are. See Weston, 2002, p. 346. Nordisk Solar Compagni issued their first lighting cataloue in 1957 (after Middelboe became head of design), and two catalogues from 1958 feature the Sundowner (P251) and Tivoli (P254 & P256) pendants alongside other Utzon designs. Nordisk Solar Compagni, 1958a, p. 6, and Nordisk Solar Compagni, 1958b, pp. 112–113. The Halsskov lamp (No. 0.5301: the ceiling version of the Tivoli lamp without the top shade) is also included in the catalogue (ibid., p. 22). The 1978 and 1981 catalogues from Nordisk Solar Compagni show all these models still in production, while many other Utzon lamps had at this point been discontinued (see, for example, the lamps in Nordisk Solar Compagni, 1981, pp. 12–13).
7   In Utzon's house in Hellebæk, there are a couple of Tivoli pendants with the large exterior shade divided vertically into two colour sections. Jan Utzon explains: 'My father had a friend who was a painter [Povl Schrøder (1894–1957)], and he asked him to paint about 20 Tivoli pendants in different ways. The test lamps were then hung above the coffee tables in our living room at varying heights. They were only up for a few days, then they were taken down again; it was simply an experiment' (Jan Utzon, 7 June 2019).
8   The fashion designer Christian Dior presented his New Look collection in the spring of 1947.
9   Jan Utzon, 7 June 2019.
10   The idea was to allow people to buy shades in different colours and combine them any way they liked. Jan Utzon explained that one of the reasons why the Sundowner was not initially as popular as the Tivoli pendant was that people did not want to assemble the lamp themselves: 'Later, of course, we got used to that, but at the time, people preferred to receive it pre-assembled in the box' (Jan Utzon, 7 June 2019).
11   Trumpet lamp No. P. 240, 'Satchmo', 1957, designed for Nordisk Solar Compagni, presented at Landsforeningen Dansk Kunsthaandværk's Annual Exhibition in 1957 (photos from the association's archives; Designmuseum Danmark's library archive; Nordisk Solar Compagni, 1958b, p. 99). Around this time, Utzon created other lamp designs with exotic names: Lotus, Bellevue, Maroc, Tokyo and Japan as well as the Kineser (Chinese) pendant, which is reminiscent of the previously described designs (see pp. 50 and 58). These latter lamps are shown in Kemp & Lauritzen, 1954, in the above-mentioned catalogues from Nordisk Solar Compagni and in Weston, 2002, pp. 346–347. Utzon did not come up with the Sundowner name himself; it was the suggestion of an electrician (perhaps with an affinity for cocktails?), and Utzon immediately liked it, he said to Bløndal. Bløndal adds that the name EL SE for the bedside bracket lamp reflects Utzon's sense of humour (Bløndal, 24 June 2018) (because of its pun on the Danish words for 'electricity' (el) and 'see' (se), which put together can be read as the Danish woman's name Else). This small bracket lamp had a turnable white interior shade that also switches lamp on and off when it is rotated (see, for example, Nordisk Solar Compagni, 1958b, p. 52). Jan Utzon remembers the lamp from his childhood: 'My father had made a bedside lamp that my sister and I had next to our bunkbeds. By opening or closing a shade we could switch the lamp on and off' (Jan Utzon, 7 June 2019).
12   Utzon in Tøjner, 2004, p. 15.

Poul Henningsen:
Tivoli lamp

1   PH explained in 1942 that the principle was 'to create a horizontal light that is not visible from above and which does not light up the terrain at a luminance level that is visible from the air. In addition to illuminating walking persons and standing objects better, this also adds an illumination that contributes to the atmosphere'. Henningsen, P., 1942, p. 80.
2   Henningsen, S., 1944, p. 272. In May 1944, while PH was in Sweden, his son, the architect Simon Henningsen, spoke about the changes to the Tivoli lamp. Simon Henningsen worked at Tivoli together with his father, and in 1948 he replaced PH as the amusement park's chief architect.
3   Henningsen, P., 1945, p. 424.
4   Henningsen, P., 1949b, p. 709.
5   The story is based mainly on Nørregaard et al., 1994, pp. 255–260, and on Henningsen, S., 1944, pp. 271–272, Henningsen, P., 1942, pp. 80–82, and Dybdahl, 2006, pp. 198–199.
6   Henningsen, P., 1949b, pp. 708–709.

Arne Jacobsen:
AJ lamp

1   The notion of the Gesamtkunstwerk, the total work of art, was originally conceived by the opera composer Richard Wagner in the mid 19th century to signify a work of art where all artistic genres,

forms and expressions come together in a coherent whole. In the art nouveau style of the Wiener Werkstätte (Vienna Workshops) and, later, in Bauhaus functionalism, the concept reflected a desire for agreement between a building's form and content with the purpose of creating an appropriate setting for the life in and around the building. As a total work of art, the SAS Royal Hotel may be seen as an expression of Jacobsen's desire to exercise complete aesthetic control and, not least, as a demonstration of the wide scope of his talent. See Thau and Vindum, 2002, p. 30. In its overall design, the building draws on inspiration from Gordon Bunshaft's Lever House and Mies van der Rohe's Seagram Building, both in New York.
2	Today, the wall lamp also swivels, which improves its functionality. Originally, the base was made of cast iron, the socket section of brass, and the tilt shade of iron. The shade was soldered to the socket section, and the lamp was finished with lacquer. Today, all the components are steel. Originally, the lamps were available in light grey, black or dark brown. Thau & Vindum, 2002, p. 475; Mathias Bøgeholdt, 30 December 2022.
3	The paragraph is based on Thau and Vindum, 2002, pp. 62–63, and Dybdahl, 2006, pp. 206–207.
4	Both models had the same exterior lampshade but different interiors, as the large model had an interior shade and a single bulb emitting downwards light. Three bulbs mounted in the space between the shades had their light reflected both down and out through the slits in the top of the shade. Most of the light thus struck the tabletop. The bulbs in between the shades and the central interior bulb could be switched on or off separately. The smaller model only had the three light bulbs. This also meant that the lamp was glare-free if it was hung high. Later, the three-bulb solution was changed to a single 100-watt incandescent light bulb. The smaller version was first launched in 1962 and was first used at St Catherine's College, where the pendants hung low over coffee tables. Mathias Bøgeholdt, 30 December 2022; Thau & Vindum, 2002, p. 475.
5	The SAS Royal Hotel is now considered one of Jacobsen's principal works. During the 2000s, the hotel enjoyed a renaissance as a hotspot for design aficionados. Today, only room 606 remains with the original interior. Although only some of the furniture in this museum room was actually used in the original hotel rooms, it still offers an opportunity to experience the characteristic collisions of cubic and organic forms. None of the lamps discussed here were used in the hotel rooms, which instead had Eklipta lamps in the ceiling, special sliding wall lamps in nickel-plated metal with coloured Plexiglas shades and the Royal floor lamp with a specially designed textile shade, a nickel-plated stand and a blue-painted based. Mathias Bøgeholdt, 30 December 2022.
6	Thau and Vindum, 2002, p. 8.
7	Jacobsen made this comment in an interview, 'Portræt af en professor' (Portrait of a Professor), in the Danish newspaper *Information* on 20 August 1959 in connection with his appointment to professor at the Royal Danish Academy of Fine Arts, School of Architecture; reproduced in Thau and Vindum, 1998, p. 172.

Poul Henningsen: PH 5

1	PH in a Louis Poulsen ad from 1930.
2	Henningsen, P., 1958a, p. 1565.
3	In 1959, a variant was launched that emitted more light through the gap between the upper shades. This made the pendant lamp more suitable for hanging high and lighting up a larger area with a considerably higher luminance level. See Nørregaard et al., 1994, p. 274.
4	Henningsen, P., 1966, p. 2458.
5	Møller, V.S., 1980, p. 5.
6	Jørstian, 1994a, p. 6.
7	See Signe Lykke Littrup in Dybdahl, 2016a, p. 61. According to Louis Poulsen's sales department – and perhaps not surprisingly in a time that celebrates authenticity – in spring 2019, the classic PH lamp series PH 3/2 (the numbering system is explained in Poul Henningsen: PH lamp, note 5, p. 240) had climbed to the number one spot. Still, the PH 5 remains the most common model in Danish homes.
8	Henningsen, P., 1958a, p. 1564.
9	Ibid., p. 1563.

Poul Henningsen: Artichoke lamp

1	PH in Koppel, 1958, p. 1573.
2	Koppel, 1958, p. 1570. In the quote, Koppel called the Langelinie Pavilion a functionalist building. A review in *Arkitekten* stated that Koppel's pavilion was a 'restrained and sparse variant of the so-called international functionalism, which Arne Jacobsen was the first and most accomplished exponent of' (Hansen, 2017, p. 120). Both the Langelinie Pavilion and Jacobsen's SAS Royal Hotel, Copenhagen's first skyscraper, are characterized as being in the international style – the postwar style that found its purest manifestation in the new skyscrapers.
3	PH in Koppel, 1958, p. 1573.
4	Enevoldsen and Enevoldsen, 1958, p. 94.
5	Raizman, 2003, p. 264.
6	Koppel, 1958, pp. 1572–1573.

Jørgen Bo and Vilhelm Wohlert: Louisiana pendant

1	Bo graduated from the Royal Danish Academy of Fine Arts, School of Architecture, in 1941, Wohlert three years later. In autumn 1956, they were commissioned to design the new art museum, a task they would work on for 33 years before the final extension was completed. On Bo and Wohlert's early careers, see, for example, Sheridan, 2017, pp. 42–52. Jensen writes, 'Until the Louisiana project of 1957–1958, Jørgen Bo and Vilhelm Wohlert had been independent architects. From then and until sometime during the 1960s, they had a shared office. In the long run, however, their strong individual personalities caused them to split up and form separate architectural firms' (Jensen, 1986, p. 184).
2	Bo and Wohlert, 1958, p. 48.
3	Bo and Wohlert wrote in 1958 that this was preferable to 'ordinary overhead lighting, as the light strikes the walls, making them the dominant surfaces in the room, an effect that is heightened by the dark floors and ceilings' (ibid., pp. 47–48).
4	Louisiana, 2018. See also Sheridan, 2017, p. 122. Kjeld Kjeldsen, a curator at Louisiana and probably the person who knows most about the design of the museum, explained that Wohlert appears to have designed the lamps alone, both the small copper lamps and the large lamps designed specially for Louisiana (Kjeld Kjeldsen, 8 August 2019). This is confirmed by the architects Andreas Hansen and Alfred Homann, who worked in Wohlert's firm. When Homann joined Wohlert's firm in 1976, he was involved in the design of yet another, major expansion of Louisiana and thus gained intimate knowledge of the museum, its furnishings and the distribution of tasks between the two lead architects (Alfred Homann, 3 June 2019). However, while the Louisiana pendant was in production, Louis Poulsen consistently attributed it to both architects; see, for example, *LP & Co. NYT*, 1973, p. 3386.
5	Wohlert's bracket lamp is quite similar to Arne Jacobsen's bracket lamp from the SAS Hotel – too similar, in Jacobsen's opinion, according to Homann (8 August 2019).
6	Louisiana, 2018. In the retail edition, nylon grating was added to the Louisiana pendant (ibid.).
7	Louis Poulsen attributed the small spherical lamp to both Bo and Wohlert (Olsen in *LP & Co. NYT*, 1963, p. 2161). Wohlert designed an earlier spherical glass lamp, the Satellite pendant, Louis Poulsen, 1959.
8	Information about the exhibition was found in the 'Lighting' folder in the library archive of Designmuseum Danmark. According to the Le Klint company, the bracket lamp was installed in Niels Bohr's honorary residence at the Carlsberg factory estate, where Bohr lived from 1931 to 1962 (see https://www.leklint.dk/da-DK/Nyheder/Smuk-kending-vender-tilbage.aspx?Action=1&PID=1187). In 1956–1957, Wohlert oversaw a major renovation of Bohr's summerhouse in Tisvildeleje, on the north coast of Zealand, including the structural and interior design of a separate guest house. See Sheridan, 2017, pp. 66–67. Søren Andersen, marketing manager at Le Klint, showed a line-drawing sketch of the lamp included in the plans for the summerhouse (Søren Andersen, 12 August 2019). The lamp was used in both the main house and the guest house. An updated version of Wohlert's bracket lamp was launched in 2018.
9	Jensen, 1986, p. 185.
10	Wohlert taught architecture at the Royal Danish Academy of Fine Arts, School of Architecture, in 1944–1946, at the University of California, Berkeley, in 1951–1953

and again at the Academy in 1953–1959. In 1968–1986, Wohlert was a professor of architecture. In 1959, Bo was appointed associate professor of architecture and the following year professor at the Academy, a position he held until 1989. Thus, in addition to their joint projects, the two architects also crossed paths at the Academy. However, while Wohlert was inspired by Kaare Klint from his student days, Bo was influenced by Kay Fisker (see Sheridan, 2017, pp. 42 and 47).
11   Bo and Wohlert, 1958, p. 48.

Verner Panton: Topan

1   Panton was briefly married to PH's stepdaughter, Tove Kemp. See Engholm, 2005, p. 17.
2   Paragraph based on Møller, S.E, 1980, p. 3947, and Engholm, 2005, pp. 16–20.
3   Kirsten Ørskov, who met her future husband, Torben Ørskov, at a party in spring 1955, where Panton was also a guest, says, 'Back then, Verner was living in his VW van in front of Torben's flat in Peder Skrams Gade. When Torben went out for fresh bread in the morning, he tapped on the windscreen, and then Verner came in to shower in the flat. At the time, they had done one joint project, some short little candlesticks made of a triangular piece of iron where the three points were bent down to form legs, and then there was a little brass cuff in the middle. They were intended to be placed together in clusters due to their triangle shape. Torben was making these candlesticks and selling them in his first little shop, in Vingårdsstræde. Until then, the only other project Torben had been involved in was the Krenit bowl' (Kirsten Ørskov, 24 July 2019). Torben Ørskov formed Ørskov & Co. in 1953 and established the design shop Form & Farve (Form & Colour). The Krenit bowl (1952–1953) was designed by Herbert Krenchel based on an idea by Ørskov. See more about the bowl in Brun Petersen, 2016a, pp. 154–157.
4   The 'Lighting' folder with photos from the Association of Danish Crafts in the archive of the library at Designmuseum Danmark.
5   Kirsten Ørskov, 24 July 2019.
6   Paragraph based on Engholm and Michelsen, 2018 pp. 30–33 and 56–58.
7   Henningsen, P., 1961c, pp. 1858–1859. PH's comment that the lighting in the restaurant broke no new ground in technical terms applies to another pendant lamp that looks like a Topan shade turned upside down on a ring with a flat reflector plate on top. This pendant was produced by the Norwegian manufacturer Arnold Wiig's factories. See a small photo of the lamp in Henningsen, P., 1961c, p. 1857. In the review of the restaurant, PH also wrote that 'one will have to cover one's ears due to the din of two-tone harmonies and circles and squares' (ibid., p. 1856).
8   In January 1961, *LP & Co. NYT* presented the Topan pendant to a professional audience in shiny aluminium and pale grey lacquer. Topan was fitted with an ordinary E27 socket intended to hold a 75-watt standard incandescent light bulb or – if the client wanted the lamp without the mesh – with a chrome-capped light bulb. Louis Poulsen recommended the pendant for display lighting in retail spaces and shop windows (Henningsen, P., 1961c, p. 1858). Later, the pendant also appeared in orange, red, turquoise and blue. Today, Topan is produced by &Tradition.
9   Henningsen, P., 1961c, pp. 1858–1859.

Lars Eiler Schiøler: Pearlshade

1   The original Heiberg lamp was an oil lamp with an angular base, a so-called moderator lamp, which emerged during the 19th century. In Denmark, it was nicknamed the Heiberg lamp after an 1870 painting by the Danish artist Wilhelm Marstrand showing the Heiberg family (famous for achievements within Danish theatre and literature) seated around a table with such a lamp on it. The popular lamp design was later converted to electricity and sold by several manufacturers. The angular (not patented) base, which was originally made in both opal glass and porcelain, now also came in a ceramic version from Søholm Keramik (Søholm Ceramics) and others. See also p. 16.
2   When Lars Eiler Schiøler joined the company, a fruitful partnership, where Høyrup was in charge of business decisions, while Schiøler was responsible for design and production. P.J. Høyrup became a private limited company in 1968, with Høyrup as the main shareholder and Schiøler as a minority shareholder (Uffe Schiøler, 'Hoyrup Light Revisited').
3   Lars Eiler Schiøler had not yet acquired a vacuum machine in the mid 1950s but invented his own makeshift system, which worked perfectly. The problem was the plastic available at the time: when the finished shades were exposed to heat from the incandescent light bulb, especially with added heat from sunlight, they simply collapsed, says Lars Eiler Schiøler's son Uffe Schiøler (31 July 2019).
4   The expensive vacuum-forming machine was purchased in 1959 in connection with a move to bigger facilities in Gladsaxe, near Copenhagen, according to Uffe Schiøler. He also explained that the models developed during the late 1950s were successfully put into production, as the plastic was now more heat-resistant. The vacuum-formed and very affordable lamps were successful export articles. The Apollo 280 model in particular was popular in Finland, 'because it was reminiscent of a high-end Finnish glass lamp' (ibid.). The glass lamp in question is the Finnish artist and designer Yki Nummi's (1925–1984) Innolux Lokki, or Skyflyer, pendant from 1960, which also used vacuum-formed shades in opalized acrylic. See Fiell and Fiell, 2005b, pp. 62–63.
5   Uffe Schiøler, 31 July 2019.
6   Pearlshade is a cold-pleated lamp. As soon as the pleated waffle-pattern sheet came out of the machine, it was cut into the appropriate lengths. Sewn together and finally bent around a mould.
7   Participation in the annual lighting fairs in Gothenburg, Hannover and Paris led to a successful export business.
8   IKEA was founded as a mail-order company by Ingvar Kamprad (1926–2018) in 1943; in 1948, the company added furniture to its product line. In 1943, the Swedish department store NK had introduced flat-pack self-assembly furniture, but the real breakthrough for this concept came when IKEA introduced the first self-assembly furniture piece in 1956, the LÖVET (Foliage) table (Wickman, 2009, unpaginated [pp. 36, 40 and 48]). Kamprad opened the first physical IKEA store two years later, in 1958, in Älmhult, Sweden, while the first Danish IKEA shop opened in Ballerup, north of Copenhagen, in 1969. For the lighting company P.J. Høyrup, IKEA subsequently became an even bigger client and remained an important retail partner until the late 1970s. 'Our use of the flat-pack concept was also what enabled us to export to so many countries – the box only contained a shade and a metal mount for an electric socket, but it didn't have a socket and cord, which made everything much easier, because it didn't require any certifications [in Denmark a D label provided by DEMKO, certifying that the electrical components were safe], and then people could assemble them at home. Some exporters, however, actually assembled the lamps and sold them that way' (Uffe Schiøler, 31 July 2019).
9   Ibid. P.J. Høyrup's catalogue from 1970 showed five self-assembly models; the rest came assembled, but by 1976 almost all the lamps were self-assembly models. By then, Pearlshade was no longer in production. In 1976, Uffe Schiøler designed the self-assembly lamp Cactus, which came in several different sizes and colours and became a big export success. In 1978, the company was divided in two, and Uffe Schiøler continued to sell the P.J. Høyrup lamps under the name HoyrupLight until the company closed in the mid 1980s. Uffe Schiøler concludes about his father that 'he was a good designer, was able to read the market and knew how to exploit the technical possibilities. From the 1950s, a time when lighting was still very dim, he lit up living rooms' (ibid.).
10   Ibid.

Hans J. Wegner: Wegner pendant, Model JH604

1   Wegner in Holmsted Olesen, 2014, p. 13. Additional information in the section is similarly based on Holmsted Olesen, 2014, p. 13, and on personal communication with Wegner's daughter, the architect Marianne Wegner, on 24 May 2019. Although Wegner attended the School of Arts and Crafts in Copenhagen from 1936 to 1938, he never completed his degree there. When he later returned to the school, it was as a teacher.
2   The Copenhagen Cabinetmakers' Guild held the first of their annual exhibitions in 1927, in part in an attempt to promote Danish furniture design in response to the growing import of cheap furniture copying existing styles. At these

exhibitions, Wegner presented those of his furniture designs that were manufactured by the Copenhagen cabinetmaker Johannes Hansen. 'My father soon established a regular partnership with Johannes Hansen. He did take part in the exhibitions in 1938 and 1939, but in cooperation with other cabinetmakers. In fact, he didn't exhibit in 1940, the only year from 1938 to 1966 when he didn't participate.' From 1950, Wegner also worked with five other manufacturers; these designs were presented elsewhere, including the annual furniture fair Købestævnet in Fredericia. Wegner thus designed new pieces for all six manufacturers almost every year, says Marianne Wegner (24 May 2019).

3   The rise-and-fall pendant JH1 was first exhibited at the 26th Guild exhibition at the Danish Museum of Art & Design (now Designmuseum Danmark) on 26 September to 12 October 1952 (Jalk, 1987, pp. 212–213).

4   Marianne Wegner, 24 May 2019.

5   Like Wegner, the architect Frits Schlegel, who in 1928 had designed his first lamps in cooperation with the architect Vilhelm Lauritzen (see p. 40), only designed a small number of lamps. However, as Vibeke Anderson Møller notes in her 2004 book about Schlegel, his 1956 rise-and-fall pendant for Lyfa (previously Kjøbenhavns Lampe- og Lysekronefabrik) was his most successful luminaire. Anderson Møller, who studied the many Lyfa catalogues, notes that, at the time, Lyfa had several rise-and-fall pendant lamps in production, but that Schlegel's version stood out by remaining in production at Lyfa for more than 20 years (Møller, 2004, pp. 187–188).

6   For example, the JH1 was included in Wegner's retrospective exhibition in New York in 1959. See Holmsted Olesen, 2014, p. 66. 'There are photos where the exterior of the JH1 is painted white, perhaps in an attempt to make it less dominant, since a general criterion in the selection of lamps for the Guild exhibition stands was that the lamps must not "overshadow" the furniture' (Marianne Wegner, 24 May 2019).

7   According to Johannes Hansen's files, versions with black, red, light blue and light grey paint were approved, but whether they were all produced is unclear. Marianne Wegner knows of versions in black and light blue and a variant in polished brass with an egg-shaped brass pulley. At the 1964 Guild exhibition, Wegner exhibited a 70-cm version of the pendant above a large, round dining table. It was never put into production, but along with the table it wound up in the Wegner family's own dining room. Wegner used the smaller version above all the different desks and drawing tables in the house, says Marianne Wegner: 'The drawing tables were big, because we used T-squares and set squares and always drew chairs to full scale. All other workshop drawings were made in the size the tables allowed. The electric cord for the rise-and-fall pendant was fitted with a metal hook attached to a longer, ceiling-mounted metal rail. That let us move the lamp, so the light fell exactly where we needed it. That is very important when you work on high-precision drawings' (Marianne Wegner, 24 May 2019).

8   In the 1980s, Louis Poulsen had to abandon the pulley feature, as the fabric cover on the cord risked wearing through with heavy use, causing a short circuit. Hence, for a number of years, Louis Poulsen produced and sold the Wegner pendant without the pulley feature, which made the grip – the entire lower part of the bracket – pointless. When Pandul took over production, it was on the condition that an attractive and reliable solution was found. The redesign thus included a pulley feature built into an enlarged canopy (Marianne Wegner, 24 May 2019).

9   Wegner in *Politiken*, 1964. Quoted from Holmsted Olesen, 2014, p. 95. Since 2023, The pendant has been in production for Carl Hansen & Søn.

Poul Henningsen: Contrast lamp

1   PH in Bundgaard, 1966, p. 16.

2   In 1962, PH explained that while all his other lamps had overlapping shades, which cast a shadow on the lower edge of each shade, this part of the Contrast lamp emits an even light without these shifts in luminance. See Henningsen, P., 1962, p. 2037, and Nørregaard et al., 1994, p. 281.

3   PH explains that he chose red and blue to tone down 'the yellow centre', exactly as in the PH 5 pendant (Henningsen, P., 1962, p. 2036).

4   The paragraph is based on Henningsen, P., 1962, pp. 2035–2037, Dybdahl, 2012, p. 83, and Nørregaard et al., 1994, p. 281. The bracketed terms are PH's own (Henningsen, P., 1962, pp. 2036–2037). That the lamp was really three lamps in one was most obvious, said PH, when it was observed from slightly below (ibid.).

5   Henningsen, P., 1961a, p. 112. The detailed review of PH's lamps in the book celebrating his centenary, *Light Years Ahead*, explains why the Contrast lamp was so complicated to make and, hence, so expensive: each lamp required about 130 layers of paint and lacquer, each of the ten shades lacquered in six different sections (Nørregaard et al., 1994, p. 282).

6   PH in Bundgaard, 1966, p. 18. PH rebuked not only the architects but also the consumers who also ought to know – and live and light their homes – better, since architects would continue to design 'interesting' forms until 'the consumers liberate themselves from their traditional perceptions of lighting and begin to demand higher quality from the manufacturers, who are, after all, more or less compelled to produce what is in demand' (ibid.).

7   This PH 5 model proved less popular than the PH 5 pendant and was discontinued by Louis Poulsen in the mid 1980s. A final triple-shade table model that was launched just before PH's death in 1967 was more successful. With a chromed metal frame, it matched the high-tech interior design style of the 1970s, and its exclusive and spectacular appearance made it a good fit for the offices of the 1980s yuppie generation. See Nørregaard et al., 1994, p. 283, Dybdahl, 2012, p. 83, and *Bo Bedre*, 1966, no. 11, front page.

8   Henningsen, P., 1962, pp. 2036–2037.

Simon P. Henningsen: Divan 2

1   Quote used by the design studio employees in connection with Simon Henningsen's 50th birthday. From Louis Weisdorf's archive.

2   Louis Weisdorf, 2 May 2019.

3   Roos, 2015.

4   The architect Louis Weisdorf, who assisted Simon Henningsen in the redesign of Divan 2, prepared the design drawings of the Divan 2 lamp and took part in all the meetings concerning the production of the lamp, says that Brødrene Bjerg's metalware company produced the Divan 2 lamp for Lyfa (Louis Weisdorf, 2 May 2019). The Divan 2 lamp was also installed in the Georg Jensen shop on Fifth Avenue in New York in 1964 (Roos, 2015).

5   Louis Weisdorf, 2 May 2019.

6   Lyfa ad in *Bo Bedre*, 1962, no. 5, p. 113. The garden lamp was only available in a green-and-yellow version.

7   Henningsen, S., 1970. Quote used by the design studio.

Henning Koppel: Petronella

1   Excerpt from advertisement text about Petronella in *Bo Bedre*, 1963, no. 12, p. 83, among others.

2   For example, the architect Mogens Voltelen wrote in 1948 in *Dansk Husmoderleksikon* (Danish Housewives' Encyclopaedia), 'Where there is no electric lighting, kerosene lamps are the most common form of lighting' (Voltelen, 1948, p. 193). In 1964, the historian Michael Schrøder wrote, 'Thousands of beautiful kerosene lamps are still found in people's homes. And (…) new kerosene lamps are being produced and sold in growing numbers. There is agreement that with their live flame, they bring an atmosphere to the living room' (Schrøder, 1964, p. 199).

3   Anker Tiedemann, 25 June 2017.

4   Text in an ad from 1962 that was shown, in various layouts, in *Bo Bedre*, 1962, no. 6, p. 79, and 1962, no. 7, p. 67.

5   Møller, H.S., 1975, p. 91.

6   Petronella was first presented in the article 'Bedstemors lampe' (Granny's Lamp) in Rohweder, 1962, no. 6, pp. 44–46. While Petronella was priced at DKK 87, a PH 5 pendant, by comparison, cost DKK 175. By 1963, the price tag on the PH 5 had increased to DKK 197, and the Petronella cost DKK 92.50 (*Bo Bedre*, 1963, no. 6, p. 21, and 1963, no. 12, p. 83).

Jo Hammerborg: Orient

1   The 26-year-old Hammerborg Nielsen spoke of the two inspiring professors at the Royal Danish Academy of Fine Arts in an interview with a journalist from *Randers Amtsavis* in 1946. At the time, he had attended the Academy for three semesters: 'I learnt the goldsmith's trade

but picked up painting at the age of 20. I thought it might be a fleeting passion, but I just have to paint. (…) I soon realized that I had to get into the Academy if I wanted to make something of it' (ibid.). About his training as a silversmith: in July 1943, the 'silversmith Johs. Hammerborg Nielsen' received his diploma from the A.B.C.-Skolen for Tegning (A.B.C. School of Drawing). From 3 May 1943 until 26 January 1944, he worked as a silversmith at Hejl & Co. Sølvvarefabrik in the Danish city of Randers, as documented by a recommendation dated 2 July 1948, which highlights his 'good aptitude for drawing' (documents from the Hammerborg family's archive).
2   Henni Hammerborg, 5 July 2019. See also Hansen and Petersen, 2005, p. 94.
3   Henni Hammerborg explains that her husband was always called 'Johs' by his family and friends, 'but at Fog & Mørup, there already was an employee called Johannes Nilsen, so they needed to distinguish between the two men. Also, when the company began to export to the United States, among other places, it was helpful to have an abbreviated form. He gave up "Nielsen" completely' (Henni Hammerborg, 5 July 2019).
4   For example, Koppel's silver jug nicknamed the Pregnant Duck is from 1952, his fish dish is from 1954 and his eel dish is from 1956. See Hjortkjær in Dybdahl, 2016a, pp. 146–149.
5   *Elnyt*, 1962, p. 7.
6   Ibid. The article further mentioned that Orient came in two sizes, 22.5 cm and 34 cm in diameter, in either copper or aluminium. This is also clear from Fog & Mørup's lighting catalogue from 1963. A few years later, Hammerborg designed a drop-shaped Orient lamp base. See, for example, Fog & Mørup, 1978.
7   The brass shades had a yellow interior, while the copper ones were orange, producing a warm golden light.
8   That this hobby was also helpful in relation to his (lamp design) practice is clear from a brief article in *Rødovre Avis* (Rødovre Newspaper) titled 'De flyver selv' (They Do Their Own Flying), which describes how Fog & Mørup could fly out to meet retailers because both 'Head of Sales J.C. Jørgensen and the famous Danish lamp designer Jo Hammerborg' had a pilot's licence. Thus, they could quickly 'take off to reach both clients and warehouses rapidly and stay up to date on varying customer preferences and the selection on the shelves' (undated clipping from *Rødovre Avis* from the mid 1960s in the Hammerborg family's scrapbook).
9   Hammerborg was both a highly experienced pilot and parachutist, and at the time of his last, fatal jump on Bornholm in 1982, he had done more than 1,100 jumps.
10   Chr. H-m., 1946. An undated newspaper clipping from the Hammerborg family's archive. In 1943–1947, Hammerborg Nielsen displayed his paintings and drawings in an annual solo exhibition at the Randers Hotel. Catalogues from these exhibitions are in the family's archive.

Jens Møller-Jensen: Albertslund Post

1   The large housing development consists of three-storey blocks around a canal. From this centre, two-storey terraced houses, one-storey atrium houses, nurseries and schools were dispersed throughout the area, while a city centre was placed next to the train station. In keeping with prevailing ideals during the 1960s, pedestrians were kept completely separate from wheeled traffic. The principles that shaped Albertslund South took form under the leadership of the architect and city planner Peter Bredsdorff (1913–1981), who was inspired by the English garden cities. The atrium house theme, which was known from southern Europe, was inspired by the Arab kasbah and probably also by Jørn Utzon's Kingo Houses and Fredensborg Terraces, which had been built a few years earlier.
2   See Dybdahl, 2006, p. 204.
3   Mansfeldt, 2006, p. 5.
4   See Møller, H.S., 1975, p. 220. Jens Møller-Jensen originally trained as an instrument maker but then enrolled at the Royal Danish Academy of Fine Arts, School of Architecture, and thus made the Albertslund Post while he was still a student.
5   Mansfeldt, 2006, p. 5.
6   Møller, H.S., 1975, p. 224.
7   Ibid. Jens Møller-Jensen (8 May 2019) confirms that this remains a source of irritation.
8   Ibid. Jens Møller-Jensen (8 May 2019) underscores again that they were able to cut the cost by two thirds. Lisbeth Mansfeldt (2006), then showroom manager at Louis Poulsen, wrote that several companies were in play as manufacturers of the Albertslund Post, including Lyfa and Louis Poulsen. The latter company won the contract with an unbeatable cost price of DKK 0.50 (Mansfeldt, 2006, p. 6)! A total of 1,200 of the lamps were installed in Albertslund South. See Louis Poulsen's Albertslund Post catalogue, 2019, p. 3.
9   Jens Møller-Jensen established his own design firm in Nyhavn, Copenhagen, in 1967. He retired some years ago, and the company is now continued by his son, Peter Møller-Jensen (b. 1967). In Danish, design is sometimes referred to as *formgivning* (form-giving), but Jens Møller-Jensen views his own work as 'design': 'Design is a solution to a problem, and that's what I did; I solved a problem!' (Jens Møller-Jensen, 8 May 2019).
10   Møller, H.S., 1975, p. 226.
11   Jens Møller-Jensen, 8 May 2019.

Friis & Moltke: Pendant

1   After his graduation, Moltke initially stayed in Copenhagen, while Friis joined the architectural firm C.F. Møller in Aarhus. When Friis was able to take on smaller projects in addition to his work for C.F. Møller, he convinced Moltke, his friend from the Academy, to come to Aarhus, where they soon began to make plans for founding their own firm. Not until 1957 were the two architects able to work full-time in their own firm, Friis & Moltke (interview with Knud Friis, *Berlingske*, 5 April 2008; Mikkel Bahr, 20 June 2019).
2   Moseng, Andersen and Poulsen, 2004, p. 28.
3   DR, 1976.
4   Moseng, Andersen and Poulsen, 2004, p. 28, and Mikkel Bahr, 20 June 2019. Poulsen's plumbing firm later became Trepol (3 x Poulsen), which is known today for its collection of cooker hoods (ibid.).
5   Mikkel Bahr, 20 June 2019.
6   The firm's collaboration with Lampas began in 1973, and the first Friis & Moltke pendants were produced. The lamp series was presented at Bella Center in the *LUXPO* exhibition in 1975. See Berentzen, 2000, p. 2. Among other features, Rix added the later iconic signage lighting and mailbox. Rix initially headed the firm's design department, and after a reconstruction in 1994 he became the owner of the independent company Friis & Moltke Design (Moseng, Andersen and Poulsen, 2004, p. 28). Today, the limited company is an integrated part of Friis & Moltke.
7   Mikkel Bahr, 20 June 2019. Lampas was founded by the engineer Kjell Berentzen (b. 1942) in 1971.
8   This model, Lampas 6, was later developed into a full signage series. Its firm also provided the main inspiration for Rix when he later designed the Lampas mailbox (Berentzen, 2000, p. 8).
9   The outdoor wall lamp, which was named Lampas 5 in 1975, is now marketed by Lampas under the name Liber L5U. Hidden behind the curvy galvanized-aluminium shade are a socket and bulb, mounted on the back plate and covered by a glass globe to keep the lamp vandalism- and waterproof. The shade and reflector direct the light upwards and downwards along the wall behind the lamp.
10   The Friis & Moltke pendants now come in seven sizes: three from the FM1954 series and four from the FM2014 series. The pendants were relaunched in a collaboration between Friis & Moltke and Rewired, a sub-brand under the Frandsen Group, which specializes in relaunching classic Danish lighting designs. The Friis & Moltke pendants were the first to be relaunched by Rewired, says Lone Kudsk, the Frandsen Group's head of marketing, 27 June 2019. In 1982, Rix designed the Minneapolis lamp for Friis & Moltke's interior design of Hotel Scanticon in Minneapolis, Minnesota. Friis & Moltke's current head of design and partner, the architect Mikkel Bahr, has updated Rix's lamp to match contemporary lighting technology and requirements. It was recently put into production by Rewired. It shows a kinship with the original geometric universe but is far from the brutalist expression, which also does not define Friis & Moltke's other designs now, in 2019: 'Today, our approach is a little different. In our small design department, we are very aware that we possess a substantial design legacy but also that our main focus has to be the future. This balance is very interesting' (Mikkel Bahr, 20 June 2019).
11   Ibid.

12   Joint statement by Friis and Moltke in *Interview med Århus arkitekterne Friis og Moltke* (1976).

Finn Juhl: Table lamp

1   Wivel, 2004, pp. 10–14.
2   In 1991, the architect Acton Bjørn (1910–1992) spoke to design researcher Lars Dybdahl about his time as an employee in Vilhelm Lauritzen's firm together with Juhl, among others. Bjørn emphasized that it was Juhl who had worked on the brass record-player bracket lamp and on the VL38 table lamp, which uses the same lampshade (Lars Dybdahl, March 2019); see also Dybdahl, 2006, pp. 270 and 540, and Lund, 1994b, p. 247. It should be added that Juhl was very interested in Gunner Asplund's work, and this lampshade has clear references to that on Asplund's 1937 bracket lamp at Gothenburg City Hall. Juhl mentions 'Asplund's famous Gothenburg City Hall lamp' in Juhl, 1947b, p. 539.
3   Juhl was head of the School of Interior Design in 1948–1955 and can be credited with the more international outlook that came to characterize teaching at the school. His tenure also marked an important period in the school's history, with many trendsetting interior designers among the graduates. In 2000, the school was renamed The Danish Design School in a merger with the School of Decorative Art (Lytken, 2013, pp. 8–12).
4   Juhl never abandoned his functionalist home interior design ideals, which were fully demonstrated in his own home in Ordrup, north of Copenhagen, one of his few building designs. It is a consistent manifestation of the ideals of the time, the architectural setting forming a perfect harmony with the layout and interior design of the rooms, the colour scheme and the influx of light. Many of his famous furniture designs were created for this specific setting. See Hansen, 2009.
5   Juhl's assistant in this project, the interior designer Marianne Riis-Carstensen, has explained that the ceiling light fittings were a given; their design was determined by the Americans. However, she and Juhl selected the colours: 'The challenge for the ceiling was to design a colour palette with blue, orange, yellow, green and red light fittings. Initially, I prepared a proposal using the light red that appeared in a gouache by Vilhelm Lundstrøm that Finn owned and was very fond of and was hoping to include. However, I wasn't satisfied with the result, so I also prepared an alternative proposal. That was the more beautiful, and ultimately, that is the one we used' (Lytken, 2019, p. 52).
6   See Hansen, 2009, pp. 112–113. In Ifversen and Lyngbye Pedersen, 2013, p. 109, it says that the dual-direction lamp was manufactured by Mogens Voltelen. Christian Bundegaard does not include it in his comprehensive list of Juhl's designs (see Bundegaard, 2018, pp. 251–263). According to Marianne Riis-Carstensen, Voltelen was a lighting consultant, while Fog & Mørup produced the bracket lamps, which were specially designed for this project. Riis-Carstensen is also certain that the lamps and the large wall clock were the last interior items to be designed (Marianne Riis-Carstensen, 29 April 2019).
7   See Dybdahl, 2006, pp. 207–208.
8   Onecollection produced Finn Juhl's lamps until 2016, at which time the rights were transferred to Louis Poulsen. At the time of writing, Louis Poulsen has not put the lamps into production.
9   Juhl, 1954, pp. 140–141.

Louis Weisdorf: Conch

1   Louis Weisdorf, 2 May 2019.
2   Ibid.
3   Weisdorf was employed in PH's studio in connection with the 1958–1959 renovation of the Alléscenen theatre in Frederiksberg. Weisdorf's subsequent employment at Verner Panton's studio was related to Panton's 1959–1960 interior design of the Astoria Hotel in Trondheim, Norway. Of his earliest projects for PH and Panton, Weisdorf explains, 'PH needed a draughtsman, as that wasn't really a skill he mastered. My first task was to help design the theatre seats, which was actually one of my first design to be realized. It was a one-legged chair that you could swivel in any direction, depending on what was happening on stage. At one point, Verner Panton also came into the picture, because he needed assistance when he did the interior design of the Astoria Hotel in Trondheim, where everything had to done in his style. That was rather unique. I thought it was exciting. Among other things, I did the drawings of the Cone chairs for him' (Louis Weisdorf, 2 May 2019).
4   Ibid.
5   Ibid.
6   Steinhal, 1964. Weisdorf underscores, 'There was a photo in *Politiken* of my cardboard model of the Conch. Ditzel had never seen the lamp "live."' She contacted Panton in Switzerland, but he did not regard Weisdorf's lamp as a copy.
7   PH quotes in the paragraph: Louis Weisdorf, 2 May 2019. Weisdorf says about the production of the Conch lamp, 'When Tivoli wanted to order the lamps, I showed the model to Lyfa, but they said that the lamp was unfeasible. We were already collaborating with the metalworks factory Brødrene Bjerg, which made Simon's Divan 2 lamp, and when I showed them the lamp, they said immediately that it wasn't going to be a problem, so I wrote to Lyfa asking if they would produce the impossible lamp; they did. So the Brødrene Bjerg factory made it on commission for Lyfa' (Louis Weisdorf, 2 May 2019).
8   Ibid.
9   Ibid.
10 Ibid.
11 Ibid.

Jacob E. Bang: Bang pendant

1   https://www.holmegaard.dk/designere/oevrige-designere/jacob-e-bang.
2   Kay Fisker designed the Danish pavilion together with the architect Tyge Hvass. Jacob E. Bang was the construction manager for the Paris exhibition (Lassen and Schlüter, 2002, p. 21).
3   Bang in Tiedemann and Karlsen, 1961, p. 15.
4   Bang in 'Glas. Orientering ved Begyndelsen af en ny produktion' (Glass. Introduction at the Beginning of a New Production Run) in *Nyt Tidsskrift for Kunstindustri* (New Magazine for Industrial Art), 1928, quoted in Lassen and Schlüter, 2002, p. 22.
5   Hogla is an abbreviation for Holmegaard glassworks. For a detailed description of Hogla with a focus on production technology and its place in cultural context, see Dybdahl, 2016c.
6   Mogens Voltelen in Voltelen, 1928, p. 11. The vertical ad on the page reproduces Bang's words (in a slightly different order): 'Appropriate, strong, beautiful, affordable' (ibid). The design scholar Lars Dybdahl points out that although *Kritisk Revy* contained articles and ads for modern industrial art from both Denmark and other countries, few other items apart from the PH lamp receive favourable mention – but Bang's beer glasses did (Dybdahl, 2016c).
7   During the 1920s, Bang was Holmegaard's first in-house designer and had the position of art director until 1948. After a 15-year hiatus from glass design, Bang was appointed art director at the glassworks Kastrup Glasværk in 1957. It was during his tenure here that Bang first turned his hand to lamp design.
8   While designing the Bang pendant, Bang also made a few other models, with Kreta (Crete) being the best known. At Fog & Mørup, Chief Designer Jo Hammerborg worked with Bang to turn the mouth-blown shades into pendants to be included in Fog & Mørup's product line. A Fog & Mørup brochure from 1964 shows both the Bang and Kreta lamps. The brochure mentions that Bang is available in coral, ocean blue, midnight blue and opal, while the 37-cm-tall Kreta was available in 'heliotrope, olive, grey or opal' (Fog & Mørup, folder, 1964; from the Hammerborg family's archive). The glass shades were placed on a small metal plate attached to the cord with locking screws to support the weight of the fairly heavy shades.
9   Bruun, 2015, p. 14. In his prolific production, Bang created both elegant art glasses and anonymous industrial jars. One example of the latter is the octagonal ketchup bottle for the Danish condiments manufacturer Bähncke (1936) (ibid.).
10 Bang, 1949, p. 6.

Andreas Hansen: Pine Cone lamp, Model 153

1   Andreas Hansen, 17 July 2019. The architect Ole Wanscher (1903–1985) was the professor of furniture and spatial design at the Royal Danish Academy of Fine Arts when Hansen was a student at the Academy. Hansen's first time there was brief, but he later returned to the School of Architecture and for many years taught drawing there (ibid.).
2   Andreas Hansen, 17 July 2019. Hansen also described the history and chronology to Schmidt, 1968b, unpagi-

nated [p. 23]. Other aspects of the story about the beginnings of the collaboration with Allan Bock and Le Klint are told in Dalby, 2008, pp. 59 and 62.
3   Ibid.
4   Ibid. Also described by Hansen to Schmidt, 1968b, unpaginated [p. 24].
5   The name Pine Cone lamp was used, for example, in a Le Klint ad in *Bo Bedre*, 1964, no. 10, p. 173.
6   Only a few coloured lamps were made, and they never made it into the shops, because it was difficult to get the colour or the gold to adhere to the plastic shade (Andreas Hansen, 17 July 2019).
7   Ibid.
8   Andreas Hansen, 17 July 2019. In 1968, Hansen had five different folded lampshades on sale. See Schmidt, 1968b, unpaginated [p. 23]. Later Hansen also designed glass bases for the classic Le Klint shades, which were blown by the glassblowers at the Odense branch of the Holmegaard glassworks – the same city where the Le Klint shades were folded.
9   For example, Hvidt & Mølgaard created the Orgelpibe (Organ Pipe) (1963), Diamant (Diamond) (1964) and Krystal (Crystal) (1969) for Le Klint. For more on Hvidt & Mølgaard's design, see Dalby, 2008, pp. 63–64.
10 Andreas Hansen to Schmidt, 1968b, unpaginated [p. 23].
11 Andreas Hansen, 17 July 2019.
12 Ibid.

Verner Panton: Shell lamp

1   Marianne Panton, 28 March 2019. Marianne and Verner Panton's secretary Rina Troxler underscored that the lamp premiered at the Frankfurt Fair, not the fair in Cologne, as it is often claimed (ibid.).
2   See Vorre, 2008, p. 188.
3   Henningsen, P., 1961c, p. 1858.
4   The pendant was designed in 1960, but in August 1961 PH wrote in *LP & Co. NYT* that Louis Poulsen is 'working on some new items (...) a new lamp by Verner Panton, the Visor lamp', which had recently been presented in *Mobilia* magazine along with some chairs by Panton (ibid., p. 1917). Four months later, the Visor pendant No. 16568 was presented as a new product in *LP & Co. NYT*: 'Verner Panton has designed a new lamp ...' (Henningsen, P., 1961b, p. 1948). In the four black-and-white photos that show the white pendant in varying positions against a black background, the parallel to the Moon is striking. The space age had begun: the Russians launched the Sputnik satellite in 1957, later that year the Russian space dog Laika was the first living creature to orbit the earth, and in 1961 the Russian cosmonaut Yuri Gagarin followed. In a special 1966 issue on lighting, *Bo Bedre* presented the lamp as the Moon pendant (Gottlob, Hübbe and Rasmussen, 1966, p. 83).
5   Verner Panton, quoted in Møller, S.E., 1980, p. 3950.
6   Marianne Panton, 28 March 2019. The Shell lamps were created during a hectic time in the couple's life, when they married and moved into their home in Basel. See Engholm, 2005, p. 28.
7   Verner Panton in Bernsen, 2003, p. 50.
8   Ibid.
9   Ibid. and Engholm and Michelsen, 2018, p. 100.
10 The shells were circular, as were the connecting steel rings and the metal ring they were suspended from and rested on. Marianne Panton emphasizes that 'Verner was the first person ever to make a lamp like that, with both aluminium and mussel discs' (28 March 2019). Since, a wide range of more or less successful copies have emerged. Today, the original Panton Fun lamps are produced, in the different variants, by Verpan, following a close collaboration with Marianne Panton to ensure that they have exactly the right shape and sound. Peter Frandsen, CEO of Verpan, explains that the biggest model Verpan makes is the Fun 8, which has 6,000 shells and 50,000 stainless-steel rings. The lamp is two metres tall and one metre wide (Peter Frandsen, 5 July 2019). The Moon pendant is also in production today by Verpan, a subsidiary in the Frandsen Group.

Bent Gantzel-Boysen: LamPetit

1   Møller, S.E., 1966, p. 2443.
2   *Fyns Tidende*, October 1966, quoted in ibid., p. 2445.
3   Dybdahl, 2006, p. 2018.
4   Personal communication with Bent Gantzel-Boysen's widow, Dorit Gantzel-Boysen, and their daughters, Gitte and Janne Gantzel-Boysen, on 6 April 2019 in the family home, where two modified PH 5 lamps are installed: despite his great respect for PH, Gantzel-Boysen, ever the perfectionist, adapted his own PH lamps to what he considered the right incandescent light. A PH 5 installed above a table traps a great amount of light, and so it makes sense that Gantzel-Boysen, among other modifications, removed the metal base plates in his two lamps to make them shine a direct light on the tabletop without producing glare. Gantzel-Boysen was so close with PH that he and his wife were present at PH's 70th birthday party in 1964.
5   Advertisement, *LP & Co. NYT*, no. 311, 1967, p. 2554.
6   *Ekstrabladet*, October 1966, quoted in Møller, S.E., 1966, p. 2443.
7   Panton had nothing to do with LamPetit, according to Dorit Gantzel-Boysen; Panton's widow, Marianne Panton; and Rina Troxler, Panton's secretary for many years. A possible source of the confusion may be that Louis Poulsen never mentioned Gantzel-Boysen by name in their ads for the lamp. Around 1970, magazine ads for the lighting company showed photos of LamPetit alongside other lamps, including Panton's Flowerpot and PH's PH 5 and PH 4/3. Gantzel-Boysen is the only designer who is not mentioned by name in these ads (see, e.g., *Bo Bedre*, 1969, no. 4, p. 10).
8   *Fyens Stiftstidende*, October 1966, quoted in Møller, S.E., 1966, p. 2445.

Jo Hammerborg: Trombone

1   The Hammerborg family recently compiled a list based on the lamps mentioned as Jo Hammerborg designs in Fog & Mørup's catalogues, but the list is far from exhaustive because Hammerborg designed many lamps for the company that were not attributed to him. This according to Hammerborg's widow, Henni, and their daughters, Gry and Marlene Hammerborg (5 July 2019).
2   Ibid. Henni Hammerborg (b. 1938) also explains that Jo Hammerborg left nothing to chance in the design of his own home: 'When I first visited his flat on the 15th floor in Brøndbyøster, I entered a bright, modern, simple living room with designer furniture – including some of Børge Mogensen's furniture. I came from a home with dark furnishings, so this was very different. No bric-a-brac was allowed, except for a few select items, mostly in glass. Gradually I was able to exert a little influence and make a cosy living room. But one day when I returned home, new furniture had been put in; it was designed by Wegner and matched the Børge Mogensen dining table. I knew that new furniture had been ordered, but I had no say in what it was' (ibid.). Henni Hammerborg mentions that it was important for her husband that his lamps in Fog & Mørup's catalogues were shown alongside modern designer furniture, because they were designed for exactly that sort of context.
3   It is a characteristic of many of Hammerborg's lamps that in addition to downwards light they also radiate light towards the ceiling and thus contribute to the general lighting in the room. The Studio lamp, which was designed as a wall lamp, had the same feature.
4   For the wedding, a long 'sabre arch' was formed in front of the church. While the colleagues from Fog & Mørup raised Studio floor lamps, Jo Hammerborg's friends from the KB Tennis Club presented raised tennis rackets (ibid.).
5   The lamp head swings 45 degrees in one direction and 180 degrees in the other, explains the Hammerborg family (ibid.).
6   Ibid.
7   Jo Hammerborg was instrumental in Fog & Mørup's success as a lighting manufacturer during the 1960s and 1970s. In 1978, Fog & Mørup was taken over by the competing firm Lyfa, and Hammerborg set up a studio in his home, where he continued his work. In 1980, he went into business for himself, a venture that was facilitated by the royalties he received for his many lamp designs. As described on p. 84, he sadly passed away only two years later. Jo Hammerborg created an impressive number of lamps for Fog & Mørup, including lamps for the Royal Porcelain Factory (now Royal Copenhagen) and Holmegaard glassworks. See, for example, Hansen and Petersen, 2005, p. 94. One example of a popular Hammerborg lamp based on geometric forms is the Nova pendant (Fog & Mørup, 1963). It consists of four shade rings, and like many of Hammerborg's lamps it had shades in copper,

brass or aluminium with a coloured interior in order to provide a golden light. Here too, Hammerborg used the feature of not only painting the inside of the smallest shade, which was closest to the light bulb, white for maximum reflection but also adding a dark grey band to soften the downwards light. The distribution of light in this model was so accomplished that it won first prize in the 1965 design competition Concurso Nacional de Diseño Industrial in Buenos Aires, besting PH's design for Louis Poulsen.
8   Henni Hammerborg, 5 July 2019.

Benny Frandsen:
Ball Model 1300

1   Benny Frandsen, 20 August 2019.
2   Ibid.
3   Ibid.
4   Ibid. Frandsen adds that the tool was created as an examination project by the son of the owner of the sub-supplier Thisted AluminiumIndustri, now AB Metal, who was training to become a wood-cutting machinist. It was fairly unique because the ballshape was so difficult to manufacture. The sub-suppliers also lacquered the balls. Initially, the shells were all iron; later, shells in spun aluminium were added (ibid.).
5   Ibid.
6   Daells Varehus, 1973, pp. 214 and 215.
7   Benny Frandsen, 20 August 2019. Frandsen explains that like most manufacturers at the time, he used numbers because they made the certification process easier. In acquiring the D-label from DEMKO, it was simpler to obtain certification for a numbers sequence: 'If I had named them after cities or given them girl's names, each individual lamp had to go through a separate approval process. The certificates were provided by state institutions, both in Norway and in Denmark, and it was both time-consuming and very costly to obtain these approvals.' Frandsen adds that to this day, many Norwegians know what sort of lamp a Model 1300 is. Why it was 1300 and not some other number, 'I honestly don't remember' (ibid.).
8   Ibid.
9   Ibid. The factory later began to make its own LED bulbs for the magnet lamps because 'the bulbs on the market were too big, they protruded slightly, while ours were small enough to remain hidden inside the shade. Initially, we delivered the lamp with a bulb, but today there are many manufacturers making small, high-quality bulbs, so we leave it to them' (ibid.).
10 Frandsen's first production was launched in 1968 in the basement of the family's home in Skanderborg, in eastern Jutland. Today, the factory is placed some 30 km south, in Horsens. From these modest beginnings, the factory now occupies 8,200 square metres. The Frandsen Group also includes the subsidiary Verpan, dedicated to lamps and furniture designed by Verner Panton, and the project section Frandsen Projekt, which in 2016 launched Rewired as a sub-brand under the Frandsen Group. Frandsen, 2018, pp. 132–133, and information from Lone Kudsk, marketing director, Frandsen Group, 27 June 2019, and Benny Frandsen, 20 August 2019.
11 Benny Frandsen, 20 August 2019.

Verner Panton:
Flowerpot

1   Excerpt from a poem by the Danish poet Olaf Gynt (1909–1973) written in April 1971 and printed in Gynt, 1971, p. 2914.
2   In 1968, the lamps had textile cords, five years later, in Panton's spirit, they were replaced with coloured plastic cords. Mathias Bøgeholdt, 30 December 2022; Carin Panton, 16 January .2023.
3   Henningsen, P., 1928, p. 68. When he designed the lamps for the Kom-Igen inn (see p. 72), Panton had already created a pendant with a hemispherical lower shade. Thus, the form is based not only on the round shape of his early Louis Poulsen lamps but also on this upturned reflector.
4   Møller, S.E., 1968a, p. 2591. The architect Svend Erik Møller also wrote the review of the exhibition in *Mobilia*. See Møller, S.E., 1968b, unpaginated [pp. 42–49].
5   Bernsen, 2003, p. 52.
6   There were ads for the Flowerpot lamps in *Bo Bedre*, 1969, no. 4, p. 109, and 1969, no. 5, p. 175, and a new ad in *Bo Bedre*, 1969, no. 11, p. 93.
7   See examples of concepts for cluster installations in a schematic by Louis Poulsen, reproduced in Engholm and Michelsen, 2018, p. 153. Panton also used large groups of Flowerpot lamps in his design of the Hamburg office for the German weekly magazine *Der Spiegel* (about the building, see p. 110), and in the Varna restaurant in the Danish city of Aarhus, 112 Flowerpot lamps lit up the stairs to the toilets and public telephones in the basement (Møller, S.E., 1972b, p. 3950).
8   According to Marianne and Carin Panton, any reference to pot smoking from Panton would have been unintentional. Panton was not into drugs of any sort, so the reference will have been to flowers, either indiviudally or in a bouquet. Carin Panton, 16 January 2024.
9   'Stor mønstret Flowerpot', 1970, no. 3, p. 2801. Here, it is also mentioned that a white version of the 'big brother of the Flower-Pot' was launched, and that these models had been presented at the furniture fair in Cologne in January 1970 (ibid.). A large monochrome version had already been presented at the *Visiona* exhibition in 1968 (Møller, S.E., 1972a, p. 3240).
10 Flowerpot was awarded the German design award Gute Form Bundespreis (Federal Prize for Good Form) in 1972.
11 Panton in Møller, S.E., 1972b, p. 3950. In addition to the mentioned sources, the article is also based on Hvidberg-Hansen, 2000, p. 106, Engholm, 2005, p. 43, and Dybdahl, 2006, pp. 214–217. After being discontinued for a period, like almost all Panton's lamps, Flowerpot was relaunched during the 2000s, initially by Unique Interieur and subsequently by &Tradition, which still sells the series, both the pendant and two table lamps.

Sven Middelboe:
Verona

1   Sven Middelboe was the older brother of the designer Rolf Middelboe (1917–1995), who, unlike Sven, trained as an artist at the School of Arts and Crafts and had a career as a graphic designer (Bruun et al., 1979, p. 409).
2   Publisher Torsten Bløndal, 24 June 2019. In 2002, Bløndal published an Utzon monograph that was written in collaboration with Utzon. Bløndal interviewed Utzon and Middelboe and heard this story from both of them. See also Weston, 2002, pp. 347 and 422, note 17. It is part of the story of Middelboe and Utzon's relationship that Utzon designed a home for Middelboe and his wife by Furesøen lake in Holte, north of Copenhagen. The house was built in 1952–1953. It was mounted on stilts to provide an optimal view of the lake. Utzon described climbing up into a tree and saying to Middelboe that he should really elevate the building to get exactly that view – and so he did (Torsten Bløndal, 24 June 2019). About the house, see Weston, 2002, pp. 68–73. Photos on p. 73 shows that Utzon's Tivoli, Sundowner and Sunlighter pendants were used in the house.
3   Bruun et al., 1979, p. 410.
4   Thorkild Thage Jørgensen, 12 July 2019. The former CEO Thorkild Thage Jørgensen (b. 1944) is the son of Harald Jørgensen, the then CEO and co-owner of Nordisk Solar Compagni, who in 1955 employed Middelboe. Bruun et al., 1979, writes that Middelboe had designed lighting exhibitions at 'La Boutique Danoise in Paris, in London, Oslo and Gothenburg and at the Hannover fair every year since' (Bruun et al., 1979, p. 410). A photo from Nordisk Solar Compagni's stand at the 1956 Hannover fair appears in Weston, 2002, p. 346. 'He exhibited both his own designs and everybody else's, including Jørn Utzon's,' added Jørgensen (12 July 2019), which is also evident from the photo in Weston, 2002.
5   Nordisk Solar Compagni's first lighting catalogue was issued in 1957. A large catalogue from 1959 shows Pagode in three sizes and lists it as being available in red, yellow, black or terracotta.
6   In design, Nord-Lys is reminiscent of the other Nordisk Solar Compagni pendant Minisol (Mini Sun), designed by K. Kewo. This harmonious pendant, made up of strictly geometric shapes – a hemisphere above a cylindric stair formation – was a big hit for the company, says Jørgensen (12 July 2019). He was not able to assign a more specific design year to either Minisol or Nord-Lys. Nite-cap has some similarity to the Phister bracket lamp, which was designed by Hans Due for Fog & Mørup. Phister and Minisol are mentioned here because they are often erroneously attributed to Middelboe.
7   After searching through photos and other materials, Sven Middelboe's family concluded that the lamp much have been designed in 1968. Louise Eidemak, granddaughter of Sven Middelboe, 14 January 2024.

8   Nordisk Solar Compagni, 1978a. Nordisk Solar Compagni's 1978 lighting catalogue included 11 different ceiling lamps by Sven Middelboe. One stands out, both due to its fascinating form and because it is the only one to have its own name: Verona. In 1978, Verona was made in two sizes and three metal and colour combinations. Nordisk Solar Compagni's larger 1978 catalogue features Verona in four sizes. Shortly after, the company added one more size, two models for installation directly on the ceiling with three or five shades, respectively, and a table lamp. These additions are evident from Nordisk Solar Compagni's catalogue from 1981. The Verona pendant exists in two variants, their main distinction between slight variations in the shape of their top shades.
9   From 1941 to 1967, PH wrote for Louis Poulsen's magazine *LP & Co. NYT*, including offering specific descriptions of his luminaires; naturally, a lighting designer, such as Middelboe, will have read and learnt from these articles.
10   Thorkild Thage Jørgensen, 12 July 2019. Middelboe was attached to Nordisk Solar Compagni's lighting design department as design and exhibition director until he retired at an advanced age. Jørgensen confirms that Nordisk Solar Compagni produced lamps until 1998.
11   Slogan in Nordisk Solar Compagni, 1978a, p. 2.

Torsten Thorup and Claus Bonderup: Semi

1   Torsten Thorup, 30 April 2019. At Fog & Mørup, the experienced designer and head of design Jo Hammerborg helped the two young architects perfect the dimensions.
2   Ibid.
3   Dybdahl, 2006, pp. 50–53.
4   Ibid.
5   Torsten Thorup, 30 April 2019.

Verner Panton: Spiegel Fittings

1   Møller, H.S.H, 1990, p. 107. See also von Vegesack and Remmele 2000, p. 365. Pavillon de Marsan is at the north-western end of the Louvre Palace. Since 1905, Pavillon de Marsan and the adjacent buildings have housed Le Musée des Arts Décoratifs (Museum of Decorative Arts) and thus also the Centre de Création Industrielle (Centre of Industrial Creation). The exhibition *Qu'est ce que Le Design?* was shown from 24 October to 31 December 1969 (http://www.idref.fr/03297583X). Jens Bernsen har fejlagtigt skrevet, at denne udstilling fandt sted i Centre George Pompidou, men selv om planlægningen af museet begyndte i 1969, var det først i 1977, at Renzo Piano og Richard Rogers bygning blev indviet (Bernsen 2003: 48 versus https://www.centrepompidou.fr/fr/Le-Centre-Pompidou/L-histoire).
2   Møller, S.E., 1969, p. 2692. Remarkably, Møller also writes that the square light fittings had many potential uses: their perforated surface made them suitable for air conditioning, and with an insulating backing they could be used for sound-dampening (ibid.).
3   Ibid. The fittings were also installed as a luminous wall in the yard of the Spiegel building.
4   *Visiona II* followed *Visiona 0* (1968) and *Visiona I* (1969).
5   Bernsen, 2003, p. 68, and Engholm, 2005, pp. 41–43.
6   Henningsen, P., 1927, p. 82.
7   Sparke, 1999, p. 266.
8   Møller, S.E., 1969, p. 2696.

Verner Panton: Ilumesa

1   Hvidberg-Hansen, 2000, p. 114. The Spiral lamp was also made in a version where three spheres are suspended one under the other, the SP3. Here, both the sculptural effect and the lighting are particularly impactful, like sunlight shining on a flowing waterfall.
2   Møller, S.E., 1972, p. 3242.
3   'Nyt lys på vej fra Køln', 1970, p. 2781. In *LP & Co. NYT*, no. 340, 28 March 1970, it is announced that Ilumesa is now being launched in Danish retail shops.
4   Ibid.
5   Panton in Møller, S.E., 1980, pp. 3948 and 3950.
6   'Nyt lys på vej fra Køln', 1970, p. 2781.
7   Gottlob, 1970, p. 45. Ilumesa, on the other hand, was a very expensive lamp, which cost about the same as three PH 5 lamps.
8   Panton, 1991 p. 15.

Verner Panton: VP Globe

1   Louise Campbell, 13 March 2013.
2   'Nyt lys på vej fra Køln', 1970, p. 2781.
3   Ibid.
4   Ibid., p. 2782. In 1972, the pendant is mentioned in Louis Poulsen's magazine *LP & Co. NYT* as the VP Globe ('Tre producenter, én designer', 1972, p. 3244).
5   This paragraph is based in part on Dybdahl, 2006, p. 217.
6   As a homage to PH, Panton designed the VP Europa lamp system in 1977 including pendant, table and floor lamps. They are clearly a paraphrase on PH's lamp system. In his 2003 monograph on Panton, Jens Bernsen described VP Europa as 'A PH-lamp drawn in one line, made in one process, and in glass' (Bernsen, 2003, p. 82). The lamps were also produced with classic glass shades and shiny metal bases, but the mouth-blown glass shades made them very expensive, heavy and fragile, and after a few years they were discontinued.
7   'VP-kuglen', 1975, p. 3542.
8   Panto was put into production by Louis Poulsen in 1977 and is now in production by Verpan, like the VP Globe. It now also comes with a diameter of 40 cm but no longer in the less manageable 60-cm version (Peter Frandsen, CEO of Verpan, 5 July 2019).

Bent Karlby: Pantre

1   Bent Karlby in Lyfa 1949, p. 1.
2   Møller, 2014, p. 89.
3   Lyfa advertisement in *Bygge og bo. Tidskift for danske hjem*, 1959, no. 4, p. 4. Reproduced in Møller, 2014, p. 89. The Mosaik lamps had a stringently geometric form, but the 25-cm-high pendant, whose metal shade was available in multiple colours, was not least intended for clusters of two or more lamps to be assembled into festive decorations, depending on the buyer's preference; some of the possible combinations were presented in the Lyfa advertisement.
4   Karlby, 1942, p. 77.
5   Ibid.
6   Panton, 1991, p. 15.
7   The light from the bulb is reflected from the back of the rings and light up the coloured front plate to give rise to a slightly diffused annular pattern.
8   Karlby, 1942, p. 76.
9   Most of Karlby's lamp designs were manufactured by Lyfa, but he also created lamps for ASK, A. Schrøder-Kemi. See Møller, 2014, pp. 96–97.
10   Hans Schrader, Karlby's grandson, 18 June 2019. The text is largely based on Andersson Møller's 2014 monograph *Arkitekten og designeren Bent Karlby* (The Architect and Designer Bent Karlby). I also received valuable input from Hans Schrader and his wife, Anne Vibeke Mortensen.

Michael Bang: Parasol

1   Michael Bang in Holmegaard Glasværk, 1980, p. 5. Bang added in 1980, 'I consider myself neither an artist nor a designer. Working with a team of glass-makers, the soloists, my role is to visualize an idea and give it form in the material of glass' (ibid., p. 4).
2   As Bang put it in 1980, 'I am not sure I would have been here today, had my father not worked in glass' (ibid., p. 5).
3   Ibid.
4   Ibid., p. 4.
5   Ibid., p. 5.
6   Rolino from 1971 is a more angular version of Parasol; both have a corbel at the top of the cylindrical column. In this top section, covered by the coloured shade, the bulb is placed out of view behind the white opal glass, illuminating the shade, which also reflects the light down towards the column and the tabletop. Another 1970 model was the Bowler.
7   Lassen & Schlüter, 2002, p. 52. Holmegaard had a long-standing tradition for making glass shades, and when Jacob E. Bang created his glass pendants during the early 1960s, it was similarly only the shades that were blown at the glasswork; at the time, all the lamps were finished and assembled at the respective lighting factories. Jacob E. Bang's lamps were designed for Fog & Mørup. See p. 94.
8   Susanne Outzen, curator at Museum Sydøstdanmark (Museum of South-Eastern Denmark), explains that Astronaut and Parasol were included in Holmegaard's

catalogues from 1973 to 1976, after which time they were discontinued. Victoria first appears in a 1973 catalogue and was discontinued by the end of 1989 (Susanne Outzen, 10 July 2019). The prevailing trend now was minimalism, but in the many summerhouses and, later, conservatories, there was still room for nostalgic idyll. The year after the launch of Victoria, another retrospective luminaire appeared, designed for the Danish Postal and Telegraph Service, P&T. The 75-cm-tall P&T table lamp consists of an adjustable iron frame that holds a pendant shade, with direct reference to a traditional shoemaker's pendant. The shade is opal white with dark green flash. No humour here; the form is sober and clean. See Lassen & Schlüter, 2002, pp. 69 and 178.
9   Etude from 1971 and Mandarin from 1983 are two of the lamps which became popular items in white opal glass. Etude was also made in a version with aubergine-coloured flash.
10   Michael Bang in Holmegaard Glasværk, 1980, p. 5.
11   Ibid.

Poul Christiansen: SinusLine Model 172A

1   Poul Christiansen, 23 April 2019.
2   Ibid.
3   Ibid.
4   Ibid.
5   Ibid.
6   Ibid. Christiansen explains how he found the solution with the sinusoid curve: 'I scored a long, continuous line, and based on that I drew several parallel curves with different oscillations at a given distance to the first. When the shade was folded, a sphere emerged' (ibid.).
7   Christiansen says that he proposed names referencing celestial bodies – Sirius, Corona and Luna – to Le Klint's director, but they were considered a little too 'lofty' for the clientele; instead, a consensus formed around the name SinusLine, from sinusoid, for the series. See Dybdahl, 2006, p. 53.
8   Concerning his choice of building design (rather than other aspects of design, all of which were included under 'architecture' in Denmark at the time) as his field, Christiansen says, 'That is what a progressive architecture student had to choose at the time.' It is also important to add that Christiansen was a student at the Academy during the time of the youth rebellion, when the university hierarchy and the rigid and old-fashioned traditions were under attack: 'Design had an aura of dusty conservatism; the good story about Kaare Klint's furniture school was a thing of the past, to us. Design was associated with commercialism. Just as today, the focus is on saving the planet by incorporating sustainability; we wanted to liberate the world from capitalism, but I simply couldn't curb my urge to create these designs. But I wanted to be a building architect; design was just a hobby to me. Back then, following in Kaare Klint's footsteps with Le Klint played no big role; that's something I thought much more about later' (Poul Christiansen, 23 April 2019).
9   Ibid.

Verner Panton: Panthella

1   'Panthella bord- og standerlamper', 1972, p. 3238. This ad mentions the three-way bulb offering 60, 100 and 150 watts; other ads say 60, 100 and 160 watts – see, e.g., *LP & Co. NYT*, August 1971, p. 2929, and these are indeed the correct levels. The tri-light bulb was discontinued in the early 1990s, but today Panthella comes with a stepless dimmer switch (see note 8).
2   Sparke, 1999, p. 204.
3   At Louis Poulsen, Panton had developed a close relationship with Bent Gantzel-Boysen, who was the head of Louis Poulsen's design team. In 1966, Gantzel-Boysen had developed LamPetit under his own name, which offered two different light levels. See p. 100.
4   See Bernsen, 2003, p. 82, and Engholm, 2005, p. 44.
5   In September 2016, a small table lamp model with three light levels was launched. The new model had a metal shade and was available in 11 colours, selected from Panton's palette. Today, the lamp has stepless dimming.
6   The Danish Louisiana Museum of Modern Art showed the exhibition *Vision and Reality. Conceptions of the 20th Century* from 21 September 2000 to 14 January 2001.
7   Louis Poulsen discontinued production of Flowerpot, VP Globe and the Moon pendant in the early 1980s, while Panthella has remained in continuous production. The others are currently in production by &Tradition and – the majority – by Verpan. Much has been written about Panton. Interested readers will find information about his many designs in von Vegesack and Remmele, 2000, and Engholm and Michelsen, 2017.
8   Panton, 1991, p. 17.

Bent Gantzel-Boysen: Unispot

1   Dybdahl, 2006, p. 217.
2   The Lytespan conductor rail was introduced in 1967 as a flexible lighting system for display windows, offices, schools, exhibition halls, museums and so forth. The rail was a brilliant solution to the problem of the wall-mounted electric sockets being rarely where they were needed. With this system, spotlights (or, for that matter, PH lamps) could be mounted on ceiling rails wherever they were needed here and now and later moved or supplemented with additional lights, as needed. Luminaires are simply plugged into a socket mounted on the rail, which closes the circuit (Olsen, 1967, p. 2483).
3   'Hannover-Messen 1973', 1973, p. 3307.
4   Alring, 1981, p. 111.
5   SorteLouis is described as a new product in Stephensen, 1974.
6   Dorit Gantzel-Boysen, 6 April 2019.
7   Stephensen, 1974, pp. 3439–3440. 'Even if SorteLouis comes at a price, something we elderly view with seriousness, it is still one of the most affordable quality luminaires.'
8   Butler's lampshade, like the shade on the IT lamp, is an elliptic reflector. Mounted on a black rod, it is easily directed at the intended target. The rod stands on a three-part base on castors with covers matching the colour of the lampshade, which came in contemporary trendy colours: brown, orange and yellow. The lamp can thus be wheeled around the home to where it is needed – hence the name Butler. As many as three lamps could be mounted on the rod. See, e.g., Stevensen, 1974, p. 3440.
9   Bent Gantzel-Boysen is mentioned by name, for example, in Jens Barslund, 'Shopping', *Bo Bedre*, 1984, no. 1, p. 7. Unispot was presented as coming from 'Louis Poulsen's Development Department', see, e.g., *LP & Co. NYT*, no. 380, December 1973, p. 3490.
10   Bent Gantzel-Boysen's IKEA lamps: CIRKEL pendant and table lamp (1979), BANJO series (1980), RAMP shelf lighting (1982), LIRA/ACKORD floor and table lamp (1982), GALAX pendant (1982), DUETT pendant (1983), ARIA/ACKORD floor and table lamp (1983), SONAT wall lamp (1984), SONAT/KORUS series (1985) and VÄXA plant lighting (1987).
11   'Unispot', 1971, pp. 2902–2903.

Jørgen Gammelgaard: Tip Top pendant

1   Mollerup, 1995, pp. 4 and 15–19.
2   Karin Gammelgaard, 15 May 2019.
3   Ibid. The specific light bulb remains unknown, but at the time several tubular incandescent bulbs existed. Most of them were small, but some were long – for example, opalized versions (resembling a candle) that could be used with a mirror. As *Bo Bedre* wrote in 1966, these tubular light bulbs had 'as many different names as there are companies to make and sell them' (Gottlob, 1966, p. 140).
4   After the death of cabinetmaker Johannes Hansen in 1961, his youngest son, the cabinetmaker Poul Hansen, took over the company, Johannes Hansens Møbelsnedkeri. In the early 1970s, he launched the sub-brand Design Forum, which focused on young and modern design. In 1982, Poul Hansen sold Design Forum.
5   Karin Gammelgaard describes how initially the attempt was made to string the shades together with thin steel ball chains, which gave it a look that was closer to the original Samoan lamp, where the shades were held together with fishing line. Ultimately, however, Jørgen Gammelgaard and the manufacturer agreed to use more stable spacers in metal tubing (Karin Gammelgaard, 15 February 2019).
6   Remy-Jensen, 1980b, p. 37.
7   Nielsen, J., 1988, p. 72.

Henning Koppel: Bubi

1   Hannah Koppel explains that her young son, Adam (b. 1966), was wearing a white 'strawberry hat' with a roll edge (Hannah Koppel, 29 May 2019). In form, the bust and the lamp are quite similar.
2   Louis Poulsen's ad was shown in *Bo Bedre*, 1963, no. 12, p. 83, among other places.
3   It has not been possible to find any ads for Bubi or any mention of the lamp in Louis Poulsen's magazine *LP & Co. NYT* from the relevant years. The question is how many lamps actually made it out of the factory.
4   Claus Juhlin, owner of the lighting company Pandul, 21 May 2019. Hannah Koppel says that Louis Poulsen gave up its right to produce and sell the pendants in 1988 (Hannah Koppel, 29 May 2019).
5   Claus Juhlin, 21 May 2019. After the death of Claus Juhlin in 2022, Pandul was bought by Carl Hansen & Søn in i 2023.
6   Koppel in Kaiser, 2000, pp. 79–82. Hannah Koppel describes that it was the legendary TV reporter Flemming Madsen who in the 1970s elicited this reply from Henning Koppel when Madsen kept probing at Koppel's view on the ideals of functionalism in relation to his large and very expensive silver dishes (fish dish, 1954, and eel dish, 1956) (Hannah Koppel, 29 May 2019). According to DR, the programme was aired on 12 November 1971.
7   Koppel in Schmidt, 1968a, unpaginated [p. 20].
8   Claus Juhlin, 21 May 2019. Henning Koppel died in 1981, and Bubi was relaunched and modified in consultation with his daughter, the sculptor and ceramicist Hannah Koppel.
9   Claus Juhlin, 21 May 2019.
10   Koppel in Schmidt, 1968a, unpaginated [p. 20].

Hans Due: Optima

1   Hans Due (5 August 2019) explains that he began his apprenticeship in a graphic design studio in 1958. Four years later, certificate in hand, he enrolled at the Graphic Arts Institute of Denmark, from which he graduated in 1964. Next, he went to Paris, where he worked mainly with photography. After his Parisian sojourn, Due returned to Denmark, where he worked with graphic design, both as an employee and as a freelance designer; in 1974, he founded his own company, Due Design AS. Due began to experiment with lighting design around 1970, in connection with exhibition design projects. His first lamp design to be put into production was manufactured by Artela, a spherical luminaire inside a transparent acrylic cylinder. Although it proved more of a decorative item than an effective lamp, it sparked his interest in lighting (Hans Due, 5 August 2019).
2   Ibid.
3   Ibid.
4   Optima was available on the retail market as a wall lamp, a table lamp and two floor lamps with either one or two shades. The four models were named Optima 1, 2, 3 and 4. In addition, the series included the pendant lamps Optima 5, 6 and 7, with diameters of 20, 50 and 60 cm. Later, a fourth pendant was added, measuring 35 cm. The colours remained the same: white, yellow and brown. Due also wanted to produce a version in polished aluminium, but only a small number of aluminium lamps were made, for use in his own studio.
5   In 1974, the Optima series was supplemented with the Formel lamp series, inspired by the traditional shoemaker's lamp, whose geometric metal shade consisted of a cylinder and a wide truncated cone. The Formel series was produced in several colours and in polished aluminium.
6   Hans Due, 5 August 2019.
7   Ibid.
8   Ibid. Due had originally intended Phister as part of a series of metal luminaires including wall, table and floor models with a movable lamp head. Ultimately, only the one version was made, in light grey, yellow, green, brown and red plastic (ibid.)
9   Due's original dream was to become a visual artist, and he accomplished this dream. Throughout his career, he has worked with sculpture and painting, and since 2005 he has dedicated his time exclusively to art.
10   Hans Due, 5 August 2019.

Hans Jørgen Berthel and Hans Erik Vestergård Schmidt: H 63 Abo Mag

1   Fiell and Fiell, 2005a, pp. 9 and 58–59. The Italian designer Vico Magistretti (1920–2006) created the small spherical night light Eclisse (1965–1966). See, e.g., Fiell and Fiell, 2005a, pp. 110–111.
2   In June 1961, the factory owner Hans Jørgen Berthel established the company Abo Metalindustri (Abo Metal Industry) in Lyngby, north of Copenhagen, and when Berthel moved to Randers in 1969, the company moved too. During this period, the company grew and become a limited company with Berthel as production director. In the company, Berthel, who had completed his training as a metal grinder in 1958, worked not only with lamp production but more generally with braziery, although the lamps gradually took over. Berthel came up with the name Abo because he liked the sound of it and, not least, because the spelling gave the company top listing in the alphabetized telephone directory. Schmidt, who was 18 years his senior, joined the company in 1972. He had managerial experience from many years in the fishery industry. In 2019, Berthel says about his business partner that 'we complement each other well, we pulled together!' (Hans Jørgen Berthel, 7 May 2019).
3   Ibid. See also Berthel, 2019, p. 25.
4   Hans Jørgen Berthel, 7 May 2019.
5   Ibid. At the time, the annual Scandinavian lighting fair was held in Gothenburg; later it moved to Bella Center in southern Copenhagen. By then, Berthel had participated in 19 consecutive Gothenburg fairs. The fairs were important, as companies would often be able to fill up their order books for an entire year.
6   Ibid. Essentially, the design was jointly developed, but Vestergård Schmidt had the main responsibility for the design, while Berthel was mainly in charge of practical aspects, including making sure the lamp worked and securing its certification.
7   Hans Jørgen Berthel, 7 May 2019.
8   Berthel, 2019, p. 27.
9   Unlike a chrome-capped bulb, this solution was a loose bulb shield that was attached to a standard light bulb, but the effect was the same.
10   Hans Jørgen Berthel, 7 May 2019.
11   The D-label, certifying that an electrical device was safe to use, was (and is) issued by DEMKO (now UL International Demko). Berthel personally lacquered the first 100 lamps; the main problem was to ensure a sharply defined edge between the white interior and coloured exterior. Berthel managed, using a spray gun and a record player spinning at 78 rounds per minute with a specially made rack for the ball in the centre. Later, both the ball-shaped shades and the bases were finished at the industrial paint shop Randers Industrilakering (ibid.).
12   See Daells Varehus, 1974, p. 223. Confronted with the photo from the catalogue, Berthel confirms: 'We delivered the three brown magnetic lamps, original H63s, as they came into the world; you can recognize them on the chromed magnetic housing and the familiar design. Any other, similar lamps were not from Abo' (Hans Jørgen Berthel, 27 June 2019). As early as the previous year, in 1973, ball-shaped luminaires were shown in the department store catalogue, both in a pendant version and mounted on a stem (see Daells Varehus, 1973, pp. 214–215), but these had nothing to do with Abo, Berthel confirms. At the 1973 Gothenburg fair, Daells Varehus bought the lamps at DKK 49 apiece, 'but then each lamp had to be delivered in a separate box'. In the 1974 autumn catalogue from Daells Varehus, the price was set at DKK 58 (p. 223). Abo was later able to reduce the production cost of each lamp drastically, in part by making the backing in a synthetic material; the savings were translated into a lower retail price. For a more detailed description of the lamps and the changes that enabled the price cut, see Berthel, 2019, pp. 29–31. In the spring 1978 catalogue from Daells Varehus, the H63 is shown in eight colours, all with a grate. By then, the price had dropped to DKK 51 (Daells Varehus, 1978, p. 222).
13   A bigger version of the magnet lamp was launched, the H163, which had an E27 socket instead of the E14 that was used in the H63. Among the other models were Abo pendant, Abo stat ('stand', a floor or table lamp) and Abo klem ('clamp', a lamp that was attached to a rod by means of a clamp). Initially, the H63 came lacquered in eight different colours, but from time to time the selection changed. At one point, Berthel fell in love with a particular shade of pink, which was used on 1,000 ball-

shaped shades. The pink lamps proved impossible to sell until the sales rep took a lamp to an electrician's shop in the rowdy and slightly seedy street Istedgade in central Copenhagen – here, 1,000 lamps were moved in less than two years (Hans Jørgen Berthel, 7 May 2019).
14   Ibid.
15   By 1982, what began as a one-man business in 1961 had a staff of 24 men and 100 women. See Berthel, 2019, p. 43. Five years later Abo was taken over by Lyfa.
16   Berthel, 2019, p. 25.

Louis Weisdorf: Multi-Lite

1   Louis Weisdorf, 2 May 2019.
2   Ibid.
3   Ibid.
4   Ibid.
5   Ibid.
6   Turbo and Multi-Lite remained in production until 1978, when Lyfa acquired Fog & Mørup and overhauled the product line. In 1991, after yet another takeover, Lyskær–Lyfa put the Turbo pendant into production without first consulting Weisdorf, even renaming it Regina. Weisdorf sued the company, and production was discontinued. As early as 1971, Weisdorf had designed a Multi-Lite floor lamp, which was never realized: 'In my collaboration with Gubi, I designed the necessary changes, just as I contributed to the later table lamp, which took quite a bit of discussion' (Louis Weisdorf, 2 May 2019).
7   Louis Weisdorf, 2 May 2019.

Hans J. Wegner: Opala

1   Wegner in Holmsted Olesen. 2014, p. 39. 'That's the way it was back then. If you were an employee, the boss's name was on everything you did. But it was definitely my father who personally designed all the furniture for the offices' (Marianne Wegner, 24 May 2019). For the City Council Chamber, a pendant was designed in frosted glass where the light source is placed in a rounded bowl facing up. The light is thus emitted upwards into an upper shade which diffuses and reflects the light into the room. A photo of the lamp is included in Holmsted Olesen, 2014, p. 39. Perhaps this lamp inspired the very different – and very rare – ceiling lamp JH605. This latter lamp has a diameter of 118 cm with a brass frame and the light source shining up inside a conical acrylic bowl so that the light strikes an upper shade made of moulded wood painted white. The lamp, intended for outdoor use, was designed for Johannes Hansen, and in 1969 it was presented at Bella Center, hung above a large round table with six Net chairs, JH719. See Holmsted Olesen, 2014, p. 70.
2   Marianne Wegner, 24 May 2019.
3   Marianne Wegner trained in building architecture at the Royal Danish Academy of Fine Arts, School of Architecture, in 1966–1973, in 1973, she joined Hans J. Wegner's design firm, and from 1974 she worked there full time. 'I had 20 years with my father in the studio, and ultimately we were able to have a completely seamless generational changeover, because all the manufacturers knew me, so I was ready.'
4   Ibid.
5   Ibid. See also Holmsted Olesen, 2014, p. 85.
6   Abrahamsen et al., 1976a, p. 3598. About the competition and the winning project, see F.R., 1975, p. 3563, and Abrahamsen et al., 1976a, pp. 3595–3599. In the latter source, the lamp is listed as being designed by 'architect MAA Hans J. Wegner. Assistant: architect Marianne Wegner' (ibid., p. 3598).
7   Uwe Iwersen, 23 April 2019. The lamp is also in fairly wide use in Kolding and Aalborg, among other Danish cities. In Tønder, the well over 100 streetlights are installed on main street, in the square by the church and in the 'green ring' (Marianne Wegner, 24 May 2019).
8   Claus Juhlin, the then owner of the Danish lighting manufacturer Pandul, acquired the rights to manufacture and sell the Opala series in 2006 and implemented a number of updates in cooperation with the Wegner family. Among these updates, the base on the table and floor lamps was diminished in size. As the thinner base no longer has room for a switch, all the models now have an inline cord switch instead. Pandul also introduced new variants, which existed as drawings but had never been produced, or only in very limited numbers. One of these was the small Opala table lamp, which Louis Poulsen produced for Wegner in the early 1980s exclusively for one of Scanticon's large hotel and conference centres in the United States. Another was the small Opala pendant, which had not previously been in production because the top of this smaller lamp did not have room for the sophisticated balancing mechanism that Wegner had invented for the larger pendant. Pendant lamps easily hang askew, and for aesthetic reasons Wegner did not want to use the common solution of a stabilizing tube around the first 10–15 cm of the cord above the shade. Instead Wegner designed a balancing mechanism in the rounded top of the lamp that stabilized each individual lamp before it was delivered to the customer. In 2006, the new manufacturer developed a simple and effective solution for the small Opala pendant, which was thus ready for launch (Claus Juhlin, 24 May 2019). From 1993, Wegner no longer worked hands-on in the studio, but he remained involved in the projects. He died in 2007. Today Wegner's daughters, Eva and Marianne Wegner, manage their father's design legacy. Since 2023, Opala has been produced for Carl Hansen & Søn.
9   Møller, H.S., 1975, p. 109.

Torsten Thorup and Claus Bonderup: Pendant No. 1, Calot and Confetti

1   Torsten Thorup, 30 April 2019.
2   Claus Bonderup and Torsten Thorup in Vistensen, 1991, p. 4.
3   Remy-Jensen, 1980a, p. 30. Nils Kristiansen, who came from a position at Fog & Mørup, founded the lighting company Focus in 1975.
4   Torsten Thorup, 30 April 2019.
5   Ibid.
6   Remy-Jensen, 1980a, p. 30.
7   Claus Bonderup and Torsten Thorup in Vistensen, 1991, p. 40.

Alfred Homann, Nyhavn Wall

1   F.R., 1975, p. 3563.
2   Abrahamsen et al., 1976a, pp. 3596 and 3603. A total of seven entries received prizes. Hans J. Wegner and Marianne Wegner won first prize (see p. 136), Peter Bysted won second prize (see p. 162), while Alfred Homann and Ole V. Kjær came third (ibid., pp. 3598–3603).
3   Alfred Homann, 3 June 2019. The competition entry included a larger series of lamps, all part of the same family, but only the wall lamp and a pendant were put into production (ibid.).
4   Ibid.
5   Gunmetal (also called red brass) is a copper alloy with a high copper content, from 58 to 85%.
6   Alfred Homann, 3 June 2019.
7   Ibid.
8   Ibid.
9   Using the same lighting principle, Homann developed a lamp for the square by Roskilde Cathedral (1983). A few years later, the lamp was included in Louis Poulsen's standard product line. Later, the medium-sized light Nyhavn Boulevard, a bollard lamp and a Maxi wall lamp were added to the company's selection (ibid.).
10   Alfred Homann, 3 June 2019.

Torsten Thorup and Claus Bonderup: Floor Lamp and Table Lamp

1   Barslund and Helles, 1982, p. 6. Anne Bay, director of the Danish Lighting Center, explains that the GU10 socket and other sockets used for the bipin halogen bulb are mentioned in IEC 60061, the International Electrotechnical Commission's standard for lamp caps and holders, from 1969. Vivi and Erik Sørensen, who have had the electrician's workshop and lamp shop El-Hjørnet in Godthåbsvej in Frederiksberg since 1974, say that halogen was just beginning to play a role when they opened their shop but was only really embraced by the Danish public from around 1980 (Anne Bay, 3 and 4 May 2019).
2   Torsten Thorup, 30 April 2019.
3   Ibid.
4   Ibid.
5   The floor lamp was initially named the Fusionslampen (Merger lamp), because it was designed around the time when the Royal Porcelain Factory, Georg Jensen and the Holmegaard glassworks merged to become Royal Copenhagen. For use in the shops, the lamp was also made as a wall lamp. Later, a white-painted floor lamp was launched on the retail market.
6   The light source that was placed in the lamp bowl was initially a halogen bulb but was later replaced by LED lights.

In front of the light source, there is an opal-glass disc that prevents glare, even though the lamp was not intended for people to look directly into the light.
7   In 1996, the lighting company Focus was renamed Focus-Tema and in 2000 renamed to the current Focus Lighting. The founder of Focus, Nils Kristiansen, died in 2011.
8   Barslund and Helles, 1982, p. 9.

Ebbe Christensen and Sophus Frandsen after PH: Charlottenborg 6½-6

1   As early as 1927, PH had mentioned a four-shade lamp in a patent application, but the four-shade lamps that he presented at the exhibition *Dit Hjem* (Your Home) at Forum in 1931 were a recent design. See Nørregaard et al., 1994, pp. 241–242. The PH lamps were named after the sizes of the shade set. Generally, a shade set was described as a fraction that is equal to 1; for example, 4/4 indicates an upper shade of 40 cm and its matching middle and lower shades with a combined diameter of 40 cm. The shades were in a mutual ratio of 3:2:1. However, any upper shade could be combined with middle and lower shades (which always go together) from smaller lamps, which led to 'odd' shade sets with names like 4/3, 3/2 and 2/1 (Ulla Riemer, head of LP Academy, 7 August 2019). In 1931, PH called his four-shade lamp 4–4½/4. Thus, this four-shade lamp had a fourth, upper shade with a diameter of 45 cm, while the top shade in the 'classic' triple-shade design was 40 cm (the shades below it were in the normal ratio of 3:2:1). This relates to the name 6½–6 for the new 1980 variant for Charlottenborg – that is, a top shade of 65 cm with a 60-cm shade below it.
2   The paragraph is based on Nørregaard et al., 1994, pp. 242–243. The lamp was never commercially successful, and the four-shade pendant variant was discontinued, as were several other models during the first half of the 1940s (ibid.).
3   See note 2.
4   Møller, H.S., reprinted in *LP & Co. NYT*, no. 448, 1980, p. 3964.
5   Ibid.
6   Lund, 1994a. This small base disc is easily removed when the bulb is replaced if the user wants more downwards light.
7   In 1984, Christensen and Frandsen created a smaller version of the pendant: 5/4½ for the Concert Hall Aarhus.
8   From 1976, Christensen and Frandsen ran a joint architecture consultancy. Together with Mogens Voltelen, they co-edited the book *PH om Lys* (PH on Light) (1974). Voltelen had worked with PH early on as sub-editor for *Kritisk Revy* from 1927, the year when Voltelen left the Royal Danish Academy of Fine Arts, School of Architecture. Voltelen was an employee of PH's and later of Vilhelm Lauritzen's in 1937–1947; among other engagements, he was involved as a lighting consultant for Finn Juhl's interior design of the Trusteeship Council Chamber at the United Nations' headquarters in New York (p. 90). Voltelen should be recognized, not least, for his contributions as a lecturer and head of the Lighting Laboratory at the Royal Danish Academy of Fine Arts, School of Architecture, from 1940 to 1978. About Voltelen, see also p. 50.
9   The Fibonacci pendant was first presented in an advertisement in *Dansk Kunsthaandværk* (Danish Crafts), no. 1, 1961; see Dybdahl, 2006, pp. 204 and 540.
10   In the design of the Fibonacci pendant, Frandsen had made it possible to adjust the height of the bulb slightly by means of a screw on the cylinder to achieve the optimal position based on the height at which the pendant was hung.
11   Fibonacci numbers are a sequence where each number is the sum of the two preceding ones. The principle applies to many natural phenomena and was first described by the Italian mathematician Leonardo Fibonacci (1170–ca. 1250).
12   All the shade rings were painted white on the inside for optimal reflection. The pendant was also available in a completely white version. The description of the lamp is based on Dybdahl, 2006, p. 204, and Houston Wilson, the owner of Danish Vintage Design, 6 August 2019. Wilson has disassembled and reassembled the luminaire repeatedly and is thus intimately familiar with the construction.
13   The architecture critic Henrik Sten Møller (1938–2019) wrote this in a review of the renovated Charlottenborg exhibition building in *Politiken*, 7 October 1980, which was reprinted in 'Ny PH-lampe på Charlottenborg', 1980, p. 3964.

Erik Magnussen: Porcelight

1   Magnussen attended what was then known as the School of Arts and Crafts (founded in 1930). In 1973, the school merged with the School of Art Industry (founded in 1875) to become the independent institution School of Decorative Art – now the Royal Danish Academy of Fine Arts, School of Design.
2   Magnussen, quoted in Jørgensen, 1986, p. 49.
3   Møller, H.S., 1975, pp. 165–166. The paragraph also draws on Stockmarr, 2008, pp. 28–29.
4   Magnussen in Jørgensen, 1986, p. 49.
5   Magnussen, quoted in Jørgensen, 1986, p. 49.

Erik Magnussen: Ship's lamp and EM oil lamp

1   Magnussen quoted in Jørgensen, 1986, p. 48.
2   Petersen, 2016b, pp. 315–317.
3   Rohweder, 1962, p. 45.
4   Stockmarr, 2008, p. 10.
5   Various burners exist for oil lamps. One of the most common is a circular burner, where the flat wick is placed inside a metal tube. Here, the chimney is tall and narrow. That provides the best light and fuel efficiency. Stelton confirms that the Ship's lamp has a circular burner as its primary light source, as did the oil lamp that was launched in 1983, while the two smaller versions from 2001 and 2002, which have the same cylindrical design, are referred to as 'decorative lamps with a wick' by Stelton (Mette Stagsted Larsen, head of marketing at Stelton, 7 May 2019).
6   In the article about Henning Koppel's kerosene lamp Petronella, the lamp is described as 'the spiritual daughter' of Koppel, because Petronella was also the name of the spiritual daughter of Saint Peter. When Magnussen is referred to as Koppel's heir in this context, it should be noted that Magnussen's first marriage was to Koppel's daughter, the designer Nina Koppel (1942–1990).
7   'Designer-pris til Erik Magnussen', 1984, p. 92. In 1987, Magnussen created another kerosene lamp for hanging on the wall in a summer cottage or in a boat and a modern, streamlined Skotlampe (Bulkhead lamp), a small ship's lamp specially designed for the sometimes turbulent conditions at sea. The latter ship's lamp was awarded the ID Prize in 1990 and was followed up the next year by the Twin Spot version intended for use as a bedside lamp in the home. Twin Spot was based on the same principle as the ship's model: the light switches on when the shade is tipped out and switches off again when the shade is lightly pushed back down. Twin Spot also pivots 360 degrees.
8   Magnussen quoted in Jørgensen, 1986, p. 48

Jørgen Gammelgaard: VIP

1   Karin Gammelgaard, 15 May 2019. See also Mollerup, 1995, pp. 13–18.
2   Mollerup, 1995, p. 18.
3   The series was also expanded with a pendant that could be positioned in a variety of angles by means of a wire attached to the shade and the lamp cord.
4   Ibid., p. 13.
5   Nielsen, 1988, p. 72.
6   The VIP lamp series was originally created in close collaboration with the manufacturer, the architect Per Skovholt, who in 1982 took over the company Design Forum from cabinetmaker Poul Hansen. In 1988, production of Gammelgaard's lamp was taken over by the lighting company Pandul, which was founded in 1986. In 2023, Pandul was bought by Carl Hansen & Søn.
7   Mollerup, 1995, p. 18.

Stig Gerlach: String Light

1   Stig Gerlach, 5 April 2019.
2   'Det hvide look', *Bo Bedre*, 1984, no. 11, p. 72–73.
3   Stig Gerlach, 5 April 2019.
4   Ibid. In a series circuit, each light bulb is mounted directly on the cord, which ran through the copper wire. In a parallel circuit, only every tenth bulb has its own copper wire. Thus, in the early parallel-circuit string lights, a series of ten bulbs switched off if a bulb burnt out. The new light bridge on the filament allowed the power to simply continue to the next bulb if one burnt out.

5 Jensen, 2014, p. 147.
6 Gerlach explains that there was also an economic interest in the product development of LED chains because there was a special tax on incandescent light bulbs. For someone buying a single bulb for a lamp, the tax was not a major expense, but a string light with 100 bulbs incurred a tax of DKK 0.75 per bulb – that is, DKK 75/€10 + VAT. LEDs, on the other hand, were exempt. However, the early LEDs Gerlach commissioned were just as expensive as the tax. Only once the production cost per diode dropped below the tax did the numbers add up. Since 2000, the string lights have been classified as 'green energy'.
7 Ibid.
8 Ibid.
9 Ibid.

Sidse Werner: Phoenix

1 It is appropriate to refer to Werner as an industrial designer, but it is doubtful whether she, as it is claimed in other contexts, actually trained at the Royal Danish Academy of Fine Arts, School of Architecture. Instead, she does appear to have taken courses at the Danish Technological Institute and to be a trained interior decorator, although it is unclear exactly where she trained. A 1977 feature article in *Politiken* mentions that she was a 'trained interior decorator, not to be confused with the higher degree of interior designer provided by the School of Interior Design' ('*Dagens portræt. Stædig pige med succes*', 1977, p. 8). In addition to the School of Interior Design, during Werner's youth it was also possible to train via the correspondence school Indendørs Arkitekt Akademiet (Interior Design Academy) and via the Indendørs Arkitekt Uddannelse (Interior Design Programme) at the Akademisk Brevskole (Academic Correspondence School) (Lytken, 2008, p. 54). Born in 1931, Werner was young at a time when far fewer women than now attained an academic degree. Today, however, there are more female than male students enrolled at the Royal Danish Academy of Fine Arts, Schools of Architecture and Design.
2 'Dagens portræt. Stædig pige med succes', 1977, p. 8.
3 Thanks to a grant from Danmarks Nationalbank's Anniversary Foundation of 1968, Werner travelled to the United States together with Leif Alring during the 1960s in order to study the new synthetic materials that were emerging. Upon their return, they immediately put their knowledge to use (ibid.). Cellulose acetate butyrate (CAB) is a clear thermoplastic polymer; see https://en.wikipedia.org/wiki/Cellulose_acetate.
4 For the lamp series, Werner and Alring had received input from Fog & Mørup's head of design, Jo Hammerborg, who was also an experienced parachutist, and the three designers actually did a joint parachute jump in connection with a commercial campaign for the Formland series. Werner subsequently took up parachuting as a regular hobby (*Politiken*, Sec. 1, 1 September 1977, p. 8). Fog & Mørup staged a concerted effort to launch the experimental humorous lamps. When the Formland series was launched in Fog & Mørup's shop at Amager Torv 8 in central Copenhagen, everyone who attended the reception was given a drinking glass that was a miniature copy of the Formland table lamp. They were made in orange glass with a white interior, had a white plastic lid and were specially made for the reception, says Henni Hammerborg, Jo Hammerborg's widow (5 July 2019). Henni Hammerborg believes the glasses were the idea of Jo Hammerborg, who had previously worked with Holmegaard; however, by 1970, Werner was attached to Holmegaard, so she may also have been involved. Susanne Outzen, curator at Museum Sydøstdanmark, has tried in vain to locate additional information. The Formland lamp series received the German design award iF in Hannover in 1971.
5 Bruun, 2015, p. 18. Werner became a regular employee at Holmegaard in 1979. Werner's Coat Tree has remained in continuous production at Fritz Hansen; for more about this, see Dybdahl, 2018, pp. 289–290, and https://fritzhansen.com/da-dk/products/accessories/9999_coattree.
6 Holmegaard's product director explained in 1973 that four years previously the glassworks had decided to focus on lamp production: 'If we want to make lamps a viable business – and we do – we need a wide selection that covers many different needs, and even though glass is good for many purposes, it is not right in every situation. (…) So diversifying into multiple materials puts us in a better position to make the most of changing fashions and to spread the risk' (Product Director J. Kirketerp in *Glaspustet* (Glassblown), December 1973, p. 8). Up until the company's last lamp catalogue in October 1984, many new lamp designs were continually added.
7 Newspaper cutting from 1973, no other date, from envelope with various newspaper cuttings about Werner from Designmuseum Danmark's archive. Skibslampen had a rise-and-fall feature; it came in three sizes and was available in both brass and aluminium. Over the following years, Werner also designed the metal pendants Ballerina and Stavlampen (the Torch). Ballerina had a sweeping organic shade under a tall funnel. The shape echoes a ballet skirt flaring out from a very slender waist. With its light concentrated by a long cylinder, Stavlampen was particularly suitable as a spotlight.
8 Werner in Holmegaard Glasværk, 1981b, p. 7. See also Holmegaard Glasværk, 1981a, p. 11.
9 Werner in Holmegaards Glasværk 1982b, p. 5. In the article, the inclusion of a light source in the lamp base itself was described as 'unusual'. Indeed it was a novelty in a Danish Holmegaard context. However, as early as 1954, the Irish artist Max Ingrad (1908–1969) had created the glass lamp Model 1853 (for Fontana Arte) with a light source in both the glass base and behind the glass shade. See Fiell and Fiell 2005a, p. 512.
10 Werner in Holmegaards Glasværk 1982b, p. 5.
11 See Lassen and Schlüter, 2002, p. 53. All the lamps were made by the glassblowers at Odense Glasværk, which was a sub-section of Holmegaard after 1965. In its exterior form, Phoenix bears some resemblance to the Italian designer Angelo Mangiarotti's Lesbo glass table lamp (Artemide, 1966–1967), but in an important difference, Mangiarotti mounted the light bulb at the metal base of the closed lamp, and the light is solely diffused through the glass. See, e.g., Fiell and Fiell, 2005b, p. 114.
12 See note 4.
13 Werner in Holmegaards Glasværk 1982b, p. 5.
14 See Bruun, 2015, p. 18, and Lassen and Schlüter, 2002, pp. 52–53.
15 Werner in Holmegaards Glasværk 1982b, p. 5.

Alfred Homann: Rappe Louis

1 While Homann was a student employee in Professor Vilhelm Wohlert's architecture studio, he was also involved in the renovation of the Church of Our Lady in Copenhagen, a project that also involved the design of new luminaires (Alfred Homann, 3 June 2019).
2 Ibid.
3 Over the years, Homann's design and architecture office has handled projects ranging from building architecture to furnishings and lighting: 'Many of my building designs included bespoke furnishings, and lighting design was generally a natural component' (ibid). In 2002, Homann received the Weber lighting award from the Danish Lighting Center in recognition of his contributions to the development of luminaires and their incorporation into architectural solutions.
4 Ibid.
5 Ibid.
6 Ibid.
7 Full-page advertisement for Louis Poulsen; see, for example, *Bo Bedre*, 1989, no. 11, back cover.
8 Homann's 50 luminaires for Louis Poulsen fall into ten product series: Rappe Louis, Nyhavn, Strata, Homann Væg (Wall), Pulsar, Kipp, AH system, AH Wall, AH Mini and Homann Park.
9 Alfred Homann, 3 June 2019.
10 Ibid.

Piet Hein: Sinus lamp

1 In 1933, Hein presented two Funco lamps and the Ra lamp at the *Opfinderens Udstilling* (Inventor's Exhibition), where the Ra lamp attracted most of the attention (see p. 48).
2 Hein describes this in the portrait film *Piet Hein, Roholt og Tyrrestrup* (Piet Hein, Roholt and Tyrrestrup), DR (Danish Broadcasting Corporation), 19 March 2006. See also Kristiansen, 2015, p. 85.
3 Later Hein designed several candleholders and constellations. Today, the candleholders are among the most iconic Piet Hein designs, with more than 1.7

million sold in Denmark alone (Kristiansen, 2015, p. 85). The number was confirmed by Anni Knudsen, chief archivist at Piet Hein (28 May 2019).
4   Kristiansen, 2015, p. 97.
5   Ibid., p. 100. The Super pendant was installed at Dansk Folkeferie's four new holiday parks in the 1970s (ibid.). The pendant was listed as No. 163529 in the catalogue from Lyfa – Fog & Mørup, a company created in a takeover in 1978.
6   Ibid., p. 101.
7   MT, 1995, p. 14.
8   The lamps were then put into production by Uniline. The Holmegaard glassworks took over production of Uniline lamps in 2003. In 2008, Holmegaard was closed, and the lamps are now produced by Piet Hein.
9   Piet Hein © *grook* (written between 1978 and 1980). Reproduced with kind permission from Piet Hein A/S Middelfart.

Peter Bysted:
Rubbie

1   Peter Bysted, 31 May 2019.
2   The Danish sculptor Bjørn Nørgaard (b. 1947) had created a series of sculptures expressing social criticism, including a millennium version of the Little Mermaid: *The Genetically Modified Little Mermaid*.
3   Peter Bysted, 31 May 2019.
4   Ibid.
5   Bysted founded the design and communication firm Bysted A/S in 1987. Rubbie was designed and produced in this firm, while Louis Poulsen supplied the technical lighting components to ensure compliance with the German lighting standards when the bollard was presented in Hannover. Louis Poulsen did not begin to market Rubbie until 2010. In the meantime, alternative materials were discussed, but Bysted argued that the rubber was what gave the bollard its characteristic soft and pleasant quality. Lighting engineering adjustments were also carried out, not least, the switch to LED (ibid.).
6   Abrahamsen et al., 1976, p. 3605.
7   Peter Bysted, 31 May 2019.
8   Corten is a hard variant of steel that quickly develops a rusty surface but corrodes slowly because the surface rust forms a protective layer. The improved resistance to corrosion, compared with other types of steel, stems from the chemical composition of the material, including its copper content. In the bollard lamp, the area most exposed to corrosion is close to the ground, where the post is buried, as moisture collects in the transition between air and soil, although that is not to say this zone is delicate (https://en.wikipedia.org/wiki/Weathering_steel).
9   Peter Bysted, 31 May 2019.
10   In 2007, Bysted sold the Bysted company, which had become one of Denmark's biggest design firms. Bysted was the rector of The Danish Design School from 2007 to 2009 during the period leading up to the school's merger with the Royal Danish Academy of Fine Arts, School of Architecture, in 2010. At the time of writing, Bysted heads the consultancy firm ICONO. Lamp design is labour of love for Bysted, but some luminaires have made it into production. In 1989, Louis Poulsen launched the wall lamp Peter Plan (apart from the pun on 'Pan', the Danish *plan* also means plane), a new, flat version of a bulkhead lamp for a new type of strip light.

Sofie Refer:
Bulb

1   Sofie Refer, 6 March 2018.
2   Ibid.
3   Anodization is used to add a protective and, in Refer's use, decorative coloured layer of oxides on the aluminium. This improves the material's ability to handle corrosion and wear.
4   Sofie Refer, 6 March 2018.
5   Ibid.
6   Løkkegaard, 2006.
7   Sofie Refer, 6 March 2018.
8   Sofie Refer, 6 March 2018.

Simon Karkov:
Norm 69

1   Simon Karkov (Nielsen) had a carpenter's diploma and had also graduated from the Danish Technical College, which qualified him to enrol at the Royal Danish Academy of Fine Arts, School of Architecture, which he attended from 1954 to 1961, interrupted by his two years of mandatory military service. When he left the School of Architecture in 1961 without graduating, he was already employed by the architect J.C. Louring in Kalundborg. He stayed with Louring's firm for 11 years, the latter five as head of its Copenhagen office. Karkov was subsequently employed in a couple of other architecture firms. While a part-time teacher in Department 1 under Wohlert in 1975–1977, he also ran his own studio. Throughout his long career, Karkov worked mainly with designing and overseeing the construction of primary and secondary schools. From 1981 until his retirement in 1992, Karkov worked in the architectural department of Frederiksberg Municipality (Karkov's curriculum vitae, Normann Copenhagen's archives).
2   Ibid.
3   Poul Madsen, 28 June 2019.
4   Poul Madsen said in 2019, 'First we tried to make the lamp using Simon's original technique, but the old wooden tools weren't really working anymore, so we developed heat treatment tools and got the production started.' Poul Madsen, 28 June 2019.
5   Ibid.
6   'Puslespil med lys i', 2001, p. 23.
7   Poul Madsen describes the coverage of the lamp, including how 'a brief mention in the New York Post with a retailer's name included' led to explosive international interest overnight. Poul Madsen, 28 June 2019. Norm 69 received the 2002 Formland Award and the prize for Best Item at the 2003 IMM Cologne.
8   Ibid. Madsen and Andersen had jointly run Normann Copenhagen since 1999, and from the shop on Strandboulevarden they sold a wider range of 'bric-a-brac', as Madsen puts it. Norm 69 was a turning point and paved the way, for example, for Rikke Hagen's cognac tumblers, Claydies's Grass vase and Ole Jensen's rubber washing-up bowl. In fact, the earnings from Norm 69 helped fund the complicated product development process for the seemingly simple bowl (which is also briefly mentioned on p. 192). Within five years of the launch, Norm 69 was followed by 38 new products, all created in collaboration with established designers within their respective fields. Normann Copenhagen had become a design brand. Norm 69 has remained in production since 2001 (ibid.).
9   Simon Karkov on Normann Copenhagen's website: https://www.normann-copenhagen.com/da/Products/Lamps/Pendants/Norm-69-Lamp-Large-White-501003.
10   Ibid. In 2012, another spherical lamp was launched, based on the same principle as Norm 69: Norm 12, which has 67 components.
11   Poul Madsen, CEO and co-founder of Normann Copenhagen, 28 June 2019.

Olafur Eliasson:
Opera House Chandeliers

1   Olafur Eliasson, 12 August 2019.
2   Ibid.
3   Ibid.
4   In addition to Olafur Eliasson's light sculptures, Per Kirkeby (1938–2018) created four bronze reliefs for the Opera foyer, and Per Arnoldi (b. 1941) designed the Opera House logo, which was featured both in the floor of the foyer and in the stage curtain, also an Arnoldi design.
5   Each faceted sphere has a diameter of 285 cm.
6   Olafur Eliasson, 12 August 2019.
7   Ibid.
8   Eliasson has since used the dichromatic glass several times, for example on the facades of Harpa Concert Hall and Conference Centre (2011) in the Icelandic capital of Reykjavik. The facades were created in collaboration with Henning Larsen Architects, which designed the building.
9   Olafur Eliasson, 12 August 2019.

Louise Campbell:
Campbell

1   The information is based on an interview on 22 April 2013 with Bettina Elbæk Pedersen and Pia Knudsen, the Louis Poulsen employees who contacted Campbell and subsequently liaised with the designer. See also the Introduction
2   Louise Campbell, 13 March 2013 and 28 November 2015. Approved by Campbell on 29 April 2019.
3   Ibid.
4   Ibid.
5   Ibid.
6   Ibid.

Philip Bro Ludvigsen:
UnderCover

1   In 2000, the School of Decorative Art was renamed The Danish Design School in a merger with the School of Interior Design.

2   Ludvigsen travelled to Czechoslovakia with the designers Claus Knudsen and Thomas H. Krause. In 1992, he and Krause sold the rights to the crystal chandeliers Kapka, Jezek and Mobilia to IKEA.
3   The Le Klint Models 210, 211, 340, 375, 376, 377 and 378.
4   Philip Bro Ludvigsen, 22 March 2019.
5   Ibid.
6   Ibid.
7   The Danish textile designers Helle Graabæk and Helle Abild both designed several UnderCover interior shades.
8   Philip Bro Ludvigsen, 22 March 2019.
9   Ibid.

Cecilie Manz: Caravaggio

1   The book 101 Danish Design Icons lists Caravaggio as No. 99 on its chronological list of 20th-century iconic designs, which only includes two other lamps: PH's PH lamp from Louis Poulsen and Poul Christiansen's SinusLine pendant from Le Klint. See Jensen, 2014, pp. 406–409. Both Lightyears and Caravaggio were very successful; at the 2005 fair, Caravaggio created a real buzz, and the only photo from *Wallpaper** magazine's coverage of the fair was of the Caravaggio lamp. Going forward, Caravaggio was largely seen as synonymous with Lightyears, which in 2007 received the Danish Designmatters Award as a company that had a clear design focus and the ability to turn this focus into a healthy bottom line (Rasmus Markholt, 12 June 2019).
2   When Lars Østergaard Olsen was appointed CEO of Horn Belysning in 2004 and picked Markholt as head of design, the two men set out to reboot the company, now as Lightyears. Manz describes how her collaboration with the team began: 'They reached out and asked me if I was interested in having a lamp put into production. This was at a time when everything was still taking shape; only later was I told what the name of the company would be. I accepted because their focus was on high-quality lighting design at an affordable price, and they were very upfront about the fact that they were going to outsource production to make that possible. Few companies were open about outsourcing at the time. My brief was a lamp for private homes that would also have a potential on the contract market, and it did find a place in both contexts' (Cecilie Manz, 6 June 2019). Markholt, who was in charge of design and product development in the new company, says that since they could not offer a high salary to the designers they reached out to, they offered a royalty scheme instead, which required the designers to be willing to accept a certain risk; fortunately, Manz was (Rasmus Markholt, 12 June 2019).
3   Cecilie Manz, 6 June 2019.
4   Ibid.
5   Ibid.
6   'A Swedish company had come up with some interesting textiles for use on electric cords; we sought to develop the stitch further. Cecilie is great with this kind of detail. We were able to push the envelope for how this kind of fabric can be used to envelop a cord. Over time, we developed specialized fabrics and also bought a machine so we could weave our own textile with the right stitch. We pioneered the use of coloured cords, and that led to a very widespread trend – very quickly!' (Rasmus Markholt, 12 June 2019).
7   Manz explains in 2019, 'When the lamp designs were finished, I was asked to come up with a naming universe, and I suggested that we use artists' (ibid.). When it was time to name the table lamp, it seemed obvious to call it Mondrian as a homage to the Dutch painter Piet Mondrian (1872–1944) and his geometric forms.
8   The baroque painter Caravaggio used a contrast-rich chiaroscuro technique where a stark, dramatic light envelops figures and objects, causing them to stand out against the always dark background, while red is often used to heighten the sense of drama. In 2019, Manz says of her Caravaggio lamp: 'It's not that the Caravaggio lamp was inspired by the painter; it was a name I applied after the fact, because I saw something in the red accent, the voluminous form and the almost exaggerated highlight and deep shadow' (Cecilie Manz, 6 June 2019). See also the previous note.
9   The smallest pendant is 14.5 cm tall and has a diameter of 11 cm, while the largest measures 70.2 cm in height and has a diameter of 55 cm. Like other popular designs, Caravaggio has been widely copied, so unfortunately there are many less accomplished lamps in use.
10   See the launch text 'Caravaggio Opal af Cecilie Manz 2008' (Caravaggio Opal by Cecilie Manz 2008) from Fritz Hansen's archive.
11   Caravaggio Read was created in collaboration with Fritz Hansen, as Lightyears was acquired by Fritz Hansen in 2015 and since 1 January 2019 has also been an integrated part of the Fritz Hansen brand by name. Factual information in the text is based mainly on an interview with Cecilie Manz on 6 June 2019.
12   Cecilie Manz, 6 June 2019.
1   Jørn Utzon, 1948, in Weston, 2002, p. 11. Translated from Utzon's original text 'Arkitekturens Væsen' (The Innermost Being of Architecture), in [the artist association] Grønningen's catalogue for the 1948 Charlottenborg exhibition, pp. 19–20. Utzon's manifesto in 'Arkitekturens Væsen' outlined the basic outlook and method that guided his work throughout life (Torsten Bløndal, 24 June 2019).

Jørn Utzon: Opera

2   Based on Utzon's own statement to Bløndal, who in 2002 published the biography *Utzon. Inspiration, Vision, Architecture* (Weston, 2002, p. 347), and Bløndal, 24 June 2019. In Helsingborg, Utzon shared a studio with the brothers Erik and Henry Andersson, both architects.
3   Utzon's lamp design always began with a sketch and continued with hands-on work and experiments. Many of the designs were realized, while others piled up in the small shed he built in 1951 when he designed his own house in Hellebæk. Jan Utzon remembers the many shades and models his father kept in the shed: 'My dad always made 1:1 models and tested solutions in our house. He preferred working hands-on with the designs and was very handy; he could solve any problem. In the small shed were all these lamp experiments. My dad had modified a Nilfisk vacuum cleaner to spray a plastic material onto a mould, for example a chicken-wire form, to produce a shell. That was just one of his experiments. I also remember a lamp he had made of a thin transparent tube that he glued into a mould. It became an opal white lamp shade. It was beautiful! He did of lot of these experiments' (Jan Utzon, 7 June 2019).
4   Visir appears with a photo, name and the number P.244. It came in three two-tone variants: all three models had white side shades, while the middle shade was either red (P.244/6), black (P.244/10) or terracotta (P.244/15) (Nordisk Solar Compagni, 1958). No later catalogues have come to light that include Visir, and Jan Utzon (7 June 2019) cannot recall ever seeing the lamp, so it is likely that it was only produced in a very small number.
5   Møller, H.S., 1990, p. 123. Jørn Utzon first used these metal profiles – where the bulbs are visible, and only the sockets and cords are hidden inside the tube – as early as the beginning of the 1960s. In 1962–1963, as part of his design of the Fredensborg Terraces, Utzon created a common house in a total design that included every aspect, inside and out. Along the walls these 'garlands' were installed, which produced such a soft light that the bulbs could be unshielded. This was long before string lights began to be used indoors (except on the Christmas tree). Utzon also used them in his house on the Spanish island of Majorca (Jan Utzon, 7 June 2019).
6   Jørgen Ellegård Frederiksen, organist at Bagsværd Church, 25 June 2019. See photos of these lights in Utzon, 2005, unpaginated.
7   The new version, now named Opera, was created based on photos of the original, according to both Jan Utzon and Rasmus Markholt. In the late 1950s, Utzon had placed a rib underneath the lamp, which was not included in the new version, but the distinctive mounting screws have been preserved. The main difference is the size. Visir's dimensions were H: 19 cm x W: 23 cm (Nordisk Solar Compagni, 1958b), while the 2005 version was H: 29 cm x W: 40 cm. Due to its size, the latter version, which was made of all-white lacquered aluminium shades, was so heavy that it needed additional safety wires running alongside the cord (Rasmus Markholt, 12 June 2019).
8   In 1956, Jørn Utzon designed the Sydney lamp for Nordisk Solar Compagni, which was presented at a fair in Hannover that same year (see, e.g., Nordisk Solar Compagni, 1958b, p. 100), but he never designed a lamp specifically for the Sydney Opera House. In 1966, after a prolonged dispute with the government of New South Wales, Australia, Utzon walked

off the project, and many of his original ideas, particularly for the interior, were lost (Jan Utzon, 7 June 2019).
9   Jørn Utzon, 1948, in Weston, 2002, p. 11. With regard to the updated design solution, Markholt said in 2019 that since the CFL had since been discontinued, the original design had to be modified. The same principle was translated into a solution that matches an ordinary incandescent light bulb, which Jan Utzon approved on behalf of his father. Markholt underscores, 'I'm not afraid to make modifications, as long as we do it with respect for the original design. Some, not least collectors, want everything to stay exactly as it was, 100% original, but we have to accommodate technological changes and other developments, including higher safety standards. You have to incorporate that to make a better product and a better lighting experience, because what we sell, essentially, is good lighting' (Rasmus Markholt, 12 June 2019).
10   The Concert pendant is now available from Fritz Hansen in two sizes.

Stig Gerlach:
LED candle

1   Linnet, 2010, p. 98. The anthropologist Jeppe Trolle Linnet, who has a background in consumer studies, has focused in particular on the elusive Danish concept of *hygge*, or cosiness, in his research. It was the topic of his PhD dissertation from 2010, where he emphasizes that his was the first academic project to offer 'a thorough social and cultural analysis of the kind of atmosphere and interaction that is known as Danish *hygge*' (ibid., p. 4).
2   Stig Gerlach, 5 April 2019. Gerlach uses the common Danish term 'wax candle', because all the LED candles from Sirius have a paraffin exterior, except for the tealights, which are made of plastic due to their flat shape, which makes the use of paraffin unfeasible.
3   Ibid.
4   Ibid.
5   Ibid. Gerlach explains that the flame in the first Sirius candles did not rock, and that the slight movement has made a significant difference.
6   Ibid.
7   Ibid.
8   Ibid.

Louise Campbell:
Collage

1   Louise Campbell, 13 March, 2013. The text was approved by Campbell on 29 April 2019.
2   Ibid.
3   Campbell in *LP & Co. NYT*, no. 581, 2005, p. 16.

Tom Rossau:
TR7

1   Tom Rossau, 1 July 2019.
2   Rossau adds, 'In 2003, I made a lamp out of 20 plastic strips; the ends joined together around two cylinders. When you spun them in relation to one another, they would change shape. I repeated the principle in veneer, but that only lasted one second; there was too much tension in the wood, so it flew apart. Instead of giving up, I implemented the idea into other geometries. The result was TR4, which was followed up by TR5, TR6 and TR7. The hourglass shape has been a bestseller ever since. I sold the four veneer lamps from my own shop until I showed them at a furniture fair at Bella Center in 2006, where the response was amazing. TR5 and TR7 are still in production' (ibid.).
3   Fifteen years after the presentation at Bella Center, more than half of Rossau's lamps are sold abroad. Rossau and his staff produce and assemble the many lamps, most of which are still made in birch veneer sourced from Finland.
4   Tom Rossau, 1 July 2019.
5   Ibid.
6   Ibid.
7   Ibid.
8   Rossau also works with other materials, including plastic, paper and aluminium foils as well as dyed veneers.
9   Tom Rossau, 1 July 2019.
10   Originally, the aeroplane pendants were created as an art project for Galleri Nijenkamp in Odense as an exhibit including four 100 x 140-cm pendants with 100 planes in either anodized aluminium foil or birch veneer swirled around a centred carbon-filament bulb in organized chaos: 'The planes are based on a traditional folded paper aeroplane, but the two materials call for very different approaches. The foil keeps its shape, while the veneer has to be soaked in water before it is folded and then placed in a mould to dry for five to six days. When they come out of the mould, they are mounted on the metal rods' (ibid.). A smaller version of the highly sculptural lamp is included in Rossau's sales collection; see the main text.
11   The table lamp is part of series of four luminaires. TR36 and TR37 are based on luminous cylinders floating on frames in bent metal profiles.
12   Tom Rossau, 1 July 2019.
13   Ibid.

Poul Christiansen:
Elysion

1   Poul Christiansen, 23 April 2019.
2   Elysion was also the name of Christiansen's student association (ibid.).
3   See also Dybdahl, 2016b, p. 36.
4   Poul Christiansen, 23 April 2019.
5   Ibid.
6   Ibid.
7   Ibid.
8   Ibid.

Louise Campbell:
Snow

1   Barslund, 2008, p. 156.
2   Louise Campbell, 13 March 2013. Approved by Campbell on 29 April 2019.
3   *The chandelier can be seen at https://us.baccarat.com/en/lighting/ceiling/chandeliers/nervous-zenith-chandelier-MLNERVCH1.html.*
4   Louise Campbell, 13 March 2013.

Salto & Sigsgaard:
Nosy

1   Thomas Sigsgaard and Kasper Salto, 25 March 2019. Sigsgaard graduated from the Royal Danish Academy of Fine Arts in 1995, while Salto completed his training as a cabinetmaker in 1988 and subsequently graduated from The Danish Design School in 1994. In 2011, Salto & Sigsgaard were invited to take part in a prestigious competition to design new furniture and the interior of the Trusteeship Council Chamber in the United Nations' building in New York, which was originally designed by the Danish architect Finn Juhl in 1952. The duo won the competition, and the project is their most important and best-known collaboration to date.
2   Thomas Sigsgaard and Kasper Salto, 25 March 2019. In 1937, the Norwegian designer Jacob Jacobsen designed the Luxo working lamp, which went on to become an iconic design object and the quintessential desk lamp with more than 25 million Luxo lamps been sold worldwide (Segelcke, 1989, pp. 66–67).
3   Thomas Sigsgaard and Kasper Salto, 25 March 2019.
4   Ibid.

Salto & Sigsgaard:
Wet Bell

1   Thomas Sigsgaard and Kasper Salto, 25 March 2019. Danish Crafts launched the MINDCRAFT concept in 2008 with an exhibition at *Salone del Mobile* in Milan. It has remained active ever since and combines the specifically Danish approach to design involving MIND and CRAFT: a reflection (in the form of a message) combined with design with a high level of craftsmanship. See https://www.kunst.dk/kunstomraader/kunsthaandvaerk-og-design/initiativer/mindcraft/.
2   Thomas Sigsgaard and Kasper Salto, 25 March 2019.
3   Ibid.
4   Ibid. A honeycomb filter is an opalized plastic material with a honeycomb structure consisting of tiny elements resembling little bits of plastic straw.
5   Juicy is now sold by Fritz Hansen.
6   Thomas Sigsgaard and Kasper Salto, 25 March 2019.
7   Ibid.

Ole Jensen:
OJ lamp

1   Ole Jensen, 6 May 2019.
2   Ole Jensen's washing-up bowl (design 1996, launched by Normann Copenhagen in 2002) was featured in Erik Steffensen's 2002 monograph on Jensen in the popular series *Danske Designere* (Danish Designers) published by Aschehoug and Louisiana. In 2014, the bowl was included in Dybdahl, 2016a, pp. 378–381.
3   Ole Jensen, 6 May 2019.
4   Ibid.
5   Ibid.
6   Ibid.

7   Jensen wrote these words on 3 February 2010 before the lamps were launched (ibid.).
8   Ibid.
9   Jensen repeatedly highlighted how well the project and collaboration proceeded throughout: 'I contributed with what was my area of expertise, and Louis Poulsen contributed with theirs. We had countless meetings, and every time we made a decision about the next step, and every time we had made the best possible decision. It was a good process, and at the end we all agreed that we had a good product' (ibid.).
10 Excerpt from a text Jensen wrote about his lamps on 3 February 2010 before the lamps were launched (Ole Jensen, 6 May 2019).

Norm Architects: Milk

1   Norm Architects has received several awards, including *Bo Bedre*'s Design Award in 2014.
2   Jonas Bjerre-Poulsen, 29 May 2019. Bjerre-Poulsen explains that many of the architecture students at the Royal Danish Academy were very inspired by what was going on in the Netherlands in both architecture and design around this time. In design, the new developments included, for example, Horselamp, which is a floor lamp shaped like a life-size horse (by the Swedish design group Front) and a crystal chandelier hidden behind semi-transparent plastic foil (by Jurgen Bey), both for the Dutch company Moooi: 'That whole postmodern wave was even more intense while we were in the School of Architecture.' While the theoretical foundation was laid at the Academy, the practical aspect was shaped in the modernist Ole Palsby's studio, far removed from fashionable trends, in extension of the functional tradition. That laid the basis for Norm Architects: 'The key was to meet a need, not to create a work of art; that's fine in a gallery but not when we're talking about mass-produced design. And the time was right for what we were doing. The financial crisis struck the year after we founded Norm Architects, and then the consumer culture began to move towards what we had been, quietly, preaching, so in that sense, we got off to a good start' (ibid.).
3   Ibid.
4   Ibid.
5   Ibid.
6   Ibid.
7   Ibid.
8   Ibid.

Maria Berntsen: Design with Light lantern

1   Ibid.
2   Maria Berntsen, 25 April 2019.
3   The One series included both a pendant and a table lamp and was also made in opal glass: 'The opal glass lends it a classic appearance and produces a beautiful diffused light that is radiated mainly via the shade but also, to a smaller extent, through the base, bringing out the complete form of the lamp' (Maria Berntsen, 25 April 2019).
4   The One lamp, like other Holmegaard lamps, was discontinued when Rosendahl acquired the brand in 2008. The production of electric lighting requires a technical department, also to be able to provide customer service, and the company decided to discontinue this product line.
5   Petersen, 2005.
6   Maria Berntsen, 25 April 2019.
7   A flame-spreader burner forces the airflow through a series of holes to direct the flame outwards. This results in a large light surface.
8   When Berntsen speaks of the technical team, she is referring to the Rosendahl Design Group. Berntsen explains that they also were not used to working with oil lamps but studied the technical aspects carefully. The lantern is a brilliant engineering accomplishment, and Berntsen was closely involved throughout the lengthy development process (Maria Berntsen, 25 April 2019).
9   Maria Berntsen, 25 April 2019.

Louise Campbell: LC Shutters

1   Louise Campbell, 13 March 2013. Approved by Campbell on 29 April 2019.
2   Ibid.
3   Ibid.
4   Hedebo, 2019, p. 13.
5   Louise Campbell, 28 November 2015.

Olafur Eliasson and Frederik Ottesen: Little Sun

1   'Solar energy engineer' is Eliasson's term for Frederik Ottesen's area of expertise, says Ottesen (19 August 2019), who points out this is not a professional title one can study for at the Technical University of Denmark but that it is an apt description of his field of work. He graduated as an engineer from the Technical University of Denmark in 1995.
2   Olafur Eliasson, 12 August 2019.
3   Ibid.
4   Ibid.
5   Ibid.
6   Little Sun costs DKK 199/€24.90, and Little Sun Diamond costs DKK 235/€30 (https://littlesun.com/).
7   Slogan used for Little Sun (Camilla Kragelund, Research and Communications, Studio Olafur Eliasson, 28 August 2019).
8   Olafur Eliasson, 12 August 2019.

Anne Qvist: Outfit L905

1   Anne Qvist, 24 May 2019.
2   The text is based on information from Veksø, *Enriching Urban Life. Lighting: Outfit L905*, 2013 and from Anne Qvist, 24 May 2019. Qvist explains that the street lamp was originally designed for Lampas, which was subsequently taken over by Veksø. From 1 January 2019, Veksø decided to revive the Lampas brand, now under the name Lampas by Veksø.
3   Anne Qvist, 24 May 2019.
4   The public square in question is located in front of Mikado House in Copenhagen's university quarter by Islands Brygge.
5   Ibid.
6   Ibid.
7   Ibid.
8   Ibid.

Øivind Slaatto: Swirl

1   Øivind Slaatto, 5 April 2019.
2   Statement by PH in a Louis Poulsen ad from 1930.
3   Ibid.
4   Ibid.
5   Ibid.
6   Ibid.
7   Ibid.
8   Ibid.

Øivind Slaatto: Patera

1   Øivind Slaatto, 5 April 2019.
2   Øivind Slaatto, 5 April 2019.
3   Ibid.
4   Ibid.
5   Ibid. The 2014 Eurovision Song Contest was held in a huge former shipbuilding hall on the Refshaleøen island, in Copenhagen. Slaatto mentions that he is a former musician: before he completed his studies at The Danish Design School in 2007, he attended the Royal Danish Academy of Music. At some point, he was actually attending both schools concurrently, but eventually he chose to devote his full attention to design, rather than music. However, his approach to music helped shape his approach to the design process (ibid.).
6   Slaatto explains that it 'took five years, as Louis Poulsen diligently researched every conceivable kind of foil, until they found one that really makes the light come alive, while the lamp retains its timeless expression' (ibid.). This variant was discontinued in 2019.

Jonas Edvard: Gesso

1   Ibid.
2   Jonas Edvard, 25 March 2019.
3   Ibid.
4   Ibid.
5   Danish Crafts Collection is a well-established collection concept that presents Danish crafts and design internationally; from 1999 to 2014, it was organized by Danish Crafts, an independent institution under the Danish Ministry of Culture. In 2014, Danish Crafts merged with the Danish Agency of Culture, and until 2019 it was conducted by the Danish Arts Foundation's Committee for Crafts and Design Project Funding, with the Danish Agency of Culture and Palaces serving as the secretariat. See https://www.kunst.dk/english/art-forms/crafts-and-design/

news/danish-crafts-in-merger-with-the-danish-agency-for-culture/.
6   The noma restaurant reopened in a new location in February 2018. While the name noma is a composite of the words *nordisk* (Nordic) and *mad* (food), the name of the pendant, Gesso, is based on the word for the primer made of gypsum and animal glue used in Italian medieval painting. Today, gesso is used as the general term for any primer for wood or canvas.
7   Jonas Edvard, 25 March 2019.

Norm Architects:
Carrie

1   Frederik Alexander Werner graduated from The Danish Design School in 2015 and worked at Norm Architects while he was still a student.
2   Jonas Bjerre-Poulsen, 29 May 2019.
3   'The light is warm; the LED emits a light with a temperature of 2,700 Kelvin. We worked on it for a few years before it was ready for production, and the LED was replaced – and is still replaced – continually, so in that sense there are going to be several generations of the lamp, because it does not have a socket. A poor light source can just kill a lamp; here, we take control to ensure the light is optimized,' says Bjerre-Poulsen. In a comment on the continuous development of the LED light source, he adds, 'This technology needs to be updated, just like our smartphones, where new and better generations are constantly being put out. In furniture design, the issue of updating has been sorely neglected. It's all about having the right "original" rather than saying, "okay, based on the feedback we get from the market, what sort of improvements and adjustments can we make in production?" The idea of improving a lamp on an ongoing basis seems more natural, because it is technological, while that concept is hardly addressed in non-technological design. It should be, but that's a different discussion' (Jonas Bjerre-Poulsen, 29 May 2019).
4   Ibid.
5   Mass Light is intended to hang as a simple lamp and to be used in various formations of multiple lamps. It is available both as a single luminaire and in two variants where a total of nine lamps are assembled into a spiral-shaped or cluster formation via a canopy. The latter models are available in retail, but the Norm architects have created a wide variety of installations for their many interior design projects: 'It became an architectural tool. We created all sorts of solutions, for example placing the lamps in rows or spiralling like a spiral staircase' (Jonas Bjerre-Poulsen, 29 May 2019). Mass Light is currently available in three combinations: glass/marble, glass/brass and glass/copper.
6   Ibid.
7   Ibid. Jonas Bjerre-Poulsen explains how Norm Architects together with a number of Swedish and Danish designers visited Nepal in a project organized by the Danish aid organization Danida. In Nepal, human trafficking is a serious problem: 'Young women are lured to India, and when they return they are considered unclean and cannot return to their villages, so they end up in Kathmandu, where various aid organizations help them find work in small production companies and arrange for their children to go to school. We were a group of Danish and Swedish designers who had gone there to develop new designs. It's a big problem that they mainly make items for the tourist industry that can't be sold anywhere else. We needed to develop something that would appeal and sell in the West, and, not least, we needed to set up a lasting production. On this trip, the Socket Occasional Lamp was created, since they could not produce high-tech stuff, but a simple brass mount that can take a standard socket and become a lamp, that was within their reach. They also produce the packaging' (ibid.).
8   Ibid.

GamFratesi:
Suspence

1   Stine Gam, 17 June 2019. Fratesi says about the process, 'We usually say that absolutely every project begins with a conversation. Before we even begin to sketch, we spend a long time talking about where we want to go with it, what the point of this particular project is, what we want to achieve. Then we draw the initial sketches, create the models and go on to make computer renderings, which are merely to be considered a tool for the process because our work is very analogue, very workshop-oriented' (Enrico Fratesi, 17 June 2019).
2   Stine Gam, 17 June 2019.
3   Because a pendant needs to be stabilized to be plumb, Suspence has a stabilizing mechanism built into the shade, so that the surface remains undisrupted, as a visible pendant tube would ruin the illusion that the shade and cord are one. The shade is spun, using a traditional method, which underscores the effect of the form being drawn out and fusing with the cord (Stine Gam and Enrico Fratesi, 17 June 2019).
4   Ibid.
5   The shade has a standard E27 socket, and the bulb is easy to replace, as the large diffuser that shields the bulb is easily pushed up and removed.
6   Stine Gam and Enrico Fratesi, 17 June 2019.
7   'Bring Cosy with You,' writes the manufacturer, Fritz Hansen, on its website: https://fritzhansen.com/products/lighting/suspence_nomad?sc_lang=en-GB. Fritz Hansen took over Lightyears in 2015. Thus, today it is in this context that Suspence and Suspence Nomad are produced, and new designs are developed in collaboration with the GamFratesi design studio.
8   Stine Gam and Enrico Fratesi, 17 June 2019.
9   GamFratesi created the glass pendant Soffi for the Italian furniture company Poltrona Frau, which is world famous for its leather products. The project was therefore about designing a lamp in which leather was an important detail (ibid.).
10   Enrico Fratesi, 17 June 2019.

Anne Qvist:
AQ01

1   Anne Qvist, 24 May 2019.
2   Ibid.
3   Ibid.
4   Ibid.
5   Ibid.
6   Ibid.

GamFratesi:
Yuh

1   Enrico Fratesi, 17 June 2019.
2   Ibid.
3   As mentioned (p. 212), Fratesi is Italian, and both he and Gam, who is Danish, have received part of their training in Italy and at the Aarhus School of Architecture, where Gam graduated, while Fratesi trained in Italy. Naturally, the two cultures influence the duo's design, as the Danish tradition for architect-designed furniture meets an Italian intellectual and conceptual approach to design. Fratesi says, 'We have the same competencies, the same interests, and in a sense we have an almost symbiotic process. And that is something we really appreciate. But of course, there are also areas where we differ; we are two different individuals, bringing, respectively, a Danish and an Italian approach and method. Those differences only make it interesting, also the fact we are opposite genders, but since everything fuses into one, there will never be a sharp line. It is not easy to tell where one begins and the other takes over. It's a very important point that our design is always very honest and intimate – it cannot be broken down into its component parts' (Stine Gam and Enrico Fratesi, 17 June 2019).
4   Ibid.
5   Enrico Fratesi, 17 June 2019.
6   Gam and Fratesi explain that the specially developed LED light source can be dimmed to 15% and that the timer function makes it possible to set the lamp to switch off automatically after four or eight hours.
7   Ibid.
8   Gam and Fratesi, 17 June 2019. Rasmus Markholt, who was head of design at Louis Poulsen in 2017, says of the brief the company gave GamFratesi: 'Yuh was based on a desire for a table, floor and wall series made by a contemporary designer, where the product (the head) had some volume in order to make it a more homely and cosy product, in contrast, for example, to the NJP series [designed by Oki Sato, launched in 2015], which is more technical and more like an anglepoise lamp. They hit the bull's eye and created a great interpretation of something historical mixed with modern technology' (Rasmus Markholt, 3 July 2019).
9   Stine Gam, 17 June 2019.

Philip Bro Ludvigsen:
Hiti

1   FDB had shops all over Denmark, even in small towns, and furniture could be ordered to be picked up from any of the shops.

2   Philip Bro Ludvigsen, 22 March 2019.
3   Ibid.
4   Ibid.

Sofie Refer: Blossi 8

1   Sofie Refer co-founded the lighting company Nuura with partners Nadia Lassen and Peter Østerberg. Later, Dan Takia Petersen joined as a co-owner.
2   Sofie Refer, 6 March 2019.
3   Ibid.
4   Ibid.
5   The LED disc used in the Blossi lamp is dimmable, so both the pendant and chandelier can be dimmed from the wall switch. The table and floor lamps in the series are designed to provide a good working light: 'The light in these lamps is pretty intense, so they have a built-in dimmer. I prefer to use a fairly high lumen, so I always make the light dimmable' (Sofie Refer, 6 March 2019).
6   Ibid.
7   Shiny surfaces are expensive to make, but the shiny globe is more sustainable, which is an important priority for Refer. Frosting opal glass involves dipping the glass into an acid wash; Refer explains that many also use the procedure because tiny irregularities in the surface of the glass are conveniently removed, and that reduces glass waste. However, the process has a greater environmental impact than leaving the surface shiny and allowing the imperfections to remain (ibid.).
8   Ibid.
9   Ibid.

Design by BIG: Gople Lamp RWB

1   Jakob Lange, 13 August 2019.
2   Bjarke Ingels graduated from the Royal Danish Academy of Fine Arts, School of Architecture, in 1999, and in 2001 he co-founded the architecture firm PLOT. BIG, which was founded in 2005, now has 17 partners. Lange, who graduated from the Royal Danish Academy of Fine Arts, School of Architecture, in 2007, has worked with Ingels since 2003. By his own description, Lange spends half his time on architecture and half on design solutions: furniture, lamps and other furnishings. Based on https://big.dk/#about and Jakob Lange, partner and head of design at BIG – Bjarke Ingels Group, 13 August 2019.
3   Ibid.
4   Associate professor and biologist Stephan Wenkel, Section for Plant Biochemistry, Copenhagen Plant Science Center, University of Copenhagen, 19 August 2019.
5   Jakob Lange, 13 August 2019.
6   Ibid.
7   Standard daylight contains red, green and blue (RGB), the three primary colours of light, which produce all other colours on the spectrum through so-called additive colour mixing. The combination of red, green and blue in equal intensities produces white. This is different from the primary *pigment* colours, red, yellow and blue, which produce all other colours through subtraction and which ultimately produce black in an equal mix. See, e.g., Itten, 1991, p. 16. When pure white light passes through a prism, we can clearly see that it contains all the colours. Because plants do not need green light and while blue and red light promotes their growth, the lamp uses red and blue, as well as white light, which contains all the wavelengths. Artemide patented the special RWB technology in 2011.
8   Plants need red light to trigger the sprouting of seeds, while blue light is important for triggering bloom and again red light is needed during bloom. This complex process is based on plants having different receptors for different wavelengths. This according to Wenkel, who also explains that greenhouses have traditionally 'used white light (all colours)'. However, since plants do not need green light, the new LED solutions make it possible to leave it out. The modern lighting systems in greenhouses can 'alter the colour composition, also depending on the time of day, for example artificially adding more red light at night – like the light from the setting sun – which increases the production of auxin and thus growth' (Stephan Wenkel, 19 August 2019).

Cecilie Bendixen: Volume Yellow

1   Cecilie Bendixen, 9 May 2019. The first Hurricane Eyes were presented in the small Copenhagen gallery Galerie Another Space, but the idea of adding light to the sound-absorbing forms initially arose when Bendixen established a collaboration with Vejen Art Museum. The museum had very poor acoustics, and in an attempt to solve the problem, in close collaboration with the museum director, Teresa Nielsen, the idea arose to hang a series of large, folded textile forms from the ceiling while also having them act as lamps. Eventually, Bendixen and Nielsen developed a completely different solution for the museum. Another problem was how to reduce daylight influx from a large skylight, lest it damage the paintings, so instead the textile was used to cover the skylight, and thus both the daylight issue and the acoustics issue were solved.
2   Cecilie Bendixen, 9 May 2019.
3   Ibid.
4   Ibid.
5   Ibid.
6   Bendixen adds that a large volume is much better than several small ones, since otherwise sound just flows around the smaller volumes, like water flowing around the stones in a stream.
7   Cecilie Bendixen, 9 May 2019.

Maria Berntsen: Stay

1   'Kvindelig PH-afløser', 1993, p. 15.
2   Ibid. The Lumino shade lamp, which came both as a table lamp and as pendants in two sizes, was produced by the lighting company Design Light. The lamp cost DKK 249/€33 when it was launched. By comparison, a standard PH 5 pendant cost DKK 1435/€192 according to Louis Poulsen's retail price list from February 1993.
3   Maria Berntsen, 25 April 2019.
4   Ibid.
5   Ibid.
6   Ibid.
7   Ibid.
8   Ibid.
9   Ibid.
10   See Design For The People's website: https://www.nordlux.dk/om-os/dftp.
11   Maria Berntsen, 25 April 2019.

Olafur Eliasson: OE Quasi Light

1   Olafur Eliasson, 12 August 2019.
2   Ibid.
3   Eliasson explains how he put this knowledge to concrete use in one of his latest projects: 'When I designed Fjordenhus in Vejle [2018] together with my studio, we actually used this knowledge' (ibid.). See more about this on p. 11. Anna Wirz-Justice, who is from New Zealand, is professor emerita of psychiatric neurobiology and the former head of the Center for Chronobiology at the University of Basel, Medical Faculty.
4   Olafur Eliasson, 12 August 2019.
5   This explanation is based on Louis Poulsen's OE QUASI Press Release AW19, April 2019.
6   Olafur Eliasson, 12 August 2019. As for recycling and recyclability, 90% of the aluminium is recycled, and all the other materials used in OE Quasi Light are 100% recyclable (Louis Poulsen, 2019).
7   Ibid. The three texts on Eliasson's lamps in this book are based mainly on personal communication with Olafur Eliasson. For a more in-depth treatment of Eliasson's thoughts on light, see *LYS!* (2015), which Olafur Eliasson co-wrote with the science writer Tor Nørretranders.
8   Olafur Eliasson, 12 August 2019.

Design by BIG: La Linea

1   Jakob Lange, 13 August 2019. The terminal strips that join the quarter circle and the straight element together make countless forms and are shaped as an L, a T, an X and a straight piece, as well as an end piece to finish the form and seal up the light.
2   BIG and Artemide had written the pangram on a building at the University of Milan. The installation was part of the event Interni Material Immaterial (Jakob Lange, 13 August 2019).
3   Ibid. Lange explains that Alphabet Mini, which is a third the size of the Alphabet of Light, with 40-cm-tall letters, is in the making. 'The idea is also to reduce the price to make it much more accessible to you and me, while Alphabet of Light is more intended for a company that wants to put a big sign on their wall, because the letters are so big. Alphabet Mini is an attempt at getting as close as possible to the ambition of accommodating everybody' (ibid.).

4   In extension of the Alphabet of Light, BIG and Artemide developed Soft Alphabet, a sort of intermediate step towards La Linea. Soft Alphabet is a soft flex tube that can be fitted with an aluminium rail on the back that can be shaped into any desired form. La Linea maintains the form without this added profile.
5   Artemide has developed a light control system that is operated via an app that works for all the lighting company's LED products.
6   Jakob Lange, 13 August 2019.
7   Ibid.
8   Jakob Lange, partner and head of Design by BIG – Bjarke Ingels Group, 13 August 2019.
9   Bjarke Ingels, founder of BIG, in connection with the launch of La Linea at *Salone del Mobile Euroluce* in Milan in April 2019. Quoted at https://www.archi-panic.com/la-linea-artemide-big/.

Øivind Slaatto: Shade Pendant ØS1

1   Statement by PH in a Louis Poulsen ad from 1930.
2   Øivind Slaatto, 5 April 2019.
3   Ibid.
4   From the lighting company Shade's website: https://shadelights.com.
5   Øivind Slaatto, 5 April 2019. Slaatto adds, 'In Shade we made the light source bigger than we are used to, with the traditional electric light bulb. That reduces the light intensity per mm² while the total amount of light remains the same, because the area is bigger. In turn, this reduces the contrast between light and dark without reducing the light. We are not dazzled by light but by the contrast between light and dark' (ibid.).
6   The round Shade Node switch is an integrated part of the design solution in Shade Pendant ØS1. The smart switch can be used to switch the light on and off and dim it, and the Shade Better Light app makes it possible to program the pendant with up to eight fixed settings that can then be selected by twisting the outer ring of the Shade Node. The canopy that comes with the pendant contains a small adapter that transforms AC (alternating current) to DC (direct current).
7   Øivind Slaatto, 5 April 2019.
8   Ibid.

Interviews and literature

Below is a complete list of everyone who was interviewed for this book. Most of the interviews took place face to face, some over the telephone and a few in e-mail dialogues. The date refers to the initial interview, but in most cases there was a longer dialogue.

Lamp designers

Alfred Homann, architect, 3 June 2019

Andreas Hansen, architect, 17 July 2019

Anne Qvist, architect, 24 May 2019

Benny Frandsen, designer and owner of Frandsen Group, 20 August 2019

Cecilie Bendixen, architect and textile artist, 9 May 2019

Cecilie Manz, designer, 6 June 2019

Enrico Fratesi, architect, 17 June 2019

Frederik Ottesen, engineer, 19 August 2019

Hans Due, graphic designer, 5 August 2019

Hans Jørgen Berthel, founder and former owner of ABO, 7 May 2019

Jakob Lange, architect, partner at Design by BIG – Bjarke Ingels Group, 13 August 2019

Jens Møller-Jensen, architect, 8 May 2019

Jonas Bjerre-Poulsen, architect and co-owner of Norm Architects, 29 May 2019

Jonas Edvard Nielsen, designer, 25 March 2019

Kasper Salto, designer, 25 March 2019

Louis Weisdorf, architect, 2 May 2019

Louise Campbell, designer, interviews in 2013 and 2015, text approved 29 April 2019

Maria Berntsen, designer, 25 April 2019

Olafur Eliasson, artist, 12 August 2019

Ole Jensen, ceramicist, 6 May 2019

Peter Bysted, architect, 31 May 2019

Philip Bro Ludvigsen, architect, 22 March 2019

Poul Christiansen, architect, 23 April 2019

Sofie Refer, designer, creative director of Nuura, 6 March 2019

Stig Gerlach, CEO of Sirius Company, 5 April 2019

Stine Gam, architect, 17 June 2019

Thomas Sigsgaard, architect, 25 March 2019

Tom Rossau, designer, 1 July 2019

Torsten Thorup, architect, 30 April 2019

Øivind Slaatto, designer, 5 April 2019

Family members of designers

Bent Gantzel-Boysen's widow, Dorit Gantzel-Boysen, and their daughters, Gitte and Janne Gantzel-Boysen, 6 April 2019

Bent Karlby's grandson Hans Schrader and his wife, Anne Vibeke Mortensen, 18 June 2019

Hans J. Wegner's daughter and studio employee, Marianne Wegner, 24 May 2019

Henning Koppel's daughter Hannah Koppel, 29 May 2019

Jo Hammerborg's widow, Henni Hammerborg, and their daughters, Gry and Marlene Hammerborg, 5 July 2019

Jørgen Gammelgaard's widow, Karin Gammelgaard, 15 May 2019

Jørn Utzon's son and studio employee, Jan Utzon, 7 June 2019

Lars Eiler Schiøler's son Uffe Schiøler, 31 July 2019

Sven Middelboe's granddaughter, Louise Eidemak, 14 January 2024.

Verner Panton's widow, Marianne Panton, 28 March 2019

Verner Panton's daughter, Carin Panton, 15 January 2024.

Others

Anne Bay, engineer, director of the Danish Lighting Center, 20 September 2019

Cecilie Sand Nørholm, astrophysicist at the Tycho Brahe Planetarium, 16 September 2019

Claus Juhlin, owner of Pandul, 21 May 2019

Hanne Thomsen, historian, director of GASmuseet, 20 September 2019

Houston Wilson, owner of Danish Vintage Design, 6 August 2019

Joakim Zacho Weylandt, design archaeologist, 20 August 2019

Karin Ørskov, interior designer, 24 July 2019

Kjell Berentzen, founder and former owner of Lampas, 2 July 2019

Klavs Andersen, expert on Thykier and lamps in general, 15 January 2014

Mathias Bøgeholdt, Arne Jacobsen expert, 30 December 2022

Mikkel Bahr, architect, partner and head of design at Friis & Moltke, 20 June 2019

Nils Zeeberg, senior consultant and co-author of Byens Nips (Urban Bric-a-Brac), 10 September 2019

Peter Frandsen, CEO of Verpan, 5 July 2019

Poul Madsen, owner and co-founder of Normann Copenhagen, 28 June 2019

Rasmus Markholt, co-founder of Lightyears 2004, former head of design at Louis Poulsen and founder of Lyfa 2020, 12 June 2019

Stephan Wenkel, biologist, associate professor at the Section for Plant Biochemistry, Copenhagen Plant Science Center, University of Copenhagen, 19 August 2019

Søren Palsbo, journalist, co-author of Byens Nips, 10 September 2019

Søren Peter Kristensen, project manager at Rambøll, 20 August 2019

Thorkild Thage Jørgensen, CEO of Nordisk Solar, 12 July 2019

Torsten Bløndal, publisher, Edition Bløndal, 24 June 2019

Ulla Riemer, head of LP Academy at Louis Poulsen, 7 August 2019

References and suggested reading

Aakjær, Jeppe (1953) [1900]. 'Da Lampen tændtes – et minde fra firserne'. In *Da Lampen Tændtes og Andre Jyske Fortællinger*, pp. 9–21. Copenhagen, Denmark: Fremad.

Abrahamsen, Poul, et al. (1976a). 'Dommerkomiteens generelle bemærkninger'. *LP & Co. NYT*, no. 404, pp. 3595–3605.

Abrahamsen, Poul, et al. (1976b). 'Dommerkomiteens generelle bemærkninger – Forslag no. 75'. *LP & Co. NYT*, no. 404, p. 3610.

Abrahamsen, Poul, et al. (1976c). 'Idékonkurrence om belysning'. *LP & Co. NYT*, no. 404.

Albertslund Lygte – Ikonisk Lygte Klar til Fremtiden (2019). https://www.catalogue.louispoulsen.com/DK/albertslund-lygte/. Louis Poulsen catalogue.

Alring, Leif (1981). 'Lamper er mere end lys'. *Skønne Hjem*, no. 3, p. 11.

Andersen, Hans Christian (1949a) [1870]. 'The Candles'. In *The Complete Andersen*. New York, NY: The Limited Editions Club. https://andersen.sdu.dk/vaerk/hersholt/TheCandles_e.html.

Andersen, Hans Christian (1949b) [1868]. 'Godfather's Picture Book'. In *The Complete Andersen*. New York, NY: The Limited Editions Club. https://andersen.sdu.dk/vaerk/hersholt/GodfathersPictureBook_e.html.

Advertisement for LamPetit (1967). *LP & Co. NYT*, no. 311, p. 2554.

Baagøe, Johan Hedemann (1965). *Lamper og Lysestager. Belysningen gennem tiderne*. Copenhagen, Denmark: Thaning & Appel.

Baldwin, Neil (1995). *Edison. Inventing the Century*. New York, NY: Hyperion.

Bang, Jacob E. (1949). 'Glasset i hjemmet'. In Sigvard Bernadotte and J. Lehm-Laursen (eds.). *Moderne Dansk Boligkunst*. Næstved, Denmark: Holmegaards Glasværk. Reprint.

Barslund, Jens (2008). 'Lyspunkter i en mørk tid'. *Bo Bedre*, no. 11, pp. 156–168.

Barslund, Jens, and Helles, Vibeke (1982). 'Nu kan de få spændende nyt lys i hele huset'. *Bo Bedre*, no. 11, pp. 6–17.

Belysning. Collection of photos from Landsforeningen Dansk Kunsthaandværk. From the archive of the Library at Designmuseum Danmark.

Bendixen, Tine (2000). 'Hun bryder det muliges grænser'. *Alt for Damerne*, no. 48, pp. 128–136.

Berentzen, Kjell (2000). *Lampas i Al Sin Enkelhed. In All Simplicity*. Copenhagen, Denmark: Danish Design Centre.

Bernsen, Jens (2003). *Verner Panton – Space:Time:Matter*. Copenhagen, Denmark: Danish Design Centre.

Berthel, Hans Jørgen (2019). *Abo Assentoft 8900 Randers 1961–1982*. Denmark: Hans Jørgen Berthel.

Berthelsen, Jens (ed.) (ca. 2006). *Vilhelm Lauritzen. En moderne arkitekt*. Copenhagen, Denmark: Bergiafonden, Aristo.

Bo, Jørgen, and Wohlert, Vilhelm (1958). [about Louisiana]. *Mobilia*, no. 38, pp. 47–48.

Boesdal, Ove (ed.) (1934). *Det Danske Hjem*. Copenhagen, Denmark: Nyt Nordisk Forlag Arnold Busck.

Boesdal, Ove (1931). *Hvordan Skal Vi bo? Vejledning i sund og naturlig boligindretning*. Copenhagen, Denmark: C.A. Reitzel.

Braae, Karen (ed.) (1948). *Dansk Husmoderleksikon, vol. I*. Denmark: Standard Forlaget.

Bruun, Mette (2015). '10 Designere På 100 Dage'. Exhibition catalogue. *Liv og Levn*, no. 29. Næstved, Denmark: Næstved Museum.

Bruun, Vibeke, et al. (eds.) (1979). *Dansk Kunsthåndværker Leksikon*, vols. 1 and 2. Copenhagen, Denmark: Rhodos.

Bundegaard, Christian (2018). *Finn Juhl. Life, Work, World*. Copenhagen, Denmark: Strandberg.

Bundgaard, Kirsten (1966). 'PH om Lys'. *Bo Bedre*, no. 11, pp. 16–19.

Campbell, Louise (2004). *The Story behind Campbell* (DVD). From Louis Poulsen's archive.

Chr. H-m. (1946). 'Man maa undvære meget, naar man først har den lyst. Interview med den unge Maler Johs. Hammerborg Nielsen'. *Randers Amtsavis*. Undated newspaper cutting from the Hammerborg family's archive.

Clemmensen, Tove (1965). 'Et københavnerhjem fra klunketiden'. In *Nationalmuseets Arbejdsmark 1963–1965*. Copenhagen, Denmark: National Museum of Denmark.

Crone, Axel (1892). *Kunsten at Møblere sin Lejlighed*. Copenhagen, Denmark: Gyldendal.

Crowley, John E. (2001). *The Invention of Comfort. Sensibilities & Design in Early Modern Britain & Early America*. Baltimore: The Johns Hopkins University Press.

'Da folk græd i Gothersgade' (1982). *Ingeniøren*, 10 December, pp. 12–13.

Daells Varehus (1978). *Forår 1978*. Copenhagen, Denmark: Daells Varehus, p. 222. Spring catalogue.

Daells Varehus (1974). *Efterår 1974*. Copenhagen, Denmark: Daells Varehus, p. 223. Autumn catalogue.

Daells Varehus (1973). *Efterår 1973*. Copenhagen, Denmark: Daells Varehus, pp. 214–215, 222 and 223. Autumn catalogue.

'Dagens portræt. Stædig pige med succes' (1977). *Politiken*, Sec. 1, 1 September, p. 8. Newspaper cutting from the archive of Designmuseum Danmark.

Dalby, Mette Strømgaard (2008). *Le Klint Design – Håndværk – Historie*. Denmark: KreativGrafisk Forlag.

'Den ideelle Belysning' (1921). *Vore Damer*, no. 24, unpaginated [p. 33].

'Det hvide look' (1984). *Bo Bedre*, no. 11, pp. 72-73.

Dybdahl, Lars (2018). *Furniture Boom. Mid-Century Modern Danish Furniture 1945–1975*. Copenhagen, Denmark: Strandberg.

Dybdahl, Lars (ed.) (2016a). *101 Danish Design Icons*. Copenhagen, Denmark: Strandberg.

Dybdahl, Lars (ed.) (2016b). *Dansk Design Nu*. Copenhagen, Denmark: Strandberg.

Dybdahl, Lars (2016c). 'Ølglasset til "Danmarks Hansen"'. In Dybdahl (2016a).

Dybdahl, Lars (2012). 'Hele Dagliglivets indhold. PH's design og designkritik'. In Hans Hertel (ed.). *Poul Henningsen Dengang og Nu. Lysmageren i nyt lys*, pp. 65–84. Copenhagen, Denmark: Gyldendal.

Dybdahl, Lars (2008). 'Scientific management i "hjemmets fabrik"'. In Lars Dybdahl and Ida Engholm (eds.). *Design. Køkkenet*. Copenhagen, Denmark: Gyldendal.

Dybdahl, Lars (2006). *Dansk Design 1945–1975*. Copenhagen, Denmark: Borgen.

Dybdahl, Lars (1987). '"Virkelig kunstindustri" – dansk industridesign i mellemkrigstiden'. In Finn H. Lauridsen (ed.). *Festskrift til Vagn Dybdahl*, pp. 91–118. Aarhus, Denmark: Universitetsforlaget.

Elnyt – til Forbrugerne – fra Elværket (1962), no. 3.

'En nyhed' (1961). *LP & Co. NYT*, no. 241, pp. 1948–1949.

Enevoldsen, Birgit, and Enevoldsen, Christian (1958). *Brugskunst. Møbler, textiler, lamper*. Copenhagen, Denmark: Arkitektens Forlag.

Engholm, Ida, and Michelsen, Anders (2018). *Verner Panton. Environments, Colours, Systems, Patterns*. Vienna, Austria: Phaidon.

Engholm, Ida (2005). *Verner Panton*. Copenhagen, Denmark: Ascheoug.

'Farvernes hemmelighed' (1913). *Vore Damer*, no. 7, unpaginated [p. 15].

F.R. (1975). 'LP udskriver konkurrence'. *LP & Co. NYT*, no. 400, pp. 3363–3564.

Fiell, Charlotte, and Fiell, Peter (2005a). *1000 Lights. 1879 to 1959*. Cologne, Germany: Taschen.

Fiell, Charlotte, and Fiell, Peter (2005b). *1000 Lights. 1960 to Present*. Cologne, Germany: Taschen.

Filskov, Niels (1917). 'Belysning'. *Hjemmet*, no. 45, pp. 881–882.

Fisker, Kay (1950). 'Den funktionelle tradition. Spredte indtryk af amerikansk arkitektur'. *Arkitekten* (reprint), no. 1–2, pp. 69–100.

Fog & Mørup (1978). *Lampekatalog 1978/79*. Copenhagen, Denmark. From the Hammerborg family's archive.

Fog & Mørup (1970). *Formland*. Copenhagen, Denmark: Fog & Mørup. PR folder. From the Hammerborg family's archive.

Fog & Mørup (1964). PR folder. Copenhagen, Denmark: Fog & Mørup.

Fog & Mørup (1940). *Den Blå Bog*. Copenhagen, Denmark: Fog & Mørup.

Fog & Mørup (1939–1941). Catalogue. Copenhagen, Denmark: Fog & Mørup.

Folkmann, Mads Nygaard (2007). *Louise Campbell*. Humlebæk and Copenhagen, Denmark: Louisiana and Ascheoug.

Frandsen, Benny (2018). *FABRIKKEN*. Copenhagen, Denmark: Frandsen Group.

Freeman, June (2004). *A Cultural History. The Making of the Modern Kitchen*. Oxford, England: Oxford International.

Frydensberg, Kim (ed.) (2019). 'Stjernehimlen'. *Politiken*, Sec. 1, 6 September, p. 10.

Gad, Peter Urban (1949) [1947]. *Klunketiden paa en Anden Maade*. Copenhagen, Denmark: H. Hagerup.

Garnert, Jan (1993). *Anden i Lampan. Etnologiske perspektiv på ljus och mörker*. Stockholm, Sweden: Carlsson.

Garrett, Elisabeth Donaghy (1990). *At Home. The American Family 1750–1870*. New York, NY: H.N. Abrams.

Gelfer-Jørgensen, Mirjam (2013). *Influences from Japan in Danish Art and Design, 1870–2010*. Copenhagen, Denmark: Arkitektens Forlag.

Gottlob, Anette (1970). 'Spar penge, ha' det sjovt. Lamperne laver vi selv'. *Bo Bedre*, no. 10, pp. 40–45.

Gottlob, Anette (1966). 'Er pæren i orden?'. *Bo Bedre*, no. 11, pp. 76–77 and 140.

Gottlob, Anette, Hübbe, Lone, and Rasmussen, Gerda Ørsted (1966). 'Lampeleksikon'. *Bo Bedre*, no. 11, pp. 80–85.

Gynt, Olaf (1971). 'Digt til Flowerpots pris'. *LP & Co. NYT*, no. 353, p. 2914.

Hansen, Harriet M., Petersen, Flemming, and Wistoft, Birgitte (1991). *Elektricitetens Aarhundrede, Bind 1*. Copenhagen, Denmark: Danske Elværkers Forening.

Hansen, Johannes Hedal (2017). *Eva og Nils Koppel*. Copenhagen, Denmark: Strandberg.

Hansen, Ove (1994). 'Lighting Engineering Terms'. In Jørstian and Nielsen (1994), pp. 298–300.

Hansen, Per H. (2009). *Finn Juhl og Hans Hus*. Charlottenlund and Copenhagen, Denmark: Ordrupgaard and Gyldendal.

Hansen, Per H., and Petersen, Klaus (2005). *Den Store Danske Møbelguide*. Copenhagen, Denmark: Lindhart og Ringhof.

Hansen, Willy (1930). 'Stockholmsudstillingens Boligafdeling'. *Arkitektens Maanedshefter II*, pp. 147–160.

Harkær, Gorm (2010). *Kaare Klint, vol. 1*. Copenhagen, Denmark: Klintiana.

Hedebo, Lars (2019). 'Hæder til Louise Campbell' (Accolade for Louise Campbell). *Politiken*, 24 February 2019, Sec. 3, p. 13.

Heiberg, Edvard (1929). 'Fremtidens Hus er Bluff'. *Vore Damer*, no. 39, unpaginated [pp. 13–14].

Heiberg, Edvard (1927). 'Hvordan har De det?'. *Kritisk Revy*, no. 1, pp. 31–34.

Heiberg, Edvard (1925). 'Udstilling for dekorativ kunst. Paris 1925'. *Byggekunst*, no. 12, pp. 181–184.

Hein, Piet (1936). 'Ra-Lampen'. *Arkitekten Ugehæfte*, vol. 38, pp. 9–11.

Henningsen, Poul (1974) [1928]. *PH om Lys*. Edited by Ebbe Christensen, Sophus Frandsen, Steen Jørgensen and Mogens Voltelen. Copenhagen, Denmark: Rhodos.

Henningsen, Poul (1966). 'Hvordan PH-lampen blev til'. *LP & Co. NYT*, no. 300, pp. 2453–2458.

Henningsen, Poul (1963). [Untitled]. *LP & Co. NYT*, no. 266, p. 2158.

Henningsen, Poul (1962). 'Kontrastlampen. En PH nyhed for 1962'. *LP & Co. NYT*, no. 252, pp. 2035–2039.

Henningsen, Poul (1961a). 'Dialog om lamper'. *Mobilia*, no. 72, pp. 107–112.

Henningsen, Poul (1961b). 'Nattens nyheder – organ for Krybskytter'. *LP & Co. NYT*, no. 237, pp. 1915–1917.

Henningsen, Poul (1961c). 'Restaurant Astoria, Trondheim'. *LP & Co. NYT*, no. 230, pp. 1855–1859.

Henningsen, Poul (1960). 'Tanker omkring et skohorn …'. *Mobilia*, no. 54, pp. 21–22.

Henningsen, Poul (1958a). 'En klassisk nyhed'. *LP & Co. NYT*, no. 196, pp. 1563–1569.

Henningsen, Poul (1958b). 'En omvendelse, tre fire væsentlige ting, 6 spektre'. *Mobilia*, no. 33, pp. 22–35.

Henningsen, Poul (1954a). 'Kære Vilhelm Lauritzen'. *LP & Co. NYT*, no. 149, p. 1185.

Henningsen, Poul (1954b). 'Omgang mod naturen med kunstnerretten'. *LP & Co. NYT*, no. 148, pp. 1171–1173.

Henningsen, P. (1949a). 'Belysningsarmaturer'. *Dansk Kunsthaandværk*, vol. 22, pp. 199–200.

Henningsen, Poul (1949b). 'Tivolilampens konstruktion'. *LP & Co. NYT*, no. 90, pp. 707–712.

Henningsen, Poul (1947). 'Krig paa Kniven eller rimelig Konkurrence'. *LP & Co. NYT*, no. 66, pp. 535–536.

Henningsen, Poul (1946). 'En løsning af papirlampens problem'. *LP & Co. NYT*, no. 62, pp. 503–505.

Henningsen, Poul (1945). 'Belysningens kunst'. *LP & Co. NYT*, no. 52, pp. 423–426.

Henningsen, Poul (1943). 'Den permanente'. *LP & Co. NYT*, no. 22, pp. 171–173.

Henningsen, Poul (1942). 'PH Tivolilampen'. *LP & Co. NYT*, no. 12, pp. 80–82.

Henningsen, Poul (1941). 'Glødelampens historie'. *LP & Co. NYT*, no. 3, unpaginated.

Henningsen, Poul (1928). 'P.H. Lampen i Hjemmet'. In *Det Ideale Hjem. Dets skønhed, hygge og bekvemmelighed*, p. 68. Copenhagen, Denmark: Hage & Clausens Forlag.

Henningsen, Poul (1927). 'Rummets belysning – med særligt Henblik paa Anvendelsen af P.H.-Lampen'. *Kritisk Revy*, no. 2, pp. 67–102.

Henningsen, Poul (1926a). 'Le Corbusier'. *Kritisk Revy*, no. 1, pp. 50–55.

Henningsen, Poul (1926b). 'Moderne belysning af rum'. *Kritisk Revy*, no. 1, pp. 60–82.

Henningsen, Simon P. (1944). 'Mere Lys i Tivoli'. *LP & Co. NYT*, no. 33, pp. 271–272.

Holmegaards Glasværk (1982a). 'Kinaform og Chintz'. *Glas & Mennesker*, September, p. 5.

Holmegaards Glasværk (1982b). 'Lampefamilier og minipendler'. *Glas & Mennesker*, September, p. 5.

Holmegaards Glasværk (1981a). 'Apoteker-lamper'. *Glas & Mennesker*, no. 5, pp. 10–11.

Holmegaards Glasværk (1981b). [Untitled]. *Glas & Mennesker*, no. 4, p. 7.

Holmegaards Glasværk (1980). 'Michael Bang'. *Glas & Mennesker*, no. 2, pp. 4–6.

Holmegaards Glasværk (1973). 'Nye Søstærke lamper'. *Glaspustet, Personaleblad for Kastrup og Holmegaard Glasværker A/S*, December, pp. 8–9.

Holmsted Olesen, Christian (2014). *Wegner. Just One Good Chair*. Copenhagen, Denmark: Strandberg.

Holst, Helge, and la Cour, Poul (1904). *Menneskeaandens Sejre. Opfindelsernes historie i omrids*. Copenhagen, Denmark: FREM Det Nordiske Forlag.

Hvidberg-Hansen, Poul (2000). 'The Source of Light'. In von Vegesack and Remmele (2000), pp. 100–131.

Høst, Ole (1982). *Danske Kulturplanter*. Denmark: DSR Forlag.

Ifversen, Karsten R.S., and Lyngbye Pedersen, Birgit (2013). *Finn Juhl i FN – et Dansk Mesterværk i New York*. Copenhagen, Denmark: Strandberg.

'Ilumesa' (1970), *LP & Co. NYT*, no. 340, p. 2802.

Illustreret Tidende (1878), no. 998, p. 63.

Interview med Århus-arkitekterne Friis og Moltke (1976). Originally broadcast 15 August. Denmark: DR (Danish Broadcasting Corporation).

Itten, Johannes (1991). *Farvekunstens Elementer*, 8th edition. First Danish edition 1977; originally published in German in 1961 as *Kunst der Farbe*. Copenhagen, Denmark: Borgen.

Iwersen, Uwe (2019). 'Wegner får egne lamper foran fødehjemmet'. *JydskeVestkysten*, 23 April. https://www.jv.dk/toender/Wegner-faar-egne-lamper-foran-foedehjemmet/artikel/2708823.

Jacobsen, Carl (1912). *Belysningsteknikkens Historiske Udvikling*. Denmark: Kunsthistorisk Samling Nielsen & Lydiche.

Jakobsen, Hans (2012). *Notat om To Tegninger fra Utzon-Arkivet, som Blev Vist på Udstillingen 'Jørn Utzons Skitser og Modeller' i Perioden 04.08.2012–02.09.2012 på UTZON CENTER i Aalborg*. Eight-page memo found in Henrik Lund Larsen and &Tradition's archive.

Jalk, Grete (ed.) (1987). *Dansk Møbelkunst Gennem 40 Aar*, vols. 3 and 4. Taastrup, Denmark: Danish Technological Institute.

Jensen, Charlotte Louise (2014). *What Is Energy Efficient Light? A Socio-Technical Analysis of Lighting in Transition*. PhD dissertation. Aalborg, Denmark: Aalborg University.

Jensen, Hans-Christian (2016). 'Dansk design i globaliseringens tidsalder'. In Dybdahl (2016a), pp. 406–409.

Jensen, Johannes V. (1973) [1908]. *Bræen. Myter om Istiden og det Første Menneske*. Copenhagen, Denmark: Gyldendals Tranebøger.

Jensen, Knud W. (1986). *Mit Louisiana-Liv*. Copenhagen, Denmark: Gyldendals Bogklub.

Jørgensen, Jørgen (1986). 'Vi drikker Store Bælts-kaffen af hans kopper'. *Bo Bedre*, no. 1, pp. 48–49.

Jørgensen, Lisbet Balslev (1994). 'Vilhelm Lauritzen 1894–1983'. In Berthelsen (ca. 2006), pp. 8–118.

Jørgensen, Steen, and Jørstian, Tina (1994). 'Lighting Logic. The PH Lamp – The Solution to the Problems of Lighting'. In Jørstian and Nielsen (1994), pp. 117–160.

Jørgensen, Steen, Jørstian, Tina, and Nielsen, Poul Erik Munk (1994). 'The Taming of the Light. From Prisms to Reflective Shades'. In Jørstian and Nielsen (1994), pp. 75–116.

Jørstian, Tina (1994a). 'PH lampen. Tre krumme skærme – indbegrebet af moderne belysning'. *LP & Co. NYT*, September, pp. 3–6. Theme issue titled 'PH 100 Lys og design'.

Jørstian, Tina (1994b). 'The PH lamp as a Type. Fads and Classics'. In Jørstian and Nielsen (1994), pp. 161–206.

Jørstian, Tina, and de Waal, Allan (1994). 'The Quality of Light. PH on the Problems Associated with Lighting'. In Jørstian and Nielsen (1994), pp. 59–74.

Jørstian, Tina, and Nielsen, Poul Erik Munk (eds.) (1994). *Light Years Ahead. The Story of the PH Lamp*, Copenhagen, Denmark: Louis Poulsen.

Juhl, Finn (1954). *Hjemmets Indretning*. Copenhagen, Denmark: Thaning & Appel.

Juhl, Finn (1947a). 'Bing & Grøndahl, Amagertorv 4'. *LP & Co. NYT*, no. 69, pp. 558–562.

Juhl, Finn (1947b). 'Om belysningen i hans hjem'. *LP & Co. NYT*, no. 66, pp. 537–540.

Juhl, Finn (1946). 'Sorry Sir – vi har ikke flere af de runde!'. *LP & Co. NYT*, no. 63, pp. 517–518.

Kaiser, Birgit (1992). *Den Ideologiske Funktionalisme*. Copenhagen, Denmark: Gad.

Kaiser, Niels-Jørgen (2000). *Henning Koppels Verden*. Copenhagen, Denmark: Gyldendal.

Karlby, Bent (1942). *Bo for To. Haandbog i Hjemmets Indretning*. Denmark: Henry Clausen.

Keiding, Lis Marie (ed.) (2003). *Miljøfaktorer i Danskernes Hverdag – med Særligt Fokus på Boligmiljø*. Copenhagen, Denmark: National Institute of Public Health.

Kemp & Lauritzen (1954). *Hjemmets Belysning* (PR brochure). Albertslund, Denmark: Kemp & Lauritzen. From the Collection of Pamphlets and Corporate Publications, Royal Danish Library.

Kjær, H.A. (H.A.K) (1923). 'Lamper'. In *Salmonsens Konversationsleksikon, vol. 15*, 2nd edition, pp. 300–301. Copenhagen, Denmark: J.H. Schultz Forlagsboghandel.

Klint, Kaare (1930). 'Undervisning i Møbeltegning ved Kunstakademiet'. *Arkitekten Månedshæfte*, no. 10, pp. 193–203.

Klint, Kaare (1921). 'Kommunens nye Gadelygter'. *Arkitekten*, no. 10, pp. 345–348.

Koppel, Nils (1958). 'Langeliniepavillonens belysning'. *LP & Co. NYT*, no. 196, pp. 1570–1573.

Kornum, Birgitte Rahbek (no year). 'Lyset påvirker din søvn'. *Magasinet Sundhed*. http://magasinet-sundhed-dk/lyset-paa-virker-din-soevn/.

Kristensen, Erik (ed.) (2006). *Elektricitetens Pionerer*. Copenhagen, Denmark: Dansk El-Forbund.

Kristiansen, Erik (2015). 'Designeren'. In Harsløf, Olav (ed.). *Piet Hein Verdensdanskeren*, pp. 80–114. Copenhagen, Denmark: Gyldendal.

Kritisk Revy (1926), no. 1, p. 1.

'Kvindelig PH-afløser' (Female Successor to PH) (1993). *Bo Bedre*, no. 10, p. 15.

'Lampereklame' (Lamp Advertisement) (1926). *Kritisk Revy*, no. 3, p. 29.

'Lampeskærme – Modeller fra Magasin du Nord' (1913). *Vore Damer*, no. 16, unpaginated [p. 24].

Lassen, Erik, and Schlüter, Mogens (2002). *Dansk Glas 1925–1985*. Copenhagen, Denmark: Nyt Nordisk Forlag Arnold Busck.

Lauritzen, Vilhelm (1954). 'Har der været rationelle armaturer på markedet …'. *LP & Co. NYT*, no. 149, pp. 1184–1185.

Lauritzen, Vilhelm, and Schlegel, Frits (1930). 'Fritsches Læselampe'. *Arkitekten Ugehæfte*, p. 191.

Le Corbusier (1986). *Toward a New Architecture*. New York: Dover Publication. Originally published in French in 1923; in English in 1927.

Lees-Maffei, Grace (2008). 'Professionalization as a Focus in Interior Design History'. *Journal of Design History, Special Issue. Professionalizing Interior Design 1870–1970*, vol. 21, no. 1, pp. 1–18.

Linnet, Jeppe Trolle (2010). *Interweavings. A Cultural Phenomenology of Everyday Consumption and Social Atmosphere Within Danish Middle-Class Families*. Odense, Denmark: University of Southern Denmark.

Littrup, Signe Lykke (2016). 'Lysets økonomi – PH–lampen'. In Dybdahl (2016a), pp. 58–61.

Louis Poulsen (2019). *OE QUASI Press Release AW19*, April. Copenhagen, Denmark: Louis Poulsen.

Louisiana (2018). *Louisiana 1958–2018. Design by Vilhelm Wohlert*. Humlebæk, Denmark: Louisiana.

Lund, Morten (2008). *Fra Radiohus til Musikkonservatorium*. Copenhagen, Denmark: The Royal Danish Academy of Music.

Lund, Morten (1994a). 'Lauritzens lamper og PH's polemik'. *LP & Co. NYT*, no. 543, pp. 10–17.

Lund, Morten (1994b). 'Vilhelm Lauritzens moderne rum'. In Berthelsen (ca. 2006), pp. 206–319.

Lundqvist, Søren, and Brænne, Jon (2009). *Edvard Heibergs Eget Hus. I.H. Mundts Vej 16*. Copenhagen, Denmark: Realea.

Lundstrøm, Johannes (2016). Fra markedsplads til messehal. Toga Partner.

Lyfa (1949). *Katalog no. 3. Belysninger tegnet af Bent Karlby* (Lyfa Catalogue No. 3. Luminaires Designed by Bent Karlby). Copenhagen, Denmark: Lyfa.

'Lysgave fra Aalestrup til kronprinsparret' (2004). *Nordjyske*, 10 April. https://nordjyske.dk/nyheder/lysgave-fra-aalestrup-til-kronprinsparret/d8c11683-6081-4fe9-b5cf-b4b8e6b694e9.

Lytken, Malene (2019). *Marianne Riis-Carstensen – et Farverigt Liv*. Denmark: Private edition.

Lytken, Malene (2016). *Lys og Lamper i de Danske Hjem. Sagkundskabens formidling af en formålstjenlig kunstbelysning*. Copenhagen, Denmark: Royal Danish Academy of Fine Arts, Schools of Architecture, Design and Conservation.

Lytken, Malene (2013). 'The Professionalisation of Women and Interior Design in Denmark'. *Journal of Interior Design*, vol. 38, no. 3, pp. 1–19.

Lytken, Malene (2008). *Skolen for Boligindretning. Kvindernes og boligindretningens professionalisering*. Copenhagen, Denmark: University of Copenhagen.

Løkkegaard, Anne Marie (2006). 'Refer+Staer "Vi designer de ting, vi længes efter"'. *Berlingske*, Sec. Boligen, 25 June. https://www.berlingske.dk/bolig/referstaer.

'Må vi præsentere Petronella' (1962). Louis Poulsen advertisements. *Bo Bedre*, no. 7, pp. 67 and 79.

Madsen, Flemming (1971). Interview with Henning Koppel originally broadcast 12 November. Søborg, Denmark: DR (Danish Broadcasting Corporation).

Mansfeldt, Lisbeth (2006). 'Albertslundlygten'. In Janstrup, Jette, et al. (eds.). *Glimt fra Albertslunds Historie. Årsskrift for 2006*. Albertslund, Denmark: Albertslund Lokalhistorisk Forening.

Meyer, Karl (K.M.) (1924). 'Lys'. In *Salmonsens Konversationsleksikon*, vol. 16, 2nd edition, pp. 176–177. Copenhagen, Denmark: J.H. Schultz Forlagsboghande.

Mobilia (1958), no. 38.

'Moderne Belysning' (1936). *Bygge og Bo*, no. 6, pp. 20–21.

Mollerup, Per (1995). *Jørgen Gammelgaard, Kunstindustrimuseet 1995*. Catalogue for exhibition at the Danish Museum of Art & Design, now Designmuseum Danmark, 23 February–2 June 1995.

Moseng, Kari, Andersen, Camilla Bank, and Poulsen, Mogens Brandt (2004). *I Al Enkelhed. Friis & Moltke 1954–2004*. Aarhus, Denmark: Aarhus School of Architecture.

MT (1995). 'Et dansk multitalent runder halvfems'. *Bo Bedre*, no. 11, p. 14.

Møller, Henrik Sten (1990). *Fra Vor Egen Tid – 100 Års Boligidealer*. Copenhagen, Denmark: Gad.

Møller, Henrik Sten (1975). *Dansk Design. Danish Design*. Copenhagen, Denmark: Rhodos.

Møller, Svend Erik (1980). 'Portræt af en arkitekt'. *LP & Co. NYT*, no. 446, pp. 3947–3950.

Møller, Svend Erik (1972). 'Her er et helt nummer om Verner Panton. Oplevelser på Varna'. *LP & Co. NYT*, no. 366, pp. 3239–3245.

Møller, Svend Erik (1969). 'Spiegel-huset i Hamburg'. *LP & Co. NYT*, no. 329, pp. 2691–2697.

Møller, Svend Erik (1968a). 'Verner Panton i Køln'. *LP & Co. NYT*, no. 316, pp. 2587–2591.

Møller, Svend Erik (1968b). 'Verner Pantons Bayer-ship'. *Mobilia*, no. 151, unpaginated [pp. 42–49].

Møller, Sven Erik (1966). 'Det Nye Louis Poulsen-Barn' (The New Louis Poulsen Baby). *LP & Co. NYT*, no. 299, pp. 2443–2445.

Møller, Vibeke Andersson (2014). *Arkitekten og Designeren Bent Karlby*. Copenhagen, Denmark: Forlaget Rhodos.

Møller, Vibeke Andersson (2004). *Arkitekten Frits Schlegel*. Copenhagen, Denmark: Arkitektens Forlag.

Møller, Vibeke Andersson (2003). *Stellings Hus*. Denmark: Fisker.

Møller, Viggo Sten (1980). 'Brugskunst og funktionalisme'. In *Form og Funktion*, Sophienholm, pp. 52–55. Lyngby, Denmark: Sophienholm. Exhibition catalogue.

Nielsen, Jens (1988). 'Jørgen Gammelgaard – Troldmandens lærling'. *Bo Bedre*, no. 9, 72–73.

Nielsen, Poul Erik Munk, and de Waal, Allan (1994). 'The Spread of the PH Lamp. Sales Curves and Didactic Advertising'. In Jørstian and Nielsen (1994), pp. 207–228.

Nordisk Solar Compagni (1981). Vejen, Denmark: Nordisk Solar Compagni. Catalogue 1981. From The Collection of Pamphlets and Corporate Publications, Royal Danish Library.

Nordisk Solar Compagni (1978a). Vejen, Denmark: Nordisk Solar Compagni. Catalogue 1978. From Torsten Bløndal's archive.

Nordisk Solar Compagni (1978b). *Loftsbelysninger*. Denmark: Nordisk Solar Compagni. Catalogue 1978. From The Collection of Pamphlets and Corporate Publications, Royal Danish Library.

Nordisk Solar Compagni (1958a). *Armatur Solar*. Vejen, Denmark: Nordisk Solar Compagni. Catalogue 1958. From The Collection of Pamphlets and Corporate Publications, Royal Danish Library.

Nordisk Solar Compagni (1958b). *Belysninger*. Vejen, Denmark: Nordisk Solar Compagni. Catalogue 1958. From Torsten Bløndal's archive.

'Ny PH-lampe på Charlottenborg' (1980). *LP & Co. NYT*, no. 448, p. 3964.

'Nyt lys på vej fra Køln' (1970). *LP & Co. NYT*, no. 338, pp. 2781–2782.

Nørregaard, Kurt, Jørgensen, Steen, Hansen, Ove, and Nielsen, Poul Erik Munk (1994). 'From the PH Lamp to the PH 5. Variations on a Theme 1926–67'. In Jørstian and Nielsen (1994), pp. 229–292.

Nørretranders, Tor, and Eliasson, Olafur (2015). *Lys! OM lys i livet og liv i lyset*. Copenhagen, Denmark: Forlaget Tor.

O.W. (1930). 'Belysningsudstillingen i Tivoli'. *Arkitektens Ugehæfter*, pp. 184–186.

Olsen, Erik (1974). 'En LP-Nyhed'. *LP & Co. NYT*, no. 384, p. 3429.

Olsen, Erik (1963). 'Gyldendals Ekspeditionsbygning – arkitekterne Jørgen Bo og Vilhelm Wohlert'. *LP & Co. NYT*, no. 266, pp. 2159–2161.

Olsen, Erik (1967). 'Lytespan-Concord'. *LP & Co. NYT*, no. 303, p. 2483.

'Originale elektriske Lamper' (1921). *Vore Damer*, no. 21, unpaginated [p. 38].

Palsbo, Søren, and Zeeberg, Nils Kristian (1974). *Byens Nips – om Brandhaner, Lygtepæle og Andet Godt*. Copenhagen, Denmark: Sporvejshistorisk Selskab.

Panton, Verner (1991). *Lidt om farver. Notes on Colour*. Copenhagen, Denmark: Danish Design Centre.

'Panthella bord- og standerlamper' (1972). *LP & Co. NYT*, no. 365, p. 3238.

Petersen, Anja (2005). 'Maria Berntsen'. *Berlingske*, Sec. Boligen, 30 October. https://www.berlingske.dk/bolig/maria-berntsen.

Petersen, Trine Brun (2016). 'Perfekt geometri og generøse former. Krenitskålen'. In Dybdahl (2016a), pp. 154–157.

Petersen, Trine Brun (2016b). 'Termokanden med den ophængte vippeprop'. In Dybdahl (2016a), pp. 314–317.

'Puslespil med lys i' (2001). *Bo Bedre*, no. 11, p. 23.

Raizman, David (2003). *History of Modern Design*. London, England: Laurence King Publishing.

Rasmussen, Erik L. (1934). 'Lysteknik og belysningslegemer'. In Boesdal (1934), pp. 73–85.

Remy-Jensen, Jo (1980a). 'De kaster nyt lys over tingene'. *Bo Bedre*, no. 3, pp. 30–31.

Remy-Jensen, Jo (1980b). 'Han tegner møbler efter boligens mål'. *Bo Bedre*, no. 10, pp. 36–37.

Roholt, Anders, and Tyrrestrup, Mikkel (2006). *Piet Hein*. Biopic as part of the documentary series *Store Danskere*, originally broadast 19 March. Søborg, Denmark: DR (Danish Broadcasting Corporation).

Rohweder, Birte (1962). Bedstemors lampe. *Bo Bedre*, no. 6, pp. 44–46.

Roos, Ole (1964). *PH Lys*. Denmark: Laterna Film. https://filmcentralen.dk/museum/danmark-paa-film/film/ph-lys#.

Roos, Trine (2015). 'Solgt på auktion'. *Politiken*, 1 February.

Roux, Caroline (2013). 'Prism Break'. *Wallpaper**, May, pp. 96–98.

Rudberg, Eva (1999). *Stockholmsutställningen 1930*. Stockholm, Sweden: Stockholmia.

Rumford, Count. B. (Benjamin Thompson, Count of Rumford) (1875) [ca. 1806]. 'Of the Management of Light in Illumination'. In *Complete Works*, vol. 4, pp. 101–168. Boston, MA: American Academy of Arts and Sciences.

Rybczynski, Witold (1986). *Home. A Short Story of an Idea*. London, England: Simon & Schuster.

S.E.M. (1966). 'Det nye Louis Poulsen-barn'. *LP & Co. NYT*, no. 299, pp. 2443–2445.

Schivelbusch, Wolfgang (1995) [1983]. *Disenchanted Night. The Industrialization of Light in the Nineteenth Century* (1983). Berkeley, CA: University of California Press.

Schiøler, Uffe. *Hoyrup Light Revisited*. http://schiolers.dk/.

Schmidt, Torben (1968a). 'Interview med Henning Koppel om et spændende produktudviklingsarbejde'. *Mobilia*, no. 153, unpaginated.

Schmidt, Torben (1968b). 'Foldede lampeskærme af Andreas Hansen'. *Mobilia*, no. 150, unpaginated [pp. 23–29].

Schrøder, Michael (1968). *The Argand Burner. Its Origin and Development in France and England 1780–1800*. Odense, Denmark: Odense University Presse.

Schrøder, Michael (1964). *Olielampen i den Vestlige Verdens Kulturområde*. Copenhagen, Denmark: Spektrum.

Segelcke, Nanna (1989). *Norsk Kvalitet*. Oslo, Norway: Dreyer.

Semper, Gottfried (2006) [1852]. 'From Science, Industry, and Art'. In Mallgrave, Harry Francis (ed.). *Architectual Theory – Volume I. An Anthology from Vitruvius to 1870*, pp. 540–544. London, England: Blackwell.

Sheridan, Michael (2017). *Louisiana – Arkitektur og Landskab*. Humlebæk, Denmark: Louisiana.

Simon Karkov's curriculum vitae in Normann Copenhagen's archive.

Sommer, Kai (1929). 'Fremtidens Bolig. En samtale med Arkitekt Edvard Heiberg'. *Vore Damer*, no. 29, unpaginated [pp. 7–8].

Sparke, Penny (1999). *A Century of Design. Design Pioneers of the 20th Century*. London, England: Mitchell Beazley.

Steffensen, Erik (2002). *Ole Jensen*. Copenhagen and Humlebæk, Denmark: Aschehoug and Louisiana.

Steinhal, Herbert (1964). 'Tivoli bliver to tønder land større'. *Politiken*, 29 March.

Stephensen, Hakon (1974). 'SorteLouis er min ven'. *LP & Co. NYT*, no. 386, pp. 3439–3440.

Stockmarr, Pernille (2008). *Erik Magnussen*. Humlebæk and Copenhagen, Denmark: Louisiana and Lindhardt og Ringhof.

Stoklund, Bjarne (2003). *Tingenes Kulturhistorie. Etnologiske studier i den materielle kultur*. Copenhagen, Denmark: Museum Tusculanum.

'Stor mønstret Flower-Pot' (1970). *LP & Co. NYT*, no. 340, p. 2801.

Store Danskere. Poul Henningsen (2012). Documentary, directed by Lone Leegaard. Søborg, Denmark: DR (Danish Broadcasting Corporation).

Sørensen, Leif Leer (2000). *Edvard Heiberg og Dansk Funktionalisme – en Arkitekt og Hans Samtid*. Copenhagen, Denmark: Arkitektens Forlag.

Thau, Carsten, and Vindum, Kjeld (2002). *Arne Jacobsen*. Copenhagen and Humlebæk, Denmark: Aschehoug and Louisiana. From the series Danske designere.

Thau, Carsten, and Vindum, Kjeld (1998). *Arne Jacobsen*. Copenhagen, Denmark: Arkitektens Forlag.

The Great Exhibition (1995). *A Facsimile of the Illustrated Catalogue of London's 1851 Crystal Palace Exposition*. London, England: Gramercy.

Theilgaard, R. (1915). 'Belysning'. In *Salmonsens Konversationsleksikon, vol. 2*, pp. 897–902. Copenhagen, Denmark: J.H. Schultz Forlagsboghandel.

Theilgaard, R. (1923). 'Lamper'. In *Salmonsens Konversationsleksikon, vol. 15*, 2nd edition, pp. 297–300. Copenhagen, Denmark: J.H. Schultz Forlagsboghandel.

Thomsen, Hanne (2011). *Gas – fra den Sorte til den Grønne og Ud i det Blå*. Copenhagen, Denmark: Gasmuseets Forlag.

Thorndahl, Jytte (2000). 'Da natten forsvandt – om lys før der kom lys'. *Lys*, no. 4, pp. 34–38.

Tiedemann, Anker (2011). *Historien om Dengang vi fik Danskerne til at Bo Bedre*. Denmark: M.T. Press.

Tiedemann, Anker, and Karlsen, Arne (1961). 'Dansk Brugskunst'. In Zahle, Erik (ed.). *Hjemmets Brugskunst. Kunsthåndværk og kunstindustri i Norden*, pp. 9–22. Copenhagen, Denmark: Hassings Forlag.

'Tivoli-lampens ånd' (1970). *Politiken*, 21 August. Newspaper cutting from Louis Weisdorf's archive.

'Topanpendel' (1961). *LP & Co. NYT*, no. 230, p. 1858.

Tornbjerg, Jesper (2014). 'Lys gør en masse ved mennesker'. *Nyhedsbladet Dansk Energi*, no. 3, p. 7.

'Tre producenter, én designer' (1972). *LP & Co. NYT*, no. 366, pp. 3244–3245.

Troels-Lund, Troels Frederik (1914) [1884]. *Dagligt Liv i Norden i det Sekstende Aarhundrede. VI Bog. Hverdag og Fest*, 4th edition. Copenhagen, Denmark: Gyldendal.

Tøjner, Poul Erik (2004). 'Arkitektur som menneskeligt velbefindende – Jørn Utzon i samtale med Poul Erik Tøjner 6. februar 2004'. *Louisiana Revy*, no. 2, pp. 6–15.

'Unispot' (1971). *LP & Co. NYT*, no. 352, pp. 2902–2903.

Utzon, Jørn (2005). *Jørn Utzon Logbog, vol. II Bagsværd Kirke*. Hellerup, Denmark: Edition Bløndal.

Veksø (2013). *Enriching Urban Life. Lighting. Outfit L905*. Kolding, Denmark: Veksø. PR brochure.

Vistensen, Karen (1991). 'De leger sig til succes'. *Bo Bedre*, no. 1, pp. 40–41.

Voltelen, Mogens (1948). 'Petroleumslampe'. In Braae (1948).

Voltelen, Mogens (1941). 'Radiohuset'. *LP & Co. NYT*, no. 2.

Voltelen, Mogens (1928). [Untitled advertisement]. *Kritisk Revy*, no. 2, p. 11.

von Holstein-Rathlou, Emil (1934). 'Ra-lampen i Københavns Kødby'. *Ingeniøren*, no. 8, p. IX. From Piet Hein's archive.

von Holstein-Rathlou, Emil (1930). 'Belysningsudstillingen i Tivoli'. *Arkitektens Ugehefter*, pp. 184–186.

von Vegesack, Alexander, and Remmele, Mathias (eds.) (2000). *Verner Panton, the Collected Works*. Weil am Rhein: Vitra Design Museum.

'VP-kuglen' (1975). *LP & Co. NYT*, no. 397, p. 3542.

Vorre, Birgit (2008). *Boligen i det 20. Århundrede. Indretning og brug*. Copenhagen, Denmark: Nyt Nordisk Forlag.

Waagepetersen, Christian (1969). *Lysekroner i Skandinavien. Fra gotik til klunketid*. Copenhagen, Denmark: Gyldendal.

Wanscher, Ole (1930). 'Kunstindustrien paa Stockholmsudstillingen'. *Arkitektens Maanedshefter, II*, pp. 139–149.

Wanscher, Wilhelm (1921). 'Kommunens Gadelygter'. *Arkitekten*, no. 8, pp. 293–294.

Weistrup, Torben (2018). 'Skal PH's gamle gadelampe lyse over Slotsholmen?'. *Berlingske*, Sec. 3, 15 December, pp. 20–22.

Weston, Richard (2002). *Utzon. Inspiration, Vision, Architecture*. Hellerup, Denmark: Edition Bløndal.

Wickman, Kerstin (2009). 'Design Historian, on a Furniture Store for Everyone'. In *IKEA at Liljevalchs konsthall 2009*, pp. 32–61. Stockholm, Sweden; Liljevalchs. Exhibition catalogue.

Wille, Elisabeth (2010). 'Boligens nye stilikoner. Derfor elsker vi Louise Campbell'. *ALT for Damerne*, no. 7, pp. 68–69.

Wilmann, Preben (1974). 'PH på Sophienholm'. *LP & Co. NYT*, no. 387, pp. 3451–3457.

Wistoft, Birgitte (1991). *Rundt om Edison. Da Verden og Danmark blev elektrisk*. Copenhagen, Denmark: Elmuseet.

Wivel, Henrik (2004). *Finn Juhl*. Humlebæk and Copenhagen, Denmark: Louisiana and Aschehoug.

Woaz, Franz (1881). 'Den elektriske Udstilling i Paris'. *Illustreret Tidende*, no. 1148, pp. 645–650.

Zalewski, Barbara (2000). *Under Kronen*. Copenhagen, Denmark: Lindhardt og Ringhof.

Index

&
&Tradition 42, 60, 128, 140, 142, 146, 152, 158, 164, 166, 194, 196, 210, 224

A
Abo Mag, Model H 63 132
Stelling House 42
AJ lamp 64
AJ reading lamp 64
AJ pendant 64
Albertslund Post 86, 142
Albertslund Wall 86, 142
Alphabet of Light 230
Alring, Leif 156
Andersen, H.C. 14, 20–21
Andersen, Jan 166
Andersson, Henry 176
Angle pendant 226
Apiales 220
Apoteker pendant 156
AQ01 214
Argand lamp 15–16, 18–19, 20, 22
Argand, François-Pierre Ami 15–16
Arnfred, Tyge 86
Artemide 222, 230
Artichoke lamp 29, 68
Asplund, Gunnar 25
Astronaut 120

B
B&G pendant 52
Baccarat 20, 186
Bahr, Mikkel 88
Ball Double 104
Ball, Model 1300 104, 112
Bang & Olufsen 204
Bang pendant 94
Bang, Jacob E. 24, 94
Bang, Michael 94, 120, 156
Bauhaus lamp 26
Bay, Anne 12
Bellevue 42
Bendixen, Cecilie 224
Beoplay A9 204
Berlin, Boris 122, 184
Bernadotte, Sigvard 58
Berntsen, Maria 29, 196, 226
Berthel, Hans Jørgen 134
Bibliotek lamp 156
BIG, Bjarke Ingels Group 222, 230
Big Flowerpot 106
Bing & Grøndahl 50, 52, 90, 138, 148
Bjerre-Poulsen, Jonas 194, 210
Blossi 8 220
Bo, Jørgen 70, 96
Bock, Allan 96, 122
Bohr, Niels 70
Bombardment chandelier 44
Bonderup, Claus 108, 140, 144
Bulb 164
Butterfly 74
Bysted, Peter 162
Baagøe, Johan Hedemann 13–14

C
Cactus lamp 96
Calabash 184
Calot 140
Campbell pendant 170, 180
Campbell, Louise 170, 180, 186, 198
Caravaggio 174
Carl Hansen & Søn 140
Carrie 210
Charlottenborg 6½-6 146
Chevreul, Michel Eugene 16
China lamp 58

Christensen, Ebbe 146
Christensen, Rudolf 22
Christiansborg ring chandelier 52
Christiansen, Poul 96, 122, 172, 184
Clausen, Ludvig 34
Collage 180, 186
Collage 450 180
Collage 600 180
College of Advanced Technology 34
Colombo, Joe 112
Concert 176
Conch 92
Confetti 140
Contrast lamp 78
Cour, Poul la 17, 19
Cylinda-Line 150–151

D
Dahlerup, J.V. 21–22, 31
Danish Association of Architects 40, 42
Danish Technical College 72
David Thulstrup Architects 208
Davys, Humprey 19
Dell, Christian 42
Den Permanente 44, 122
Design by BIG 222, 230
Design For The People by Nordlux 226
Design Forum 128, 152
Design With Light-lantern 196
Die gute Industrieform 110, 136
Ditzel, Nanna 92, 156
Divan 2 80
Due, Hans 132
Duett 126, 128
Dybdahl, Lars 100

E
Eames, Charles 112
Edison, Thomas 16, 19–20, 22, 29
Edvard, Jonas 11, 208
Eliasson, Olafur 11, 168, 200, 228
Elysion 184
EM oil lamp 150–151
EM77 vacuum jug 150
Enevoldsen, Birgit 68
Enevoldsen, Christian 68
Engelhardt, Knud V. 148, 198

F
F. Mogensens Jernstøberi 21
Facet 136
Fan lamp 96
Faradays, Michael 19
Fatso 170
Fibonacci pendant 146, 204–207
Fibonacci, Leonardo 204
Filskov, Niels 14, 18
Finn Juhl pendant 90
Finn Juhl table lamp 90
Fisker, Kay 25, 94
Floor Lamp (by Thorup og Bonderup) 144
Flowerpot 106, 112, 114, 124, 180
Flying Saucer lamp 160
FM pendant 88
FM1954 88
FM2014 88
Focus 140, 144
Fog & Mørup 46, 84, 94, 102, 110, 126, 132, 146, 156
Forme Utile 140
Formland 156
Forum lamp 38
Frandsen Retail 104, 132
Frandsen, Benny 104
Frandsen, Inge 104
Frandsen, Sophus 146

Fratesi, Enrico 212, 216
Friis & Moltke 88
Friis, Knud 88
Fritzsche, C.E. 40
Fritzsche's reading lamp 41
Fritzsche's Universal lamp 40-41, 50
Fruit Lantern, Model 101 56
Frølich, Lorenz 20
Fun series 98
Funco 160
Fællesforeningen for Danmarks Brugsforeninger 218

G
Gad, Emma 21
Gad, Peter Urban 22
Galaxy lamp 160
Galerie Maria Wettergren 224
Gam, Stine 212, 216
Gamfratesi 212-214, 216
Gammelgaard, Jørgen 128, 152
Gammelgaard, Karin 128
Gantzel-Boysen, Bent 100, 126, 132
Gantzel-Boysen, Dorit 126
Georg Jensen 82-85, 130, 144, 218
Gerlach, Stig 154, 178
Gesso 208
Giant Diamonds 206
Globe lamp 114-115
Goethe lamp 42
Gople Lamp RWB 222
Gople Mini 222
Gropius, Walter 25-28
Guðmundsdóttir, Dögg 218

H
Halsskov 60
Hammerborg, Henni 102
Hammerborg, Jo 84, 102, 132
Hammershøi, Vilhelm 15-16
Hansen, Andreas 96
Hansen, Fritz 84, 156, 160, 174, 214
Hansen, Johannes 76
Hansen, Willy 25
Hay 180
Heiberg lamp 15-16, 74
Heiberg, Edvard 24-28, 42
Hein, Piet 48-49, 160-161
Henningsen, Simon P. 80, 92
Herløv, Erik 86
Hippokrates 12
Hiti 218-219
Holmegaard glassworks 94, 156, 196
Holst, Helge 17, 19
Homann, Alfred 142, 158
Horn Belysning 46
Hurricane Eyes 224
Hvass, Tyge 25
Hvidt, Peter 96
Høyrup, Preben Johan 16, 74

I
Ice 164
Ice Blue 164
IKEA 74, 110, 126, 128
Ilumesa 112
Ingels, Bjarke 222, 230
Isfahan cover 172
Isola, Maja 172

J
J. Lüber 98, 114
Jacob Blegvad's architecture firm 140
Jacobsen, Arne 11, 42-43, 50, 64-65, 72, 124, 128, 138, 150, 216
Jalk, Grete 128, 152

Jefferson, Thomas 15
Jensen-Klint, P. V. 54, 56
Jensen, Carl 27
Jensen, Johannes V. 13-14
Jensen, Kim Weckstrøm 172
Jensen, Knud W. 70, 158
Jensen, Ole 192
JH-1 76
JoGa 152
Jucker, Carl Jakob 26
Juhl, Finn 28, 50, 52, 56, 90
Juhlin, Claus 130
Juicy 188, 190
Jørgensen, Axel 84
Jørgensen, Torkild Thage 146

K
Karkov, Simon 166
Karlby, Bent 29, 58-59, 118
Kastbjerg, Klaus 164
Kastor 84
Kiel, Ole 218
Kjær, Ole V. 142
Kjærholm, Poul 128
Kjøbenhavns Lampe- og Lysekronefabrik 44, 48
Klint, Esben 172
Klint, Kaare 24, 26, 54-56, 58, 70, 94, 96, 172, 184, 214
Koch, Mogens 126
Konkret 208
Koppel, Eva 66
Koppel, Henning 82, 84, 134, 152
Koppel, Niels 66
Krause, Thomas 172
Københavns Belysningsvæsen 34
Kaastrup-Olsen, Jens 82

L
La Linea 31, 230
Lampas 88, 202
LamPetit 100
Lange, Jakob 222, 230
Larsen, Henning 110, 140, 168
Lassen, Flemming 50
Lassen, Mogens 42
Lauritzen, Vilhelm 40-42, 50-53, 58, 60, 90, 218
LC shutters 98
Le Corbusier 25, 27-28, 38
Le Klint 54, 56, 58, 70, 92, 96, 122, 172, 184, 204, 218
Le Klint shade, model 153 96
Le Klint, models 395 and 396 172
Le Klint, Model 204 (the Toadstool) 70
LED candle 178
Lelli, Angelo 134
Lightyears 174, 176, 184, 188, 190, 212, 214
Linnet, Jeppe Trolle 178
Little Sun 200, 228
Little Sun Charge 200
Little Sun Diamond 200
Louis Poulsen 18, 25, 28, 34, 36, 38, 42, 44, 50, 52, 56, 62, 64, 66, 68, 70, 72, 76, 87, 82, 86, 90-98, 100, 106-114, 116, 124-126-127, 130, 140, 142-146, 148, 158, 162, 170, 180, 186, 192, 198, 206, 216, 228
Ludvigsen, Philip Bro 172-173, 218
Lumino 226
Lund, Morten 52
Lundstrøm, Vilhelm 80, 84
Luxo 52, 188
Lyfa 48, 58, 76, 80, 90, 92, 110, 118, 128, 136, 160

M
Madsen, Poul 166
Magnussen, Erik 148-151
Maison & Object 208
Manz, Cecilie 174
Marimekko 172
Marstrand, Wilhelm 16
Mass Light 210
Mathsson, Bruno 160
Maurer, Ingo 182
Menu 194, 210
Meyer, Hannes 28, 38
Middelboe, Sven 60, 108
Milieu 84
Milk 194
Model 1 (by Tage Klint) 54
Model 177 A (by Louis Weisdorf) 92
Model JH1 (by Hans J. Wegner) 76
Moderator lamp 16
Mogensen, Børge 218
Mollerup, Per 152-153
Mondrian (by Cecilie Manz) 174
Moon pendant / Visir 92, 98, 106
Mosaik 118
Multi-Lite 136-137
MUUD 144
MyMoon 186
Møller, Mærsk Mc-Kinney 168
Mølgaard-Nielsen, Orla 96
Møller-Jensen, Jens 86, 142
Møller-Jensen, Viggo 86
Møller, Erik 142
Møller, Henrik Sten 82, 86, 139, 146-147
Møller, Svend Erik 113-114
Møller, Vibeke Andersson 118

N
Nemo-Cassina 190
Nervi, Pier Luigi 122
Nervous Zenith 186
Nielsen, Elmar Moltke 88-89
Nielsen, Jais 46
Nite-cap 108
Nord-Lys 108
Nordisk Solar Compagni 58, 60, 126, 108-109, 176
Nordlux 226
Norm 06 166
Norm 69 166
Norm Architects 194, 210
Normann Copenhagen 166, 192
Nosy 188, 190
Nuura 222
Nyhavn-væglampen 142

O
OE Quasi Light 228
OJ lamp 192
Okholm Lighting 138
Olsen, Bernhard 20
Olympos 144
One 196
Onecollection 90
Opala 138-139
Opal-glass 5/5 lamp 38
Opera 176
Opera House Chandeliers 168
Optima 132
Orbiter 86
Orient 24, 84
Ottesen, Frederik 200
Outfit 202, 214
Outfit, model L905 202

P

Pagoda pendant 108
Palsby, Ole 194
Pan series 118
Pandul 126, 134, 143, 154
Panthella 116, 124
Panto 116
Panton, Verner 29-30, 72-73, 92, 98-99, 100, 106-107, 112-118, 124-125
Pantre 118-119
Parasol 120
Patera 206
Patera Silver 206
Peanut lamp, Model P162 58
Pearlshade 74-75
Pendant no. 1 (by Thorup og Bonderup) 140-141
Petronella 18, 82, 130, 150
PH 5 29, 66-68, 78, 116, 228
PH 6/5 28
PH Hat 78
PH's lamp system 170, 186
PH's pleated globe 56
Phister 132
Phoenix 156-157
Pine Cone lamp, model 153 96
Plate lamp 68
Poltrona Frau 212
Porcelight 148-149
Poul Henningsen / PH 12, 19, 24-30, 34-40, 44-50, 56, 58, 62-64, 66-68, 72-73, 78-80, 86, 92, 94, 96, 98, 100, 106, 108, 112, 114, 116, 124, 136, 146, 146, 166, 170-174, 176, 180, 186, 198, 204, 206, 216, 220, 228, 232
Peacock 118

Q

Quarto 140
Queen Louise 21
Queen Margrethe II 46
Qvist, Anne 202-203, 214-215

R

RA lamp 48-49, 160
Radiohus pendant 50-52, 58, 218
Raizman, David 68
Rappe Louis 158-159
Rasmussen, Erik 88
Rasmussen, Steen Eiler 128
Read series 174
Refer, Sofie 31, 164-165, 220-221
Refer+Staer 164
Reitzel, Malene 186
Rewired 88
Ring lamp 112
Rix, Ove 88
Rohe, Mies van der 28
Room for one colour 168
Rossau, Tom 182-183
Royal Copenhagen 192
Royal Danish Academy of Fine Arts, School of Architecture 26, 34, 42, 50, 60, 70, 72, 80, 86, 88, 90, 92, 94, 106, 124
Rubbie 162-163
Rumford, Count 15-16, 20
Rønn, Kasper 194, 210

S

Salone del Mobile Euroluce 110, 182, 228, 230
Schiøler, Lars Eiler 74-75
Schiøler, Uffe 74
Schlegel, Frits 40-42, 50, 76
Schmidt Hammer Lassen Architects 202
Schmidt, Hans Erik Vestergård 134-135
School of Arts and Crafts, Furniture Department 128
Schrøder, Michael 18
Semi 110-111
Semper, Gottfried 19
Septima 68, 170
Shade Pendant ØS1 232-232
Shell lamp 98-99, 106, 114
Ship's lamp (by Erik Magnussen) 150-151
Ship's lamp (by Sidse Werner) 156
Siemens 20
Silhuet 84
Sinus Line 122-123, 184
Sinus lamp 160-161
Sirius 154, 178
Slotsholmen lamp 34-35
Slaatto, Øivind 13, 204-207, 232-233
Snow 180, 186-187
Socket Occasional Lamp 210
Soffi 212
SorteLouis 126
Spiegel Fittings 112-113, 124
Spiral lamp 114
Stay 226-227
Stelling pendant 42
Stelton 150
Stephensen, Hakon 126
Stone lamp 194, 210
String light decoration 154
Struense, J.F. 21
Studio (by Jo Hammerborg) 84, 102, 132
Stær, Jakob 164
Sundowner 60
Sunflower 172
Super-Egg 160
Suspence 212-213
Suspence Nomade 212
Swing VIP 152
Swirl 204-206
System PH 36-37, 94
Søllerød pendant 50
Sørensen, Cecilie Sand 11

T

T3 46-47
Table lamp (by Bonderup and Thorup) 144, 173
Tallon, Roger 110
Tegnestuen Tekstile Rum 224
Terroir 208
The Edison Electric Light Company 20
The Pendant / Wegner pendant JH604 76-77
The Weather Project 168
Theilgaard, R. 11
Thompson, Benjamin 54
Thomsen, Hanne 18
Thomsen, Nikolaj Steenfatt 208
Thorup, Torsten 110-111, 140-141, 144-145
Thykier, Niels Rasmussen 46-47
Tiedemann, Anker 82
Tip Top pendant 128-129, 152
Tivoli lamp (by Poul Henningsen) 62-63, 80
Tivoli lamp (by Simon Henningsen) 80
Tivoli pendant (by Jørn Utzon) 60-61
Toadstool 70
Toledo 118
Topan 72-73, 98, 106, 134
TR36 182
TR7 182-183
TR747 182
Trio 154
Troels-Lund, Troels Frederik 14
Trombone 102-103
Turbo 134

U

UnderCover 172, 173
Unique Interior 164
Unispot 126, 127
Universal lamp 40-41, 50
Utzon-Frank, Einar 46
Utzon, Jan 60, 176
Utzon, Jørn 60, 61, 108, 122, 176, 177

V

Veksø 202
Velde, Henry van de 38
Verona 108, 109
Victoria 120
Viftelygte 96
VIP 152, 153
Viper 218
Visir (by Jørn Utzon) 176
Visir / Moon pendant (by Verner Panton) 92, 98, 106
VL38 52, 90
VL45 50
Voltelen, Mogens 17, 40, 50, 146
Volume Yellow 224, 225
VP-kuglen 116, 117

W

Wagenfeld, Wilhelm 26
Wannabe 168
Wanscher, Ole 25, 128
Wanscher, Wilhelm 35
Wegner pendant JH604 / The Pendant 76-77
Wegner, Hans J. 76-77, 138-139
Wegner, Marianne 76, 138
Weisdorf, Louis 80, 92, 93, 136
Werner, Frederik 210
Werner, Sidse 156
Wet Bell 188, 190
Window Projection 168
Wirz-Justice, Anna 228
Woaz, Franz 20
Wohlert, Vilhelm 70, 71, 96, 134, 158, 166
Wright, Frank Lloyd 60

Y

Yuh 216, 217

Ø

Örsjö 208
Ørskov, Torben 72, 116

Aa

Aakjær, Jeppe 17
Aalto, Alvar 28, 38, 60
Aarhus School of Architecture 162, 202, 212

Danish Lights
—1920 to Now

© Malene Lytken and Strandberg Publishing 2019, 2024
Consultant editor: Lars Dybdahl
Copy editor: Hanne Rask
Project management: Sidsel Kjærulff Rasmussen
Translation: Dorte Herholdt Silver
Proofreading: Wendy Brouwer
Picture editors: Malene Lytken, Sara Kira Wernberg-Tougaard, Sidsel Kjærulff Rasmussen, Christina Reventlov Petersen, Anna Rølle and Sandra Lyngsie Pedersen
Layout and cover design: Søren Damstedt, Trefold
The book is typeset in Object Sans
Paper: 130 g Arctic Volume White

Prepress: Narayana Press, Gylling
Printing: PNB Print
Printed in Latvia, 2024
2nd edition, 1st print run
ISBN 978-87-92596-63-5

Cover photo:
Poul Henningsen: Artichoke, photo: Louis Poulsen
and Øivind Slaatto: Swirl, photo: Kristine Funch

Copying from this book is only allowed in institutions that have an agreement with Copydan and then only in accordance with this agreement.

Strandberg Publishing A/S
Gammel Mønt 14
1117 Copenhagen K
Denmark
www.strandbergpublishing.dk

Malene Lytken (b. 1967) trained as a designer at the art academy École Nationale des Beaux-Arts de Lyon and subsequently earned an MA in art and design history at the University of Copenhagen. Following this, among other engagements, Malene taught at the Royal Danish Academy of Fine Arts, School of Design, where she also earned a PhD for the dissertation *Lys og Lamper til de Danske Hjem. Sagkundskabens Formidling af en Formålstjenlig Kunstbelysning* (Candles and Lamps in Danish Homes. The Experts' Views on Serviceable Lighting) (2016).

Photos: &Tradition 43, 164-165; Anders Sune Berg 228; Arnaud Lajeunie for *Wallpaper* magazine* 186; Artemide 222, 230; Bauhaus-Archiv, Berlin 26 v; Bent Ryberg 25; *Bo Bedre* 1967, no. 1 80; *Bo Bedre* 1969, no. 4 106 ø; Boesdal and Friis Møller: *Det danske hjem*, 1934 44; Brian Buchard 60-61, 97, 101, 111, 126-127, 135, 143, 159, 193; Bruun Rasmussen Kunstauktioner 16, 40, 47-48, 76, 78 n, 79, 82; BYENSdesign København ApS and Rambøll Danmark / Photo: Brian Buchard 35; Carl Hansen & Søn 139; Carl Jensen, *Blæksprutten*, 1943 27; Cecilie Bendixen 224; Charlotte Hauch 163; Christian B / YELLOWS 214-215; Daells Varehus catalogue, spring 1978 132; Danish Museum of Science & Technology / Photo: Jacob Thorek Jensen 18; Dansk Møbelkunst Gallery /Photo: Brahl fotografi 41; Design For The People by Nordlux 226-227; Designmuseum Danmark 46, 72; Designmuseum Danmark / Photo: Pernille Klemp 39, 91; Edison & Co. / Photo: Henrik Stahlhut 58; Else Ploug Isaksen 26 h; Erik Rasmussen 88; FDB Møbler 218-219; Federico Villa 223, 231; Frandsen Retail 104-105; Fritz Hansen 85, 174-177, 184, 190; Gamfratesi 212-213, 216-217; Giovanni Gastel 31; Gubi 110 v, 136-137; Hans Due 132-133; Hay 180; Holmegaard 156, 196-197; Hotel House of Finn Juhl, Hakuba 90; House of Design 45; Houston Wilson 74, 146; Irina Boersma 209; Jens Markus Lindhe 42; Jonas Edvard 208 v; Kbhbilleder.dk 22; Kira Brandt 67; Klassik Moderne Møbelkunst 83; Koen de Bruyn 157; *Kritisk Revy* 1926, no. 1 36; Lampas / Photo: Daniel Buchwald 203; Lampist.dk / Photo: Michael Poul Hansen 59, 116; Le Klint 54-55, 56 th., 57, 70, 92, 96, 122-123, 172-173, 185, 204-205; Little Sun / Photo: Franziska Russo 201; Lorenz Frölich 20; Louis Poulsen / Kaslov Studio 147; Louis Poulsen Lighting A/S 28-29, 34, 37-38, 51, 56 v, 62-65, 68-69, 124, 142, 158, 162, 170-171, 181, 187, 192, 199, 206-207, 229; *LP & Co. NYT* 1947, no. 69 50; *LP & Co. NYT* 1958, no. 196 66; *LP & Co. NYT* 1966-68 100; *LP & Co. NYT* 1971, no. 353 106 n; Lysfabrikken / Photo: Brian Buchard 103; Made by Hand 149; Mottlau Michael / Ritzau Scanpix 11; Much 225; Museum Sydøstdanmark / Photo: Brian Buchard 119; Museum Sydøstdanmark / Photo: Jens Olsen 118; National Museum of Denmark / Photo: Anker Tiedemann 17; National Museum of Denmark / Photo: Arnold Mikkelsen 13, 23 v.; National Museum of Denmark / Photo: John Lee and Arnold Mikkelsen 23 h.; Nationalmuseum, Stockholm 148; Nemo-Cassina 191; Nordisk Solar Co. 144; Norm Architects 194-195, 210-211; Normann 166-167; Nuura / Photo: Søren Staun Pedersen 220-221; Pandul 128-131, 138 v, 139, 152-153; Pandul / Photo: Brian Buchard 77; Philips 108 h; Piet Hein 49, 160-161; private photo, Hammerborg family 84, 102; Rasmus Koch 208 h; Rewired 89; Royal Danish Library 24, 198; Royal Danish Theatre / Photo: Lars Schmidt 169; Salon Aqua 53 / Photo: Brian Buchard; Shade 232-233; Sirius 154, 178-179; Smukt Brugt / Photo: Brian Buchard 93; Søren Nielsen 189; Stari Antik / Photo: Henrik Bjerg 81, 109, 119; Steen Rønne 138 h; Stelton 150-151; Studio Olafur Eliasson / Photo: María del Pilar García Ayensa 200; Taran Wilkhu 71; Tate Photography / Photo: Andrew Dunkley and Marcus Leith 168; *The Great Exhibition. A Facsimile of the Illustrated Catalogue of London's 1851 Crystal Palace Exposition*, 1995 19; Tom Rossau / Photo: Enok Holsegaard 182; Tom Rossau / Photo: Jesper Ray 183; Verner Panton Design 30, 73, 98-99, 107, 112-117, 125; Vintage by Riis 75; Wikimedia Commons 15; Ztijl Design 95; Aage Strüwing 52, 140, 144-145.

The publisher has attempted to trace, clear and credit all copyrights for featured illustrations. Should there be any errors or omissions, we invite copyright holders to get in touch, and they will be remunerated as if a prior agreement had been made. Further, the appropriate acknowledgement would, of course, be included in any subsequent reprints.